Russian Foreign Policy after the Cold War

Leszek Buszynski

PRAEGER

Westport, Connecticut
London

Library of Congress Cataloging-in-Publication Data

Buszynski, Leszek.
    Russian foreign policy after the cold war / Leszek Buszynski.
        p.   cm.
    Includes bibliographical references and index.
    ISBN 0–275–95585–0 (alk. paper)
        1. Russia (Federation)—Foreign relations.   I. Title.
    DK510.764.B87   1996
    327.47—dc20   96–551

British Library Cataloguing in Publication Data is available.

Library of Congress Catalog Card Number: 96–551
ISBN: 0–275–95585–0

First published in 1996

Praeger Publishers, 88 Post Road West, Westport, CT 06881
An imprint of Greenwood Publishing Group, Inc.

Printed in the United States of America

∞™

The paper used in this book complies with the
Permanent Paper Standard issued by the National
Information Standards Organization (Z39.48–1984).

10 9 8 7 6 5 4 3 2

Contents

Acknowledgments

In view of the turbulent and confusing domestic political scene in Russia since the Soviet Union began disintegrating, the writing of this book has not been an easy task. For this reason, I would like to acknowledge my debt to my Russian friends and colleagues who assisted me by obtaining material, by helping me negotiate the labyrinthian Russian bureaucracy in arranging interviews, or by spending long, stimulating hours with me in fruitful and illuminating discussion, testing and evaluating ideas and interpretations of events. Without the assistance of Slava Urlyapov, Valerii Nikolaev, Anatolii Khazanov, Valerii Titov, and many others, this book would not have been possible. My debt to my wife, Mariko, should be emphasized here for her encouragement, moral support, and her many practical contributions.

Introduction: The Foreign Policy of Disorientation

"Brave person" (*smelyi chelovek*) repeated V. A. Isaev of Moscow's Institute of Oriental Studies when he heard that the author had embarked on a study of Russian foreign policy. How, indeed, is it possible to speak of a Russian foreign policy? The many domestic critics of Boris Yeltsin's government would argue that the term foreign policy implies a sense of coherence and consistency as well as defined objectives and an identifiable strategy to attain them. These qualities, they would argue, have been noticeably absent in Moscow's relations with the outside world which have been characterized by confusion, an appalling carelessness and paralyzing conflict. They argue that what passes as foreign policy is really a series of conflicting and ill-considered moves that reflect the personal values of the actors concerned and certainly not the community. Domestic criticisms of Yeltsin's relations with the outside world have indeed been bitter and reflect the continuing battle over economic reform that was unleashed in 1992. Nonetheless, despite such criticism this study proceeds on the basis that there has been an identifiable foreign policy pursued by the Moscow government in the sense that broadly consistent positions have been adopted over the most critical issues though not without some conflicts. Domestic critics may point to the conflicts that occur within government, or between government and society, over foreign policy but they cannot deny a coherence of purpose to which they respond with varying degrees of opposition. For those critics the problem is not the absence of a foreign policy but a particular orientation, which they regard as unsuitable, inappropriate, or ill-founded.

The theme of this work is the foreign policy of a disoriented state. Disorientation has been an unfortunate characteristic of Russian society since its painful emergence from the Soviet cocoon in 1992. Few other societies have faced the traumatic shock of being relocated in new borders with the old institutions destroyed as suddenly as Russia has. As the Council of Foreign and

Defense Policy has noted in a study of foreign policy options, Russia has been reduced to four-fifths of the size of the Soviet Union, with less than half of the population.[1] Russia's neighbors in the Baltic, the west, and the south were previously constituent republics of the Soviet Union subordinate to Moscow. What were once domestic borders have become international frontiers that demand an adjustment of the behavioral patterns of the past centuries. Devising a foreign policy to match the requirements of a new geopolitical predicament would be a protracted and agonizing process even in the best of times. These, however, are not the best of times for Russia. The process of formulating foreign policy has been made all the more difficult by the difficult economic and social transformation to which Russia has been exposed.

Russia, indeed, has been subjected to the dislocatory effects of economic and political reform which have compounded the sense of bewilderment and disorientation. Russian society has been thrown into what could be the most profound crisis in its history. The Russian state has been traditionally authoritarian and paternalistic, promising a social stability underpinned by the Orthodox Church. The different social strata were bound by the obligation of service either to the landlord or the state on the basis of serfdom or the *pomest'e* (estate) system. The Soviet era may have destroyed the institutions inherited from the past but it enforced a similar collectivism and service to a political party. Russia's past made little allowance for the freedom of the individual, legality, and basic property rights as they are understood in the West. For the first time in history, Russian society at large has been exposed to the ideas of individual freedom, the rule of law, and democracy and has witnessed the crumbling of those social institutions that upheld the security of collectivism. The break with the past has been too sudden for Russian society to absorb and it is no wonder that frightened and vulnerable groups seek solace in resuscitating the collectivism of the past in the form of nationalism or communism.

The effects of the political conditioning of over 1,000 years of history cannot be easily nullified and will continue to grip sections of the population. The old believers who resisted Patriarch Nikon's ecclesiastical reforms in the seventeenth century dissociated themselves from the state and were never reconciled to it. A similar phenomenon may arise as a consequence of the current reform efforts that will create new groups of unrepentant old believers opposing and resisting the changes. Yegor Gaidar hoped that privatization would change the alignment of political forces within Russia by giving more people a stake in economic reform. According to Gaidar, beyond a certain point change would be irreversible as the social basis of the opponents of reform would contract dramatically. The transposition of theory to complex and intractable reality is rarely as smooth as the theorists of economic reform often claim. The result in Russia has been considerable chaos and uncertainty made all the more frustrating because of a recognition that there is no realistic alternative.

Russia today is suspended between the past and future like an elevator caught between floors. The centralized Soviet state and its political apparatus have been dismantled and democratic institutions, such as the legislature and the press, have been established. Nonetheless, the social and economic relations of the Soviet era persist today in the form of the monopolies and cartels that have emerged with their opposition to free market competition. Soviet style patterns of behavior that sustain monopolies, bureaucracies, and cartels and restrict the free movement of information prevent Russia's evolution to a democratic free market system of the Western variety. Soviet-style behavior continues, in the absence of Soviet political institutions, giving rise to the tensions and distortions that are characteristic of Russia today. A sad fact of life is that institutions can be destroyed overnight but their supporting values and behavior will persist for long periods of time before they weaken. As a result of the tension that has been generated between reform promoted from above and prevailing values, a paradox has arisen where a democratic government acts dictatorially pushing economic reforms by decree.

What kind of foreign policy can be expected where the future collides with the past? Main editor of *Nezavisimaya gazeta* V. Tret'yakov has observed that the search for a foreign policy in the post-Soviet era is linked with the establishment of a stable authority structure. He has claimed that unless the domestic political system is stabilized there can be no understanding of foreign policy in Russia. What passes as foreign policy, he says, has been simply the result of lobbying by interest groups and institutions.[2] To a certain extent competitive views of foreign policy can be expected of a pluralist system and an ongoing debate can be considered a healthy sign. The phenomenon noted by Tret'yakov is familiar to citizens of democratic countries and is not considered unusual. The Russian demand for clarity and coherence in foreign policy, insofar as it represents the desire to revive the certainty of the past, is somewhat misplaced under these new conditions. Nonetheless, instability and uncertainty have been more marked in Russia than elsewhere, and since her reconstitution in December 1991 there has been a merciless clash of values that may be characterized as the first stage of foreign policy formulation. Russia, indeed, has not moved beyond that first stage as government-sponsored moves into the foreign policy arena have been constantly disputed and lacking in a sound domestic foundation. It may be that as a result of this conflict a basis for long-term foreign policy may arise through confirmation of the previous ventures, their denial, or their modification.

This book is primarily a study of a conflict in foreign policy values and the impact on Russia's relations with the external world. It will identify the initially confident attempts to identify with the Western world after the collapse of the Soviet Union and the efforts to formulate a foreign policy. It will examine the conflict that has emerged between government and legislature, between government and public opinion groups, and between different branches of government itself. Some of those conflicts were narrow and personality based. Others pointed to a disturbing structural fault that separated government from wide sections of Russian society that had been unprepared for, or unconvinced by, the government's initially bold foray into foreign policy. This study will also identify emerging trends based on a recognition of the economic and geopolitical parameters of foreign policy, which will serve as a prognosis in the final chapter.

How can Russia's interests be prioritized? Two approaches have been debated. The first is thematic or issue-oriented and identifies particular areas of cooperation such as nuclear nonproliferation, economic and security multilateralism, among others. Much of Russian foreign policy activity would fall outside this scheme, however, which would focus on the Foreign Ministry's relations with the external world. The spurious assumption behind this approach is that the Foreign Ministry represents foreign policy in Russia; the influence of other agencies and important domestic political forces is neglected. The issue-oriented approach falls into the trap of identifying foreign policy with a single domestic actor, of imposing clarity and coherence where they may be absent, and of failing to examine the domestic origins of foreign policy behavior.

The second approach examines Russia's foreign policy interests in terms of a series of concentric circles that accommodate Russia's retreat from the globalism of the Soviet era. Foreign Minister Andrei Kozyrev has repudiated what he called "shallow globalism" and has emphasized contiguous regions around Russia as an area of first priority.[3] The inner concentric circle includes contiguous zones that are vital for Russia's security—Europe and the West, the Commonwealth of Independent States (CIS), and North East Asia. Beyond lies a second zone that includes the Middle East, South Asia, and Southeast Asia, which have lost their previous importance for Moscow's leaders. The third zone would include the developing world—Africa, Latin America, and the South Pacific—which is of little significance for Russia today. This book will adopt the second approach examining Russia's foreign policy in terms of three key regions as part of the area of immediate security interest—Europe and the West, the CIS, and North East Asia. It will examine Russia's interaction with these contiguous zones in terms of interagency conflict and the domestic struggle for the formulation and orientation of foreign policy.

NOTES

1. "Strategiya dla Rossii," *Nezavisimaya gazeta*, 19 Aug. 1992.

2. V. Tret'yakov, "Vneshnya politika rossii," *Nezavisimaya gazeta*, 2 Feb. 1994.

3. Andrei Kozyrev, *Preobrazhenie*, Mezhdunarodnye Otnoshenie, Moscow, 1994, pp. 48–49.

Acronyms

ABM	Anti-Ballistic Missile
APEC	Asia-Pacific Economic Cooperation
ARF	ASEAN Regional Forum
ASEAN	Association of South East Asian Nations
BMD	Ballistic Missile Defense
CBM	Confidence Building Measures
CFE	Conventional Forces in Europe
CIS	Commonwealth of Independent States
CNN	Cable News Network
COCOM	Coordinating Committee for Multilateral Export Controls
CPSU	Communist Party of the Soviet Union
CSCE	Conference of Security and Cooperation Europe
EEC	European Economic Community
EEZ	Exclusive Economic Zone
G-7	Group of 7 (Industrialized Countries)
IAEA	International Atomic Energy Agency
ICBM	Inter Continental Ballistic Missile
IEC	Inter-State Economic Committee
IMEMO	Institute of International Economics and International Relations
IMF	International Monetary Fund
LDP	Liberal Democratic Party
MITI	Ministry of International Trade and Industry
NATO	North Atlantic Treaty Organization
NPT	Nuclear Non-Proliferation Treaty
OAS	Organization of American States
PPP	Partnership for Peace Program
SLBM	Sea-Launched Ballistic Missile

SLCM	Sea-Launched Cruise Missile
SPRP	Special Privatization Restructuring Program
START	Strategic Arms Reduction Talks
STF	System Transformation Facility
TDR	Transdniester Republic
USIS	United States Information Service

Chapter 1

Foreign Policy Values

THE PROBLEM OF CLASSIFICATION

Russia has shed its superpower status as well as the accompanying foreign policy attributes that shaped the course of the Cold War era. These attributes, which formed the superpower syndrome included, as the commentator Aleksander Gol'ts noted, messianistic pretensions, imperial ambitions, and global confrontation of the West based on a universal ideology.[1] The universalism of Soviet foreign policy and everything it entailed in terms of the march of socialism and the promotion of the national liberation movement in the Third World gave certainty and predictability to Soviet behavior, and to Cold War relations in general. The loss of superpower status, however, has entailed a lapse into uncertainty for Russia and a painful effort to identify a new role in world affairs. Conceptions of Russia's new role vary considerably and have become the subject of a fundamental value conflict.

This book starts with the premise that Russian foreign policy has been the subject of a clash of values. Certain broad opinion areas can be identified that have impacted on relations with the external environment. Any categorization, however, cannot be rigid as political conditions within Russia have been notoriously fluid. Russian views of foreign policy have been readjusted or have evolved as a result of political interaction and conflict. Some opinion groups have been strengthened over time, others have fought rearguard action but have been weakened nonetheless, while others have disappeared. There are several ways in which this changeable situation may be classified.

One of the first attempts was found in the then Deputy Director (now Director) of the Institute of Africa, Aleksei Vasil'ev's 1992 article in which a conflict between Atlanticists and neo-Bolsheviks was posited.[2] The term Atlanticist denoted those who identified with the West, while the term neo-Bolshevik was applied liberally to those who opposed this policy. Vasil'ev's division of the foreign policy spectrum into just two groups was simplistic as a wide array of conflicting views was subsumed beneath the heading neo-Bolshevik. The then government adviser on political issues Sergei Stankevich introduced another dichotomy based on a conflict between Atlanticists and Eurasianists.[3] The term Eurasianist, which will be explored in subsequent pages, was understood in opposition to the predominant Western orientation of Russia's foreign policy. It signified historical continuity with Russia's past in emphasizing Asia or the Eastern direction of foreign policy. Stankevich's classification was also excessively broad. He used the term Eurasian to embrace all those who opposed the pro-Western approach whether they shared the assumptions of Eurasianism or not.

A related dichotomy was introduced by Vasil'ev when he claimed that the historical conflict between Westernizers (Alexander Herzon, Pyotr Chaadayev) and Slavophiles (Aleksei Khomyakov), which was triggered in 1836, had been replicated today in a new form. According to Vasil'ev, the modern counterpart of the Westernizers were the democrats, while the Slavophiles were represented by the supporters of state power or *gosudarstvenniki*, otherwise known as *derzhavniki* (proponents of a strong state).[4] Here again the terms *gosudarstvenniki* or *derzhavniki* encompass groups with different political inclinations that share the traditional Russian desire for a powerful Russian state. Communist or neo-Bolsheviks may be proponents of strong state power but they cannot be regarded as heirs to the Slavophiles. Aleksei Arbatov in 1993 devised a classification based on political affiliation that allowed for greater variations between extremes. Arbatov's four main groups included the pro-Westerners, the moderate liberals, the centrist and moderate conservatives, and the neo-Communists and nationalists.[5] Arbatov's classification has been the most comprehensive so far, though the terms moderate liberal or centrist, and moderate conservative may not be accurate in representing foreign policy forces.

A key issue for Russian foreign policy today is the extent to which Russia is able to cooperate with the West as a reflection of the internal process of economic transformation. The various foreign policy opinion groups have lined up in response to this issue in different ways. The Atlanticists or the pro-Western group regard internal economic reform and democratization as the highest priority, which demands close association with the West. Beyond this group are those who favor internal reform and consider themselves democrats. Though pro-Western in political orientation, the members of this group would argue that foreign policy should accommodate the geopolitical realities of Russia's predicament that conflict with the pro-Western foreign policy. They can be called geopoliticians or geostrategists. In addition, there are those who are not necessarily pro-Western in terms of political disposition and would instead focus on Asia or the East. They would argue that Russia has a particular destiny in Asia and their ideology would justify the application of the term Eurasian to their foreign policy views. Finally, at the other extreme are those who are hostile to the West and who may be regarded as neo-Bolsheviks or nationalists. The interaction between these groups and the consequent impact on foreign policy trends are outlined in later chapters.

TRADITIONALISTS VERSUS INTEGRATIONISTS

There are two opposing approaches toward foreign policy in Russia today. First, there are the traditionalists who emphasize the importance of power and military strength in foreign policy. Traditionalists vary from those who stress crude military power to the proponents of the more sophisticated balance of power strategies that can be found in the Foreign Ministry as well as in academia and journalism. A particularly popular version of the balance of power strategy has been based on the geopolitical conception of competing centers of power. Vladimir Lukin's work on this topic has strongly influenced debate on this issue.[6] According to this approach, new centers of power have emerged in the multipolar world—Germany, China, and Japan—that compete for influence with Russia. Russia seeks to maintain relevant balances in Europe, Central Asia, and the Far East to contain potential rivals and to prevent the revival of threats along its peripheries. The second approach is integrationism, which implies a break with Russia's past and traditional ways of conducting foreign policy. Integrationism is a recent phenomenon in Russia and can be traced to the Gorbachevian period of foreign policy that affirmed new thinking and promoted integration with the international system. In economic and security terms, integrationism is an effort to overcome the historical rivalries and conflicts that constitute Russia's legacy by developing harmonious relations with major regional and global actors. Proponents of integrationism decry military power and the balance of power, the pursuit of which would create tensions and conflicts with neighbors.

Traditional and modern approaches toward foreign policy compete in Russia today reflecting a deeper conflict over how Russia should relate to the external environment. The pro-Western democrats are strongly integrationist and are more inclined to see the external environment as benign rather than hostile. Nationalists and Communists are instinctively traditionalist in terms of foreign policy and regard the external environment as less than benign if not hostile. The geopoliticians or geostrategists may actually combine both approaches, regarding them as mutually supportive rather than mutually exclusive. Integrationism may be Russia's response to the West while traditionalism governs Russia's relations with other regions. The tension between these two approaches will explain some of the vacillations in Russian foreign policy behavior.

PRO-WESTERN GROUP

The Russian intelligentsia can be considered predominantly, but not completely, pro-Western. The active pro-Western group in foreign policy is a smaller group within the intelligentsia that has captured the moral high ground and the support and attention of the West. This group sees no alternative for Russia, except in terms of integration with the West, and is dismissive of views that claim a special status for Russia. Members of this group have a particular approach toward Russia's history reminiscent of Alexander Herzon and the earlier liberal Westernizers. In their view, what is regarded as specifically Russian and treasured by nationalists simply arises from isolation and distance from the West. They believe the collapse of the Soviet Union was a unique opportunity to remove the historical barriers that previously prevented Russia's integration with the West. Their identification with the West leads to their affirmation of democracy and human rights and to their call for the economic and political transformation of Russia. Foreign Minister Andrei Kozyrev, one of the leading proponents of pro-Westernism, has acknowledged his debt to Mikhail Gorbachev and to the group around him, including Aleksander Yakovlev and Georgi Shakhnazarov. Members of this group contributed to the innovations of Gorbachev's foreign policy based on integrationist assumptions such as the conception of universal international security.[7] Pro-Westerners are strategically located in government, in the Foreign Ministry, and the Presidential Apparatus. President Yeltsin has vigorously supported and defended Kozyrev but his commitment to the pro-Western course may be qualified by personal ambition and by his impulsive temperament, which defies categorization. There have been four key features of the pro-Western position.

The first feature was identification with the Western value system. Kozyrev outlined the contours of Russia's foreign policy in December 1991 when he called for a new system of values. Kozyrev proclaimed his acceptance of the priority of the individual over society, the free market, and all those values that unite the West. He declared that Russia would return to its natural allies and partners, which he identified as France, Germany, and the United States.[8] According to Kozyrev, democracy was essential for a country to reach front rank status and if Russia liberated its democratic forces within 10–12 years it would reach the front rank of countries.[9] The idea of the West as an ally, Kozyrev explained, did not imply a military relationship but adherence to common values.[10] The notion of alliance with the West found a place in Yeltsin's speech to the United Nations General Assembly in January 1992, when the president announced that Russia considered the United States, the West, and the East, not partners but allies. He declared that "our principles are clear—the supremacy of democracy, human rights, freedom, legal, and moral standards."[11]

The second feature of the pro-Western policy was the desire to promote Russia's integration into the world economy. In one of his first statements on Russian foreign policy, Kozyrev declared that Russia intended to secure the economic support of the world community and to join all the international financial institutions, such as the International Monetary Fund (IMF), that could assist its economic transformation.[12] Certainly Russia's expectation of investment and credits from the Group of 7 (G-7) countries was an important motivation behind the declaration of the pro-Western policy, which prepared the way for the announcement of the $24 billion G-7 package on 2 April 1992. Kozyrev, however, went further and in a Cable News Network (CNN) interview in September 1992 claimed that Russia needed foreign aid and a program of cooperation with the civilized world like the Marshall plan. In Kozyrev's view, a new Marshall plan would facilitate Russia's inclusion into the "family of civilized states."[13]

The third feature of the pro-Western policy was the expectation of security benefit. Conflicts along Russia's borders had erupted in the former Soviet Union. There was ongoing concern over the ethnic Russians in the newly independent states. These conflicts threatened to involve Russia in a war that could undermine democratic reform. Aware of this danger, both Kozyrev and Yeltsin pushed for an extension of the European security system Conference of Security and Cooperation Europe (CSCE) to embrace Eurasia, in a way that would remove the pressure on the fragile Moscow government in the process of reform. Kozyrev visited Bonn in January 1992 and in talks with German Foreign Minister Heinrich Genscher called for the establishment of a "single security space from Vancouver to Vladivostok."[14] Yeltsin proposed in his UN speech of the same month a "pan European security system" within which Russia's security problems could be managed.[15] In a similar vein, the pro-Western group had invested much hope in international law as a basis for regulating relations with neighbors. Kozyrev claimed that Russia was ready to sign treaties with Poland and Turkey to ensure the inviolability of the frontiers between them and to remove a possible source of tension. In this context, the Russian Foreign Ministry intended to draw on the protection of international law for Russia's borders and to ensure that every frontier would have the sanction of an international treaty.[16]

Finally, there was the assumption of Russia's great power status according to which Russia would be accepted as an equal partner of the West. The notion of equal status was reinforced by the Soviet experience. As leader of a superpower, Gorbachev had negotiated with the president of the United States and other world leaders on an equal basis and the neo-Gorbachevian presumption of equality continued to influence Russian attitudes toward foreign policy. Kozyrev declared that Russia had all the qualifications to assume a position in the G-7 as a great power and this aim became an important objective of Russia's policy toward the West.[17] In an address to Columbia University on 24 September 1992, Kozyrev claimed that Russia's loss of status due to the dissolution of the Soviet Union did not match "realities." The foreign minister identified the characteristics that made Russia a great power: human and intellectual resources, natural wealth, geographic location, and size.[18]

As a great power Russia not only had a right to be admitted to the small circle of the most developed countries, the G-7, but was to be consulted over global security issues. Kozyrev noted that both the United States and Russia had a responsibility to radically reduce their nuclear arsenals and to terminate the arms race. Negotiations over nuclear arms reductions gave Russia consultative rights and a claim to equality with the world's remaining superpower.[19] Vladimir Lukin, ambassador to the United States from 1 February 1992, claimed that Russian-U.S. relations should be of a "special kind" since the destiny of peace depends on them both.[20] Sharing this view, Kozyrev declared at the Geneva Institute of International Relations that both the United States and Russia were to ensure the settlement of all nuclear disarmament problems. He added that Russian-U.S. interaction can become the decisive factor in international security today.[21] Russia's Foreign Ministry representatives continued to propose various security and nuclear disarmament measures in the expectation that Russia would be treated as a great power.

Kozyrev gave initial expression to the foreign policy orientation of the pro-Western group in the beginning of 1992. The collapse of the Soviet Union was accompanied by a sense of exhilaration among Russia's democrats, and with the demise of totalitarianism it seemed that a new era had dawned. There were, however, major difficulties with the pro-Western position as initially formulated that resulted in its adjustment and modification over time. First, there was the obvious conflict between the declaratory universalism, the emphasis given to common values with the West, and the need to affirm great power status. Integrationism and traditionalism clashed even in the Foreign Ministry's pronouncements. Second, Russia as great power and equal of the West could never really be reconciled with Russia as aid supplicant requiring massive assistance from the G-7. Third, the effort to invoke international law and institutions as a basis for Russia's security remained unconvincing to domestic external audiences. To the latter such appeals seemed particularly self-serving while domestic critics regarded them as exercises in futility. Fourth, there were major divisions that surfaced in the pro-Western position. As a matter of practical foreign policy orientation, the European lobby group was divided from those who emphasized the importance of the United States. Further divisions arose concerning the extent to which Russia should identify with the West over all foreign policy issues, and whether Russia should show greater independence in its foreign policy.

THE GEOPOLITICIANS AND GEOSTRATEGISTS

The second opinion group includes the geopoliticians and geostrategists who believe that Russia's foreign policy should accommodate its geopolitical predicament above all. They may be democrats who are committed to the idea of a representative legislature and free press, but they insist that Russia's first task is to address the security and political problems peculiar to its geographical location. They criticize the pro-Western group for pursuing unrealizable aims without necessarily denigrating the value of those aims. The foreign policy course they advocate is one which they consider forced on Russia by geography. They may also be mild or moderate nationalists or conservatives who regard foreign policy as a realistic and pragmatic adjustment to existing conditions. National security is an imperative for the various geostrategists who have expressed opinions on foreign policy. Despite differences in their domestic political orientation, a common recognition of the significance of geopolitical or security priorities marks their outlook. Those who share these views express a particular distaste for the ideologization of foreign policy, which is a criticism leveled at the pro-Western group for placing the ideology of identification with the West above Russia's security.

Those who have argued that Russia's geopolitical situation places limits on the relationship with the West come to various conclusions about the course to be adopted by Russia, some of which are contradictory. Aleksei Vasil'ev argued that Russia could not identify with the West without impairing relations with the Islamic World. He stressed that the Islamic World was of the highest priority for Russia and that association with the West could have the effect of stimulating anti-Russian Islamic extremism or Turkic nationalism.[22] Sergei Goncharov of the Far Eastern Institute similarly argued that Russia would have to accommodate the Islamic World and China. Goncharov claimed that from a purely geopolitical perspective, Russia's diplomacy should focus on its neighbors in the Islamic World and China. He emphasized that Russia was in no position to pursue relations with the West at the expense of relations with these neighbors, a move that could result in a confrontation, which Russia could ill afford. According to Goncharov, a Russian-Western alliance of the kind Kozyrev proclaimed could result in a countervailing Islamic alliance that may even involve China.[23] Similarly, Vladimir Myasnikov argued that Russia is too removed from the West to be a part of it, and that its geostrategic position demanded an emphasis on relations with China. According to Myasnikov, China is Russia's main partner as Russia's relations with the Islamic World will be affected by fundamentalism. Myasnikov regarded both Russia and China as sharing a concern over border security and Islamic fundamentalism in which case the Asia-Pacific region becomes Russia's main foreign policy arena.[24]

Others placed the emphasis on Russia's relations with the CIS without identifying neighboring powers that may affect those relations. Andranik Migranyan of the Institute of International Economy and Political Research (and later a member of the president's Advisory Council) has been a well known proponent of the CIS as first priority for Russia. Migranyan accused the Foreign Ministry of "exchanging one ideological position for another," that is replacing Soviet ideology with Western. Migranyan argued that Russia's parlous economic condition prevented it from joining the West or from being accepted into the G-7 or the European Economic Community (EEC). He held out China as a model for Russia, a country that pursues an independent foreign policy and yet continues to receive economic and trade benefits from the West.[25] Viktor Kremenyuk, then Deputy Director of the Institute of the United States and Canada, argued that Russia's longterm interest was stability in Eurasia, which demanded the pursuit of integrationist policies in the CIS. Kremenyuk claimed that the democrats had weakened Russia by ensuring its dependence on world society whereas Russia's interests dictated that attention be given to surrounding areas. Kremenyuk coined a geopolitical maxim to rival those of Halford Mackinder when he declared that whoever controls Russia's resources will, to an extent, control the world. In his view, it was imperative that Russia maintain control over its resources and ensure that control would not pass into the hands of others.[26]

From the geopolitical perspective relations with the United States were regarded in conflicting terms. Those who emphasized the CIS, the Islamic World, or China viewed the relationship with the United States as necessary but fraught with tensions. *Krasnaya zvezda* commentator Aleksander Gol'ts argued that the United States and Russia retained the element of rivalry in their relationship because the United States had no interest in a strong Russia. Gol'ts reacted to the Pentagon document on budget planning leaked to the *New York Times* on 18 February 1992, which identified a resurgent global threat from Russia as a possibility. Though the document was subsequently revised, the impression remained that the United States regarded Russia as a potential threat. Gol'ts wrote that the United States wanted to clear the field for itself as the only superpower. For these reasons, he argued, the United States requires a "controlled crisis" in the CIS to ensure Russia's weakness. This view has gained currency among those in security circles who claim that United States and Russian interests clash.[27]

Others, however, saw a basis for geopolitical partnership between Russia and the United States. Aleksei Voskresenskii argued that in a multipolar world Russia's role may be upgraded as the United States seeks Russian support to balance a united Germany in Europe and China in the Asia-Pacific region.[28] Perhaps the best example of the concept of grand geopolitical partnership was expressed by Lt.-General Valerii Manilov, Deputy Secretary of the Security Council in July 1994. Manilov stressed that Russia and the United States together define the present stage of world development and that their partnership was essential to global security and the management of regional conflicts. Manilov's conception of a partnership differs in its geopolitical character from the pro-Western group's idea of an alliance. Whereas the pro-Western group stressed values, Manilov, and others like him, emphasized convergent geopolitical interests. In any case, Manilov noted that Russian and U.S. interests were not always compatible and observed that the CIS was an area of discord between both.[29] Manilov's panoramic geopolitical sweep revealed a neo-Gorbachevian view of Russia's role in the world based on superpower condominium. The approach has been criticized as indicative of the extent to which the old Soviet compass still steers the Soviet ship. It has been described as abstract globalism which maintains the pretence of Russia's superpower status.[30]

EURASIANISTS

Eurasianists should be distinguished from the geopoliticians despite the resemblance. Whereas the geopoliticians base their foreign policy outlook on strategic or geopolitical interests, the Eurasianists adopt a particular ideological or even Messianic approach. If the geopoliticians argue that Russia is compelled by circumstances to adopt a defined foreign policy course, which may be less than the desideratum, Eurasianists see these circumstances as the basis for an original value system or unique ideology. In the Russian tabloids Eurasianism is often misinterpreted as popularized geopolitical criticism of the Yeltsin government's pro-Western policy. Interest in Eurasianism grows as Russians search for an alternative foreign policy approach that would accommodate Russia's history, culture, and geography. The vocabulary and particular terminology of the Eurasianists has proliferated among those who cannot be regarded as Eurasianists in the strict sense.

The Eurasian movement that flourished in the Russian émigré community of the 1920s, was an attempt to affirm a special role for Russia without necessarily accepting Bolshevism, with which the Eurasianists had a distinctly ambiguous relationship. Writers such as Pyotr N. Savitskii and Nikolai C. Trubetskoi shaped the ideas of the movement as a reaction to the failure of the 1905 and February 1917 revolutions.[31] The key idea behind the movement included the notion that Russia was a bridge between Europe and Asia, and this was its special path. Accordingly, Russia was to rule a cultural unity of nations, a special world that was different from Europe or Asia. Inherent in this conception of a special path was the idea of the state as an institution based on the Orthodox faith that promoted this cultural unity, within which the individual finds his or its place as part of a symphonic whole (*simfoniya lichnost'*). The Eurasian movement, in method at least, was close to Bolshevism, and its proximity to totalitarian ideology provoked strong opposition within the émigré community.

The linguist Nikolai Trubetskoi in his work entitled *Russkaya problema* (*The Russian Problem*) accused the Russian intelligentsia of bowing before the Roman-German world and of the crime of regarding Russia as a European country. Russia's role was to join with her Asian sisters—Turkey, Persia, Afghanistan, India, and China—to lead a new liberation movement against Roman-German civilization.[32] According to Trubetskoi, Eurasianism goes beyond Slavic ethnicity and parts company with the Slavophiles. Eurasianism, says Trubetskoi, embraces all the races that constitute the Eurasian continent including Ugrofins, Samoeds, Mongols, Manchus and Turks. Trubetskoi gave a special place to the Turkic peoples in the history of Eurasia.[33] The economist and economic geographer Pyotr Savitskii claimed in his essay, *Evraziistvo* (*Eurasianism*) that Eurasia constituted a special world including the Russian Far East, East Siberia, Central Asia, Persia, the Caucasus, and Asia Minor. This world was united in itself and separate from the countries of the southeast or the south.[34] The philosopher Nikolai Alekseyev argued in his essay, *Evraziitsy i gosudarstvo* (*Eurasianists and the State*) that Eurasians would have to establish their own state based on the sovereignty of the nation in which the ruling party should implement the government program. Alekseyev predicted that a revolt would take place against Soviet Russia executed by groups sympathetic to Eurasianism, or by Eurasianists themselves who would introduce a new age.[35]

From the Eurasian morass of conflicting ideas, two stand out as relevant for foreign policy orientation. First, the Eurasian world that Russia was a part of was culturally and historically distinct from the European world. Second, it was an illusion of the Russian intelligentsia or nobility to imagine that Russia could be part of Europe. The Eurasianists saw European civilization as a structure imposed on Russia by Peter I that had no real or lasting roots in Russian soil. Second, Russia's task was to focus attention on the Eurasian world, which was its natural environment, and to desist from regarding Europe as its highest priority. Within that Eurasian world the Turkic-Islamic states along Russia's southern borders, as well as China, should receive the highest priority.

Eurasianism was strongly criticized within the émigré community and failed to obtain widespread support. The writer Nikolai Berdyaev in 1927 labeled the Eurasianists Bolshevik agents who demanded the subordination of the individual to "Utopian statism."[36] The historian Aleksander Kizevetter in 1925 derided Eurasianism as a mood masquerading as a system that in his view was a negative reaction to the Great War and the emergence of Bolshevism in Russia. Kizevetter chided the Eurasianists for their conflicting ideas and their unfortunate disregard of historical facts.[37] The Eurasianists continued to publish a journal called *Evraziiskoi khroniki* from 1925–1934 but otherwise were stigmatized within the émigré community by the resemblance of their views to Bolshevism.

Eurasianism has been revived in Russia today through the writings of the ethnographer Lev Gumilev (1912–1992). Gumilev spent 30 years with the Faculty of Geography at Leningrad University working on Turkish-Mongolian history from a non-Eurocentric perspective. Gumilev's Eurasianism was distinct from that propounded by the émigrés in the 1920s as it arose independently. His books popularized Eurasianism in the early 1990s, which resulted in the publication of articles by the early Eurasianists in the journals *Nash sovremenik* and *Elementy*. Gumilev developed a theory of ethnogenesis claiming that Eurasia was forming what he called a super ethnos that would embrace Slavic, Turkic, and Mongol peoples. He criticized what he regarded as hostile historical interpretations of the Mongols in Russian history. Gumilev claimed that the Turks and Mongols could be Russia's sincere friends as opposed to the English or the French.[38] In an appeal to Russia to desist from Eurocentrism, Gumilev cited Trubetskoi's comment that it was the repressed dream of every European to destroy all culture but his own, which would then be universalized.[39] He argued that Eurasian unity was a higher priority for Russia than alliance with the West, a unity that traditionally had been opposed by Catholic Europe, the Muslim South, and China.[40] Gumilev has been criticized for geographical determinism and for historical inaccuracy but his views continue to have an impact in a country that is searching for an identity.

Eurasianism today serves to justify a variety of views in relation to the former Soviet Union and at least five interpretations have been noted in different political contexts: first was the idea of a Russian Eurasian state involving the integration of Slavic and Turkic peoples as proposed by the émigré theorists of the 1920s–1930s; second was the Gumilev approach involving a unity of Mongol, Turkic, and Russian peoples; third was Andrei Sakharov's proposal for a federation of nations based on the U.S. model; fourth was the neo-fascist conception of an alliance of all former Soviet states against the United States; fifth was the idea of the reconstruction of the Soviet Union supported on the basis that the Soviet Union was an expression of Eurasian civilization, and that the Soviet system was the "best possible model to reflect the Eurasian condition."[41] Eurasianism from this point of view came to symbolize a political or historical community embracing Russia and the former Soviet Union. The Eurasianists saw themselves as opposing the pro-Western group, who supposedly sacrificed Russia's claim to be part of a special civilization in order to join Europe, they predicted Russia's rejection by the West and its reorientation toward Eurasia.[47]

Many of the ideas of the Eurasianists have been utilized by political leaders, commentators, and scholars alike as a basis for a foreign policy that would reflect Russia's history and geography. In a letter to Boutros Boutros Ghali, Yeltsin claimed that Russia could fulfill the role of a bridge between Europe and Asia.[43] When Yeltsin addressed the South Korean Parliament in November 1992 he again referred to Russia's role as a bridge.[44] Commentator Aleksander Gol'ts thought that Russia should strive to emerge as the center of Euro-Asian integration. Russia, in his view, could stimulate the integrative process between a united Europe and the Asia-Pacific region.[45] Fedor Burlatskii claimed that Russia could not be a great power without establishing order in Eurasia, and that Russia's major priority should be the establishment of "Eurasian house," not as an empire but as a democratic community.[46] Others argued that Russia had a special mission in Eurasia not only as an arbitrator or mediator in conflicts but as a patron.[47] In the spirit of traditional Russian Messianism others saw Russia's greatness in its mission to reconcile East and West. Success in this endeavor would depend on Russia's ability to establish a community of equal partners in the Eurasia.[48] Throughout these ideas is the theme that the Eurasian status of Russia is the basis of its claim as a great power and that Moscow cannot turn its back on Eurasia without turning its back on history.[49]

In terms of influence on political figures, Eurasianism can count on Sergei Stankevich as a proponent. Stankevich was Russia's government adviser and a designated adviser to Yeltsin on political issues. Stankevich was an advocate of strong and effective government power and a proponent of an evolutionary approach to economic reform. His view of foreign policy entailed a balance of Western and Asian orientations and emphasized the need for Russia to strengthen relations with Asia. He argued that the collapse of the Soviet Union left Russia geographically removed from the center of European international life and that Russia should strive to be economically independent by developing relations with the former Soviet Union. Directly referring to Eurasian themes, Stankevich stated that Russia must find a synthesis of the Slavic and Turkish, Orthodox and Muslim elements that have played such significant roles in Russia's history.[50] Stankevich also argued that domestic political developments in Russia supported Eurasianism in opposition to the Europeanization of Russia.

The term Eurasianism has had widespread appeal even though the body of ideas that support it is largely unknown. The discussions in the tabloids as well as scholastic journals, demonstrate a continuing interest in the movement among the Russian public. Eurasianism presents an alternative to the pro-Western course, which to many entails Russia's continuing humiliation, without embracing the ugly and unpalatable extremes of nationalism or neo-Bolshevism. It is an affirmation of Russia's sense of historic mission for a population that has been historically conditioned to believe in a separate path for Russia. In practical foreign policy terms, Eurasianism would also entail distance from the West, and the West's endorsement of Eurasia as a separate political community, but not hostility or confrontation. Critics, however, regard Eurasianism as a comforting illusion that is exploited to justify a hegemonic role for Russia in the former Soviet Union.

NATIONALISTS, NEO-BOLSHEVIKS, AND COMMUNISTS

Finally, irreconcilably opposed to the pro-Western group are the nationalists and neo-Bolsheviks who regard Yeltsin's coterie of democrats as traitors to Russia or to the idea of the Soviet Union. The nationalists have targeted Kozyrev in particular for conducting a foreign policy described as the passive duplication of Western initiatives. Kozyrev was criticized for continuing the capitulationist foreign policy course of Gorbachev and Eduard Shevardnadze that has hastened Russia's decline.[51] Sergei Baburin and Nikolai Pavlov have been prominent among the nationalist opposition to the pro-Western course. Both were members of the Supreme Soviet *Rossiya* faction that was formed in 1990 and called for the rebirth of Russia on the basis of self-determination when it was still part of the Soviet Union. Both Baburin and

Pavlov were conspicuous by their firm opposition to any deal with Japan involving the disputed territory. Vice-President Aleksander Rutskoi adopted nationalist positions over various issues and was a thorn in Yeltsin's side until his removal from his position after he joined the Supreme Soviet's rebellion against Yeltsin in October 1993. Rutskoi was selected by Yeltsin to be vice-president in June 1991 and justified his trust by his defense of the Supreme Soviet building with Yeltsin in August 1991. Rutskoi, however, became a defender of the ethnic Russians in the former Soviet Union and a supporter of Ruslan Khasbulatov and the Supreme Soviet against Yeltsin.

Several nationalist groups have also influenced public attitudes over foreign policy. The Russian National Assembly—*Russkoi natsionalni sobors*—formed in February 1991 and intended to embrace a wide group of nationalist organizations (monarchists, patriotic associations, the Cossacks Union, the National Republican Party of Russia, and even representatives from the Russian Christian movement) called for the revival of a great Russia. The Russian National Assembly did not recognize Russia's present borders as natural and appealed for the reconstitution of Russia within its historical borders.[52] Its first congress was held in June 1992 and attempted to unify all Russian patriotic forces. A mixture of themes resulted from the congress, however, including Eurasianism and global revolution, which demonstrated the extent to which incompatible groups had been brought together for the occasion.[53]

Vladimir Zhirinovsky's Liberal Democratic Party (LDP) was possibly the most prominent of all the nationalist groups if only because of Zhirinovsky's ability to capture the headlines. Mayor of Saint Petersburg Anatolii Sobchak claimed that Zhirinovsky was a politburo creation and a product of Gorbachev's desire for controlled political parties to participate in multiparty elections. The LDP was created in December 1989 but Sobchak could not confirm whether the party itself was a KGB-sponsored organization, or whether it was simply favored by Soviet authorities once the politburo in March 1990 decided in favor of multiparty elections.[54] *Izvestiya* investigative reporters, however, noted that Zhirinovsky traveled abroad eight times in 1991 with ample funds, raising their suspicions.[55] Zhirinovsky contested the presidential elections of 12 June 1991—he came third after Yeltsin and Nikolai Ryzhkov with 7.81 percent of the vote, around 7 million votes. Zhirinovsky's initial statements on foreign policy were deliberately outrageous. He declared the Baltic states part of Russia and that Russia had an interest in parts of Turkey, Iran, and Afghanistan.[56] He declared that Russia should be restored to its national borders—without Poland.[57] Zhirinovsky was a friend of Gerhard Frey, leader of the right wing German People's Union, and with him declared that the Oder-Neisse frontier with Poland was not the last word in history. Zhirinovsky led an LDP delegation to Iraq in November 1992 where he called for Iraq to remain an ally of Russia. He criticized Yeltsin's policy of supporting the West's position in relation to Iraq as the "treacherous policy of the present Russian leadership with respect to the Iraqi people."[58]

A more coherent foreign policy view was included in the LDP party program based on the party's third congress of 19 April 1992. Section 6 of that program covers foreign policy and calls for agreement between the world powers over the demarcation of spheres of influence. The U.S. would have Latin America and the Caribbean Sea, Europe would have West Africa, Russia would have Afghanistan, Iran, Turkey, and Japan, and China would have South Asia and Oceania. Zhirinovsky's views were developed in two publications. In *Poslednii brosok na yug* (*Last Rush to the South*) he turned his attention to Turkey, Iran, and Afghanistan, which he claimed would become part of Russia if his party could dictate policy. Their borders, wrote Zhirinovsky, would be Russian southern borders.[59] In a later publication, *Poslednii vagon na sever* (*Last Wagon to the North*), Zhirinovsky criticized what he saw as the "anti-national direction of Russian diplomacy." He called for Russia's reconstitution within its "historical borders" and for the former Soviet Union to be regarded as an exclusive sphere of Russia's vital interests.[60]

Among the Communists and neo-Bolsheviks were at least nine Communist groups that joined the 29th congress of the Communist Party in August 1992. The various groups could not agree on a common platform and representatives from the Russian republics opposed the recreation of the All-Union Soviet Communist Party. Nina Andreyeva's All Union Communist Party of Bolsheviks (with a membership of about 35,000) called for the restoration of the Soviet Union and condemned Yeltsin's government. Andreyeva was catapulted into fame (or notoriety) when her letter criticizing Gorbachev's reforms was published in *Sovetskaya Rossiya* on 12 March 1988. She has since pressed for the maintenance of relationships with former Soviet allies and has visited North Korea in pursuit of this aim. The neo-Bolshevik organizations are divided and small, and congregate on the margins of political life.

More significant was Gennadi Zyuganov's Communist Party of the Russian Federation that gained 13.59 percent of the vote in the December 1993 elections. As he prepared for the 1993 elections Zyuganov outlined his party's foreign policy platform in which there was no place for Marxist-Leninist ideology. The doctrine of the confrontation of socialism and capitalism was absent though the policy platform identified the United States as a hegemon in international affairs. A series of recommendations followed that could hardly be characterized as particularly Communist. National interest was the proclaimed key concept for foreign policy, which should be based on healthy national pragmatism and the norms of international law. The collapse of the Soviet Union eliminated the previous geopolitical equilibrium between the great powers of which Russia was one of the guarantors. Russia should, accordingly, develop relations with China, India, and the Third World to restore equilibrium against the hegemonic United States. The platform claimed that Russia's Left wanted no confrontation with the West, but regarded the unipolar world as against its interests. The Communist Party held its third congress on 22 January 1995 and produced an updated version of the party platform that returned to the theme of confrontation between socialism and capitalism. The program emphasized the re-establishment of the Soviet Union and its traditional interests and position in the world.[61] Zyuganov emphasized in his book *Derzhava*, that the Russian Left "does not seek confrontation with the West" and that the aim was to seek "wide collaboration with the governments of the West in various fields and on the basis of equality and mutual advantage." Zyuganov's priorities in foreign policy included the restoration of the Soviet Union on a voluntary basis and Russia's re-emergence as a great power. Unless Russia is able to find its rightful role as a great power other powers, most notably China, may fill the resultant vacuum.[62]

FOREIGN POLICY ACTORS

The various opinion groups, depicted above, express themselves through particular institutions or agencies that influence foreign policy. The pro-Western position has its supporters in the Presidential Apparatus and the Foreign Ministry. Nationalists and Communists can be found in the legislature and to some extent in the military. Geopolitical views, however, are not limited to any particular institution and are found in all in varying degree. The correspondence between institution and foreign policy attitude is inexact as institutions reflect social divisions at large. Within Russian government, decision-making has been conducted somewhat haphazardly and unsys-tematically, which has been in part a reflection of Yeltsin's personal habits as well as a product of the institutional vacuum created by the collapse of the previous party-based administrative structure. Yeltsin tended to rely on Gennadi Burbulis, who was first vice premier and state secretary until he was removed from these positions in November and December 1992 respectively. Yeltsin credited Burbulis with unarguable authority as the real head of his cabinet. He claimed that all administrative issues involving the ministries were resolved through Burbulis who also participated in the establishment of the Presidential Apparatus.[63] Nonetheless, a systematic approach toward decision-making was absent even with Burbulis in control. It was Oleg Rumyantsev (head of the Supreme Soviet's Constitutional Committee) who declared that the battle for access to the president decides policy, "those that win the battle are those who inform the president."[64] Kozyrev himself revealed that it was an acute struggle to have access to Yeltsin but claimed that his own access was assured.[65] The absence of coordination at the highest level explains to a large extent the policy discrepancies that arise between government representatives that have been interpreted as evidence of internal conflict.

The Presidential Apparatus

Pro-Westernism was promoted by the Presidential Apparatus, a bastion of radical democrats and reformists, as well as the Foreign Ministry. The Presidential Apparatus was a sprawling organization headed since July 1991 by Yuri Petrov who revealed in an interview that it employed some 2,000 people.[66] Yeltsin brought Petrov from his own city of Sverdlovsk where he was Obkom first secretary and subsequently party central committee member and ambassador to Cuba. In March 1993, information about the structure of the apparatus appeared in the Russian press according to which there were 31 sections and centers. The three analytical centers included general policy, which covered foreign policy, and was then headed by Sergei Stankevich; social and economic policy; and special presidential programs. The apparatus included protocol, press service, and organization departments as well as an archives section and a library.[67] Petrov was dismissed by Yeltsin in January 1993 because his Communist background made him anathema to the liberals and democrats—his links with the Communists in the 7th Congress of Peoples's Deputies in December 1992 made him a liability. He was replaced by Sergei Filatov, the first deputy speaker of the Supreme Soviet and Ruslan Khasbulatov's deputy and enemy. Filatov brought into the Presidential Apparatus his radical democratic colleagues such as Vyacheslav Volkov and Pyotr Filippov who was made head of the Analytical Center for Social and Economic Policy. Nonetheless, the Presidential Apparatus has not been a united body and there have been reports of clashes among the radical democrats themselves, and between Volkov and Head of the Control Department, Yuri Boldyrev.[68] More recently, reports indicated a clash between democrats and conservatives that showed that the Presidential Apparatus was subject to the same political divisions as other bodies in Russian society. Some in the apparatus were concerned about what they regarded as the excessive pro-American tilt in Russia's foreign policy, others were linked to conservatives and sought to have Sergei Filatov replaced by a more conservative figure.[69]

The Foreign Ministry

The Russian Foreign Ministry became a shadow of the Soviet Foreign Ministry. Because of reduced hard currency support from the government, diplomatic representation was reduced in 10 countries in April 1992, mainly in Africa and Papua New Guinea. Skilled and experienced personnel began to leave the Soviet Foreign Ministry after August 1991 seeking higher wages in the private sector. Kozyrev claimed that 15–30 people annually left the Soviet Ministry in the 1980s. In 1993 around 500 personnel left, while in the first quarter of 1994 71 diplomats and 31 technical workers resigned.[70] As this author was informed by disgruntled officials, the wages and conditions of service cannot compete with private business. Deputy Minister for Personnel Sergei Krylov complained that the most talented employees under the age of 35 had left and that a new generation of Foreign Ministry staff had not been formed.[71] The Foreign Ministry has been deprived of the talent to uphold the pro-Western line and provide necessary depth in policy. Kozyrev's pro-American line has provoked hostility within some sections in the Foreign Ministry—those dealing with the Middle East and the Arab world in particular—and several deputy ministers and departmental directors have been known to seek allies elsewhere.

The Security Council

The Security Council is an example of an abortive attempt to establish control over decision-making through the creation of an extensive administrative structure. It was intended to function according to the model of the U.S. National Security System and to introduce regularity and coherence into Russian decision-making. Russian liberals viewed the emergence of the Security Council with concern as it has been regarded as a Soviet institution that functions on the basis of an anachronistic Soviet conception of national security. It accumulated a secretariat and advisory body that has access to independent sources of information other than that provided by the ministries. Nonetheless, the attempt to regularize decision-making failed as the Security Council was transformed into a personal organ of the president.

Mention of the Security Council was included in Article 5(9) of Yeltsin's Constitutional amendments of 24 April 1991 that stated that the president was its head, and that its structure and powers were to be defined by the law of the country. Promulgated under the Security Act of 5 March 1992, the Security Council's task was to examine the internal and external threats to security, to meet in the case of crisis or extraordinary situations, and to prepare recommendations for the president. At that stage, its composition included the president, Vice President Rutskoi, State Secretary Burbulis, Defense Minister Pavel Grachev, External Intelligence Director Yevgennii Primakov, Security Minister Viktor Barannikov, Presidential Adviser Dmitri Volkogonov, and Security Council Secretary Yuri Skokov. Yeltsin's speech at the first session of the Security Council on 20 May 1992 indicated an intention not to re-create the secrecy of Soviet style decision-making. Yeltsin emphasized that the Security Council would work according to law and would not conflict with the constitutional structure of power that had arisen since the Soviet collapse. The intention was to ensure that national security decision-making would not be undertaken by a body above the legislature, executive, or judiciary in isolation from the rest of society. At that first session the Security Council's agenda included the concept of security on which Russia would operate as well as the composition of the Security Council itself.[72]

Yeltsin's decree of 7 July 1992 (no. 747) outlined the Security Council's role and function: Point (1) of that decree specified that Security Council recommendations would be formalized in presidential decrees; Point (2) stated that executives of federal ministries, agencies, and government bodies in the provinces "shall take exhaustive measures to implement decisions of the Security Council." They were required to issue instructions relating to these decisions "within two days on the receipt of the decisions of the Security Council"; copies of those instructions were to be sent to the Security Council. Point (3) empowered the Security Council's secretary to monitor implementation of these decisions as well as presidential decrees relating to security. The secretary was also required to coordinate the activities of executive bodies in the implementation of these decisions.[73] Sergei Filatov subsequently revealed that there were initially five voting members whose positions were formalized under the decree. They were the president, vice president, Yegor Gaidar, Yuri Skokov, and Filatov. All others were nonvoting members.[74]

Despite Yeltsin's initial intentions, his decree elevated the Security Council to a key role as a controlling institution. It acted according to a broad concept of security above the ministries and below the president to which it reported directly. There were few spheres of government activity that could not fall within the Security Council's jurisdiction according to this all-encompassing understanding of security. Initially, the Security Council met every Wednesday to review current issues of the day and provide the president with the necessary information in relation to those issues.[75] Yuri Petrov emphasized that the Security Council dealt with strategic development and not the day-to-day issues which were the government's concern. According to Petrov, the Security Council was intended to be a consultative body, a view that was hardly justified by its actual functions.[76] The decision to cancel President Yeltsin's trip to Japan was made during a Security Council meeting on 9 September 1992. Concerns were raised in relation to the manipulation of information and data that was fed to the president as the Security Council assumed a monopoly of information. Commentators feared that through the control of information the president could be induced to accept particular courses of action. An example raised was the appointment of then Major-General Aleksander Lebed' as commander of the 14th Army in Moldova in July 1992. Yeltsin was apparently against the appointment but was required to accept a fait accompli when the general took command of the army during an explosive situation there. Later Yeltsin confirmed the appointment on the basis of documents and information prepared by the Security Council.[77]

An important factor in the rise of the Security Council was Yuri Skokov—its first secretary. Skokov was associated with the Communist-conservative wing of Russian politics and had appointments as first deputy premier of the Russian Federation (1990–1991) and adviser to the president. Skokov was regarded as a proponent of strong state power (*derzhavnik*) by the liberals and democrats and one whose talents related to the infighting and power accumulation that was characteristic of the Soviet system. He was confirmed in the position of secretary of the Security Council in April 1992 and reportedly joined Yuri Petrov to study the American national security system as a model. Skokov clashed with both Burbulis and Kozyrev who opposed the expansion of the Security Council, which became a source of constant criticism for the democrats. As an indication of his views Skokov arranged for the preparation of a document entitled *Programma natsional'noi bezopastnosti (A Program of National Security)* that called for the deployment of the armed forces anywhere in the world to prevent the United States from gaining military advantages, and which cast Russia in the role of a balancing factor against the United States.[78] This document was prepared before Yeltsin's visit to Washington in June 1992 but was not approved by the Security Council and ultimately disappeared. Skokov was also responsible for military appointments making his role in the appointment of Aleksander Lebed' critical.

Skokov erected an administrative structure that threatened to marginalize the Foreign Ministry entirely and brought together convinced nationalists and *derzhavniki*. Kozyrev began to attack what he called the war party that was pushing Russia into conflicts in the CIS, Moldova, and South Ossetia.[79] Kozyrev subsequently identified Rutskoi as the leader of the war party and was attacked within the Security Council, which discussed the issue of his removal as foreign minister.[80] Kozyrev retaliated and lobbied Yeltsin to ensure that the Foreign Ministry would retain control of foreign policy. When Yeltsin spoke to the Foreign Ministry collegium (a gathering of its highest officials) on 27 October 1992, he promised that the Foreign Ministry would act as coordinator for all of Russia's foreign relations, economic as well as political.[81] According to the president's decree of 8 November 1992 (no. 663), the Foreign Minister was granted these coordinating powers that extended to all ministries, committees, and authorities of Russia. It embraced the dissemination of information on foreign policy that required Foreign Ministry approval, as well as all treaties and agreements concluded in the name of the Russian Federation.[82]

Nonetheless, in one of those contradictory decisions (for which he has become notorious) Yeltsin allowed Skokov to reverse the situation on 16 December 1992. Yeltsin's decree created an interdepartmental commission for foreign policy and security under the Security Council which, as Yevgennii Ambartsumov declared, became a second Foreign Ministry.[83] Yeltsin's decree was apparently drafted under Skokov's supervision; it covered the composition, structure, and functions of the new commission at the head of which was Skokov himself. The commission's membership included key government ministers responsible for foreign policy and security. Representatives from the Defense and Foreign Affairs Committees of the Supreme Soviet could be included in discussions subject to agreement. The commission analyzed trends in international relations and identified potential and actual threats to Russia's security. All military and political decisions relating to foreign policy, defense, or security in general were subject to the commission's approval. The commission was also given the right to correct the Foreign Ministry's position and was responsible for drafting Yeltsin's speeches in this area. On paper at least, Skokov had achieved his ambition of controlling foreign and security policy. Russian administrative realities were another matter, however, and Kozyrev persisted in his course.[84]

Rather than controlling foreign policy, the Security Council under Skokov operated to map out strategy and guidelines in a broad sense, though specific issues were brought before it for resolution according to their urgency. The Security Council acted as a coordinating body in drafting both foreign policy and defense doctrine to meet the demands of those in government and in the Supreme Soviet for clarity in these areas. The commission drafted a conception of foreign policy that was then submitted to the Security Council for discussion and approval. A meeting of the Security Council was held on 3 March 1993 which included Kozyrev, Defense Minister Grachev, Security Minister Barannikov, as well as various armed forces representatives and commanders of military districts.[85] The foreign policy concept was approved and was to be submitted to the Supreme Soviet. Yeltsin addressed the meeting and stressed that a military doctrine was required and that further delay was impermissible. The Security Council examined the completed version of the military doctrine on 3 October 1993, final approval was given on 2 November, and Russia's new military doctrine was consequently promulgated.

Skokov, however, lost his position as Security Council secretary because of his political maneuvring. On 21 March he criticized Yeltsin in a speech in the Supreme Soviet, and in May 1993 a presidential decree relieved him of his position beginning in July. Skokov was appointed chairman of the Federation of Russian Manufacturers and joined the organizing committee of the Congress of the Peoples of the USSR, which sought to re-establish the Soviet Union. The next secretary, Yevgennii Shaposhnikov, was a transitional figure and failed to receive Supreme Soviet support. Shaposhnikov wanted to give the Security Council governmental status and proposed that Yeltsin appoint him as a vice-premier.[86] Oleg Lobov was appointed Security Council secretary in September 1993 and presided over further expansion. Lobov was a first deputy premier and economics minister and combined economics experience with loyalty to Yeltsin. Under Lobov, the membership of the Security Council was expanded to 13, including the finance minister and the ministers of health, environment and justice. The professional staff was expanded to 80 with seven standing committees on: defense, foreign policy, security (economic), health, environment, public safety, information. The president's decree of 1 November 1993 (no. 1807) established an advisory body (*nauchni soviet*) that was to provide the Security Council with data and information about specific issues. Within this body, five subgroups were established on defense, foreign policy, health and ecological security, information security, government security, and the economy. The chairman of this advisory body was Vladimir Pirymov, a vice-president of the Russian Academy of Natural Sciences.[87]

One problem to emerge was the absence of legislative representation in the Security Council. Sergei Filatov had been appointed a voting member while he was first deputy chairman of the Supreme Soviet, but when he joined the Presidential Apparatus as its head the connection with the legislature was lost. After the formation of the new Federal Assembly, chairman of the new state Duma, Ivan Rybkin, and his counterpart for the new Upper House (the Federation Council) Vladimir Shumeiko, were appointed to the Security Council in May and June 1994 respectively.[88] The president's need for political support, however, has taken precedence over the need to establish stable and ordered decision-making structures. Representatives of the legislature, Rybkin and Shumeiko, have been criticized for being co-opted by the president and regarding themselves as presidential representatives in the legislature. The Security Council despite initial intentions, has become the president's personal body that functions on the basis of loyalty rather than regular procedures. Unfortunately no improvement has been noted in the rather haphazard and often erratic way that important decisions are made in Moscow as exemplified by the move into Chechnya in December 1994.

The Military

Various hypotheses of military–civil relations were developed for the Soviet Union, which in many respects posited the idea of the military as a major actor in foreign policy. Whether the relationship was characterized as value-shared or fundamentally in conflict, the military's obsession with Soviet security and its support for Third World client states gave it a major role in shaping the context of Soviet foreign policy. The military was an integral part of the Soviet system and as well as influencing specific foreign policy moves, had contributed to the formation of Soviet foreign policy values, aims, and objectives. A tendency exists in the West to regard the Russian military in much the same light as the Soviet military and more powerful and united than it actually is. The Russian military, nonetheless, has had an impact on particular areas of foreign policy while its main concern has been its survival.

The scale of the social disaster that the Russian military has faced would be difficult to overstate. Phased reductions were introduced in 1991 as the military was converted from an instrument of superpower expansion to a means of coping with regional conflicts within the borders of the former Soviet Union. Aleksander Rutskoi announced in May 1992 that the main task of the military would be local conflicts for which rapid reaction, air mobile forces, and a strategic reserve would be required.[89] Reductions included 500,000 in the first phase, as the military was to be reduced from 2.6 million personnel to 2.1 million by 1995. In the second phase, the target was 1.5 million by the year 2000.[90] Officers were laid off in large numbers beginning in 1991 without social security and without proper housing. Yeltsin's military adviser Konstantin Kobets claimed that homeless officers numbered 190,000 in 1991 and increased to 240,000 by 1992.[91] As well as those released from service by the phased reductions, there was the problem of 100,000 personnel plus 184,000 family dependents who were to be withdrawn from Germany, and an additional 40,000 military personnel and their families from the Baltic states. Housing for these returnees did not exist, though funds had been made available by the German government. Officers and their families were reduced to paupers as fixed salaries failed to keep pace with inflation. They witnessed corruption in the senior ranks as military equipment was traded for personal advantage and saw how demoralization and ill-discipline spread throughout the ranks.

Colonel Yuri Deryugin in 1994 conducted a survey within the military and claimed that the army's consciousness had been commercialized. He introduced the notion of military-commercial clans that had developed within the military and diverted it from its proper tasks.[92] These military-commercial clans involved military district and regional commanders who supplied equipment, transport, and even labor for commercial purposes. Under these conditions, basic training and discipline were increasingly ignored. Deryugin claimed that an explosive situation existed in the military that was a threat to both government and state, and which was rapidly becoming criminalized through commercial contacts with Mafia groups. Deryugin's surveys revealed that 42 percent of the officers saw no point in service and talked of leaving. He claimed that among majors and major generals some 40 percent supported radical patriotism.[93] A survey conducted in November 1992 revealed that 33 percent of officers asked wanted to see the Soviet Union restored and 66 percent wanted to see a military-based regime in Russia. Neither the size of the sample nor survey techniques were revealed.[94] Members of some 24 officers' organizations in the army that reflected patriotic sentiment to varying degrees were basically hostile toward the economic reforms and the Yeltsin government. The officers' union, which conducted a meeting in February 1993, called for Defense Minister Grachev's resignation. Grachev himself declared the union illegitimate but was no more able to restore political discipline in the officer corps than Yeltsin could manage the Supreme Soviet.

Over general foreign policy issues the military's interest has been expressed by the Moscow-based organs, the Defense Ministry, and the General Staff. The view that the United States has no interest in a strong Russia and seeks to prevent its emergence as a rival is reportedly widespread within the military. This was articulated by the then Deputy Chief of Staff Colonel General Mikhail Kolesnikov, who regarded Western policy toward Russia as contradictory, on the one hand providing assistance for Russia, on the other encouraging internal disintegration.[95] Colonel Pechorov identified a basic concern in relation to the North Atlantic Treaty Organization's (NATO) expansion in Eastern Europe and the Balkans. The fear was that through NATO Germany may again emerge as the dominant European power, in which case its territorial claims in the East would be revived.[96] In relation to nuclear arms control, the military was split and greater public opposition was voiced by nationalists and Communists in the Supreme Soviet. Those within the military who criticized the Strategic Arms Reduction Talks (START), in this case START-2, for making Russia more vulnerable were countered by those in the General Staff and the Defense Ministry who argued that Russia could not afford the cost of nuclear rivalry with the United States. Lt.-General Politsyn, Deputy Head of the Center for Military Studies, emphasized that strategic modernization was simply beyond Russia's economic capacity.[97] In relation to the territorial dispute with Japan, military representatives took part in the Supreme Soviet hearings in July 1992. The then First Deputy Defense Minister and Chief of General Staff, Viktor Dubynin, submitted the General Staff's position on the issue opposing the transfer of territory to Japan on the basis that the security of Russia's Far East would be affected.[98]

Concerning these issues, the military's role has been supplementary and hardly decisive. In relation to the Baltic states, the CIS, and immediate security policy, however, the military has had a greater impact and at times seems to have acted autonomously of central direction. Such tendencies could be seen in the agreement Yeltsin reached with Japanese Foreign Minister Watanabe in May 1992 that forces would be reduced in the disputed territory over 1–2 years. Defense Minister Grachev stated that no withdrawals were being planned.[99] Despite Grachev's opposition, however, Russian forces were scaled down in the islands. In relation to the Baltic states, the defense minister evinced a similar resistance to the withdrawal of Russian forces. Speaking at NATO Headquarters in Brussels, Grachev declared in March 1993 that the withdrawal process would be halted in the absence of measures to protect retired Russian servicemen resident in the Baltic states. He also linked the withdrawal of forces to the provision of funds for the construction of housing and social facilities for the personnel concerned.[100] The Foreign Ministry, which by then was conducting negotiations with Estonia over the withdrawal, had not been advised in advance of Grachev's statements. President Yeltsin subsequently declared that forces would be withdrawn from Lithuania, but withdrawals from Latvia and Estonia would be linked to the treatment of their respective Russian minorities.[101] Nonetheless, in view of strong Western pressure on Russia over this issue the military was in no position to prevent withdrawals indefinitely.

The military's role has been significant in relation to the CIS but it is here that it has been most fragmented and divided. Central Moscow military authorities have promoted the various proposals for a CIS military structure on the basis of the Tashkent Collective Security Treaty of May 1992. The military's interest has been to ensure central control over nuclear weapons in both the Ukraine and Kazakhstan and to prevent the escalation of local conflicts in a way that would destabilize Russia's peripheries. Central authorities have not always been able to assert control over local commanders who have developed their own personal alliances in the CIS and have traded military equipment to conflicting sides for personal profit. General Aleksander

Lebed' became a law unto himself as commander of the 14th Army after hostilities broke out in Moldova in June 1992, though he received strong political support from Moscow's nationalists. In the Abkhazi-Georgian conflict in early 1993, the Russian military was accused of being involved on both sides as Russian aircraft bombed Georgian positions and some Russian volunteers served on the Abkhazi side.[102] An *Izvestiya* report noted Russian heavy equipment passed into Georgian as well as Abkhazi hands but it was unclear as to whether deliberate policy or personal profit was the motive.[103] In relation to Tajikistan, Foreign Ministry and Defense Ministry policies were in obvious conflict. While Kozyrev called for national reconciliation with the Islamic-Democratic Alliance, which formed the opposition, the local Russian military supported Tajik Interior Ministry forces in operations against the opposition, and saw no basis for national reconciliation with them.[104]

The Intelligence Organs

The KGB was such a dominant feature of Soviet life that it is difficult for many to accept that Russian society is free of such an all-pervasive intelligence body. The KGB was too large and powerful and when its chief, Vladimir Kryuchkov, orchestrated the attempted coup of August 1991 it became an obvious threat to the Soviet leadership. On 11 October 1991, the Soviet government decided to split the KGB into three services: external intelligence, which was headed by Yevgennii Primakov; counterintelligence or the inter-republican security service; and the state commission for the defense of government borders. Other sections were separated and placed under the control of various ministries such as government communications and special forces.[105] A Security Ministry was established in January 1992 drawn from the Interior Ministry and headed by Viktor Barannikov, indicating further steps to divide the security and intelligence community. The Security Ministry was abolished in December 1993 for suspected involvement in Supreme Soviet resistance to the president in October 1993. The ministry's tasks were absorbed by the Federal Counter Intelligence Service, whose main function was to combat organized crime, narcotics trafficking, and gun running.

Primakov's External Intelligence Service reduced the scale of its activities abroad in the first year of its independent existence. Primakov declared that 30 stations abroad had been closed down as a budgetary measure and that operations had ceased in most of Africa and South East Asia. Funding for political groups abroad were curtailed and political activities were banned.[106] As a remnant institution of a once proud and infamous service, the External Intelligence Service has been considerably emasculated. Nonetheless, Primakov demonstrated an ability to influence policy as a coordinator rather than an independent actor. Primakov's speech in the Foreign Ministry's Press Center on 25 November 1993 indicated the Russian security establishment's opposition to the expansion of NATO through the Partnership for Peace Program.

Primakov's speech had reportedly been approved by the Defense Ministry and the General Staff, and signified the expression of a common interest that united the security establishment.[107]

The Supreme Soviet

Pro-Westernism as a course in foreign policy, in the way defined and implemented by Kozyrev, clashed with the conservative forces of Russian society that found expression in the Supreme Soviet. This was part of a deeper struggle for supremacy between the executive and the legislature for control over the economic and political reform process that was not resolved until Yeltsin dissolved the Supreme Soviet by force on 3–4 October 1993. Both the Supreme Soviet and the Congress of Peoples's Deputies, from which it was drawn, were products of the Soviet era and its representatives were hostile toward economic reform and deeply suspicious of Kozyrev's foreign policy. As many observers have remarked, Yeltsin should have introduced a new constitution and new elections for a reconstituted legislature after the failure of the August 1991 coup. Yeltsin lost his opportunity to make a clear break with the past and had to wait another two years before he could effect meaningful change. Under the Russian Constitution of 12 April 1978, with its many subsequent and confusing amendments, Article 104 made the Supreme Soviet the highest body of state authority. Article 2 made state bodies accountable to the Soviet of Peoples's Deputies.[108] While the Soviet Union existed, the Communist Party controlled the legislature under Article 6, which designated the Communist Party of the Soviet Union (CPSU) as the leading and guiding force of all state organizations. Once the party had been eliminated, the unifying element was lost and the stage was set for conflict between the executive and the legislature. While Yeltsin was chairman of the Russian Supreme Soviet (May 1990–June 1991) he ironically strengthened its role as part of his battle against Gorbachev and the Soviet Union. According to an amendment issued by Yeltsin dated 24 April 1991, Article 8 granted the Supreme Soviet or the Congress of Peoples's Deputies the power to cancel the decrees of the president if they contradicted either its own decisions or the Constitution.[109]

Chairman of the Supreme Soviet Ruslan Khasbulatov insisted that the Constitution gave the legislature superiority over the executive and challenged Yeltsin's government at every turn. Elected chairman on 28 October 1991, Khasbulatov emerged as an alternative executive head and foreign minister, which added to the confusion of Russian politics during this period. On 3 April 1992, Khasbulatov declared that the Supreme Soviet should be the natural opposition to government and formulated an alternative economic program from that pursued by Yeltsin's government. He criticized both the International Monetary Fund (IMF) and the U.S. for supporting Premier Yegor Gaidar, who was pushing economic reform by lifting price controls.[110] In June 1992,

Khasbulatov traveled to Saudi Arabia and sought King Fahd's cooperation to ensure that Russia's Muslims would be shielded from Iranian extremism. In August 1992, he visited New Delhi with Deputy Foreign Minister Boris Pastukhov, where he emphasized relations with India as a priority for Russia. On Russia's relations with the CIS, he declared the disintegration of the Soviet Union a tragedy, claimed that the euphoria of independence had worn off, and that the interparliamentary assembly of CIS states would stimulate regional integration.[111]

Khasbulatov stressed that Russia's foreign policy authorities did not give the CIS sufficient attention. He declared that Russia's highest priority was the CIS, and in a speech to young diplomats accredited to the CIS said that the Finance Ministry had assured him that Russian diplomats in the CIS would not be worse off financially for not having been posted to the West. Khasbulatov told the young diplomats that their mission was to transform the CIS into a confederation.[112] Khasbulatov toured the Ukraine and Belarus in March 1993 as part of his battle against Yeltsin. The chairman intended to activate the CIS interparliamentary commission to promote integration and to compensate for the supposed inadequacy of the foreign minister in this area. In the Ukraine he received a cool welcome as his Ukrainian counterpart Ivan Plyushch stressed that the Ukraine was not a member of the commission and, moreover, questioned the propriety of his visit as legislative representative.[113]

Khasbulatov maneuvred the Supreme Soviet into a position of open conflict with the executive, which in essence reflected the legislature's opposition to economic reform. Khasbulatov's former deputy Sergei Filatov accused him of acting like a dictator and "doing everything to prevent executive-legislative compromise."[114] Filatov further described Khasbulatov as a "monster," ignoring deputies' opinions, and dominating Parliament by utilizing his own administrative structure.[115] He controlled Parliament's resources including the buildings and the foreign trips made by staff, and even created his own personal militia in October 1991 without the president's permission. Khasbulatov's strength was his ability to manipulate the fears of the deputies in relation to the shock therapy Gaidar had subjected Russia. This author's interviews with deputies later revealed that many were critical of Khasbulatov's dictatorial tendencies but were concerned about their positions and alarmed by the reforms.

Khasbulatov had the Supreme Soviet issue a resolution on 13 November 1992 that gave it control over the executive. The Foreign Ministry was made subordinate to the Supreme Soviet, which also was given the power to nominate candidates for key government positions, Supreme Soviet approval was also required for all ministerial appointments.[116] A compromise was reached during the 7th Congress of Peoples's Deputies in December 1992 when Yeltsin proposed that four ministers would be appointed with Supreme Soviet consent—defense, foreign affairs, security, and interior. Through this compromise, Yeltsin wanted to ensure that the Economics Ministry would be excluded from Supreme Soviet interference. In an agreement with the Supreme Soviet, mediated by Valerii Zorkin, the head of the Constitutional Court, a formula was reached on the appointment of the premier. Yeltsin, in any case, was compelled to sacrifice Yegor Gaidar, who had been targeted by Congress, and accepted Viktor Chernomyrdin as premier.[117]

Matters came to a head in early 1993 when the president, in a speech before the Civic Union coalition, accused the Supreme Soviet of running a parallel government that acted as an obstacle to reform.[118] During the 8th Extraordinary Congress of Peoples's Deputies in March 1993, Yeltsin declared that he would rule by decree and would press for a new constitution. The deputies, in turn, considered Yeltsin's impeachment. From the perspective of the Supreme Soviet, Yeltsin was a dictator acting with foreign support who rode roughshod over Russia's constitutional organs.[119] Deputy Premier Vladimir Shumeiko claimed, however, that there had been a constitutional coup d'etat that transformed the congress into the executive and judiciary as well as the legislature.[120] The impasse was only resolved by force when Yeltsin had the Supreme Soviet building stormed in October 1993.

While it existed the Supreme Soviet was a powerful institution that exercised a major impact on foreign policy from 1992–1993. Aside from Khasbulatov, who was mainly concerned with domestic politics, other Supreme Soviet figures such as Yevgennii Ambartsumov and Oleg Rumyantsev were prominent in foreign policy. Ambartsumov was head of the Supreme Soviet's Committee on International Affairs and External Economic Relations, located in the Lower House. A balanced and prudent individual, Ambartsumov, unlike Khasbulatov, did not deliberately embark on a course of confrontation with the executive. He saw it as his role, however, to ensure that foreign policy reflected Russia's interests over specific issues. Oleg Rumyantsev, who with Ambartsumov was a member of the *Rodina* (motherland) faction in the Supreme Soviet, was head of the Constitutional Commission. In addition, there was Sergei Stepashin's Committee on Defense and Security that concerned itself with defense budgetary and finance issues.

The Foreign Ministry was concerned with cultivating relations with the key figures of the Supreme Soviet and reducing the enmity that had developed between the two institutions. The Supreme Soviet constantly questioned Kozyrev's foreign policy demanding corrections and explanations. Kozyrev appeared regularly before closed door hearings of Ambartsumov's committee, which covered such issues as the territorial problem with Japan, the Bosnian conflict, and START-2. In March 1993, Kozyrev claimed that he appeared at these hearings at least 4–5 times a year.[121] A special section in the Foreign Ministry was created for liaison with the Supreme Soviet and to lobby deputies. The head of this section, Vladimir Savel'ev, claimed that such hearings were required to prevent the appearance of the Afghan syndrome or disastrous decision-making by a narrow and isolated circle. Savel'ev stated that Kozyrev met with Supreme Soviet deputies 20 times in 1992 over foreign policy issues;

deputy foreign ministers had met with deputies at least 64 times. The Foreign Ministry, he said, does not work without the Supreme Soviet, which had already influenced foreign policy particularly toward the CIS.[122] The Supreme Soviet's concurrence was required before the Defense Ministry could dispatch additional forces to Tajikistan in July 1993 simply to avoid a political backlash from deputies who feared that the ministry was involving Russia in another Afghanistan. Before the Supreme Soviet would approve the move it called for more information about the conflict from the Foreign Ministry and the Presidential Apparatus. It even sent its own delegation to the Tajik-Afghan border to assess the situation independently before the Defense Ministry's request was endorsed.[123]

The Impact of Individuals

Stable political systems with well-defined decision-making mechanisms reduce the impact of individuals on foreign policy or limit their roles to particular institutions or agencies. Unstable or still evolving systems with ill-defined procedures allow political personalities greater influence according to the issue they invoke and the following generated. The absence of structural stability in government allowed Aleksander Rutskoi, Yeltsin's vice-president from June 1991 to October 1993, to act as a loose cannon frequently attacking government and marking out his own foreign policy agenda. In December 1991, Rutskoi acted as a foreign minister when he traveled to Iran, Afghanistan, and Pakistan and proposed negotiations to manage the conflict in Afghanistan.[124] He directly involved himself in CIS policy, declaring that the Russian government's protection of ethnic Russians in the CIS could not be regarded as interference into the international affairs of sovereign states but should be seen as security against genocide.[125] Rutskoi demanded protection for the Russians there at a time when Kozyrev insisted that strict observance of international law was required. Rutskoi attacked the Ukraine over the Black Sea Fleet and the Crimea and intervened in the Moldovan conflict demanding that Russia support the Transdniester Republic (TDR).[126] Rutskoi was an air force general and a Soviet war hero having been shot down in Afghanistan twice and his political connections with the military granted him a certain political immunity.

Valentin Fyodorov, who was governor of Sakhalin from November 1991 until March 1993, had a similar impact on Russian policy toward Japan. As chairman of Sakhalin Council, Fyodorov became a noted opponent of the transfer of any of the disputed territory to Japan. He campaigned on the issue when Gorbachev visited Japan in April 1991, and on 23 October 1991 threatened to declare independence from the Soviet Far East if the government handed over the islands to Japan. Fyodorov, certainly, contributed to the inflammation of the issue and to the widespread resistance that subsequently emerged to the idea of a territorial deal with Japan. Fyodorov was initially an embarrassment to the Foreign Ministry and those in the government who had pinned their hopes on the compromise with Japan, but he eventually became an excuse for the postponement of all such efforts. Other examples of individual impact on foreign policy include local Far Eastern governors who in 1994 protested against the border treaty that had been earlier concluded with China.

Conflict Over Foreign Policy

Foreign policy became a battleground and the above institutions and individuals participated in a way that closely mirrored the development of domestic politics. The Foreign Ministry had the initial advantage of articulating a clear policy of identification with the West while other institutions were disoriented or in a state of complete disarray. The Foreign Ministry was later attacked by the Supreme Soviet over the implications of its pro-Western policy for two reasons. First, it was criticized for failing to address the issue of Russia's relations with the CIS, and for an inability to define clearly a guiding concept of foreign policy. Secondly, it was accused of selling out Russia's interests to the U.S. or other states over issues that affected Russia directly. Such issues included the Bosnian conflict, the territorial dispute with Japan, and the proposal to sell rocket engines to India from 1992–1993. The consequence was the undermining of the Foreign Ministry as the body responsible for the articulation of foreign policy and the dilution of pro-Westernism as initially formulated.

The conflict between Foreign Ministry and Supreme Soviet for control of foreign policy manifested itself in the demand for a clear concept of foreign policy that reflected Russia's interests. The Foreign Ministry first submitted a document to the Supreme Soviet in February 1992 on the concept of Russian foreign policy that emphasized relations with the CIS as a top priority, and which included the main elements of the pro-Western position.[127] The Supreme Soviet found the concept unsatisfactory and called for its revision initiating a long struggle between both bodies over the issue. Kozyrev bemoaned the fact that diplomats in other countries were not required to reduce their flexibility by defining their policies.[128] First Deputy Defense Minister Andrei Kokoshin regarded the request for a doctrine as a clear Russian syndrome, a belief in a universal document that gives answers to every problem.[129] Behind the demand, however, was an effort to redefine foreign policy and to compel the Foreign Ministry to accommodate the Supreme Soviet.

After Kozyrev testified before Ambartsumov's committee on 30 June, the chairman decided that the Foreign Ministry had no concept of policy and that Kozyrev's approach did not suit the legislature. Ambartsumov proposed an alternative foreign policy on the basis that the former Soviet Union was an area of vital interests to Russia. Russia, he claimed, should obtain from the world community endorsement of its interests there in something resembling the Monroe Doctrine. Russia should also obtain G-7 recognition of its role in the former Soviet Union as a guarantor of security and should receive hard currency subsidies from this body to support its stabilizing role there. In bilateral agreements with the CIS states, provision's should be made for the protection of Russians there, as well as for the deployment of Russian forces. Finally, Ambartsumov pointed to China as a model of a country that pursues an independent foreign policy while maintaining stable relations with both the United States and Russia.[130] How Russia could impose itself on the CIS states in this way and obtain the approval of the world community for a Russian version of the Monroe Doctrine was not explained.

The Foreign Ministry submitted a 58–page document on the concept of foreign policy to Parliament for discussion. The existence of this document was first known in October 1992 but its circulation was strictly controlled. *Izvestiya* correspondent Stanislav Kondrashov identified its features as: an emphasis on the CIS as top priority on the agenda through intelligent policies; developing relations with Europe to eliminate Russia's isolation from the West; collaborating with the developed West, which was considered to be another major priority but not to the neglect of Russia's interests; developing a strategic partnership with the United States, which would not exclude Russia's opposition to America's imperial ambitions.[131] A condensed version of the concept was published in *Rossiiskiye Vesti*.[132] Ambartsumov, however, revealed the confusion that had emerged as two foreign policy concepts circulated between the government and the legislature. The Foreign Ministry version was sent directly to the relevant legislature committees and was not discussed in open session. After discussion in Ambartsumov's committee, the document was placed before the president for approval. The second version was prepared under Yuri Skokov's direction in the Security Council. Ambartsumov said that he was involved in its preparation but it was a closed document and after its approval by the president in March 1993 he claims he never saw it again.[133] The Foreign Ministry version still circulated, though this author found officials most reluctant to show him a full text. Deputy Director of the Institute of the United States and Canada Viktor Kremenyuk criticized it as being a product of bureaucratic interests representing the Soviet approach toward foreign policy formulation rather than a clear identification of Russia's interests. The document, according to Kremenyuk, was a statement of "bureaucratic banalities."[134]

ATTEMPTS TO ALTER DIRECTION

Several attempts were made to adjust foreign policy to accommodate the demand that Russia's interests be emphasized more clearly as a guiding principle. One obvious move was the removal of Kozyrev as foreign minister, which was rumored as early as November 1991. In February 1992, it was reported that Yuli Vorontsov would replace Kozyrev as someone better able to forge links with the outside world.[135] In July 1992, sources in the Russian government claimed that Skokov's Security Council had pressed Yeltsin for Kozyrev's removal.[136] Vitalii Tret'yakov wrote that "there is practically no doubt" that Kozyrev would soon resign as he had come under sustained attack from inside as well as outside government.[137] Finally, when Civic Union leader Arkadii Vol'skii visited Japan in December 1992 he predicted that Vorontsov would replace Kozyrev. Yeltsin was engaged in a struggle with the Congress of Peoples's Deputies and it seemed logical that Kozyrev would be sacrificed. Despite the pressure, however, Yeltsin retained Kozyrev as his presence was regarded as a signal to the West of the continuation of a pro-Western policy. As a symbol of Russia's democratic and Western aspirations Kozyrev came to be regarded as Yeltsin's sacred cow.[138]

One significant adjustment was the attempt to devise a longterm policy toward the CIS that would accommodate the sovereignty and independence of the new states. The Council on Foreign and Defense Policy, which convened under the aegis of the Foreign Ministry, highlighted this need in its report. The council, which met on 30 July 1992, was chaired by Kozyrev and included 37 members who were involved directly or indirectly in foreign policy. In a meeting attended by Ambartsumov and other Supreme Soviet deputies, officials, academics, and the editor of *Nezavisimaya gazeta,* the council emphasized the importance of the CIS as the main priority for Russia. The council's report, which was coordinated by Sergei Karaganov, pointed to a security vacuum in the former Soviet Union and identified the dangers there for Russia's security. Russia's main task was to maintain its territorial integrity for which a coherent policy toward the CIS was required to neutralize the impact of disintegrative tendencies.

The fact that this council identified the need to treat the CIS more seriously was indicative of how attitudes among Russia's foreign policy and security establishment had been influenced by the security situation. Nonetheless, the extent to which the focus on the CIS should impact on other foreign policies was a matter for debate within this group. Those who accepted the CIS as first priority for Russia for security reasons were counterbalanced by those who warned that an excessive focus on the CIS could result in Russia's provincialization. Russia should, accordingly, continue to open up to the outside world while maintaining a relationship with the West and developing relations with Asian powers.[139]

An attempt to balance the pro-Western policy was made by the Russian government toward the end of 1992 and early 1993 as Yeltsin developed relations with Asia-Pacific powers. Oleg Rumyantsev announced in September 1992 that foreign policy would be diverted from its pro-Western course.[140] Responding to the criticism that Russia's foreign policy was excessively Western in orientation Yeltsin traveled to Seoul in November 1992, Beijing in December 1992, and New Delhi in January 1993 to demonstrate that Russia's foreign policy was balanced between the West and Asia. In Beijing Yeltsin declared for the benefit of domestic audiences: "We are accused of

Americanization, of looking to the West. After the visit to South Korea this is our second breakthrough in the Asia-Pacific region. It should balance our foreign policy."[141] As a consequence, Argovski and Rumyantsev wrote that the Supreme Soviet acted as a corrective mechanism bringing foreign policy into line with Russian national interests. Until this corrective mechanism began to operate, Russia, they claimed, had sacrificed its national interests for the West.[142]

Significantly, the declaratory principles of Kozyrev's foreign policy were adjusted as a response to Supreme Soviet criticisms. In an address at the Moscow International Press Center in December 1992, Kozyrev identified new priorities that marked a departure from his policies as outlined earlier in the year. These included: an equal and special relationship with the CIS; cooperation with China; a recognition of India as a stabilizing factor in Asia; and the continuation of the relationship with the West. Kozyrev stressed that Russia had passed the stage of first acquaintance with the West and was moving to the stage of partnership.[143] Kozyrev still defended the idea of alliance with the West as providing Russia with support against the national patriots who, he claimed, wanted to isolate Russia from the rest of the world. He stressed that the alliance with the West provided Russia with the most favorable environment to defend Russia's interests, whether in terms of obtaining investment from the West or obtaining a place in Western markets for Russian products. Kozyrev conceded, however, that alliances are not without differences as was the case with the U.S. and Europe, thereby revealing a lapse of enthusiasm that did not escape his critics.[144]

Kozyrev's adjustment of views constituted an effort to deflect the political pressure without necessarily altering the fundamentals of the pro-Western policy. Yeltsin's trips to the Far East and India were attempts to protect the pro-Western policy of his government from the legislature and its many critics. The hope was that with a change in declaratory priorities and some adjustment of perspectives the pro-Western course could be secured against further domestic attack. Nonetheless, the succeeding year produced division in the ranks of the pro-Western supporters as the domestic and foreign policy costs became more apparent. Some among the pro-Western group shifted toward the geopolitical or geostrategic position, perceiving a need for the modification of foreign policy according to Russia's geographical location. Sergei Rogov, for example, now director of the Institute of the United States and Canada, was critical of what he regarded as the blind following of the United States though he supported the idea of partnership with the U.S.[145]

Perhaps the most critical split in the pro-Western camp occurred between Kozyrev and the then Ambassador to the U.S., Vladimir Lukin, who was known for his outspoken views. Lukin's foreign policy credentials were impressive. He spent 19 years with the Institute for the U.S. and Canada, 2 years with the Soviet Foreign Ministry (1987–1988) and from 1991–1992 he was the chairman of the Russian Supreme Soviet's Committee on International

Relations. It was because of Lukin that Kozyrev was selected for the position of Russia's Foreign Ministry with Deputy Foreign Minister Vladimir Petrovskii's support. Lukin became highly critical of Kozyrev's pro-US position and did not hide his feelings. According to reports, Kozyrev moved Lukin out of Moscow and later unsuccessfully attempted to move him from the embassy in Washington. Lukin conducted a seminar in Moscow on 28 August 1993 that was regarded as highly critical of Kozyrev.[146] Kozyrev apparently prevented Lukin from briefing Prime Minister Chernomyrdin before his visit to Washington in September 1993 and arranged for the briefing to be conducted by someone more loyal to his own view within the Washington embassy staff.

According to Dmitri Kosyrev, the Kozyrev-Lukin conflict was one between two conceptions of foreign policy, one pro-US and the other independent. The event that made the conflict public was the proposed sale of cryogenic rocket engines to India that the United States opposed as contravening the missile technology control regime of 1987. Kozyrev supported the United States over this issue when sanctions were imposed on the Russian agency involved—*Glavkosmos*—in May 1992. Lukin, on the contrary, defended the sale on the grounds that the missiles involved were liquid-fueled and could not be used for military purposes, and that the relationship with India was important for Russia.[147] Lukin outlined his views in various interviews when he took pains to distinguish his position from what he regarded as the subservience of Kozyrev's pro-Western policy. He distanced himself from the nationalists (whom he strongly criticized) claiming that the United States is not interested in the disintegration of Russia as the result would be a gigantic Yugoslavia with nuclear weapons. He also emphasized that the United States was opposed to a strong Russia that could be a competitor. He stressed that Russia's national interest was sometimes congruent with that of the United States but differences could not be ignored.[148]

Kozyrev's conflict with Lukin was potentially the most damaging for his foreign policy as it emerged from within the ranks of the Russian foreign policy establishment. The fact that an ambassador could openly spar with his foreign minister over these issues demonstrated the extent dissatisfaction with the Kozyrev line had spread even within the Foreign Ministry. Lukin represented not the emotional and sometimes irrational opposition to pro-Westernism, which was characteristic of the Communists or the nationalists, but an acceptable and measured position that reflected Russia's geopolitical position. In frequent statements and public appearances, Lukin articulated an alternative foreign policy that supplemented pro-Westernism with a concern for Russia's Asian interests. Lukin's alternative foreign policy entailed an adjustment of Russia's relationship with the West that brought him closer to the views of the geopoliticians or geostrategists. Kozyrev's initial version of pro-Westernism came to be regarded as fanciful, abstract, and somewhat unrelated to Russian interests. Kozyrev, indeed, would not have remained foreign minister for much longer had he not changed his views.

POST-1993 CHANGES

The events of 1993 were to change the context of foreign policy in a very critical way. First was the dissolution of the Supreme Soviet when Yeltsin ordered the army to storm the parliamentary building on 3–4 October. The removal of the Supreme Soviet and the temporary incarceration of Khasbulatov and Rutskoi eliminated a major internal challenge to the Foreign Ministry over the conduct of foreign policy. As a *Nezavisimaya gazeta* commentary put it, the last fragment of the old Soviet apparatus was finally liquidated.[149] Added to this were several other developments that strengthened the Foreign Ministry's institutional position. Yuri Skokov had been removed from his position as head of the Security Council, and his successor Oleg Lobov had little interest in foreign policy. A Foreign Ministry representative was to head the Security Council's foreign policy commission and, Kozyrev's critic within the president's entourage, Sergei Stankevich, resigned and was replaced by Dmitri Ryurikov who was more sympathetic to the Foreign Ministry position.[150]

The new Constitution, which was accepted by referendum at the same time as the new parliamentary elections of 12 December 1993, strengthened the role of the president over foreign policy and correspondingly reduced the role of the legislature. The new Constitution eliminated the difficulties of the executive's relationship with the legislature, which had generated such bitter conflict from 1992–1993. According to Article 80(3), the president defines the general direction of both internal and foreign policy; under Article 86(a) the president directs foreign policy; under Article 83(f) the president heads and forms the Security Council, the status of which was to be defined by federal law; under Article 87(1) the president was made the supreme commander of the armed forces. The Constitution created a federal assembly with two houses and under Article 95(1) the Lower House was called the State Duma with 450 representatives and the Upper House was the Federation Council. No specific powers of oversight were granted to the federal assembly under the Constitution. In terms of foreign policy, the Federation Council under Article 106 was to ratify and denounce treaties and was concerned with the "status and defense of the state borders of the Russian Federation" and with "war and peace." The State Duma under Article 103(b) was given the power to confirm the appointment of government representatives.[151] Recent commentary on the Constitution notes that the president's powers in foreign policy under Article 86 are not unrestrained, but are exercised with the participation of Parliament whose powers in foreign policy are identified in Article 106.[152]

The victory that both Yeltsin and Kozyrev won over their domestic opponents in the constitutional referendum was countered, however, by the results of the 12 December parliamentary elections in which Zhirinovsky's Liberal Democratic Party performed unexpectedly well. The LDP gathered 24 percent of the vote, ahead of Russia's Choice with 14.48 percent and Zyuganov's Communist Party with 13.59 percent. The party with the largest vote, the LDP, ended up as third largest in the Duma with 62 deputies, after

Russia's Choice with 74, and the newly formed Regional Policy Group with 66 deputies. Zhirinovsky's electoral success represented a protest against the economic reform movement, which had resulted in so much suffering, and against the fragmented democrats, who could not unite in a common platform. Neither Yegor Gaidar's Russia's Choice nor Grigori Yavlinskii's *Yabloko* Group could overcome their differences for the elections. As Kozyrev lamented, both groups thought in terms of the presidential elections and had discounted the appeal of the LDP.[153]

Zhirinovsky represented the dark forces of Russian nationalism that the democrats feared though he himself could not be taken seriously. He developed the technique of drawing attention to himself through egregious rhetoric that he subsequently repudiated or modified. In 1991 he called for the annexation of Finland, while in December 1993 he assured the Finnish news agency that he had no such intention. After having called for a new partition of Poland he explained that he only meant to criticize Poland for its ingratitude after Russia defeated the Nazis during World War II.[154] Over North Hamburg Radio he accused Germans of interfering in Russia and exclaimed, "you will get your own Chernobyl." He also threatened the Japanese saying, "We will create new Hiroshimas and Nagasakis. I will not hesitate to deploy atomic weapons."[155] Later he said he had been misinterpreted and that he only wanted to warn the West of the civil conflict that would arise if it continued to interfere in Russia. Significantly, he did not repudiate the comments directed at the Japanese.[156] Zhirinovsky toyed with the powerful symbols of Russian nationalism in order to gain attention but he was in no position, politically or temperamentally, to give that nationalism a sense of direction. He could not invoke the forces of Russian nationalism without being consumed by them and for this reason he backed away from his own rhetoric.

A new situation emerged where the Foreign Ministry was given the constitutional freedom to conduct foreign policy while being constrained politically from exercising that freedom. While the constitutional order that Yeltsin and his government attempted to foster within Russia rested on very tenuous foundations in Russian society, Kozyrev was compelled to bow to political realities. Initially, Kozyrev responded to the election results by insisting that his position would be unchanged and that the inauguration of the new Constitution ensured that foreign policy was presidential.[157] Kozyrev, however, adjusted his views to accommodate the new nationalism of the State Duma in recognition of his own vulnerability. The result was that the main exponent of Russia's pro-Western policy became hostage to domestic political forces, much reduced in terms of status, and bereft of the early enthusiasm and confidence.

The new State Duma gathered together forces of various descriptions that were broadly critical of either the pro-Western line or Kozyrev's interpretation of it. Under Article 101(3) of the new Constitution each house could form its own committees and commissions. Within the State Duma four committees were established that one way or another cover foreign policy. They are: International Affairs, headed by Kozyrev's nemesis Vladimir Lukin, the largest committee after the Budget Committee with 27 members; CIS Affairs, headed by Konstantin Zatulin, which is interested in the position of the Russians in the "new abroad"; Security, headed by Viktor Ilyukhin, which examines internal security only and has little interest in foreign policy; Defense, headed by Sergei Yushenkov, which examines issues such as nuclear proliferation, chemical weapons and holds joint hearings with the International Affairs Committee on these subjects. There was also the Committee on Geopolitical Issues headed by Viktor Ustinov, which examines ecological security, common global problems such as pollution, sea, and land borders.[158]

Nominally, Parliament could influence foreign policy in four ways. First, under Article 106(d) the power to ratify and denounce treaties was exercised when deputies refused to ratify the START-2 Treaty. Second, the Parliament could pass resolutions on foreign policy like the Supreme Soviet calling for the removal of sanctions on Serbia. The executive, however, is not bound by such resolutions but cannot ignore them entirely, particularly if they have strong support. Third, the various committees of both houses could conduct hearings into specific foreign policy issues that are attended by representatives of the Presidential Apparatus, the Foreign Ministry, journalists, and Defense Ministry officials. (In July 1995 the author witnessed the conduct of one of these Duma hearings that tended toward abstract discussions rather than debates on concrete policies.) Finally, under Article 103(a) the Duma has the power to confirm ambassadorial appointments. There have been two occasions reported when the Duma has refused to accept the president's nominations.

Nezavisimaya gazeta correspondent Mikhail Karpov claimed that all the conditions were there for a new conflict between the legislature and the president over foreign policy. Lukin had three deputies, one of whom was Aleksei Mitrofanov, the LDP's spokesman on foreign affairs. Viktor Ilyukhin was a former Communist procurator who had intended to put Gorbachev on trial for the collapse of the Soviet Union. One of his three deputies was Nina Krivel'skaya who was an LDP member. Konstantin Zatulin was a proponent of imperialism in the CIS while the Geopolitical Affairs Committee was established for the benefit of the LDP, as compensation for the government's refusal to grant Zhirinovsky a ministerial portfolio. Its head, Viktor Ustinov and his deputy Mikhail Sidorov, were both LDP members.[159] *Izvestiya* correspondent Maksim Yusin wrote that the anti-Kozyrev lobby group in the State Duma was very influential and cut across political lines. He claimed that if it came to a test some two-thirds of the Duma would vote against him.[160]

The formation of the new Duma was the occasion for the renewed expression of criticisms and attacks on the Kozyrev line as well as confident assertions of alternative courses. From his position as Duma Committee Chairman Lukin's criticisms were stinging. He lambasted what he called the infantile pro-Americanism of Russian foreign policy, which in his view was responsible for 50 percent of the result of the last elections.[161] Lukin insisted that Russia should defend its interests in relation to the West but distinguished his views from the nationalists whom he regarded as dangerous.[162] Vyacheslav Nikonov, member of Lukin's committee and head of the Subcommittee on International Security and Arms Control called for "Russian neo-Gaullism." According to Nikonov, the idea of integrating with the West was an illusion; he stressed the importance of an independent foreign policy for Russia without, however, endorsing neo-imperialism in the CIS, which he condemned.[163]

While the executive was locked in a struggle with the Supreme Soviet, it was possible to explain away the opposition as a relic from the Soviet era that would be corrected by a new Constitution, fresh elections, and a new Parliament. The resurgence of a similar opposition in the new Duma indicated that something more fundamental was at issue than the survival of an institutional relic of the Soviet era. Russian society had become sharply polarized since the dissolution of the Supreme Soviet, and those who regarded this act as a betrayal of democracy joined forces with those who reacted against the deteriorating social and economic conditions of the country. Their votes boosted the fortunes of the LDP and Zyuganov's Communist Party in the December elections in a way that Yeltsin's government could not dismiss. What followed was an effort on the part of both Yeltsin and Kozyrev to reshape their own conceptions of foreign policy to accommodate the concerns of the moderate opposition and to isolate the destructive nationalists. In this process, foreign policy views were expressed and articulated to embrace a wide variety of views from the geopolitical, the Eurasianist to the nationalist. The pure form of pro-Westernism initially espoused by Kozyrev, with its emphasis on international institutions, the UN, and human rights, lapsed.

Yeltsin's government could not retreat from the idea of association with the West as advocated by extreme nationalists; that indeed was not a serious issue as there were obvious benefits for Russia. Kozyrev defended the pro-Western course by saying that its main benefit over the past two years was that Russia had not been banished from the international arena, did not try to re-establish the empire by force and avoided the Yugoslavian syndrome on a grand scale.[164] Kozyrev's pro-Westernism could count as one of the first steps in the integration of Russia into the international system in the face of a society that had long been conditioned to regard the outside world as a threat. What were perceived by the nationalists as concessions to the West and humiliation for Russia were actually part of the process of normal integration with the international system that Kozyrev's pro-Western policy facilitated. Russia in its weakened state could not dissociate itself from the international system without the risk of complete collapse.

The pro-Western course had brought additional benefits that could not be denied. Kozyrev claimed that because of his course Russia had been admitted to international economic institutions such as the IMF and World Bank, and had received some $12.5 billion in credits. Russia had also avoided bankruptcy since the Paris and London Club of Debtors had rescheduled its debts. He added that the relationship with the West allowed Russia to defend its legal interests in economics, trade, and security and cited as examples the agreement achieved with U.S. involvement on the liquidation of nuclear weapons in the Ukraine. Kozyrev pointed to the NATO Partnership for Peace Program that for Russia was a better alternative than the immediate expansion of NATO.[165] Other benefits the Foreign Minister could have identified included nuclear arms reduction agreements (START-1 and 2) with the U.S. that allowed Russia to disengage from the nuclear arms race, and Western support for Russia's territorial integrity in the face of declarations of independence by some of its constituent republics—Chechnya, Tatarstan, and Yakutia. This support was inextricably linked with the Yeltsin government's commitment to reform. Without that commitment, pressure within the West to support Chechen self-determination, for example, would have been stronger.

What was at issue subsequently was the extent to which Russia's specific security and foreign policy interests could be harmonized with the relationship with the West. Those interests included the security of the "near abroad" and relations with non-Western states such as China, Iran, and India, countries that may be in conflict with the West over particular issues. The radical democrats and the extreme pro-Western group claimed that such specific interests would be managed within the context of the Western alliance, which for Russia had priority. The geopoliticians and geostrategists argued that Russia could pursue its security interests in the "near abroad" and its own Asian-oriented foreign policy in a way that would not undermine the pro-Western policy. The nationalists, however, insisted that Russia's immediate security interests in the "near abroad" had priority and that Russia should pursue those interests with or without Western endorsement. A nationalist view over this issue was forcefully expressed by the Armenian Andranik Migranyan who as a member of the president's advisory council called for a Russian Monroe Doctrine for the "near abroad." According to Migranyan, the "near abroad" would be a test of the solidarity of Russia's relationship with the West and whether the West could accept Russia's vital interests.[166]

The debates pushed the Yeltsin-Kozyrev view of foreign policy toward the geopolitical position as an attempt was made to grapple with the key issues that had disturbed wide sections of society. To the extent that Russia has had an official policy or a consensus on foreign policy it has become more geopolitical in orientation as the pro-Western approach is pursued together with specific security and foreign policy interests to which the West may object. Developments in 1994 revealed an emerging consensus around the need to affirm those specific interests without necessarily denying or repudiating the benefits of association with the West. Other more extreme positions continued to be expressed and forcefully advocated within government as well as without, but a noticeable convergence of views could be identified within the broader foreign policy establishment. That convergence would serve as the basis for the development and articulation of a more defined foreign policy agenda in future years.

Kozyrev's own adaptation to prevailing trends became noticeable in early 1994. Despite his initial assertion that Zhirinovsky would not change foreign policy, Kozyrev later admitted that foreign policy would be used to reduce Zhirinovsky's constituency. He accused the Baltic states of playing on the Zhirinovsky factor to demand immediate entry into NATO and stressed the need for an improvement of the social position of the Russians there.[167] Kozyrev spoke before Russian diplomats from the CIS and Baltic states and emphasized that the former Soviet Union constitutes an area of Russia's vital interests. He emphasized that one of the main strategic tasks of Russian foreign policy would be to defend Russian minority rights in the "near abroad" on the basis of dual citizenship. He also accepted the need to maintain a Russian military presence in the "near abroad."[168] Significantly, the Foreign Ministry in February 1994 prepared a series of measures to support Russians in the "near abroad" including the formation of a body to coordinate social and economic assistance on their behalf as well as more active lobbying of the CSCE and the UN.[169] When Kozyrev spoke to Russians at their cultural center in Tallinn he told them that Russia would never forget them and that with the withdrawal of Russian forces from Estonia other methods could be used to defend their interests. As a result, Kozyrev received the accolade from the conservative newspaper *Pravda* of being "sometimes a patriot."[170]

Russia, indeed, came to focus on the "near abroad" as the basis for foreign policy. Yeltsin's speech to the new Federal Assembly on 24 February 1994 reflected this emphasis in the president's first comprehensive statement on foreign policy. Yeltsin identified the nature of Russia's relationship with the outside world in terms of "the recognition of the norms and principles of international law" and the importance of defending Russia's legal interests in the context of these universal principles. Beyond that he emphasized that because of its geopolitical position Russia "has a special responsibility for stability in the multipolar world," that Russia had a special interest in the CIS, and that the establishment of a collective security system in the CIS was the first priority. Yeltsin referred to Russia's unique Euro-Asian status as a basis for the development of relations with China, Japan, India, and South Korea. Nonetheless, the president noted that the relationship with the West had become troubled by concerns about the expansion of NATO to include the Eastern European states. In this respect, the president bemoaned the absence of an effective mechanism of consultation with the West.[171]

Tension emerged between two critical areas of foreign policy as a consequence of developments during 1993–1994. Domestic political pressure and a concern for Russia's immediate security pushed the Yeltsin government into affirming the importance of the CIS. As First Deputy Foreign Minister Anatolii Adamshin stated, Russia's survival will depend on the character of its relationship with the CIS.[172] The willingness of the West to endorse Russia's role in the CIS was open to question in view of expressed concerns within the Ukraine and elsewhere in regard to a revival of a Russian empire. A Russian role in the CIS, depending of course on how that role was defined, may stimulate much tension with the West to the extent that fears are aroused in regard to Russian imperialism. How policy toward the West could be managed in the context of Russia's obvious security needs in the "near abroad" became one of the salient challenges of Russian foreign policy. Adamshin stressed that the West must understand that Russia cannot abnegate its responsibilities in the "near abroad." According to Adamshin, talk of convergence with the West should not blind Russia to the differences in the relationship.[173] Others argued that Russia has a completely different geostrategic position from the West and that there was a need for Russia to develop relations with Asian powers even if this entailed placing limits on the partnership with the West.[174]

The pro-Western course that Kozyrev had advocated represented Russia's integration into the international community, but increasingly it was compelled to compete with other policy directions toward the CIS and Asia, which were subject to geopolitical, Eurasian, and nationalist influences. The tension between Western and CIS priorities in foreign policy was exacerbated by disappointment in the pro-Western policy as NATO prepared to embrace East and Central Europe, and by concerns in relation to the security of the CIS. This tension between priorities motivated the second set of recommendations by the Council on Foreign and Defense Policy that were published in *Nezavisimaya gazeta* on 27 May 1994. The intention was to correct what was perceived as a swing away from the pro-Western policy and to prevent the emergence of nationalism or chauvinism in foreign policy. The council's recommendations included the idea of flexible diplomacy between various centers of power including China while avoiding unnecessary tension with the West. As the council included many influential figures in Russian foreign policy, its views could be regarded as reflecting the foreign policy establishment in terms of its emphasis on independence and autonomy in the context of the relationship with the West.[175]

How the pro-Western direction of foreign policy, which was initially understood as fundamental by the Yeltsin government, could be harmonized with Russia's security needs in the "near abroad," or with the Asia-Pacific will be further examined. The different opinion groups struggling for influence over foreign policy, whether pro-Western, geopolitical, Eurasian, or nationalist-Communist, have proposed various ways of managing this problem by emphasizing one direction of policy or by downgrading another. As Russia adjusts to its new geopolitical predicament and overcomes the shock of its painful birth from the Soviet Union, a broad consensus is being formed to the effect that Russia may cooperate with the West but can never be part of it while other foreign policy priorities claim its attention.

NOTES

1. Aleksander Gol'ts, "Mezhdy sverderzhavavoi i velikoi stranoi," *Rossiiskaya gazeta*, 11 Sept. 1991.

2. Aleksei Vasil'ev, "Rossiya i musil'manski mir—partnery ili protivniki?," *Izvestiya*, 10 Mar. 1992.

3. Sergei Stankevich, "Derzhava v poiskakh sebya," *Nezavisimaya gazeta*, 28 Mar. 1992.

4. Aleksei Vasil'ev, "Trudnosti predolimy," *Nezavisimaya gazeta*, 11 Mar. 1994.

5. Aleksei G. Arbatov, "Russia's Foreign Policy Alternatives," *International Security*, fall 1993, vol. 18, no. 2.

6. Vladimir Lukin, *Tsentry sily, konseptsi i real'nost*, Moscow, 1983.

7. Andrei Kozyrev, *Preobrazhenie*, Mezhdunarodnye Otnoshenie, Moscow, 1994, pp. 42–43.

8. Andrei Kozyrev, "My vykhodim na novuyu sistemu tsennostei," *Krasnaya zvezda*, 20 Dec. 1991.

9. *Krasnaya zvezda*, 20 Dec. 1991.

10. Andrei Kozyrev, "Vyzov preobrazheniya," *Izvestiya*, 31 Mar. 1992.

11. *Itar Tass*, 31 Jan. 1992.

12. Andrei Kozyrev, "Preobrazhennaya Rossiya v novom mire," *Izvestiya*, 2 Jan. 1992.

13. *Izvestiya*, 23 Sept. 1992.

14. *Tass*, 16 Jan. 1992.

15. *Itar Tass*, 31 Jan. 1992.

16. Andrei Kozyrev, "Vyzov preorazheniya," *Izvestiya*, 31 Mar. 1992.

17. *Izvestiya*, 31 Mar. 1992.

18. "Osnovnaya opasnost'—v nomenklaturnom revanshe," *Nezavisimaya gazeta*, 8 Oct. 1992.

19. Andrei Kozyrev, "Preobrazhennaya Rossiya v novom mire," *Izvestiya*, 2 Jan. 1992.

20. *Itar Tass*, 20 Feb. 1992.

21. *Itar Tass*, 12 Feb. 1992.

22. Aleksei Vasil'ev, "Rossiya i musil'manski mir; partnery ili protivniki," *Izvestiya*, 10 Mar. 1992.

23. Sergei Goncharov, "Osobye interesyi Rossii," *Izvestiya*, 25 Feb. 1992.

24. Vladimir, Myasnikov, "Vostochnyi vektor dla strany," *Krasnaya zvezda*, 23 Dec. 1992.

25. Andranik Migranyan, "Podlinnye i mnimye orientiry vo vneshnei politike," *Rossiiskaya gazeta*, 4 Aug. 1992.

26. Viktor Kremenyuk, "Vneshnaya politika Rossii: Nuzhny orientiry," *Nezavisimaya gazeta*, 17 Aug. 1993.

27. Aleksander Gol'ts, "Nam pora izbavlyatsya ot novykh mifov," *Krasnaya zvezda*, 28 Mar. 1992.

28. Aleksei Voskresenskii, "Otnosheniya v novom mire," *Nezavisimaya gazeta*, 25 Nov. 1993.

29. Valerii Manilov, "Rossiya vo Vneshnem mire," *Nezavisimaya gazeta*, 22, 26 July 1994.

30. Aleksander Vladislavlev, "Vneshnaya politika Rossii," *Nezavisimaya gazeta*, 6 May 1994.

31. L. I. Novikova, I. N. Sizemskaya (eds.), *Rossiya mezhdu evropoi i aziei; evraziiskii soblazn*, Nauka, Moscow, 1993, pp. 11–14.

32. N. S. Trubetskoi, "Russkaya problema" in L. I. Novikova, I. N. Sizemskaya (eds.), *Rossiya mezhdu evropoi i aziei; evraziiskii soblazn*, Nauka, Moscow, 1993, pp. 52–53.

33. N. S. Trubetskoi, "O turanskom elemente v ruskoi kul'ture" (1925) in L. I. Novikova, I. N. Sizemskaya (eds.), *Rossiya mezhdu evropoi i aziei; evraziiskii soblazn*, Nauka, Moscow, 1993, pp. 59–60.

34. P. N. Savitskii, "Evraziistvo" in L. I. Novikova, I. N. Sizemskaya (eds.), *Rossiya mezhdu evropoi i aziei; evraziiskii soblazn*, Nauka, Moscow, 1993, pp. 100–102.

35. Nikolai N. Alekseyev, "Evraziitsy i gosudarstvo" in L. I. Novikova, I. N. Sizemskaya (eds.), *Rossiya mezhdu evropoi i aziei; evraziiskii soblazn*, Nauka, Moscow, 1993, pp. 167–172.

36. Nikolai Berdyaev, "Utopicheskii etatism evraziitsev" in L. I. Novikova, I. N. Sizemskaya (eds.), *Rossiya mezhdu evropoi i aziei; evraziiskii soblazn*, Nauka, Moscow, 1993, pp. 301–304.

37. Aleksander Kizevetter, "Evraziistvo" in L. I. Novikova, I. N. Sizemskaya (eds.), *Rossiya mezhdu evropoi i aziei; evraziiskii soblazn*, Nauka, Moscow, 1993, pp. 266–269.

38. L. N. Gumilev, *Ritmy evrazi: epokh i tsivilizatsii*, Progress-Pangeya, Moscow, 1993, p. 31.

39. L. N. Gumilev, *Ritmy evrazi: epokh i tsivilizatsii*, Progress-Pangeya, Moscow, 1993, p. 54.

40. L. N. Gumilev, *Ot rysi k rossii*, Progress-Pangeya, Moscow, 1994, pp. 302–303.

41. Sergei Kurginyan, "Soderzhanie novogo integratsionizma," *Nezavisimaya gazeta*, 7 July 1994.

42. Vladimir Mironov, "Evraziistvo: soblazn ili shans?" *Nezavisimaya gazeta*, 26 Oct. 1994.

43. *Pravda*, 31 Jan. 1992.

44. *Nezavisimaya gazeta*, 20 Nov. 1992.

45. Aleksander Gol'ts, "Mezhdu sverkhderzhavoi i velikoi stranoi," *Rossiiskaya gazeta*, 11 Sept. 1991.

46. Fedor Burlatskii, "Evro-Aziatskii dom bez kazakhstana?" *Nezavisimaya gazeta*, 22 July 1993.

47. Yakov Plyais, "Osobennosti Rossii i ee vneshaya politika," *Nezavisimaya gazeta*, 19 Nov. 1993.

48. Aleksander Vladislavlev, "Vneshnya politika Rossii," *Nezavisimaya gazeta*, 6 May 1994.

49. Robert Yevzerov, "Evraziiskaya ideya v nezavisimykh gosudarstvakh," *Svobodnaya mysl'*, no. 14, 1993.

50. Sergei Stankevich, "Derzhava v poiskakh sebya," *Nezavisimaya gazeta*, 28 Mar. 1992.

51. Pavel Bogomolov, "Diplomatiya upadka," *Pravda*, 21 Jan. 1993.

52. *Itar Tass*, 9 Feb. 1992.

53. "K spaseniyu otechestva," *Sovietskaya Rossiya*, 16 June 1992, Sergei Modestov, "Voennaya politika russkogo natsional'nogo sobora," *Nezavisimaya gazeta*, 27 Aug. 1992.

54. *Izvestiya*, 14 Jan. 1994.

55. *Izvestiya*, 13 Jan. 1994, 21 Apr. 1994.

56. *Reuters Textline*, 19 Aug. 1992.

57. *Tass*, 9 Jan. 1992.

58. *Itar Tass*, 12 Nov. 1992.

59. Vladimir Zhirinovsky, *Poslednii brosok na yug*, Rait, Moscow, 1994, pp. 64–65.

60. Vladimir Zhirinovsky, *Poslednii vagon na sever*, Moscow, 1995, p.103.

61. See *Programma: kommunisticheskoi partii rossiiskoi federatsii* (3rd Congress, 22 Jan. 1995), Moscow, 1995; also *III s'ezd kommunisticheskoi partii rossiskoi federatsii (materialy i documenty)*, Informpechat', Moscow 1995, pp. 108–109.

62. Gennadii Zyuganov, *Derzhava*, Informpechat', Moscow, 1994, pp. 93–96.

63. *Pravda*, 25 May 1994.

64. *Rossiiskaya gazeta*, 26 Sept. 1992.

65. *Moscow News*, no. 38, 20–27 Sept. 1992.

66. *Moscow News*, no. 31, 2–9 Aug. 1992.

67. *Rossiiskaya gazeta*, 5 Mar. 1993, *Nezavisimaya gazeta*, 6 Mar. 1993.

68. *Nezavisimaya gazeta*, 6 Mar. 1993.

69. Ryurikov was identified as being disturbed over the pro-American foreign policy tilt; Viktor Ilyushin maintained links with both Yurii Skokov and Yurii Petrov. Vasilii Kononenko, "Raskol v prezidentskoi komande uvelichivaet shansy oppozitsii," *Izvestiya*, 27 Sept. 1994.

70. *Nezavisimaya gazeta*, 15 June 1994.

71. *Izvestiya*, 30 Oct. 1993.

72. Vasilii Kononenko, "Chto obsuzhdali na pervoi zasedanii soviet bezopasnost' Rossii", *Izvestiya*, 20 May 1992; Boris Sherman, "Soviet bezopastnosti provel pervoi zasedanie," *Nezavisimaya gazeta*, 21 May 1992.

73. *Moscow News*, no. 29, 19/26 July 1992.

74. *Nezavisimaya gazeta*, 10 Sept. 1992.

75. Sergei Parkhomenko, "Bezopasnost' v poslednei instantsii," *Nezavisimaya gazeta*, 8 Aug. 1992.

76. *Moscow News*, no. 31, 2/9 Aug. 1992.

77. Sergei Parkhomenko, "Bezopasnost' v poslednei instantsii," *Nezavisimaya gazeta*, 8 Aug. 1992.

78. Sergei Parkhomenko, "Nekii Skokov . . .," *Nezavisimaya gazeta*, 31 July 1992.

79. "Partiya voiny nastupaet . . .," *Izvestiya*, 30 June 1992.

80. Andrei Kozyrev, *Preobrazhenie*, Mezhdunarodnye Otnoshenie, Moscow, 1994. Rutskoi told Kozyrev, "I will not permit you to turn Russia into a doormat."

81. *Itar Tass*, 27 Oct. 1992.

82. *Rossiiskaya gazeta*, 18 Nov. 1992, *Krasnaya zvezda*, 25 Nov. 1992.

83. Yevgennii Ambartsumov, "Ya predpochitayu tsivilizovannye metodye v politke," *Rossiiskaya gazeta*, 29 May 1993.

84. On the Security Council's interdepartmental commission on foreign and security see Vladimir Orlov, "Chief of Russia's Diplomacy: Yurii Skokov," *Moscow News*, no. 7, 11 Feb. 1993.

85. *Itar Tass*, 5 Mar. 1993.

86. *Rossiiskaya gazeta*, 12 Aug. 1993. At the joint session of the Supreme Soviet on 30 June 1993 he was savagely attacked by Aleksander Rutskoi for the corrupt situation in the Soviet Army in Germany when he was Soviet defense minister, *Izvestiya*, 1 July 1993.

87. *Nezavisimaya gazeta*, 15 Feb. 1994.

88. *Radio Free Europe/Radio Liberty Daily Report*, no. 98, 25 May and no. 105, 7 June 1994.

89. Aleksander Rutskoi, "My dolzhny postroit' armiyu dostoinuyu velikoi Rossii," *Krasnaya zvezda*, 22 May 1992.

90. Aleksander Rutskoi, "My dolzhny postroit' armiyu dostoinuyu velikoi Rossii," *Krasnaya zvezda*, 22 May 1992.

91. *Nezavisimaya gazeta*, 5 Feb. 1992.

92. Yurii Deryugin, "Trevozhnye tendentsii v rossiskoi armii," *Nezavisimaya gazeta*, 24 Aug. 1994.

93. Yurii Deryugin, "Trevozhnye tendentsii v rossiskoi armii," *Nezavisimaya gazeta*, 24 Aug. 1994.

94. Major-General Vladimir Dudnik, "What to Expect from the Army at the Referendum," *Moscow News*, no. 7, 11 Feb. 1993.

95. *Itar Tass*, 30 July 1992.

96. Colonel S. Pechorov, "Geostrategicheskie ugrozi Rossii; oni realinyi ili mnimy?" *Krasnaya zvezda*, 20 Mar. 1992.

97. *Krasnaya zvezda*, 18 Mar. 1993.

98. *Nezavisimaya gazeta*, 30 July 1992.

99. *Rossiiskaya gazeta*, 23 May 1992.

100. *Nezavisimaya gazeta*, 31 Mar. 1993.

101. *Itar Tass*, 5 Apr. 1993.

102. *Nezavisimaya gazeta*, 16 Oct. 1993.

103. Sergei Mostovshchikov, "Sostoyanne voiny," *Izvestiya*, 28 July 1993.

104. *Nezavisimaya gazeta*, 20 Nov. 1993.

105. *Izvestiya*, 14, 25 Oct. 1991.

106. *Itar Tass*, 27 Sept. 1992.

107. "Opravdano li rasshirenie NATO?" *Nezavisimaya gazeta*, 26 Nov. 1993.

108. Constitution (Fundamental law) of the Russian Soviet Federative Socialist Republic (of April 12, 1978), pp. 4, 23.

109. Decree of RSFSR Congress of Peoples's Deputies on the procedure for implementing the RSFSR law, 24 Apr. 1991.

110. *Izvestiya*, 4 Apr. 1992.

111. *Itar Tass*, 20 Aug. 1992.

112. *Izvestiya*, 8 July 1992.

113. Vladimir Skachko, "Yeltsin i Khasbulatov sovernyutsya na urovne SNG," *Nezavisimaya gazeta*, 20 Mar. 1993.

114. *Itar Tass*, 16 Sept. 1992.

115. *Itar Tass*, 9, 14 Jan. 1993.

116. Jan. S. Adams, "Legislature Asserts Its Role in Russian Foreign Policy," *Radio Free Europe/Radio Liberty Research Report*, 22 Jan. 1993.

117. *Reuters Textline*, 24 Dec. 1992.

118. *Reuters Textline*, 28 Feb. 1993.

119. *Rossiiskaya gazeta*, 21 Apr. 1993.

120. *Itar Tass*, 26, 27 Feb. 1993.

121. *Nezavisimaya gazeta*, 24 Feb. 1993.

122. Vladimir Savel'ev, Vyacheslav Yclagin, "Samootchet MIDa," *Nezavisimaya gazeta*, 5 Mar. 1993.

123. "Konflikt na granitse trebuet srochnykh i tochnykh reshenii," *Nezavisimaya gazeta*, 16 July 1993.

124. *Krasnaya zvezda*, 25 Dec. 1991.

125. *Krasnaya zvezda*, 20 May 1992.

126. Yevgennii Krasnikov, "U Aleksandra Rutskogo svoya vneshnya politika," *Nezavisimaya gazeta*, 21 May 1992.

127. *Itar Tass*, 3 Mar. 1992.

128. *Krasnaya zvezda*, 26 Nov. 1992.

129. *Nezavisimaya gazeta*, 3 June 1993.

130. Konstantin Eggert, "Rossiya v roli evraziiskogo zhandarma?" *Izvestiya*, 7 Aug 1992.

131. Stanislav Kondrashov, "Orientiry novogo mira," *Izvestiya*, 30 Nov. 1992.

132. See *Rossiiskiye vesti*, 3 Dec. 1992, English language version in the *Current Digest of the Soviet Press*, vol. 54, no. 48 (1992), pp. 14–15.

133. Yevgennii Ambartsumov, "Ya predpochitayu tsivilizovannye metody v politike," *Rossiiskaya gazeta*, 29 May 1993.

134. Viktor Kremenyuk, "Vneshnya politika Rossii; nuzhny orientiry," *Nezavisimaya gazeta*, 17 Aug. 1993.

135. *Nezavisimaya gazeta*, 14 Feb. 1992.

136. *Nezavisimaya gazeta*, 10 July 1992.

137. Vitalii Tret'yakov, "Otstavka Andreya Kozyreva," *Nezavisimaya gazeta*, 31 July 1992.

138. *Itar Tass*, 3 Sept. 1992.

139. For the Council on Foreign and Defence Policy's report see "Strategiya dla Rossii," *Nezavisimaya gazeta*, 19 Aug. 1992. See also *Rossiiskaya gazeta*, 3 July 1992.

140. "Oporu nado iskat' vnutri strany," *Rossiiskaya gazeta*, 26 Sept. 1992.

141. *Itar Tass*, 17 Dec. 1992.

142. Grigorii Argovski, Dmitrii Rumyantsev, "Faktor vneshnei politiki," *Nezavisimaya gazeta*, 9 Mar. 1993.

143. *Itar Tass*, 17 Dec. 1992.

144. Andrei Kozyrev, "K slovu patriotizm prilagatel' nye ne nuzyny," *Krasnaya zvezda*, 25 Nov. 1992.

145. *Krasnaya zvezda*, 25 Mar. 1993.

146. Ivan Negov, "Vladimir Lukin i vozmozhno budet otozvan iz Vashingtona," *Nezavisimaya gazeta*, 14 Sept. 1993.

147. Dmitrii Kosyrev, "Delo ne v Lukine ili Kozyreve, a natsional'nom samosoznanii," *Rossiiskaya gazeta*, 18 Sept. 1993.

148. Sergei Filatov, "Perezhivayu za proiskhodyashchee," *Pravda*, 10 Dec. 1993.

149. Ivan Rodin, "Sovetskaya predstavitel'naya vlast' polnost'yu likvidirovna," *Nezavisimaya gazeta*, 28 Oct. 1993.

150. *Izvestiya*, 18 Dec. 1993.

151. For the new Constitution see *Izvestiya*, 28 Dec. 1993.

152. B. N. Topornina, Yu. M. Batukina, R. G. Orekhova, *Konstitutsiya rossiiskoi federatsii; kommentari*, Yuridicheskaya Literature, Moscow, 1994, pp. 420–421.

153. *Rossiiskaya gazeta*, 23 Dec. 1993.

154. *Reuters Textline*, 22 Dec. 1993.

155. *Reuters Textline*, 14 Dec. 1993.

156. *Reuters Textline*, 22 Dec. 1993.

157. Mikhail Karpov, "Vneshnaya politika Rossii ne izmenitsya," *Nezavisimaya gazeta*, 17 Dec. 1993.

158. *Vedomosti; federal'nogo sobraniya rossiiskoi federatsii*, no. 1, Jan. 1994.

159. Mikhail Karpov, "Duma i vneshnya politika R. F.," *Nezavisimaya gazeta*, 19 Jan. 1994.

160. Maksim Yusin, "Kozyrev otvergaet ul'timatum zhirinovskogo," *Izvestiya*, 26 Jan. 1994.

161. Vladimir Nadein, "Vladimir Lukin obvinyaet MID v vernosti brezhnevskoi diplomatii," *Izvestiya*, 5 Feb. 1994.

162. Vladimir Lukin, "Ot manilova k nozdrevu," *Nezavisimaya gazeta*, 14 May 1994.

163. Vyacheslav Nikonov, "Rossiiskii neogollism," *Nezavisimaya gazeta*, 24 May 1994.

164. Andrei Kozyrev, "Ne partiinye, a natsional'nye interesy," *Rossiiskaya gazeta*, 2 Feb. 1994.

165. Andrei Kozyrev, "Ne partiinye, a natsional'nye interesy," *Rossiiskaya gazeta*, 2 Feb. 1994.

166. Andranik Migranyan, "Rossiya i blizhnee zarubezh'e," *Nezavisimaya gazeta*, 18 Jan. 1994.

167. Leonid Mlechin, "Minister Kozyrev obeshchaet peremeny v vneshnei politike moskvy," *Izvestiya,* 18 Dec. 1993.

168. Andrei Kozyrev, "Za voennoe prisutstvie v sosednikh gosudarstvakh," *Nezavisimaya gazeta*, 19 Jan. 1994.

169. "MID gotovit zashchitu," *Rossiiskaya gazeta*, 18 Feb. 1994.

170. Lembit Annus, "Innogda Kozyrev—patriot," *Pravda*, 29 May 1994.

171. "Strategicheskaya tsel'—sozdat protsvetayushchuyu stranu," *Rossiiskaya gazeta*, 25 Feb. 1994.

172. Anatolii Adamshin, "Vneshnaya politika rossii," *Nezavisimaya gazeta*, 15 June 1994.

173. Anatolii Adamshin, "Vneshnaya politika rossii," *Nezavisimaya gazeta*, 15 June 1994.

174. Karen Brutents, "Neapol'ski starti politika moskvy," *Nezavisimaya gazeta*, 19 Aug. 1994.

175. "Strategiya dla Rossii 2," *Nezavisimaya gazeta*, 27 May 1994. The 49 members of the council were: Anatolii Adamshin, Yevgennii Ambartsumov, Andrei Kokoshin (First Deputy Defense Minister), Mikhail Kolesnikov (Chief of the General Staff), Vladimir Lukin, Sergei Stankevich, Sergei Stepashin (External Intelligence Director), Sergei Shakhrai (Deputy Premier), Grigorii Yavlinskii, Konstantin Zatulin (Chairman of CIS Duma Committee).

Chapter 2

Russia and the West

The relationship with the West is critical for Russian foreign policy. It touches on the central issue of Russia's national identity and influences foreign policy priorities in other areas, in the CIS, the Islamic World, or in the Asia-Pacific. The expectation of integration with the West has influenced Russian foreign policy behavior in these other regions and has made Moscow more willing to cooperate with the West. Correspondingly, fears that Russia is becoming excessively submissive to the West have strengthened the propensity to demonstrate an autonomous role in these areas, or to formulate a basis for greater independence in foreign policy.

Within the foreign policy community in Russia two views have developed in relation to the West. First, which Russia's primary relationship is with the United States as the foremost representative of the West, and that only through the United States is Russia able to maintain or elevate its status. Second, that Russia's future lies in closer integration with Europe and that the United States may be excluded. It would be a misrepresentation to portray the situation in terms of two well-defined groups in the pro-Western camp as individuals have been known to stress both views at different times. There are, however, tendencies, that may crystallize over time into something more definable. Debate and discussion between proponents of these views has been conducted within the Foreign Ministry over the past years. Kozyrev, with the strong support of Yeltsin, has emphasized the United States as Russia's major foreign policy priority, while the Foreign Ministry's Europeanists have stressed the importance of Europe. Since 1992, however, Russian foreign policy toward the West has been dominated by the United States as first priority largely based on the assumption of Russia's role as a global partner. Policy toward Europe was in many respects undifferentiated from the relationship with the United States and it was assumed that partnership relations could be extended toward Europe as well as to the United States.

EUROPE IN RUSSIAN POLICY

The European priority in Russian policy was highlighted when Kozyrev visited Germany in January 1992, and when Gennadii Burbulis visited Sweden and Brussels in January and April 1992 respectively. Burbulis promoted the European priority in Russian policy as chief spokesman of the European integrationists within Moscow. *Izvestiya* commentator Stanislav Kondrashov was a critic of what he called the America-centrism of the Foreign Ministry and predicted that the time for Eurocentrism had arrived.[1] For the European integrationists, foreign policy was to facilitate Russia's membership of key European Institutions—the European Union (EU) and the Council of Europe—as a "certificate of civilization."[2] The Security Council's version of foreign policy stated that the integration of Europe without Russia would be a blow to its vital interests, and according to this document Russia's aim was integration with European institutions.[3] Russia has applied to join the Council of Europe, which had accepted nine East and Central European states by the end of 1994, but questions about its human rights record have hindered membership. Russia has dialogue status with the EU and signed a partnership and cooperation agreement in June 1994 but continues to press for full membership.

In geopolitical terms, Russia's task for the future was to devise a satisfactory policy toward a united Germany. Soviet post-war defense strategy against Germany collapsed with the Berlin wall on 9 November 1989 leaving Moscow's geostrategists confused and in disarray. Could a united Germany be an ally or would it emerge as a threat? Would the historical conflict between Germany and Russia for influence in Eastern Europe, which is a modern version of an ancient Germanic-Slavic rivalry, continue or has that been relegated to the past? Russian figures such as Yevgennii Primakov and Vladmir Lukin have referred to the rising power of Germany without as yet expressing major concern. The Council of Foreign and Defense Policy noted that Germany may become the dominant power in Europe and that Germany's historical push toward the East will be renewed in 2–4 years. Indeed, among the Russians there have been three observable responses to the reunification of Germany.[4]

First, the integrationists assume that a united Germany could be managed within a wider European security framework that would include Russia. Russian leaders have attempted to expand the CSCE by building on the Paris CSCE Summit resolution of November 1990, which called for the recognition of common democratic values, the rule of law, respect for human rights, and the rights of national minorities. Kozyrev prepared a series of proposals for the Helsinki CSCE Summit of 10 July 1992 that envisaged the transformation of the grouping into the main vehicle of Eurasian security. The CSCE was to be designated a regional version of the United Nations with supranational powers and rapid reaction forces.[5] Despite the resistance to these proposals, Russia continued to press for the expansion of the CSCE in this way as an assurance against a united Germany.

Second, there are the collaborationists, or those who affirm Germany as Russia's major partner in Europe with all the connotations of a contemporary version of the 1922 Treaty of Rapallo.[6] The idea of a Russian-German axis is one that has been raised in Russian circles as a basis for stability in Eastern Europe and as a means to ensure Germany's participation in Russia's modernization. Germany is Russia's largest creditor and has provided Russia with $50 billion in credits and loans from 1989–1992.[7] Nonetheless, the idea of a modern Rapallo is unrealistic for a variety of reasons. The period of German-Soviet collaboration was possible under unique conditions when Germany moved away from the West; that period ended in a disastrous war and its renewal would revive European fears of another Molotov-Ribbentrop deal.

Third, there are also the advocates of a new balance of power who incline toward a relationship with France to counter a united Germany for which there have been strong historical precedents. Russia and France negotiated the alliance of 1894 based on a mutual concern over the rising power of Germany in a situation that strikes some in Moscow as similar to the present.

Views of the German-Russian relationship were distorted somewhat by the unique conditions that attended the reunification of Germany and the collapse of the Soviet position in Eastern Europe. Germany and the Soviet Union were compelled to negotiate a satisfactory basis for the withdrawal of some 380,000 Soviet troops from East Germany that required German financial assistance. The stunning effect of German reunification, which at a stroke nullified post-war Soviet strategy in Europe, resulted in confusion on the Russian side. Deeply held convictions about Germany, particularly among those who lived through World War II, were openly contradicted by events as the Soviet leadership moved toward a period of cooperation with the former enemy that may be no precedent for the future. Germany had an incentive to facilitate the withdrawal of Soviet troops that was matched on the Soviet side by the Gorbachev-Shevardnadze aspiration for a European security system that would no longer be based on confrontation.

The unexpected Soviet collapse facilitated a German-Soviet convergence of interests that may prove to be unique. Initially in late 1989 and early 1990 Gorbachev and Shevardnadze insisted on a neutral and demilitarized Germany or a reunited Germany that would have joint membership in both NATO and the Warsaw Pact. Soviet leaders quickly lost control of events while their system was moving toward its ineluctable breakdown. Gorbachev agreed with Helmut Kohl in February 1990 that the German people would decide their own future, which removed all basis for the Soviets to insist on conditional reunification. Gorbachev agreed to the united Germany's admission to NATO in July 1990 when Helmut Kohl, in turn, allowed Soviet forces to remain in Germany for 3–4 years. In September 1990 a 1994 deadline was set for the withdrawal of Soviet forces while Germany agreed to provide the Soviet Union with DM 13 billion or $8.2 billion to construct housing for returned service personnel, for the transport of Soviet forces back home, and for their retraining.

These agreements were incorporated in the Gorbachev-Kohl Agreement of 9 November 1990 when a German-Soviet non-aggression pact was signed.

German economic assistance for Russia was limited to the particular conditions of the withdrawal of forces and, moreover, was eventually reduced considerably as other priorities intervened, including the cost of German reunification. Helmut Kohl visited Moscow in December 1992 to declare support for Yeltsin's reformist course claiming that Russian-German collaboration would have consequences for Europe and would be a key element in the peaceful construction of Europe. Kohl allowed Russia an eight-year debt postponement and granted Russia an additional DM 550 million for the construction of housing in Russia for returned servicemen. The chancellor declared, however, that Germany was itself in difficulty and placed the Russians on notice that further economic assistance would be limited. In return, Yeltsin agreed to accelerate the withdrawal of forces from Germany and the deadline was moved from 31 December 1994 to 31 August 1994.[8] German interest in providing Russia with further economic assistance declined subsequently and Finance Minister Theodore Waigel told his G-7 counterparts in April 1993 that Germany had already contributed $50.8 billion and could not offer Russia additional economic assistance.[9]

In many respects, the German-Russian relationship that was established by Gorbachev and continued into the Yeltsin era was a honeymoon, signifying the termination of an era of confrontation. German economic assistance was closely tied to the withdrawal of Russian forces and the need to ensure the success of the reform movement. While those forces were still in place Russia had bargaining leverage over Germany, which had an incentive to respond with economic assistance. Germany wanted to see Russian reform succeed, as its failure could have resulted in renewed hostility and a suspension of troop withdrawal plans. Such concerns were natural at the time. Russians began to wonder what kind of relationship would be fashioned with Germany once the withdrawal of forces had removed a major incentive for German collaboration with Russia.[10] As Germany began to promote the entry of the East and Central European states into NATO, concerns were raised that for some commentators signaled the possibility of German revanchism.[11]

After Russian forces were withdrawn from Germany on 31 August 1994, Defense Minister Grachev accused Gorbachev and Shevardnadze of the "crudest political blunder,"[12] referring to the absence of housing for returned servicemen, as some 40 percent of the officers were without homes on their return.[13] Others regarded the Gorbachev-Shevardnadze agreement to a withdrawal of forces as a terrible error for different reasons. Some Russians have argued that Gorbachev and Shevardnadze could have linked Russia's withdrawal from Germany to a German commitment to an expanded CSCE that would provide assurances against a possible revival of German power and an expansion of NATO. As a consequence, Russia made a strategic concession to the West without the prospect of closer integration with Europe, and without the benefits of a multilateral security organization that would provide assurances against Germany. It is doubtful, however, that the Soviet Union at the time could have extracted any additional benefits from the Germans as Gorbachev's position completely disintegrated. In any case, once the bilateral issues of troop withdrawal and specific financial economic assistance had been resolved, reunited Germany's future became increasingly fused with NATO, behind which stood the United States.

THE UNITED STATES

At the outset the United States had greater significance for Russia's pro-Western leadership for various reasons. First and foremost, the relationship with the remaining superpower satisfied Russian national ambitions to be regarded as a great power. Yeltsin moved rapidly to ensure that Russia could assume the place of the Soviet Union in the relationship with the U.S. that Gorbachev had established. The effort to claim equality with the United States in this context was psychological compensation for the humiliations of Russia's present chaotic state and a reminder of past greatness when the two superpowers negotiated global security among themselves. Russia and the United States were bound to each other, temporarily at least, by the need to eliminate the nuclear danger as one of the vestiges of the Cold War era. The negotiation of nuclear force reductions enabled Russia to affirm the idea of partnership with the United States and gave the Americans a stake in the success of Russia's reform movement. The danger of the collapse of a nuclear-armed Russia motivated even the most skeptical of Americans to consider political and financial support for the Yeltsin government in its struggle against nationalist or Communist opponents. The United States, in this sense, could encourage international lending bodies to extend financial assistance to Russia or could promote direct private investment in Russia. The United States also provided a means of managing other powers in the Western coalition that had their own claims on Russia. In its weakened state, Russia would be vulnerable to Japanese pressure over the territorial dispute or to German demands over a host of outstanding issues relating to Russia's East and Central European interests. As long as the United States perceived an interest in supporting the Yeltsin government it could act to balance Germany in Europe or to restrain the Japanese in the pursuit of their territorial demands.

The Camp David Declaration

Yeltsin's government insisted on affirming the idea of partnership with the United States with obsessive regularity in the expectation that the relationship that Gorbachev had established with U.S. presidents would be carried over into the post-Soviet era. When Yeltsin met George Bush in January–February 1992 he signed the Camp David Declaration that enshrined the concept of alliance with the United States. The declaration was one of Yeltsin's first major steps in foreign policy revealing the intention to establish a sound foundation for continuous collaboration with the West. The Camp David Declaration proclaimed a "new alliance of partners working together against the common dangers we face." Russia and the U.S. launched a new era in their relationship and an enduring peace and friendship that "rests on lasting common values."[14] Point 6 of the declaration illustrated the extent of the partnership that included the reduction of nuclear arsenals, control over conventional weapons proliferation, the settlement of regional conflicts, and cooperation against terrorism and drug trafficking.

The strategic partnership that Yeltsin proclaimed with the United States was based on first, the common concern about nuclear stability and second, the need to support Yeltsin's reform movement and to prevent Russia's collapse. The concern about nuclear stability was basically a legacy of the Cold War era and of temporary significance. Once both countries had come to grips with the mechanics of nuclear arms reductions, the issue ceased to have its previous significance and did not require the designation "partnership." Indeed, Russia's status in U.S.'s eyes lay in its possession of a nuclear arsenal, the elimination of which would remove all basis for partnership. While Russia retained nuclear arsenal and was engaged in the process of reductions, the country continued to be important to the United States but it was a significance that diminished with time. The second issue was simply no basis for strategic partnership in any case as political and economic instability placed Russia in the position of a recipient of aid and assistance rather than a partner. In terms of the other areas of potential collaboration cited in the Camp David Declaration Russia was simply one of many partners for the United States. The idea of strategic partnership was for Russia an affirmation of status and a way to uphold a position made familiar during the Soviet era. For United States officials, however, the idea was simply diplomatic courtesy calculated to strengthen the position of a reformist government against its nationalist opponents.

Nuclear Arms Reductions

Strategic nuclear parity gave the Soviet Union a sense of equality with the United States and concomitant consultative rights over global and regional security that its leaders took for granted. Those consultative rights were enjoyed by Gorbachev when he was feted by the Western world and courted by Western leaders. Gorbachev participated in the process of reducing strategic nuclear arsenals when on 30 July 1991 he signed the START-1 Agreement, which involved a 36 percent reduction of Soviet warheads over a seven-year period, with George Bush. Subsequently, Russia's new leadership sought to go further and repudiated the notion of strategic parity in favor of the retention of a minimum nuclear deterrent. When Yeltsin visited Washington in June 1992 to launch the basis for START-2 he announced his intention to depart from nuclear parity, which Russia could not afford, and called for a minimum deterrent to deal with the unexpected that may threaten its security.[15] In a speech to the Defense Ministry in Moscow on 10 June prior to his departure for Washington, Yeltsin claimed that he would uphold parity, demonstrating his skills in manipulating his audience's expectations.[16]

The key issue for Russia was the relationship between the strategic partnership that had already been proclaimed with the United States, and the idea of nuclear parity. For Moscow's pro-Western leadership, nuclear parity was an abhorrence that was to be quickly discarded to allow Russia to find its natural home in the West. The radical democrats wanted to move rapidly toward nuclear disarmament unconstrained by what they regarded as artificial concerns about parity. For the geostrategists, however, strategic nuclear parity was a means to ensure partnership with the United States, and for the nationalists it was a symbol of Russia's status and a measure of equality. The nationalists regarded nuclear parity as a means of protection against the United States and an assurance that Russia's interests would be considered seriously. The problem resided in the fact that the status Russia claimed for itself was artificially based on its nuclear capability. Russia could not discard nuclear parity and claim equality with the United States in the absence of any other recognizable basis for that status and in this respect Yeltsin's government was pursuing a contradictory course toward the U.S. The nationalists were unrealistic in their anachronistic insistence on the preservation of parity but they were more consistent in their understanding of the basis of Russia's relationship with the U.S.

Yeltsin, accordingly, committed Russia to a new round of strategic arms reductions during his visit to Washington in June 1992, which eventually became the basis of START-2. After having told the Russian Defense Ministry audience before his departure to Washington that he would made no concessions to the U.S. Yeltsin made a number of surprising concessions to the astonishment of his Press Secretary Vladimir Kostikov.[17] Under START-1, Russia's land based heavy missile force, regarded as destabilizing by the U.S., was to be reduced from 308 SS-18's to 154. During the negotiations, the Russians had initially insisted on comparable reductions by the U.S. in return for a further reduction of this missile force. Yeltsin, however, volunteered to eliminate the SS-18's entirely without seeking comparable reductions by the U.S.; he settled for a 30 percent reduction in the U.S. sea-launched ballistic missile (SLBM) force. Yeltsin accepted the argument against reciprocal reductions on the basis that the United States required a sizable SLBM deterrent to maintain world peace.[18] Without the principle of parity to define the structure and size of nuclear arsenals, Yeltsin claimed that each country would be free to determine these factors on their own within certain parameters.

By late 1992, the basis of START-2 had been negotiated. As a cost saving measure, Russia wanted to retain the silos of those multiwarhead missiles that were nominated for destruction to house their single warhead missiles. The United States raised the demand that silos, as well as heavy missiles, be destroyed after the signing of START-1 to ensure that no government in Moscow could ever use them again. The U.S. was concerned lest Yeltsin be overthrown and a nationalist or hard line government emerge that would redeploy heavy missiles that were being phased out. At first, the U.S. resisted the demand for silo conversion but eventually conceded the issue for the sake of agreement. Ninety SS-18 silos were to be retained and converted so that they could only house smaller, single warhead missiles. The U.S. also allowed Russia the right to convert 105 SS-19 missiles, which had up to five warheads, into single warhead missiles. Russia's Supreme Soviet finally ratified START-1 on 4 November 1992 (157 for, 1 against, 26 abstentions) and the signing of the START-2 documents was made possible when George Bush visited Moscow on 3 January 1993.

Difficulties arose with the other CIS states—the Ukraine, Belarus, and Kazakhstan—that found themselves with strategic nuclear missiles after the collapse of the Soviet Union (the Ukraine was left with 176 ICBM's, Kazakhstan with 104 SS-18's). Under the Lisbon Protocol to START-1 that was signed on 23 May 1992, these CIS states were to eliminate all their strategic missiles and accede to the Nuclear Non-Proliferation Treaty (NPT) on the principle that Russia was the heir of the Soviet Union's nuclear arsenal. The United States played a key role in encouraging the other CIS states to fulfill their commitments by offering them financial incentives. All tactical nuclear weapons were removed from Kazakhstan and Belarus by February 1992 and from the Ukraine by July 1992. Under the Nuclear Threat Reduction Act of December 1991 (also known as Nunn-Lugar Act) the U.S. Defense Department provided $400 million—that in 1992 was increased to $800 million and in 1993 $1 billion—to promote the dismantling of nuclear weapons in the CIS. Belarus subsequently ratified START-1 including the Lisbon Protocol and acceded to the NPT on 4 February 1993 and received $65 million in U.S. funds for the dismantling of nuclear weapons. Kazakhstan ratified START-1 on 2 July 1992; the NPT was eventually ratified on 13 December 1993. Accordingly, Kazakhstan received $85 million in similar economic assistance.

The Ukraine, however, refused to ratify START-1 and the Lisbon Protocol despite the incentive of $175 million under the above legislation.[19] President Leonid Kravchuk at first denied that Yeltsin had the right to negotiate nuclear arms control on behalf of the CIS and insisted that all republics participate. Political paralysis within the Ukraine prevented any progress over this issue as hard line nationalists expressed nuclear ambitions, and pragmatists demanded greater financial compensation from the United States and security guarantees for the Ukraine. Russia and the United States signed START-2 without obtaining the Ukraine's endorsement of START-1 despite Bush's threat to terminate all further economic aid and assistance to the Ukraine.

During the Ukraine's Supreme Soviet hearings on START-1 and the NPT, the pronuclear lobby made itself heard calling for confirmation of the Ukraine's nuclear status as the ultimate defense against Russia. Others called for financial compensation for nuclear reductions and for guarantees from Russia that the missiles would be destroyed on their return to Russia.[20] Premier Leonid Kuchma, later Ukrainian President, even declared on 3 June 1993 that the Ukraine was an interim nuclear power pending a resolution of the issue.[21] Eventually, heavy political pressure from the West prompted the Ukrainian Supreme Soviet to ratify START-1—by 254 votes to 9 on 18 November 1993—without endorsement of Article 5 of the Lisbon Protocol according to which the Ukraine was required to accede to the NPT.[22] The Ukraine still held out for guarantees of its security and territorial integrity from both the United States and Russia, and continued to press the nuclear issue as a bargaining ploy to strengthen its position against Russia.

In a change of tactics, U.S. assistance for the Ukraine was linked to the dismantling of strategic missiles that, if completed, would make the issue virtually redundant.[23] Negotiations held in December 1993 involving the U.S., Russia, and the Ukraine resulted in the trilateral declaration signed when President Clinton visited Moscow on 14 January 1994. Under this declaration, the Ukraine was given financial and security incentives to proceed with the dismantling of its strategic missiles. Clinton promised $350 million, split equally between economic aid specifically for the Ukraine and funds for the dismantling of nuclear weapons in the CIS in general; this figure was doubled to $700 million in March 1994.[24] Clinton also promised $1 billion over 20 years for the commercial sale of uranium extracted from nuclear warheads, part of which would be granted to the Ukraine. Russia agreed to respect the Ukraine's territorial integrity and to sell oil and gas to the Ukraine below market prices. The Ukraine obtained less than the $2.5 billion it had initially proposed when negotiations began but had succeeded in involving the United States in its relationship with Russia. Without the United States, Russia would probably have been unable to resolve the nuclear issue with the Ukraine.

In any case, START-2 became the subject of much debate within Moscow security circles in relation to sacrifice of the hallowed principle of strategic parity. There were those such as Aleksei Arbatov who argued that the elimination of Russia's heavy missile force was justified but who also called for greater reductions of the U.S.'s SLBM force.[25] Others argued that Russia's main striking force had been surrendered without any prohibitions on American programs such as ballistic missile defense (BMD) and sea-based cruise missiles (SLCM) such as the Tomahawk, that would enable the U.S. to maintain a strategic advantage.[26] Others pointed out that Russia had been unfairly compelled to transform the structure of its strategic forces to meet U.S. criteria by surrendering its land based nuclear force.[27] Still others, who reacted with apprehension to the single superpower world, in which the U.S. was dominant, bemoaned the departure from parity arguing that parity had preserved peace in the Cold War.[28]

The security establishment was generally supportive of START-2 for a variety of reasons that indicated the age of strategic nuclear parity had long passed. Armed Forces Chief of Staff Mikhail Kolesnikov declared that both the Foreign and Defense Ministries supported START-2, emphasizing that never before had these two ministries worked together as they did over this issue. Kolesnikov argued that Russia's liquid-fueled missiles would have to be eliminated eventually and Russia could not afford their modernization. Russia, accordingly, obtained reductions in U.S. strategic offensive capabilities in return for something it would have to lose anyway.[29] Chief of the Strategic Rocket Forces Colonel-General Igor Sergeyev similarly argued in support of START-2 claiming that Russia no longer had the productive capacity to maintain parity with the U.S. Without START-2, Sergeyev asserted, Russia would have to disarm unilaterally.[30] Lt.-General Ananis Politsyn argued that Russia's military supported START-2 because it understood the very real difficulties that Russia faced. He argued that the modernization of strategic nuclear forces was beyond Russia's economic capacity and, moreover, Russia faced no external threat that required the maintenance of existing levels of nuclear arsenals.[31] It was also argued during the debate that the maintenance of present nuclear levels would be more expensive for Russia than reductions to lower levels.[32] After being debated within the Supreme Soviet, the START-2 Treaty was despatched in March 1993 to the International Relations and the Defense and Security Committees for further examination.[33]

The START-2 Treaty languished in the Supreme Soviet and later the Federal Assembly, a casualty of executive-legislature conflict. U.S. Defense Secretary William Perry declared that deep reductions under START-2 would not proceed without comparable reductions by Russia; this raised questions about the future of nuclear arms reductions. Perry argued for a nuclear hedge against Russia should the Cold War be revived again. Perry's request revealed that pressure existed in the U.S. to limit nuclear reductions.[34] Yeltsin attempted to give the START process further momentum when he visited Washington in September 1994. He proposed that the dismantling of strategic nuclear weapons begin immediately after START-2 was ratified.[35] Nonetheless, Russia's Federal Assembly deputies have lost the incentive to ratify the treaty while the U.S. pursues its own ballistic missile defense (BMD) program that they claim contravenes the 1972 Anti-Ballistic Missile (ABM) Treaty.

Yeltsin had attempted to use strategic nuclear arms reductions as a basis for partnership with the United States in the expectation that Russia's integration with the Western world would be facilitated. For Russia's military establishment, strategic arms reductions were a necessity in view of the obvious imperative to harmonize military capabilities with economic realities. Russia's military, however, entertained no aspirations for partnership or alliance with the United States and focused for the most part on the military and budgetary issues involved. Yeltsin's geostrategist and nationalist critics, however, perceived that the success of nuclear arms reductions would deprive Russia of partnership rights with the U.S. In their view, the willingness of the U.S. to grant Russia the status of partner was a product of respect for Russia's nuclear arsenal, which should not be surrendered easily. From this perspective, START-2 has all the makings of a bad bargain that promises to eliminate the one major lever of influence Russia has over the Western world, and a guarantee of Russia's status.

Economic Assistance for Russia

Pro-Western reformers and democrats initially expected the West to play a major role in Russia's economic transformation. It was Gorbachev who stimulated the fantasy that gripped Russian minds that Western funds would flow into Russia to revive the economy and alleviate the effects of the first years of shock therapy. Gorbachev, Yeltsin and those socialized in the Soviet system had a different understanding of economics from their Western counterparts. The Soviet system was a world of subsidies without strict financial accountability and where political and economic criteria were fused. As the Soviet Union had given economic assistance to client states on the basis of political criteria so it was expected that Russia could similarly receive support from the West. To some extent the Western world pandered to Russian demands in view of the political need to ensure Yeltsin's survival. Economic assistance on a vast scale, however, remained an illusion as Russian leaders were confronted by the demand for strict financial accountability from the West.

Political, rather than economic, criteria at first dictated Western policies of economic assistance to Russia. The massive aid packages that were promulgated had the purpose of demonstrating support for the pro-Western reformers. They were announced with dramatic fanfare and timed to coincide with particular events in Russian politics when it seemed that the reformers were most vulnerable. Subsequently, however, economic criteria intruded and the actual disbursement of the promised aid was subject to strict controls imposed by international lending agencies. The clash between political and economic criteria in the plans to extend economic assistance to Russia stimulated much debate about whether the West could have done more (or whether it had done enough). Eventually, as a learning experience for Russia's leaders it was understood that the earlier trust in the West had been misplaced for the most part and that Russia would have to depend on itself.

The first politically inspired effort to organize massive economic assistance for Russia was the joint Bush-Kohl $24 billion package of 1 April 1992. When Yeltsin visited the U.S. in February 1992 he called for the West's financial assistance claiming that a new Cold War would follow the collapse of the reform movement in Russia.[36] The Bush administration was initially skeptical and fearful of the economic black hole that Russia represented. Moreover, declarations of economic support for a country that until recently had been the U.S.'s global adversary seemed politically unwarranted in an election year. Two factors prompted the Bush administration to reverse course. The first was the domestic factor—both Richard Nixon and the then Governor of Arkansas Bill Clinton publicly called for U.S. assistance for Russia. Nixon became a vocal proponent of economic aid for Russia arguing that U.S.'s task should be the global promotion of democracy and human rights with Russia as the test case.[37] Governor Clinton addressed the Foreign Policy Association in New York on 1 April 1992 and called for a global alliance to support democracy and criticized Bush's inactivity in relation to Russia.[38] The second factor was the convening of the 6th Congress of Peoples's Deputies in Moscow in April 1992; the reformist democrats were opposed by the vested interests of post-Soviet Russia, which were antagonistic toward privatization and land reform. The package announced was intended to be a display of support for Russia's embattled reformers.

Bush timed his announcement of the $24 billion package to coincide with Governor Clinton's address. He declared that his objective was to support the democratic revolution in Russia whose defeat "could plunge us into a world more dangerous in some respects than the dark years of the Cold War."[39] The assistance package included the demands that had been earlier raised by the then First Deputy Premier Yegor Gaidar for humanitarian assistance, debt rescheduling, and a ruble stabilization fund. Accordingly, the $24 billion package included $11 billion in combined G-7 contributions, a $6 billion ruble stabilization fund, $4.5 billion in balance of payments assistance from international lending agencies such as the IMF, the World Bank, the European Bank, and the Bank of Reconstruction and Development, and $2.5 billion in debt postponement.[40] The U.S. share of this package was $4.5 billion that had already been approved by Congress in preceding legislation. In view of the contentious nature of the program the Bush administration approached Congress for a legislative endorsement of these contributions in what became known as the Freedom Support Act, eventually passed by Congress in October 1992.

Many of the details of the $24 billion assistance package had not been carefully scrutinized and the impression of a hasty effort intended to support Yeltsin in his political struggle with opponents remained. The IMF, as the distributing agency of Western largesse to Russia, had the responsibility of imposing economic criteria on Russia that G-7 leaders may have found politically sensitive. In this separation of political and economic criteria, the Russians found themselves in frustrating negotiations with a body indifferent to the political issues involved. When Gaidar began negotiating for the first tranche of IMF assistance in April 1992 the conditions were revealed, including a reduction of the budget deficit from 17 percent to 5 percent of gross domestic product (GDP) by the end of the year, a reduction of inflation to 10 percent monthly, the legalization of private property, an increase in the price of energy to world market levels, a strict fiscal policy to limit subsidies to inefficient enterprises and bankruptcy legislation.[41] On 5 July 1992 the IMF finally agreed to provide Russia with its first credit of $1 billion, transferred in August 1992. Under its director Michel Camdessus, the IMF had initially desisted to offer credits as Yeltsin refused to release energy prices. Moreover, beginning in June 1992 the Russian Central Bank, which was under the control of the Supreme Soviet, dispensed vast ruble subsidies to Russian industry and agriculture and canceled some 2 trillion rubles in accumulated enterprise debt.[42] This action was taken, as First Deputy Premier Vladimir Shumeiko explained, to prevent the total collapse of Russian industry. It openly clashed with IMF monetarist prescriptions for Russia. Nonetheless, political pressure from the Bush administration caused the IMF to accommodate political criteria and at least agreed to the disbursement of the first tranche of economic aid. Because of this pressure Michel Camdessus flew to Moscow in July 1992 to negotiate with Gaidar announcing that the IMF would adopt a special approach toward Russia.[43] The disbursement of the $6 billion ruble stabilization fund was suspended, however, pending the introduction of monetarist reforms outlined above.

Yeltsin had declared, at the G-7 meeting in Munich in July 1992, that $24 billion would not save Russia and that direct investment was required from all sources up to several hundred billion dollars.[44] There was a great discrepancy between the expressed hopes and the small amounts that were either disbursed by the IMF or extended bilaterally by G-7 governments in short-term loans. The IMF accordingly became a target of attack. Georgi Arbatov accused the neo-Bolsheviks of the IMF of imposing alien and undemocratic rules on Russia. He also claimed that the IMF adopted an approach more relevant for the Third World than for Russia.[45] Nixon declared that the IMF was not competent for the political task on hand, which went beyond narrow financial interests, an argument echoed by adviser to the Russian government, Jerry Sachs. On the other side of the argument there was the genuine concern that financial aid would be wasted in subsidies to inefficient industries or be siphoned off to bank accounts in the West as part of Russia's capital drain. In addition, the IMF could not bestow special status on Russia without jeopardizing its programs in other developing economies. In any case, the event that tilted the balance for the Bush administration was Yeltsin's willingness to agree to sweeping strategic arms reductions during his visit to Washington in June 1992.[46] Yeltsin's concessions in strategic nuclear weapons had the effect of ensuring greater U.S.'s political support for his position to the point of influencing the IMF to view Russia in a different light.

The second public declaration of economic support for Russia was under the Clinton administration. President Clinton emerged as a champion of Russia and a supporter of Yeltsin in his struggle with nationalist and Communist opponents. Clinton's belief that a democratic revolution was sweeping the world after the Cold War era elevated Russia to the position of prime test case. Clinton wanted to ensure that Yeltsin's reforms would triumph and the urgency of the task was intensified by Yeltsin's conflict with Khasbulatov and the Supreme Soviet in early 1993. Efforts were made within the Supreme Soviet to have Yeltsin impeached, the word "impeachment" subsequently entered into the Russian language. The Clinton administration confronted the dilemma of deciding whether to focus primarily on Yeltsin as the agent of reform or whether to broaden the area of support within the reform movement. The Bush administration's support for Gorbachev was held up by critics as an example of what happens when policy becomes linked to a single person. Lee Hamilton, Chairman of the House Foreign Affairs Committee, and Sam Nunn, Chairman of the Senate Armed Services Committee, were both vocal in criticizing the administration for its narrow support of Yeltsin.[47] Coordinator of humanitarian assistance to the CIS, Richard Armitage predicted that Yeltsin's time was coming to an end. Armitage later retracted his comments but was removed from his position as the impression was created that the Clinton administration was preparing to ditch Yeltsin. Indeed, the Clinton administration could not broaden its support for the reform movement without impairing Yeltsin's position at a critical juncture, and had no option but to continue with the previous policy.

The dilemma faced by the Clinton administration was intensified when on 20 March 1993 during a meeting with Helmut Kohl, Yeltsin raised the possibility of dissolving the Supreme Soviet and ruling by decree. Yeltsin was a popularly elected president, the first in Russia's history, while the Supreme Soviet was composed of deputies who had been nominated by the Communist Party machinery and who had not faced free elections. It seemed clear where Clinton's priorities lay. He had already declared that the U.S. would not oppose the dissolution of the Supreme Soviet but would not support the use of force.[48] A different nuance was expressed by Secretary of State Warren Christopher after Yeltsin had sounded out Helmut Kohl. In an address to the Chicago Council for Foreign Relations on 22 March Christopher described Russia as the "greatest strategic challenge of our time." The secretary of state declared that the United States would support Yeltsin as long as he acted peacefully and guaranteed civil liberties. Russia, he stressed, must remain a democracy.[49]

Clinton's task was to prepare the American public for his planned program of economic assistance for Russia after he had campaigned on the basis of strengthening the American economy. In a radio address on 3 April 1993, Clinton explained that "Russia's rebirth is in the economic interest of American tax payers" and stressed the dangers that would arise if "Russia were to revert to its old ways or plunge into chaos." America, declared Clinton, "must mobilize the world on behalf of peace and reform in Russia."[50] In his Annapolis address of 1 April, Clinton had to adjust his campaign pledge of giving priority to domestic issues. He declared that America could not be strong at home unless it was actively engaged in the world, which was a casuistical reversal of his earlier emphasis on the domestic economy.[51] Support for Russia became Clinton's top foreign policy priority for three reasons. First, there was the need to ensure the success of democracy in that country on which American security depended. Second, there was a need to engage Russia in what Clinton called global problem solving to eliminate regional conflicts and to build a better world. Third, Russia's economic growth would provide opportunities for American business.

Russia could expect no better friend in the White House, given the constraints of official duties and other competing priorities, all of which demanded urgent attention. It was this personal commitment that led Clinton to prepare the ground for the Vancouver Summit with Yeltsin from 3–4 April 1993. The summit was intended to be a demonstration of support for Yeltsin, who faced a referendum on his leadership on 25 April. Clinton declared a $1.5 billion aid scheme for Russia that was to be funded from unspent appropriations. Seventy-five percent of these funds were to be distributed to the private sector where, according to Clinton, there was a proven mechanism for its effective disbursement to avoid waste. These funds were to be directed toward specific sector areas and were to be carefully monitored. On 15 April, Clinton announced an additional $1.8 billion for Russia as supplementary appropriations from the defense budget and foreign aid program. Every item in the foreign aid program was reduced except aid for Egypt and Israel, revealing the extent to which Russia had affected foreign assistance priorities.[52] During the Vancouver Summit Clinton stressed that he would also press the United States's G-7 partners to do more for Russia as part of a coordinated program of economic assistance. If Clinton could spread the burden of support among the members of the G-7, congressional and domestic criticisms of his plans to assist Russia would also be reduced.

Clinton's efforts to mobilize the world community in support of Russia were revealed at the Tokyo meeting of G-7 leaders on 8–9 July 1993. The Tokyo G-7 meeting declared a monumental $43.4 billion program of assistance for Russia that gathered all existing programs together with the addition of a new proposal. Some $15 billion of this package was designated debt relief and $28.4 billion included bilateral loans, currency stabilization, and support for necessary imports. The G-7 meeting also approved a change to enable the IMF to dispense funds to Russia despite its inability to satisfy strict economic criteria. A systematic transformation facility (STF) of $3 billion was established as a new feature of the program according to which funds could be disbursed on the basis of the Russian government's pledge to continue with reform. The creation of the STF was made possible by an agreement between Russia's Finance Minister Boris Fyodorov and the Russian Central Bank to limit subsidies to industries, an unenforceable agreement in any case. The Russian government's budget deficit then was estimated at 20 percent of GDP and inflation had reached 2,000 percent annually, certainly no grounds for IMF funding on economic criteria. In addition, the G-7 meeting promulgated a $3 billion Special Privatization and Restructuring Program (SPRP) that was to be managed by international financial institutions and would assist in the modernization of large Russian firms. The SPRP was to provide equity loans and export credit support for specially targeted enterprises.[53] Five hundred million dollars of this fund was to be provided by governments in the form of bilateral assistance, the American share was $125 million.[54]

Subsequently, however, the urgency was removed and the need for the Clinton administration to make such a public display of support for Russia lapsed. The focus of G-7 attention was no longer on the so-called life-and-death struggle of democracy in Russia but on the practical details of the economic support program. Economic assistance ceased to be at the center of the West's relations with Russia and the dramatic pronouncements of the Bush era and early Clinton administration became a thing of the past. The situation in Russia was stabilized somewhat after Yeltsin forcibly dissolved the Supreme Soviet in October 1993. The Western world, for the most part, may have been alarmed by the methods used by Yeltsin but was otherwise relieved by the elimination of the obstacle to reform and the promulgation of a new constitution. Warren Christopher said in Moscow on 23 October 1993 that the U.S. does not easily support the suspension of parliaments "but these are extraordinary times; Yeltsin's steps were in response to extraordinary circumstances."[55] Yeltsin's future was no longer in the balance and it seemed as though he would survive. Western assistance became a factor in Russia's domestic politics, contributing to the polarization of Russian society and the nationalist backlash as epitomized by increased votes for Zhirinovsky in the December elections.

It may have been difficult for Western leaders to appreciate the fact that high profile pronouncements of economic assistance could have had negative consequences for Russia's domestic politics. A frequent complaint heard in Russia was that little was seen of the promised aid, much of which amounted to an adjustment of national accounts with no tangible effect on people's lives. Yevgennii Ambartsumov claimed that unfulfilled promises of Western aid bred cynicism within Russia and affected public opinion negatively.[56] Even after the Tokyo G-7 meeting, which endorsed a change of lending criteria for the IMF, negotiations dragged on over the dispensing of a second tranche of $1.5 billion. The Clinton administration continued to press the IMF to draw funds from the STF to assist Russia, but the IMF still insisted on economic criteria.[57] More importantly, the *Izvestiya* commentator Stanislav Kondrashov claimed that Western aid was being used as an instrument in the executive's struggle with the legislature, or as he put it "firewood on the fire of Russia's conflict." Kondrashov wrote that Western aid emboldened Yeltsin in his conflict with the Supreme Soviet pushing him toward dictatorial methods.[58] Proponents of this view in Moscow would argue that Western support for Yeltsin contributed to the appearance of Zhirinovsky.

Disappointed expectations in what Kondrashov regarded as manna from Heaven compelled Yeltsin's government to adjust its approach toward the

West. First Deputy Premier Vladimir Shumeiko argued, even before the Vancouver meeting, that Russia did not need Western aid, it would simply add to the burden of Russia's debts. Shumeiko claimed that debt postponement was the most significant contribution the West could make to Russia's economic reform.[59] The first deputy premier thought that Russia could export natural resources to the West to generate the capital for economic development; a course that has been advocated by Russian and Western economists for some time. Kozyrev declared that Russia did not require new aid from the West and called for the following measures: debt postponement; the implementation of the ruble stabilization fund to arrest inflation; the lifting of Coordinating Committee for Multilateral Export Controls (COCOM) restrictions on trade; and the gradual integration of Russia into the G-7.[60] Minister of Finance Boris Fyodorov argued for specific measures to support small businesses through the formation of a reform fund.[61] The then Minister of External Economic Relations Sergei Glaziev thought that the priority of priorities was Russia's access to the EU market and an end to discriminatory trade policies against Russia.[62]

The Russian government's attitude had shifted from what opponents called the mendicant mentality, which entailed the demeaning soliciting of Western credits, toward the idea of promoting the internal conditions for Russia's development. Yeltsin raised specific demands for the lifting of COCOM restrictions when he met Clinton in Vancouver and at the Tokyo G-7 Summit. COCOM, as a body that controlled trade to Communist countries via the domestic legislation of its 17 members, was subsequently terminated in March 1994. At the Tokyo G-7 meeting Yeltsin focused of ending trade discrimination and called for a timetable allowing at least 10 years for the removal of discriminatory legislation against Russia.[63]

In relation to debt rescheduling, Yeltsin made a point of insisting that unlike the Bolsheviks, who repudiated Russia's debts after 1917, his government would affirm its obligations. Under an agreement with the CIS, Russia assumed liability for the Soviet Union's $70 billion debt to various creditors. Russia again found an ally in the United States that supported its demand for a moratorium on debt interest payments and for rescheduling. These demands only marginally affected the United States as it held a small percentage of Russia's debt. Germany, however, held around 50 percent of Russia's external debt and opposed Russia's demands advocating the negotiation of new loans as a substitute.[64] Russia's debt service bill for 1992 according to IMF estimates was $20.5 billion, and it was expected to increase to $39 billion in 1999. Over half of Russia's export earnings would be directed to debt interest payments every year, representing a considerable drag on the economy.[65] On 2 April 1993 the Paris Club of Russia's creditors agreed to a 10-year debt postponement with no payments for the first five years. Deputy Premier Aleksander Shokhin declared that this act was the West's first major step in support of Russia's reform.[66] In June 1994 the Paris Club again rescheduled Russia's debts (which had swelled to $80 billion, $45 billion of which was owed to the Paris Club), this time over a 15-year period with no payments for the first three years.[67] No similar agreement was reached with Russia's creditors in the London Club that held the remainder of its debts.

The United States's attention moved away from high profile politically inspired economic assistance packages toward specific measures intended to promote particular areas of the Russian economy. In October 1993, Warren Christopher emphasized privatization as the key to economic reform and declared that U.S. assistance projects would focus on the privatization of Russia's industry. Moreover, the Western world in general began to emphasize economic criteria once again now that the political danger to Yeltsin had subsided.[68] G-7 financial ministers met in Frankfurt in February 1994 but offered nothing new for Russia and reaffirmed existing programs. G-7 ministers noted that substantial financial assistance in the form of debt rescheduling, export credits, and loans had been provided and emphasized that other elements could be disbursed if necessary conditions are in place. Ministers also agreed that a program of social support was essential to enhance public acceptance of the reform but stressed that such funding would have to come mainly from domestic Russian sources. Ministers insisted that substantial debt rescheduling would await agreement between Russia and the IMF over the economic stabilization plan.[69] G-7 ministers linked the further development of assistance programs for Russia to IMF-Russian negotiations as a reprimand to the Russian government for its unwillingness or inability to reduce inflation and the budget deficit. Agreement was eventually reached with the IMF for the disbursing of a second tranche of $1.5 billion on 20 April when Premier Chernomyrdin agreed to reduce inflation to 7 percent by the end of 1994. By September 1994, positive indicators emerged in the Russian economy to the extent that the IMF was at last considering the disbursement of the $6.25 billion ruble stabilization fund that had been proposed in 1992.[70] On 10 March 1995, the IMF announced the disbursement of this fund that had been delayed by the Chechen war, but in monthly rather than quarterly tranches to enhance accountability.

The 20th G-7 meeting in Naples from 8–9 July 1994 simply endorsed previous approaches toward Russia while pointing to other areas of assistance that could be expanded. The economic communiqué noted that Russia had not made adequate progress in implementing the reform program. Nonetheless, an increase in special drawing rights from the IMF was under consideration for Russia as well as further loans from the World Bank.[71] A two-pronged strategy had emerged that focused on particular areas of Russia's economy where economic assistance would have the greatest impact in the promotion of reform. Privatization was one area targeted and the U.S. government claimed that most of its aid to Russia was being directed through private channels through the SPRP or other programs. The second area to receive attention was Russia's oil industry regarded as the generator of the Russian economy. Six-hundred and ten million dollars was granted in 1992 and on 29 June 1994 an additional $500 million was announced for pipeline improvements and environmental protection.[72]

What was achieved? There has been no agreement about the actual amounts disbursed given the uncoordinated nature of the effort to assist Russia. The communiqué from the Naples G-7 meeting of June 1994 claimed that some $30 billion of the $43.4 billion declared had been advanced.[73] U.S. Treasury Undersecretary Lawrence Summers claimed that $22 billion had been disbursed, most of which was debt rescheduling. Without this factor the figure was reduced to $7 billion from 1992–1994.[74] Professor Jerry Sachs, who was the Russian government's adviser until January 1994, calculated that $23 billion had been disbursed from 1992–1993 in the form of short-term credits to Russian state trading bodies at commercial interest rates.[75] Figures from Russian financial sources differ again giving a total of $17.8 billion from 1992–1994, $10.5 billion for 1992, $4.5 billion for 1993 and $2.8 billion expected for 1994.[76] Jerry Sachs has echoed Russian views outlined previously that the great discrepancy between announced intentions and the relatively small amounts disbursed contributed to an anti-Western backlash.[77] According to Sachs, the failure lay in the inability of the IMF to promote reform adequately and the task should have been assumed by a political body such as the G-7. It is difficult to imagine, however, the G-7 laying down conditions for economic assistance that would have been substantially different from those imposed by the IMF in view of the fear of rampant corruption in the Russian system. The problem resided in the Russian inability to accept large scale economic aid and the absence of institutions and safeguards that would ensure that the assistance would be utilized effectively. That problem may have been compounded by the absence of coordination and strategic direction within the Western economic assistance effort to the extent that a proper reckoning could not be made. Nonetheless, the basic constraint was on the Russian not the Western side.

Fundamentally, Western economic assistance programs for Russia were peripheral to its economic development and could not substitute for indigenous efforts. Political and economic purposes were initially confused in the Western program that explains to a large extent the grandiose declarations of support and the haphazard coordination of the disparate programs. The need at the time was to demonstrate Western support for an embattled president. Russian expectations were naturally stimulated and the impression was created of an open-ended commitment. When the time came to disburse the aid, economic criteria were disclosed and Western governments invoked a financial prudence that belied the earlier political purpose. It is no wonder then that Russian responses were cynical and skeptical and that the great promises of support may have had the opposite effect on the Russian people to that which was intended. A carefully prepared program developed and coordinated by the United States from the start could have targeted particular strategic areas of the Russian economy to stimulate growth. The separation of political and economic purposes at the outset would have done much to prevent the disillusionment that subsequently arose in Russia in relation to Western aid efforts and would have shown greater results over the longterm.

Strategic Partnership with the United States

What kind of strategic partnership could Russia establish with the United States? Inherited from the Gorbachev era, the notion of strategic partnership soothed wounded Russian pride and offered relief for frustrated national ambitions by providing a basis for Russia's great power aspirations. Russia had achieved strategic nuclear arms reduction agreements with the United States and the cooperative momentum generated in this area was to spill over into other areas that would ensure Russian influence. Nonetheless, the START process was stalled by Russia's Parliament and there was no basis for assuming that nuclear arms reductions would lead to collaboration in other areas. Fundamentally, the idea of Russia as a strategic partner of the U.S., and Russia as major aid recipient were contradictory and Yeltsin could not escape this fact. It was asserted that Western aid programs were temporary and that Russia would soon be on its feet again, but Russia's lapse of status belied this hope. Russia was no longer a superpower, yet Russian leaders for the most part acted as if they had not noticed.

The United States initially cooperated with Yeltsin in his desire to be treated as the leader of a great power. What for the United States was an artificial and illusory elevation of Russia's status for a particular diplomatic purpose became a narcotic for the Russian leadership and later an irritant for Western leaders. The specter of President Yeltsin continually asserting Russia's role as a great power was comical for some, puzzling for others, and simply tragic for the rest. Nonetheless, Western leaders understood that confirmation of Russia's great power status was a political as well as a psychological need for Yeltsin, without which he would become politically vulnerable for having presided over Russia's collapse as an international actor.

It was for this reason that Kozyrev would talk about the United States and Russia as two countries possessing nuclear arsenals and exercising tremendous and unique influence in different parts of the globe.[78] Yeltsin pushed for Russia's membership of the G-7, though how Russia as aid recipient could justify its position alongside the donors of the G-7 was never explained. The United States was an ally over this issue and in July 1992 George Bush spoke of Russia's unique status and advocated its inclusion into the G-7, against the opposition of both John Major and Helmut Kohl.[79] Yeltsin was able to participate in the deliberations of the third day of the Munich G-7 meeting of July 1992. At the Tokyo G-7 meeting his requests that the G-7 sign a political declaration with Kozyrev met with a cold rebuff.[80] At the Naples G-7 meeting of July 1994, Yeltsin was allowed to participate in the political discussions but was excluded from the economic deliberations.[81] When Yeltsin visited Washington in October 1994, the notion of alliance with the United States was again reaffirmed. He then reiterated that Russia and the United States were two great powers and dismissed the idea of the United States as the world's only superpower as unacceptable. Yeltsin declared that international issues should be managed by Russia and the U.S. on an equal footing.[82]

Yeltsin's strength in insisting on equal status with the United States was paradoxically his weakness. While he was regarded as a reformist leader battling with obstructionist forces in Russian politics, he was encouraged by the United States and his excesses were condoned. The existence of Russia's nuclear arsenal and the understandable desire on the part of the West to prevent the hemorrhage of nuclear material into the hands of terrorists, intensified the need to support Yeltsin as the one major ally within Russia that the West could rely on. Russia's instability and weakness enabled Yeltsin to claim a relationship with the United States and the West in general that it would otherwise not be entitled to on the basis of economic criteria alone. The Russian leadership was accordingly allowed certain benefits that flowed from the assumption of strategic partnership.

In terms of the economic assistance program visions were not matched by actual performance. Nonetheless, Russia benefited from having the United States as its patron because it was the U.S. leadership galvanized the world community behind the need to support Russia. The United States influenced international lending institutions to extend financial assistance to Russia at a time when economic indicators dictated restraint. Both the Bush and Clinton administrations prompted the IMF to dispense funds to Russia on the basis that the political situation allowed its special treatment. Both administrations remonstrated with the Europeans, the Germans in particular, to reschedule Russia's debts and have conditionally supported Russia's entry into the G-7. The financial benefits were not as vast as expected but without United States's support for Yeltsin, Russia would have received considerably less from all sources. American leadership stimulated the hopes of the international community in relation to the ultimate success of the democratic revolution in Russia and made governments and lenders more willing to propose assistance than they otherwise would have been. The United States has also acted as role model for Russia's democrats providing a sense of direction and inspiration for Russia's political and economic reformers.

Most important as far as foreign policy is concerned, has been the United States's willingness to restrain and counterbalance Japan. Here again the United States has acted as an ally of Russia in deflecting political pressure and demands that Russia in its weakened state would have had difficulty in managing. Had Japan's territorial dispute with Russia been a strictly bilateral affair, Russia would have confronted greater pressure from the Japanese side, and the consequences of not settling the dispute would have been greater than they were. The Japanese were grudging participants in the G-7 plans to assist

Russia given that they had linked economic assistance packages to a settlement of the territorial dispute. The Japanese objected to Bush's $24 billion package, claiming that it was premature and that its implementation would be a disincentive for Russia to negotiate a settlement to the territorial dispute.[83] Japan acted to have the territorial dispute mentioned in G-7 political communiqués hoping that the G-7 would be a diplomatic means to press Russia to negotiate the issue. Western leaders, in turn, pressed the Japanese to extend greater economic assistance to Russia, and the G-7 became a means of neutralizing Japanese pressure on Russia.[84] In an article that prompted Clinton to support Russia, Nixon wrote that Japan should cease asking for the return of the disputed territory because of the danger that if Yeltsin failed "they will never get the islands back."[85] Western leaders generally followed this approach, and in the 1993 G-7 political declaration there was no mention of the territorial dispute that had appeared in previous G-7 declarations (1991–1992). Japanese Foreign Minister Kabun Mutô complained that Russia and the U.S. gang up against Japan, which seemed to have become the common enemy of both.[86]

GEOPOLITICAL TENSIONS WITH THE WEST

The idea of strategic partnership with the United States was a response to a particular set of circumstances that arose after the collapse of the Soviet Union, which cannot be expected to endure. Russian democrats stretched their hands to the West for support and encouragement in their efforts to transform Russian society and their suppression under the Soviet Union endowed this need with greater intensity and urgency. The notion of a partnership with the United States tended to gloss over the very real foreign policy differences that were subsequently revealed, most serious of which was the clash of geopolitical interests that emerged within Europe. Proponents of geopolitics would support Samuel Huntington's argument that the West and Russia constitute separate civilizations and that "conflict between civilizations will be the latest phase in the evolution of conflict in the modern world." Huntington proposed that the dividing line between Western civilization and Orthodox-Slavic civilization is the most "significant dividing line in Europe."[87] Huntington subsequently qualified his views, saying that conflict between civilizations was not necessarily inevitable.[88] Quite apart from the difficulty of defining what constitutes a civilization, the characterization of the West and Russia as separate civilizations ignores the continuing impact of the West on Russia and the shared heritage of Christianity. Modern Russia has been closely tied to Western civilization in a way that confirms the idea of linked rather than separate civilizations.

Clashes of interest between Russia and the West have been revealed in Europe and, while not justifying the idea of a clash of civilizations, certainly point to renewed geopolitical tensions. Historical factors stimulate the geopolitical differences that have emerged between Russia and the West over concrete issues in Europe such as the Bosnian crisis, Russia's relationship with the newly-independent Baltic, Central European states, and the future course of NATO. These issues impact immediately on the relationship with the United States as the Western coalition leader and main proponent of all that the West stands for. Yeltsin's government may have expected that a strategic partnership with the United States would mitigate (or even overcome) the geopolitical tensions in Russia's relationship with Europe. Nonetheless, Russia cannot form a relationship with the United States independently of Europe, to which the United States is bound by the terms of the Western alliance. Ultimately, the ties within the Western alliance are stronger than those between Russia and the U.S.

The Bosnian Crisis

Russia's role over the Bosnian crisis cannot be regarded as a civilizational clash based on the Orthodox-Western division popularized by Huntington. Domestic political forces within Russia, within the Supreme Soviet, and elsewhere attempted to portray the issue in these terms but the reality of Russia's diplomatic position was more complicated. Russia's pro-Western leadership attempted to utilize the Bosnian crisis to demonstrate to the West that Russia could play a meaningful part in conflict resolution in the Balkans. The intention was to implement closer collaboration with the West to justify the demand to be included in the G-7 and great power security deliberations, not to alienate the West by supporting Orthodox Serbia in its ambitions as was demanded by Russia's nationalists. The issue demonstrated the arousal of popular nationalist opinion in Russia but also its limited impact on foreign policy in complicated circumstances.

Russia's commitment to the pro-Western position was put to the test over the Bosnian crisis. The Supreme Soviet accused the Foreign Ministry of deserting the Serbs as Russia's traditional allies when Russia first voted to support sanctions against Serbia in the UN Security Council on 30 May 1992. Kozyrev declared that the Supreme Soviet vote to terminate sanctions on Serbia was an action against the international community and identified an alliance between Russia and Serbian "national patriots."[89] Kozyrev's opponent over this issue was Yevgennii Ambartsumov who pressed for greater balance in Russian foreign policy. Ambartsumov complained that the Foreign Ministry looked at this issue through the eyes of the West and that sanctions should be applied to all of the warring sides, not just the Serbs.[90] Ambartsumov and Oleg Rumyantsev subsequently traveled to Serbia and met Serbian leaders including Slobodan Milosevic. They warned that the Supreme Soviet would push the Foreign Ministry to change its position over the Serbs and pointed to the danger of Islamic revanchism that threatened Russia from the south.[91] On 26 June 1992, Kozyrev explained the Foreign Ministry's position before a joint sitting of the Supreme Soviet, defending Russia's adherence to international sanctions, but demonstrating that Russia had acted in favor of their mitigation.[92]

Serbian leaders appealed to Russia's Supreme Soviet for support on the basis of Slavic-Orthodox solidarity, and in response deputies insisted on supporting the Serbs as Russia's traditional ally in the Balkans. On 16 December 1992, a resolution was passed by the Supreme Soviet calling for sanctions on all parties to the Bosnian conflict, Russia to use its veto if the UN Security Council reached the point of considering military intervention into the conflict, and humanitarian assistance for Yugoslavia. Deputies demanded that Russia act unilaterally to assist Yugoslavia without considering the UN position.[93] *Izvestiya* correspondent Maksim Yusin wrote that this was the Supreme Soviet's first major assault on Kozyrev's foreign policy. Subsequently, the legislature continued in the same vein demanding an end to sanctions against Yugoslavia and calling on the Russian government to place this issue on the agenda of the Security Council. If the other Security Council members refused to accept this change then the deputies demanded that Russia annul its signature to the original resolution imposing sanctions on Belgrade.[94] In July 1993, the Supreme Soviet appealed directly to the world community to terminate sanctions against Yugoslavia. Russian diplomats were reportedly embarrassed by the emotive language of the appeal that came after Serbia's Parliament petitioned the Russian legislature for support.[95]

Russia's diplomacy over the Bosnian crisis was affected by domestic political pressure and attempts were made to demonstrate balance. Russia supported the Vance-Owen plan of 27 October 1992 that envisaged a partition of Bosnia into Serb and Muslim areas. In May 1993, Russia clashed with the United States over this issue as the Americans opposed any partition of the status quo that would reward the Serbs for their aggression.[96] Similarly, Russia opposed President Clinton's plan to lift the arms embargo on Bosnia to allow the Muslims to arm themselves against the Serbs. Deputy Foreign Minister Anatolii Adamshin declared that Russia would veto any such resolution in the UN Security Council.[97] These events were portrayed within Russia as instances where Russia was asserting itself diplomatically against the West. Neither could be regarded in terms of conflict with the West as in both cases Russia had European support. The Vance-Owen plan was a Western creation and had British and French support; both Britain and France also opposed the lifting of the arms embargo.

The greatest disappointment for Russia occurred in 1994 when NATO launched air strikes against the Bosnian Serbs on five separate occasions. Russia discovered that its so-called traditional alliance with the Serbs was a creation of rhetoric with little contemporary basis. On 5 February 1994, the Bosnian Serbs unleashed a mortar attack on a Sarajevo market and on 9 February NATO served them with an ultimatum to withdraw their heavy weapons beyond 20 kilometers of Sarajevo.[98] Yeltsin expressed his annoyance that Russia had not been consulted about NATO's ultimatum and Zhirinovsky threatened retaliation against the West if the Serbs were attacked. Yeltsin became personally involved in the Bosnian crisis and directly contacted Serbian leader Slobodan Milosevic and Bosnian Serb leader Radavan Karadzic promising Russian protection if their forces surrendered their heavy weapons.[99] The Bosnian Serbs backed down and the Russians claimed a great victory.[100]

Russia subsequently became closely involved in the search for a diplomatic settlement on the basis of its ability to influence the Serbs, which had supposedly been demonstrated over Sarajevo. Russia's special envoy, Vitalii Churkin, called for a cease-fire and a settlement based on a Bosnian Serb partial surrender of territory.[101] Nonetheless, continued Bosnian Serb pressure on Gorazde resulted in further NATO air strikes, which the Russians could not avert, on 12 March and 10 April. Churkin claimed that he had received Karadzic's assurances that the assaults on Gorazde, designated a "safe haven" for Muslims by the UN Security Council on 4 July 1993, would end. Nonetheless, the Serbs continued with the attacks and the Russians reacted bitterly. Maksim Yusin described the event as a serious diplomatic defeat for Russia as it became apparent that the Serbs had manipulated the Russians to gain more time for their offensive to succeed.[102] The Serbs may have calculated that Russia as their traditional ally could be relied on to construct a greater Serbia and to ward off pressure from the West.[103] Churkin declared that the Serbs were no longer trustworthy and Russian opposition to further NATO air strikes (executed on 20 April, 22 September and 21 November 1994) dissipated.

Russia's so-called influence over the Serbs had been proved illusory and its diplomatic position merged with that of its Western counterparts over most, but not all, issues. At the Geneva meeting of foreign ministers on 13 May 1994, which included Kozyrev, Warren Christopher, Klaus Kinkel, and Douglas Hurd, a new plan was unveiled that entailed the division of Bosnia into a federation. The Bosnian Serbs, who controlled 70 percent of the country, were to be granted 49 percent.[104] At this meeting, Russia emerged as no special protector of Serbian interests. Further attempts by Russia were made to induce Slobodan Milosevic to cut ties with the Bosnian Serbs and to accept international monitoring of Serbia's border with Bosnia. Kozyrev's visit to Belgrade in August 1994 was the occasion for the promotion of this proposal, which Milosevic rejected for reasons related to the nationalist opposition he faced. Moscow had utilized every lever with the Serbs with little success, demonstrating that civilizational or cultural ties do not necessarily lead to alliances. Despite the evident sympathy that existed for Serbia within Russia, domestic political pressure had minimum impact on Foreign Ministry diplomacy over an issue that was largely removed from internal politics. The same could not be said about the Baltic States.

The Baltic States

The issue of the Baltic states—Estonia, Latvia, and Lithuania—and their relationship with Russia quickly became an emotive one for both sides as the Soviet Union disintegrated. On the Baltic side, there was the sorry history of Soviet annexation and occupation under the Molotov-Ribbentrop Pact of August 1939. The Baltic states consider themselves an extended part of Europe due to their Catholic or Lutheran affiliation. Economics and demography, however, have introduced complicating factors as the Baltic states were strongly dependent on Russia for trade and energy. Lithuania derived 97 percent of its energy supplies from Russia—approximately one-third of Latvia and Estonia's trade was with Russia. The period of Soviet occupation had altered the ethnic composition of the Baltic states as the Russian population increased. In 1992 the percentage of Russians in Lithuania (population 3.75 million) was 9.4 percent; in Estonia (population 1.5 million) 30.3 percent; in Latvia (population 2.6 million) 34.0 percent. For Estonia and Latvia in particular, many of the Russians who had settled there were regarded as occupants who threatened the ethnic basis of society. Independence was perceived as the opportunity to rectify this injustice. For Russia, however, irrespective of the reasons that brought the Russians to the Baltic states, their rights were to be protected. The desire of the Baltic states to reorientate themselves toward the West and to reduce the ethnic Russian presence became a domestic political issue within Russia.

The initial pro-Western course of Yeltsin's government demanded that the issue of the Baltic states be removed as an irritant in relations with the West, and with Germany and the United States in particular, which had strongly taken up their cause. Both insisted that the former Soviet forces stationed there (130,000 in 1991) were incompatible with Baltic sovereignty and should be removed as rapidly as possible. Within Russia, two approaches emerged in relation to the Baltic states. The pro-Western democrats regarded the issue as a means to build trust and confidence with the West. Yeltsin's government reaffirmed the Soviet commitment of September 1991 to negotiate the status of forces there. This commitment accompanied the Soviet recognition of the independence of the Baltic states. Russian minorities were to be protected according to the norms of international law and within the context of European institutions such as the CSCE. The nationalists such as Rutskoi and the Russian Unity (*Russkoe yedinstvo*) group in the Supreme Soviet had no trust in Western norms and regarded the Russian troop presence in the Baltic states as a lever to extract concessions for the Russian minorities. It was the Eurasianist Sergei Stankevich who first claimed that the Baltic states were indulging in ethnic cleansing against the Russian minorities. Stankevich declared that the West had no sympathy for the Russians and that Russia would have to follow the Turkish example when it invaded Cyprus in 1974 to protect the Turkish minority.[105] Competing pressures from the two groups explained to a considerable extent Yeltsin's wavering course over this issue.

Between 1992, when bilateral negotiations began over the withdrawal of Russian forces, and 1994 relations were inflamed by several developments. The emergence of Zhirinovsky as a political force after the December 1993 elections provoked alarm in the Baltic states prompting them to call on NATO for protection.[106] The Baltic states also objected to the use of the term "near abroad" (*blizhnee zarubezh'e*) by the Russians. They had rejected membership to the CIS and any multilateral relationship with Russia and regarded the idea of the "near abroad" as a declaration of a Russian right of influence over their territory. That impression was reinforced by the views of Andranik Migranyan, who as a member of the president's council expressed his views of the Baltic states in *Nezavisimaya gazeta*. According to Migranyan, Gorbachev made the fatal error of recognizing the independence of the Baltic states immediately after the abortive coup of August 1991. Migranyan claimed that Baltic independence should have been linked to a resolution of outstanding issues such as the rights of the Russian minorities. He described the Baltic states as racist regimes that intended to push the minority Russians back to Russia and lamented Western indifference to their plight.[107]

Under intense pressure from the United States and Germany, Yeltsin's government negotiated force withdrawal agreements with the three Baltic states. The West made a clear distinction between the Baltic states, which were regarded as part of Europe and therefore were to be strongly supported, and Muslim Chechnya, regarded as part of Russia. When Yeltsin declared on 29 October 1992 that the withdrawal of forces from the Baltic states would be suspended pending a resolution of the states of Russian minorities the West reacted strongly. Yeltsin responded to the Estonian Nationality Law, subsequently amended, which limited citizenship to those who were citizens before 1938 and their descendants. NATO pressed for a complete withdrawal without conditions while the U.S. Congress threatened to link a Russian withdrawal of forces to the granting of economic assistance under foreign aid legislation.[108] According to German Foreign Minister Klaus Kinkel, Germany felt a special responsibility to rectify the injustices of the Molotov-Ribbentrop Pact and consequently pressed for the unconditional withdrawal of Russian forces.[109]

Russia first reached a withdrawal agreement with Lithuania, which suggests that political difficulties were to some extent a function of the size of the Russian minority. Of the three Baltic states Lithuania had the smallest percentage of Russians. Lithuania gave its Russian minority the right to citizenship after independence subject to conditions that were basically acceptable to Russia. Agreement was reached on 8 September 1992 for the withdrawal of Russian forces by September 1993. The defeat of the nationalist Sajudis led by Vytautas Landsbergis in the elections of 25 October 1992 brought into power Algirdas Brazauskas, leader of the former Communists in the Lithuanian Democratic Party. A deteriorating economy was behind this election defeat, and Brazauskas accordingly announced his policy of maintaining economic ties with Russia. Despite the Lithuanian demand for monetary compensation for the years of Soviet occupation, Yeltsin declared his satisfaction with Lithuania praising its respect for the human rights of the Russian minority.[110] Russian forces were withdrawn from Lithuania by 31 August 1993 and the agreement was seen as an example for the more difficult negotiations with Latvia and Estonia.[111]

Negotiations over the withdrawal of Russian forces in Latvia and Estonia continued to involve the problem of a shortage of housing for returning Russian servicemen as well as the question of Latvia's Citizenship Law (the first version was promulgated before the elections of June 1993). This version severely restricted the Russian right to citizenship based on the exclusion of those and their descendants who were not citizens before 1940 as well as their dependents. Other issues involved the future status of the Skrunda Radar Station, which the Russians wanted to maintain, as well as claims to former Soviet property. An agreement was reached between Yeltsin and Latvian President Guntis Ulmanis on 30 April 1994 according to which Russian forces were to be withdrawn by 31 August 1994. Latvia agreed to provide social guarantees to 22,320 retired Russian servicemen. Russia obtained access to the Skrunda Radar Station for an additional four years and agreed to pay $5 million in rent annually. The head of the Russian delegation in negotiations with Latvia, Sergei Zotov, declared that the agreement removed an obstacle from Russia's cooperation with the CSCE and strengthened its international position.[112] Latvia continued working on new drafts of its citizenship law.

More difficult were the negotiations with Estonia which were complicated by two factors. First, the initial Estonian refusal to accept any Soviet military retirees intentionally excluded by the Nationality Law. Second, the Estonian territorial claim on Russia had been negotiated with the Bolsheviks under the Treaty of Tartu of 2 February 1920. This treaty awarded Estonia part of Russian Pskov Oblast, which is mainly populated by Russians today. After Estonia's incorporation into the Soviet Union in 1940 this area was detached from Estonia and returned to Russia. The Russians recognize only Estonia's present borders as stipulated by the bilateral treaty of 12 January 1991 under which the Soviet Union accepted Estonia's independence. In the Russian view, this treaty superceded the Treaty of Tartu, which was a product of civil war politics. The territorial claim has been pushed by Estonian populist parties and was incorporated in Article 122 of the 1992 Constitution according to which Estonia's borders follow those outlined in the Treaty of Tartu.[113] Voices in Latvia have been raised in support of a similar claim under the 1920 Treaty of Riga, but President Guntis Ulmanis has refused to raise the claim officially.

From the Russian perspective, the Estonians were deliberately provoking trouble in the expectation that the West would support them to the hilt, even to the point of endorsing their territorial claims. From the Estonian perspective, Russian demands were overbearing and exorbitant. Not only did the Russians demand social guarantees for military retirees but also a $23 million housing subsidy for servicemen and their families compelled to move from Estonia, and compensation for supposed ecological damage to the army's property.[114] Chief Russian negotiator with the Estonians, Vasili Svirin, accused them of attempting to forge a mono-ethnic state.[115] Defense Minister Pavel Grachev played into Estonian hands when he declared on 6 May 1994 that Estonia was practicing apartheid and announced that the Russian military presence there would be increased.[116] Grachev's fit of pique caught Russia's diplomats by surprise and only succeeded in focusing the Western world's attention on the issue. The West pressed Yeltsin to come to an agreement with Estonia and to avoid tension that could jeopardize the G-7 Naples meeting. British Foreign Secretary Sir Douglas Hurd in Moscow on 23 May and President Clinton in the Latvian capital Riga on 6 July both rejected the Russian linkage between a withdrawal of forces and the treatment of the Russian minority.[117]

Both sides engaged in considerable posturing (in the process of bargaining with the Estonians) refusing the demand that all military retirees be accepted. The extent of the posturing was revealed when Estonian President Lennart Meri traveled to Moscow and concluded an agreement on 26 July 1994 for the withdrawal of Russian forces by 31 August. Estonia agreed to grant residency rights to 10,689 military retirees, excluding those considered a danger to Estonian security, namely former KGB and other security personnel. A committee was to be formed, including CSCE representatives, to examine applications for residency permits.[118] The agreement still required ratification by both parliaments but the issue had been resolved and the Russian withdrawal from Latvia and Estonia was made to coincide with the final withdrawal of forces from Germany.

The Russians had conceded their more extravagant demands under Western pressure. It was difficult for Russians to surrender influence in the Baltic states as Viktor Parshutkin, Press Secretary to the Duma Committee on International Affairs demonstrated. Parshutkin claimed that Russian diplomacy had no understanding of Russian interests, that Russia had been ejected from the Baltic states against its will, and that Russia should be more assertive there to defend its interests.[119] Russia asked the CSCE Commissioner for National Minorities in Estonia to examine the situation of the Russians there and a report was issued that found no grounds for complaint in any case. While the Western world finds no fault in the treatment of Russian minorities in the Baltic states, there are those in the Duma who claim that Russians are being victimized and claim the West has double standards on human rights.[120] Other issues will also trouble Russia's relations with the Baltic states. Estonia's territorial claim has not been settled and in June 1994 Russia constructed markers on its side of the border as a practical response. There is also the issue of transit access through Lithuania to the Russian enclave of Kaliningrad where the Russian military presence disturbs Poland and Germany. European institutions such as the CSCE or the West European Union may become involved in monitoring transit arrangements to Kaliningrad in which case bilateral problems with Lithuania may be avoided.

The anxiety of the Baltic states in relation to Russia is understandable, particularly as unstable conditions in Russia make it difficult to determine whether Russia would ultimately accept their independence. The Baltic states lost their independence through a German-Russian deal which was a product of unusual circumstances when predatory regimes emerged concurrently in both Germany and Russia. Those circumstances are unlikely to be repeated, and the steady integration of the Baltic states with Europe strengthen their position in relation to possible nationalistic backlashes in Russia.[121] No doubt the West has a troubled conscience about the three Baltic states in view of their experience of Soviet occupation. This will probably spur their integration into both the European Union and eventually NATO.

The Expansion of NATO

No more troubling issue has emerged for Russia's relationship with the West than the expansion of NATO, which in many respects points to the geopolitical limits of the partnership that the pro-Westerners had advocated. The collapse of communism has resulted in an expansion of the West, the core area of which was included in NATO during the Cold War years, to embrace those countries in the East that had shared common Western values. Recently former Soviet satellite states in Eastern Europe, as well as the Baltic states, have moved to rejoin the Western community. The area known as the Western community is being extended to encompass these newly independent states as they prepare for membership in the West's major institutions. Historically, Russia has dominated border states and has demanded deferential behavior and accommodation of its interests. Now that these border states are set to join the wider Western community Russia cannot expect to reimpose the previous relationships on them without disturbing relations with the West and the United States.

NATO's eastward movement throws Russia into an acute dilemma that goes to the core of its foreign policy orientation and sense of identity. Russia's pro-Western orientation stemmed from an understanding that Russia's security would be enhanced through the creation of security multilateralism to enclose the Eurasian continent. The emphasis placed by the West on NATO has challenged the value of the pro-Western position in Russia, and has increased the ranks of the geopolitical or moderate nationalist camps. The expansion of NATO may undermine the pro-Western foreign policy orientation and could create a situation in which nationalist groups less disposed toward the West control foreign policy.

The issue cuts through nebulous and captivating notions of partnership, and compels Russia to focus on the structure of its relationship with the West. The debate over the issue will at least remove deceptive mirages about Russia's collaboration with the West requiring both pro-Westerners and nationalists to reassess their positions. Pro-Western democrats who thought in terms of an all too glib partnership have been compelled to recognize that the Western embrace stops short of Russia, and that the idea of partnership is not necessarily reciprocated. For those whose sense of identification with the West was based on protestations of fidelity to Western principles, this comes as a sobering experience and a reminder of the deeper security and political issues that underlie foreign policy. Nationalists and Eurasianists who assumed that Russia was a separate world and could somehow survive autonomously have been compelled to recognize the dangers of Russia's isolation in the event of NATO's expansion eastward.

The debate within NATO circles about the future role of the alliance arose in 1993 in response to the Visegrad Group—Poland, Hungary, Czech Republic, and Slovakia—and Baltic interest in joining NATO. Significantly, when Yeltsin visited Warsaw on 25 August 1993, he declared that his sympathy with Poland's desire to join NATO would not run counter to Russian interests.[122] Yeltsin's views differed from those of Defense Minister Grachev, who in an interview with the Polish press agency on 23 August stated that Russia could not allow Poland to join NATO.[123] In the discussions that followed Warren Christopher and the Germans were in favor of expanding NATO. Deputy Secretary of State Strobe Talbott sent a memo dated 17 October to Christopher claiming that NATO's expansion would be tantamount to neo-containment of Russia. Secretary of State altered his view. A White House cabinet meeting on 19 October resulted in Clinton's endorsement of the more restrained approach.[124] Accordingly, on 20 October Defense Secretary Les Aspin proposed the idea of a partnership for peace program (PPP) that was subsequently endorsed by NATO's defense ministers. The PPP was to entail military cooperation but not actual membership of NATO for the Central/East European states. Nonetheless, the Copenhagen meeting of the North Atlantic Assembly in the same month pointed to future directions. The assembly called on NATO to articulate the terms and conditions and accession to the alliance by European states "that have achieved stable market-orientated economics," and to establish the procedures by which accession could be achieved.[125] The Partnership for Peace Program was formerly endorsed at the Brussels NATO Summit of 10–11 January 1994. The declaration from the summit reaffirmed "that the alliance remains open to the membership of other European countries." Under Point 1K of the declaration, NATO would consult with members in the event of a threat to their territorial integrity and would develop joint military exercises and cooperation in other defense matters.[126]

The key issue for the West was whether and to what extent Russian objections to NATO should be accommodated. Concerns in relation to the Russian response obviously weighed heavily with the Americans, resulting in the conversion of the initial movement to expand the alliance eastward in a phased approach, starting with the Partnership for Peace Program. Objections were raised that enlargement would simply dilute the alliance and paralyze its decision-making, that ethnic communal disputes would disrupt the alliance as a consequence of its expansion, and that potential members were unprepared for membership in terms of their military procedures, forces, and capabilities. The proponents of enlargement argued, however, that hesitation simply encouraged the Russian nationalists and gave them dangerous veto power over the alliance that strengthened their position domestically. NATO, accordingly, had a moral obligation to support the newly established democracies of Central and Eastern Europe, accentuated by the political instability of Russia and the danger of a relapse into authoritarianism. Moreover, NATO could adjust its decision-making to take account of expanded membership by replacing the principle of unanimity with the majority rule. The alliance could also act as a stable framework for the resolution of ethnic and communal disputes and could prevent their escalation.[127]

The debate within NATO triggered a similar prolonged debate within Moscow as to the appropriate response. In late October 1993, in a message to Mitterand, Yeltsin claimed that Russia did not regard NATO as a threat but would regard enlargement as an unproductive development that would result in Russia's isolation.[128] A more comprehensive response was delivered on 25 November by Yevgennii Primakov when he expressed the views of Russia's security establishment at the Foreign Ministry Press Center. Primakov did not openly contradict Yeltsin by claiming that enlargement was a threat, but his remarks indicated that the security establishment was deeply troubled. Enlargement, he said, brought NATO close to Russia's borders, in which case Russia's defense posture and strategy that had been developed on the absence of external threat would require review. Primakov emphasized that enlargement would create a barrier between Russia and the rest of the continent that could stimulate anti-Western opinion in Russia and undermine the reform movement. He stressed the alternative of a wider European security structure that had been promoted by the Russian government at the outset. He called for the creation of a post-Cold War multilateral security organization that would embrace NATO, the CSCE, and the UN.[129]

Views of NATO varied considerably within Moscow. Russia's military and conservatives could hardly reconcile themselves to NATO's continued existence after the termination of the Cold War, and imprinted on their minds was the idea of NATO as a threat. The then Deputy Chief of Staff Mikhail Kolesnikov told the Council of Security and Foreign Policy on 3 July 1992 that the longterm interest of NATO was not served by the rise of a new power in the former Soviet Union and that Russia could be NATO's new rival.[130] Similar views have been aired since reflecting the military's perception of NATO as a relic of the past which has been unjustifiably perpetuated.[131] The Foreign Ministry had promoted the idea of wider Eurasian multilateral security structure and the challenge to this idea represented by enlargement of NATO pushed it into the Primakov-defined consensus.

With the promulgation of the PPP, the debate intensified within Moscow. Opposition views centerd on three key objections. First, the issue of Russia's status. Russia was a nuclear power whose status demanded something more than membership to a program on the same level as other much smaller states.[132] Second, membership would conflict with and undermine the role of the CIS that was essential for Russia's security. Third, membership would conflict with China and the Islamic World where, according to the Russian perception, concern about the West had been stimulated since the end of the Cold War. This last factor was repeatedly articulated in discussions about NATO and was regarded as a significant restraint on Russian actions. Other points raised included the fear that Russia would lose its position as arms supplier to the Central European states if they conform to Western weapons standards and that the Bosnian crisis discredited NATO as a means of resolving communal conflict.[133] Those that argued for Russia's membership of the PPP pointed out that Russia would be dangerously isolated if it refused to join and, indeed, by the end of March 1994 twelve states had joined the program, including Poland on 2 February and the Ukraine on 8 February. The argument that only by joining the program could Russia hope to influence it was decisive and explained the government's basic agreement to the program. The subsequent discussion revolved around the terms and conditions of Russia's membership.

Hearings on the issue were conducted in the Duma's Defense Committee in April 1994 where the prevailing view was in favor of conditional membership. Sergei Yushenkov, the Committee Chairman, called for special status for Russia as a nuclear power in the PPP and declared that it should be regarded as a step toward an all-European security structure.[134] Of special interest were the views of Vladimir Lukin who thought it humiliating for Russia to stand in a line to join the program, and who also demanded a special status for Russia. Lukin subsequently insisted on attaching three conditions to Russia's membership of the program: Russia's responsibilities in the CIS should be accommodated; the nature of the collaboration with the West should be defined more clearly; and the role of Russia's military command should be identified. Lukin was particularly concerned about China's reactions, stating that Russia should convince China that it was not entering a military block directed against it and that a security relationship should be negotiated with the Chinese.[135] Concerns were also raised by Konstantin Zatulin, Head of the Duma Committee on the CIS, and Lt.-General Leonid Ivashov, Secretary to the CIS Council of Ministers, that the program would undermine security cooperation in the CIS. Ivashov, in particular, saw the program as a dangerous alternative to CIS security cooperation, which would eliminate the basis for collective security under the Tashkent Treaty of May 1992.[136] Ivashov claimed that the CIS militaries had negative views of the program and that it was plainly not in Russia's interests to join. Deputy Chairman of the Duma Committee for Defense, Aleksei Piskunov, claimed that membership to the program would deprive Russia of the ability to influence events in the CIS effectively and would destroy the Tashkent Collective Security Treaty. Nonetheless, Piskunov also saw no alternative for Russia but membership.[137]

During the hearings, the Foreign Ministry's Yuri Ushakov (Director of the Department of Europe) and the Defense Ministry's Maj.-General Pavel Zolotarev both spoke to the deputies in favor of membership, indicating a consensus between their institutions over this issue. Vyacheslav Nikonov, Chairman of the Duma's Subcommittee on International Security and Arms Control, claimed that the program would allow Russia influence over the further development of NATO; would give Central and East European states greater security against Russia; and would overcome the civilizational barrier with Europe permitting Russia's integration into world society. Russia, he argued, had no choice but to join the program in view of the fact that several CIS states had become members and that refusal on Russia's part would entail exclusion from other integrative steps with Europe.[138] Yeltsin reflected the general consensus that emerged by the end of April 1994 and claimed that Russia was in favor of joining but with a supplementary protocol that would confirm its unique position.[139]

The idea of the supplementary protocol was subsequently dropped in the face of NATO resistance. U.S. Defense Secretary William Perry emphasized that there would be no special status for Russia but he did not exclude the idea of a separate agreement to define Russia's relationship with NATO.[140] That special relationship would be reflected in Russia's involvement in the political deliberations of the G-7, announced by Warren Christopher in April 1994.[141] Defense Minister Grachev declared Russia's agreement to the program when he spoke to NATO defense ministers in Brussels on 24 May. Grachev stated that Russia was preparing a "framework document" that would follow its membership to the program and would formulate a "mechanism of consultation" over security issues.[142] Russia joined the PPP on 22 June in the understanding that it would eventually lead toward a wider European structure and that its collaboration with NATO was to stimulate this development. Point 2 of the Joint Russian-NATO communiqué, which was issued on the occasion of its accession, noted that both sides "agreed to develop an extensive individual partnership program corresponding to Russia's size, importance and capabilities."[143]

The Partnership for Peace Program was simply a means of gaining time for NATO as the crucial issue of Russia's relationship with the alliance was avoided. Pressure from the Central and East European states for full membership in the alliance could not be resisted for too long. Polish President Lech Walesa had pressed NATO for a schedule to identify the stages of Poland's gradual entry into NATO.[144] Germany has been a persistent advocate of Central European membership—Poland, Hungary, Czech republic—to be followed by the Baltic states. Duma Deputy Boris Fyodorov claimed that Russia could apply for membership in NATO as a way of testing the intentions of its

Western partners.[145] Among Russia's democrats the surprising belief arose that Russia could neutralize NATO by joining it. This was first heard in official circles in early 1992.[146] Duma Subcommittee Chairman Vyacheslav Nikonov also thought that Russian membership in NATO was a way of removing the civilizational barrier with Europe.[147] Nonetheless, European attitudes are opposed to Russia's admission into NATO, and justifiably or otherwise reinforced that civilizational barrier. German Defense Minister Volker Rühe has stated that Russia cannot be integrated into either NATO or the European Union, and that its situation was completely different from that of the East European states.[148] Rühe expressed the view that the collapse of Russia's position in Europe was not a consequence of an internal transformation of values and ambitions within Russia, but of external factors, in which case Russia had no place in Europe.[149]

The eventual accession of Central Europe and the Baltic states into NATO would confirm Russia's worst fears in relation to the construction of a *cordon sanitaire* around it. For this reason, the new Ukrainian President Leonid Kuchma warned the West against the rapid expansion of NATO when he visited Washington in November 1994.[150] The consequences could indeed be far-reaching and may involve a collapse of the rudimentary democratic institutions that Russia has established and a reversion to authoritarianism. In this condition, Russia could emerge as a backward delinquent state that would side with the enemies of the West. An alternative expressed by Russia's security establishment is a mutual agreement on spheres of influence between NATO and the CIS with a consultative mechanism between them. Deputy Secretary of Russia's Security Council Lt.-General Valerii Manilov expressed the idea of NATO and the CIS as component structures within a universal collective security system.[151] Lt. General Leonid Ivashov endorsed this idea emphasizing the importance to Russia of a Eurasian collective security system that would form the basis of Russia's collaboration with NATO.[152] Russia's security establishment tended to think in terms of condominium between blocs, NATO, and the CIS, as a legacy of the Soviet era.

There are several reasons why the idea of condominium in this sense is simply unrealistic. First, Central and East European states oppose the idea or anything that resembles a mutual recognition of spheres of influence given that their interests would be sacrificed as a consequence. Poland and the Baltic states are countries that lost their independence as a product of such policies in the past and are extremely sensitive to any possible return to the idea of German-Russian condominium in Europe. Estonian President Lennart Meri has voiced his concern about the possibility of U.S.-Russian condominium, which would result if both sides issued guarantees of Central and East European security as Kozyrev had earlier proposed. Meri insisted that NATO was the preeminent instrument of European security and that there was no need to construct umbrella security organizations that would weaken the alliance.[153]

Second, the West opposes the idea of endorsing mutual spheres of influence that is obviously incompatible with the economic and security integrative developments that have swept Europe since the Soviet collapse. Russia is simply unable to exert exclusive influence in the former Soviet Union as the newly-independent states there develop their own relationships with the West. Russia alone could not resolve the problem of the Ukraine's resistance to START-1 and, indeed, had it attempted to do so, the Ukraine may have conceivably emerged as a nuclear power. Only through the involvement of the U.S. was the trilateral agreement possible that allowed the Ukraine to engage in nuclear disarmament. The Ukraine, after all, has emerged as the fourth largest recipient of U.S. aid after Israel, Egypt, and Russia with total U.S. aid amounting to $900 million.[154] Western oil companies negotiated with Azerbaijan and Kazakhstan directly, removed Russia from its previous position of retaining exclusive access to the oil fields of the CIS. Those Russians who complained about the U.S. intention to push Russia out of the post-Soviet South, or the effort to establish "pro-U.S." regimes in the CIS, or who thought that American penetration of the CIS could "trigger a conflict in U.S.-Russian relations" had little understanding of events.[155] The CIS states sought closer relations with the U.S. as an alternative to Moscow for security or economic reasons, or as a demonstration of independence. When Yeltsin visited Washington in September 1994 the issue of Russia's role in the CIS was raised with the Russian side demanding the West's recognition of a special peace-keeping role there. The Americans made it clear that it refused to endorse the idea of spheres of influence and insisted that a Russian role be consistent with UN resolutions and international law.[156] The German position over this issue, as expressed by Foreign Minister Klaus Kinkel on 21 June, was also unmistakably opposed to the idea of special Russian interests in the CIS.[157]

Alternative means had to be negotiated that would avoid confirming Russia's nightmare of a creeping *cordon sanitaire* without endorsing the idea of separate spheres of influence. Kozyrev sent letters to CSCE chairman, NATO, EU, and the West European Union in July 1994 proposing that the CSCE be upgraded as the overriding security organization for the Eurasian continent. He called for the creation of an executive organ under the organization with permanent membership, which would be supplemented by its own secretariat.[158] The Russian Foreign Ministry proposed that the CSCE be converted into a central coordinating body that would oversee the CIS, NATO, and all other European institutions including the EU.[159] The proposal was raised at the Prague meeting of CSCE officials on 14 September 1994 but received no support.[160]

The Russian proposal simply provoked the same objections as the Europeans were yet unprepared to accept the subordination of European institutions to an amorphous body. Any proposal to upgrade the CSCE in this context would give Russia veto power over NATO and other European bodies, which the Europeans rejected.[161] Domestic political forces in both Russia and the U.S. acted on the situation in a way that complicated the issues further. A Republican victory in the U.S. congressional elections of 8 November 1994 undermined Clinton's policy of accommodating Russia. Jesse Helms, eventually Chairman of Senate Foreign Relations Committee, was particularly hostile toward economic aid for Russia. Mitch McConnell, Chairman of the Senate Appropriations Committee, sought to link aid to Russia to its behavior in the CIS. The Clinton administration devised a two-track strategy to manage Russia as a response to competing domestic, European, and Russian pressures. To facilitate the entry of Central and East European states into NATO, the administration intended to strengthen the CSCE as a conflict resolution and peace-keeping organization. A strengthened CSCE was a partial answer to Russian demands and a means to deflect Russian hostility toward the expansion of NATO.[162] Russian reactions against NATO was evident as it became increasingly clear that the alliance was not to be deflected from its course. At NATO's ministerial meeting in Brussels on 1 December 1994 the first NATO-Russia dialogue was instituted. Warren Christopher declared that NATO's expansion would be "steady, deliberate, and transparent" and would be linked to an upgraded role for the CSCE.[163] Kozyrev, however, refused to sign the accompanying documents relating to the development of the PPP with Russia and the NATO-Russia relationship beyond the program.[164]

Matters came to a head at the Budapest CSCE Summit, 5–6 December 1994. Yeltsin's address of 5 December was regarded as the most strident since the collapse of the Soviet Union. Yeltsin warned against "plunging Europe into a cold peace" and again emphasized the need to strengthen the CSCE as the overarching security organization for Eurasia. Yeltsin demanded that the West recognize the CIS as a security organization responsible for the former Soviet Union and declared that if NATO were pushed to Russia's borders it would be too easy "to bury democracy in Russia."[165] Both Clinton and Helmut Kohl, however, spoke against the idea of spheres of influence that had been persistently promoted by the Russians.[166] Nonetheless, Yeltsin's tirade notwithstanding, the Budapest Summit adopted measures for a role expansion for the CSCE that Russia should have encouraged by promoting a better atmosphere. As of 1 January 1995 the name of the organization was changed to the Organization for Security and Cooperation in Europe (OSCE) to reflect the transition from a conference to a more durable organization. Point 8 of the Budapest Summit Declaration stated that the organization "will be a primary instrument for early warning, conflict prevention and crisis management in the region." Point 9 indicated the organization's intention to develop new capabilities including a peace-keeping capability as well as strengthening of its decision making bodies.[167]

Reactions to the Budapest Summit were surprisingly similar. The liberals and democrats characterized the Budapest conference as a sharp defeat for Russian diplomacy. In their view, Russia could not prevent the admission of new members to NATO and could only influence the situation for the better by ensuring that it stays on the democratic path.[168] Those who represented the nationalist position also regarded the Budapest conference as a defeat, but for different reasons. Andranik Migranyan wrote that that the alliance was bent on expansion, which Russia had not been able to prevent in any case.[169] Others linked the expansion of NATO with pressure from the Republican Congress and the rising power of Germany within Europe. Lamented the authors of one commentary, the West has no faith in Russian democracy and believes that Russia will become the "chronic sick man of Europe" who has to be isolated by a *cordon sanitaire*.[170]

Russian reactions to the Budapest Summit contributed to a general hardening of position toward the United States that was observable in late 1994, particularly as Russian forces moved into Chechnya on 11 December. The Duma's four committees on foreign policy—international affairs, defense, geopolitics, and security—met in December to consider a response to Clinton's address to Congress on 20 October 1994 entitled "The National Security Strategy of the United States of America." The Duma committees had been angered by American warnings against the use of force in the CIS while the U.S. freely occupied Haiti on 19 September. The committees criticized the U.S. for arrogating to itself the right to use force without restraint and complained that the U.S. ignored Russia and without it could not maintain international stability.[171] A move toward nationalism within the Duma was a consequence of these events, which the democrats and liberals were largely powerless to avert.[172]

The proposed expansion of NATO would jeopardize areas of collaboration already negotiated with Russia in a way that would affect European security. First, deteriorating relations with the West entail a greater emphasis on maintaining nuclear arsenals, not reducing them. Vladimir Lukin claimed that in the event of NATO's expansion to Russia's borders, Russia would require a strong nuclear guarantee that would place the future of the START-2 Treaty in doubt. Second, there would be pressure to adjust Russian defense strategy to what is perceived as a new division of Europe. This could mean a greater emphasis on tactical nuclear weapons and perhaps medium range ballistic missiles in an effort to compensate for a new military imbalance in Europe, which would be the consequence of NATO's expansion.[173] Third, the Conventional Forces in Europe (CFE) Treaty would be jeopardized accordingly. The CFE was signed between NATO and the Warsaw Pact on 19 November 1990 and was adjusted to the collapse of the Communist bloc by the Tashkent Collective Security Treaty and the Oslo meeting of 5 June 1992. The treaty established limits to conventional weapons in various zones of Europe from the Atlantic to the Urals. The Russian Foreign Ministry has insisted that the expansion of NATO threatens the CFE limits, as an obvious imbalance would be created between an expanded NATO and Russia. Moreover, the Russian military has claimed that the CFE sublimits prevent increased deployments of forces in the North Caucasian military district where the danger of instability is greatest. The West has resisted Russian pressure over this issue, which has intensified because of the Chechnya operation. The Foreign Ministry has threatened a unilateral revision of the treaty, which according to Director of Press and Information Grigori Karasin, prevents Russia from ensuring its own security.[174]

Russia's relations with third countries can also be an issue affecting the relationship with the West. Moscow has the option of developing relations with states that are in conflict with the West as a way of gaining diplomatic advantages, or reducing Western pressure for NATO's expansion. In this context, Moscow's relationship with China and the domestic pressure to strengthen relations with that country will be further explored. Russia's ties with Iran which are a product of policy toward the Islamic World, have served a similar purpose. The U.S. has been concerned about Russian arms sales to that country and over 1992–1993 two kilo class diesel submarines were delivered to Iran under a 1988 contract concluded with the Soviet Union. In September 1994 Yeltsin promised the U.S. that no new arms agreements would be concluded with Iran despite the pressure from Russia's arms manufacturers.[175] U.S. attention turned to Moscow's agreement with Iran, signed on 8 January 1995, for the sale of two nuclear reactors for a total contract price of $800 million.[176] The United States insisted that the agreement would assist Iran in its clandestine nuclear program and demanded that it be rescinded. The Russian leadership regarded American pressure as another attempt to gain a commercial advantage. NATO's expansion would strengthen the Russian propensity to seek compensatory diplomatic leverage by developing relations with China and Iran.

Russia's concerns about NATO's expansion have been shared by France to some extent. France may play a role in terms of balancing and countering pressure from the United States and Germany for the alliance's expansion. The French have been less enthusiastic about the prospect in view of their concerns about a new division in Europe, and among NATO members have demonstrated a greater willingness to accommodate Russia. Kozyrev visited France in early December 1994 and stressed the theme of European contribution to European security, which was an effort to exploit NATO differences.[177] Chairman of the French National Assembly Philip Segen visited Moscow and spoke to the Duma about the need for a European security system that would avoid the division of Europe. The French visitor told the deputies that the rapid expansion of NATO threatened the stability of Europe and indicated a possible basis for further cooperation between France and Russia.[178]

NATO's absorption of the Central and East European states would affirm a civilizational barrier between Russia and Europe. Russia's pro-Western democrats would be discredited and left to their own devices to face the nationalist forces of Russian society. NATO cannot deny membership to the other part of Europe that was previously under Soviet domination. Various combinations are possible, however, that will avoid a stark polarization between Russia and the West that could be exploited by Russia's nationalists. Integrative links between Russia and Europe could be promoted with various institutions, as well as the CSCE, such as the European Union or the West European Union, which would reduce the impact of NATO's expansion. For the stability of Europe, the two processes should be promoted concurrently so that the emphasis should be gradually moved from NATO to a wider all-European integrative process.

RUSSIA AND THE WEST—THE FUTURE

The decision to expand NATO has had an observable impact on Russia's relations with the West that will be significant for the future. The benefits of the proclaimed partnership with the United States were perceived to decline, however, when the U.S. began to push for NATO's expansion. To the extent that the Russians regard NATO's expansion as U.S. driven the interest in affirming a strategic partnership with the United States will weaken. Vladimir Lukin expressed Russian disenchantment with the U.S. when he remarked that the purpose of U.S. strategy is to push Russia out of Europe.[179] Russian interest may move toward Europe and developing diplomatic ties with those NATO members such as France who share Russia's concerns about the division of Europe. Russia's internal crisis was the basis for the special relationship with the United States that both Yeltsin and Kozyrev proclaimed in 1992–1993. As long as both the Bush and Clinton administrations feared the collapse of the reform movement with all its consequences the United States acted as a global patron of Russia. In this context, Russia's global status was artificially elevated and what was a product of temporary circumstances was taken as permanent condition by those around Yeltsin. The consequence was disillusion with the U.S. when the internal crisis subsided, when the Clinton administration ceased to lavish attention on Yeltsin, and when the U.S. began to promote NATO's expansion. At this point it was painfully understood that the United States had no need for a global partner in Russia and that America's commitment to the Western community was stronger than its relationship with Russia. Russian disenchantment with the United States is a product of an exaggerated conception of Russia's role in world affairs, which was a legacy of the Soviet era, rooted as it has been in the historical isolationism of the Russian and later Soviet experience. The dissipation of this illusion will in time compel Russia to give greater priority to Europe and to the development of integrative links with European institutions.

NOTES

1. Stanislav Kondrashov, "Orientiry novogo mira," *Izvestiya*, 30 Nov. 1992.
2. Lev Brunin, "Rossiya stuchitsya v dveri evropeiskogo kluba," *Nezavisimaya gazeta*, 8 May 1992.

3. Vladislav Chernov, "Boris Yeltsin utverdil kontseptsiyu o vneshnei politiki RF," *Nezavisimaya gazeta*, 29 Apr. 1993.

4. "Strategiya dla Rossiya," *Nezavisimaya gazeta*, 19 Aug. 1992.

5. Sergei Samulov, Sergei Geivandov, "Bezopastnost' Evropy: variant SBSE," *Rossiiskaya gazeta*, 7 July 1992.

6. Christoph Bluth, "Germany and the Soviet Union: Towards a New Rapallo?"

7. Aleksander Polotskii, "Ukreplyaetsya os Rossiya-Germaniya," *Nezavisimaya gazeta*, 20 July 1993.

8. *Izvestiya*, 14 Dec. 1992, Leonid Velekhov, "Kol' prikhodit El'tsinu na vyruchku," *Nezavisimaya gazeta*, 18 Dec. 1992.

9. *Itar Tass*, 14 Apr. 1993.

10. Yevgennii Bovkin, Boris Vinogradov, *Izvestiya*, 13 May 1994.

11. Sergei Palii, "Spasenie rossiiskoi kuznitsy oruzhiya'...," *Rossiiskaya gazeta*, 14 Oct. 1993.

12. *Radio Free Europe/Radio Liberty Daily Report* (168), 5 Sept. 1994.

13. See statement by Pyotr Shirshov, Chairman of Federation Council's Security and Defence Committee, *Radio Free Europe/Radio Liberty Daily Report* (176), 15 Sept. 1994.

14. *New York Times*, 2 Feb. 1992; Vladislav Drobkov, "Ot N'yu Iorka do Kemp Devida," *Pravda*, 3 Feb. 1992.

15. *New York Times*, 16 June 1992.

16. *New York Times*, 16 June 1992.

17. Vladislav Drobkov, "Sezon vizitov," *Pravda*, 18 June 1992.

18. *New York Times*, 16 June 1992.

19. James Goodby, "Dismantling of Nuclear Weapons: Building Confidence and Partnership," *U.S. Dept. of State Despatch*, 26 Apr. 1993, vol. 7, pp. 288 290.

20. Vladimir Skachko, "Slishkom mnogo protivorechii," *Nezavisimaya gazeta*, 27 Apr. 1993.

21. *Itar Tass*, 6 June 1993.

22. *Izvestiya*, 20 Nov. 1993.

23. *USIS*, 28 Dec. 1993.

24. *New York Times*, 4 Mar. 1994.

25. Aleksei Arbatov, "START II, Red Ink, and Boris Yeltsin," *Bulletin of the Atomic Scientists*, Apr. 1993.

26. Lt.-General Viktor Starodubov (retired), "Amerikanskii schet ne pokhozh na Russkii," *Pravda*, 6 Jan. 1993.

27. Viktor Linnik, "SNV-2 devyat voprosov v noch' pod rozhdestvo," *Pravda*, 6 Jan. 1993.

28. Colonel-General Achelov, "Doveryayu faktam," *Pravda*, 11 Feb. 1993.

29. Pavel Fel'gengauer, "Genshtab rossiiskoi armii poddezhivaet SNV-2," *Nezavisimaya gazeta*, 11 Jan. 1993.

30. *Itar Tass*, 27 Apr. 1993.

31. *Krasnaya zvezda*, 18 Mar. 1993.

32. Aleksander Lin'kov, "Ne postupilas' Rossiya interesami," *Rossiiskaya gazeta*, 12 Jan. 1993.

33. *Itar Tass*, 3 Mar. 1993.

34. *New York Times*, 15 Mar. 1994.

35. *USIS*, 28 Sept. 1994.

36. *Pravda*, 3 Feb. 1992.

37. See Richard Nixon, *Seize the Moment: America's Challenge in a One Superpower World*, Simon and Schuster, New York, 1992, pp.74–77.

38. *New York Times*, 2 Apr. 1992.

39. *New York Times*, 2 Apr. 1992.

40. *USIS*, 3 Apr.1992.

41. *Izvestiya*, 27 Apr.1992.

42. *Itar Tass*, 21 Aug. 1992.

43. *Izvestiya*, 6 July 1992.

44. *Rossiiskaya gazeta*, 10 July 1992.

45. *New York Times*, 7 May 1992, *Itar Tass*, 24 Oct. 1992.

46. *New York Times*, 19 June 1992.

47. *New York Times*, 21 Mar. 1993.

48. *New York Times*, 14 Mar. 1993.

49. *New York Times*, 23 Mar. 1993.

50. *Weekly Compilation of Presidential Documents*, 12 Apr. 1993, vol. 28, no. 14, p. 531.

51. *Weekly Compilation of Presidential Documents*, 5 Apr. 1993, vol. 29, no. 13, p. 513.

52. *Congressional Quarterly*, 29 May 1993, p. 1370.

53. See testimony of Lawrence H. Summers, Undersecretary for International Affairs, U.S. Treasury. *Impact of IMF/World Bank Policies Toward Russia and the Russian Economy*, Hearings before the Committee on Banking, Housing and Urban Affairs, U.S. Senate, Washington DC., 8 Feb. 1994, pp. 49–50.

54. Nikkei, 12 July 1993, *Reuters Textline*.

55. *USIS*, 24 Oct. 1993.

56. *Itar Tass*, 13 Mar. 1993.

57. *The Guardian*, 28 Aug. 1993.

58. Stanislav Kondrashov, "S'ezd v Moskve i vstrche v Vankuvere," *Izvestiya*, 19 Mar. 1993.

59. *Itar Tass*, 29 Mar. 1993.

60. *Itar Tass*, 23 Mar. 1993.

61. *Itar Tass*, 10 Apr. 1993.

62. "ES–Rossiya protivorechiya narastayut," *Pravda*, 15 Sept. 1993.

63. *Nezavisimaya gazeta*, 10 July 1992.

64. *New York Times*, 21 Sept. 1992.

65. *Reuters Textline*, 6 Aug. 1993.

66. Aleksei Portanski, "Pervyi akt global'noi podderzhki rossiskikh reform," *Izvestiya*, 8 Apr. 1993; also *Rossiiskaya gazeta*, 5 June 1993.

67. *New York Times*, 5 June 1994.

68. *USIS*, 24 Oct. 1993.

69. *USIS*, 1 Mar. 1994.

70. *Japan Times*, 19 Sept. 1994.

71. *USIS*, 14 July 1994.

72. *Radio Free Europe/Radio Liberty Daily Report* (323), 30 June 1994.

73. *USIS*, 22 June 1994.

74. See testimony of Lawrence H. Summers, *Impact of IMF/World Bank Policies Toward Russia and the Russian Economy*, p. 13.

75. See testimony of Jerry Sachs, *Impact of IMF/World Bank Policies Toward Russia and the Russian Economy*, p. 75; also "Towards *Glasnost* at the IMF," *Challenge*, May/June 1994.

76. *Radio Free Europe/Radio Liberty Daily Report* (91), 13 May 1994.

77. Testimony of Jerry Sachs, *Impact of IMF/World Bank Policies Toward Russia and the Russian Economy*, p. 47.

78. *Itar Tass*, 5 Apr. 1993.

79. *Izvestiya*, 3 July 1992.

80. *The Independent*, 10 July 1993.

81. *Radio Free Europe/Radio Liberty Daily Report* (129), 11 July 1994.

82. *Radio Free Europe/Radio Liberty Daily Report* (189), 5 Oct. 1994.

83. *New York Times*, 5 Apr. 1992.

84. Pavel Golub, "Bol'shaya semerka obespokoena rossiisko-yaponskii krizisom," *Izvestiya*, 11 Sept. 1992.

85. Richard Nixon, "Clinton's Greatest Challenge," *New York Times*, 5 Mar. 1993.

86. *Kyodo*, 12 July 1993, *Reuters Textline*.

87. Samuel P. Huntington, "The Clash of Civilizations?" *Foreign Affairs*, summer 1993, vol. 72, no. 3.

88. Samuel P. Huntington, "Russia and the West: Clash of Civilizations?" *Moscow News*, (10) Mar. 11/17 1994.

89. *Izvestiya*, 30 June 1992.

90. *Rossiiskaya gazeta*, 29 May 1993.

91. Makism Yusin "Deputaty Ambartsumov i Rumyantsev prizyvayut Moskvu k soyuzu s Belgradom," *Izvestiya*, 11 Aug. 1992.

92. *Izvestiya*, 27 June 1992 and 21 Sept. 1992.

93. Maksim Yusin, "Verkhovnyi soviet gotovit reviziyu vneshnei politiki Rossii," *Izvestiya*, 18 Dec. 1992.

94. Maksim Yusin, "Rezolutsiya rossiiskogo parliamenta po yugoslavii tolkaet moskvu k mezhdunarodnoi izolyatsii," *Izvestiya*, 20 Feb. 1993.

95. *Izvestiya*, 24 July 1994.

96. Sergei Gryzunov, Andrei Baturin, "Rossiiskaya initsiativa vstrechena v Vashingtone so skeptitsizmom," *Nezavisimaya gazeta*, 21 May 1993.

97. *Reuters Textline*, 29 June 1993.

98. *New York Times*, 13 Feb. 1994.

99. *Nezavisimaya gazeta*, 19 Feb. 1994.

100. See "Slovo moskvy okazalos reshayushchim," *Rossiiskaya gazeta*, 22 Feb. 1994. Alex Pushkov wrote that Russia "scored the greatest victory," had used the opportunity "brilliantly" and without its mediatory effort the tough NATO stand "would have triggered full scale war in southern Europe." "Russia Confirms Great Power Status," *Moscow News* (8), 25 Feb./3 Mar. 1994.

101. *Washington Post*, 30 Mar. 1994.

102. Maksim Yusin, "Serby nanosyat zhestokii udar po prestizhu rossiiskoi diplomatii," *Izvestiya*, 20 Apr. 1994.

103. Andrei Baturin, Sergei Gryzunov, "V Belgrade nadeyutsya, chto Moskva pomozhet sozdat velikuyu serbiyu," *Izvestiya*, 4 Mar. 1994.

104. *Radio Free Europe/Radio Liberty Daily Report* (93), 17 May 1994.

105. Sergei Stankevich, "Rossiya uzhe sdelala anti imperskii vybor," *Nezavisimaya gazeta*, 6 Nov. 1992.

106. *Nezavisimaya gazeta*, 17 Dec. 1993.

107. Andranik Migranyan, "Rossiya i blizhnee zarubezh'e," *Nezavisimaya gazeta*, 18 Jan. 1994.

108. *New York Times*, 31 Oct. 1992.

109. *International Herald Tribune*, 10 Mar. 1994.

110. *Itar Tass*, 5 Apr. 1993.

111. *Nezavisimaya gazeta*, 15 May 1993.

112. Sergei Zotov, "Diplomatiya i vyvod voisk," *Nezavisimaya gazeta*, 30 Aug. 1994.

113. *Rossiiskaya gazeta*, 18 Mar. 1994.

114. *Nezavisimaya gazeta*, 12 Mar. 1994.

115. *Nezavisimaya gazeta*, 12 Mar. 1994.

116. *Radio Free Europe/Radio Liberty Daily Report*, (88), 9 May 1994.

117. *Radio Free Europe/Radio Liberty Daily Report* (97), 24 May 1994, and (127), 7 July 1994.

118. *Izvestiya*, 30 July 1994.

119. Viktor Parshutkin, "O chem zhe dogovorilis' dva mudrykh prezidenta," *Nezavisimaya gazeta*, 27 Aug. 1994.

120. Viktor Parshutkin, "O chem zhe dogovorilis' dva mudrykh prezidenta," *Nezavisimaya gazeta*, 27 Aug. 1994.

121. See Carl Bildt, "The Baltic Litmus Test," *Foreign Affairs*, Sept./Oct. 1994, vol. 73, no.5.

122. *International Herald Tribune*, 26 Aug. 1993.

123. Zbigniew Brzezinski, "The Premature Partnership," *Foreign Affairs*, Mar./Apr. 1994, vol. 73, no. 2.

124. *International Herald Tribune*, 8 Jan. 1994.

125. Bruce George, *After the NATO Summit: Draft General Report*, North Atlantic Treaty Organization, Public Data Service, 26 May 1994.

126. *Declaration of the Heads of State and Government Participating in the Meeting of the North Atlantic Council Held at NATO Headquarters, Brussels on 10–11 January 1994*, p. 2.

127. See Tamas Wachsler, *NATO and NAA, Enlargement: Draft Special Report*, NATO International Secretariat, Nov. 1994.

128. Mikhail Karpov, "Kozyrev po frantsii," *Nezavisimaya gazeta*, 21 Oct. 1993.

129. "Opravdano li rasshirenie NATO," *Nezavisimaya gazeta*, 20 Nov. 1993.

130. Pavel Fel'gengauer, "Voennye ozhidayut vmeshatel'stva," *Nezavisimaya gazeta*, 1 Aug. 1992.

131. *Krasnaya zvezda*, 9 Sept. 1993.

132. See Andranik Migranyan in *Nezavisimaya gazeta*, 15 Mar. 1994.

133. Andranik Migranyan in *Nezavisimaya gazeta*, 15 Mar. 1994.

134. *Nezavisimaya gazeta*, 18 Mar. 1994.

135. *Nezavisimaya gazeta*, 21 Apr. 1994.

136. Ivan Rodan, "Budushchee SNG i partnerstvo vo imya mira," *Nezavisimaya gazeta*, 15 Apr. 1994; Vladimir Mikheyev, "Deputy Dumy okhotno raspustili by NATO," *Izvestiya*, 16 Apr. 1994.

137. *Rossiiskaya gazeta*, 21 May 1994.

138. Vyacheslav Nikonov, "Partnerstvo vo imya mira," *Nezavisimaya gazeta*, 7 Apr. 1994.

139. *Nezavisimaya gazeta*, 26 Apr. 1994.

140. *Radio Free Europe/Radio Liberty Daily Report* (98), 25 May 1994.

141. *International Herald Tribune*, 27 Apr. 1994.

142. Vladimir Peresada, "Tak budet li ravnopravnoe partnerstvo?" *Pravda*, 27 May 1994.

143. *NATO Review*, Aug. 1994, vol. 42, no. 4, p. 5

144. *Radio Free Europe/Radio Liberty Daily Report* (100), 27 May 1994.

145. Boris Fyodorov, "Rossiya dolzhna vstupit' v NATO," *Izvestiya*, 6 Sept. 1994.

146. Aleksei Arbatov, "Rossiya i NATO: Nyzhny li my drug drugu," *Nezavisimaya gazeta*, 11 Mar. 1992.

147. Vyacheslav Nikonov, "Rossiya i NATO," *Nezavisimaya gazeta*, 14 Sept. 1994.

148. *Financial Times*, 10/11 Sept. 1994.

149. *Financial Times*, 28 Sept. 1994.

150. *Radio Free Europe/Radio Liberty Daily Report* (222), 23 Nov. 1994.

151. Valerii Manilov, "Rossiya vo vneshnem mire," *Nezavisimaya gazeta*, 26 July 1994.

152. Vyacheslav Kozerov, "Partnerstvo vo imya—chego?" *Rossiiskaya gazeta*, 25 Mar. 1994.

153. Lennart Meri, "Estonia and peace keeping," *NATO Review*, vol. 42, no. 2, Apr. 1994.

154. *Radio Free Europe/Radio Liberty Daily Report* (222), 23 Nov. 1994.

155. Liana Minasyan, "Amerikanskaya diplomatiya aktiviziruetsya u yuzhnykh granits rossii," *Nezavisimaya gazeta*, 10 Mar. 1994.

156. *USIS*, 29 Sept. 1994.

157. *Radio Free Europe/Radio Liberty Daily Report* (117), 22 June 1994.

158. Dmitri Gornostaev, "RF, vydvinula novuyu programmu dla SBSE," *Nezavisimaya gazeta*, 30 July 1994.

159. *Radio Free Europe/Radio Liberty Daily Report* (137), 15 July 1994.

160. *Radio Free Europe/Radio Liberty Daily Report* (177), 16 Sept. 1994.

161. See Klaus Kinkel's view, *Radio Free Europe/Radio Liberty Daily Report* (100), 27 May 1994.

162. *New York Times*, 27 Oct. 1994; *International Herald Tribune*, 16 Nov. 1994.

163. *Opening Statement of U.S. Secretary of State, Warren Christopher at the Meeting of the North Atlantic Council, NATO Headquarters, Brussels, Belgium*, 1 Dec. 1994.

164. *New York Times*, 8 Dec. 1994.

165. *Radio Free Europe/Radio Liberty Daily Report* (249), 6 Dec. 1994, and (250), 7 Dec. 1994, also *Financial Times*, 6 Dec. 1994.

166. *New York Times*, 8 Dec. 1994.

167. CSCE Budapest Document 1994, "Towards a Genuine Partnership in a New Year," *Budapest Summit Declaration*, OSCE Secretariat, Prague Office, Dec. 1994.

168. "Budapesht videl bolee svetlye dni nashei diplomatii," *Izvestiya*, 7 Dec. 1994.

169. Andranik Migranyan, "Vneshnaya politika rossii katastroficheski itogi trekh let," *Nezavisimaya gazeta*, 10 Dec. 1994.

170. Mikhail Dmitriev, Gennadii Yevstaf'ev, "Istoricheskoe reshenie o rasshirenie NATO," *Nezavisimaya gazeta*, 31 Dec. 1994.

171. *Nezavisimaya gazeta*, 10 Dec. 1994.

172. *Nezavisimaya gazeta*, 14 May 1995.

173. Aleksander Konovalov, "K novomu razdelu," *Nezavisimaya gazeta*, 7 Dec. 1994.

174. *Izvestiya*, 29 Dec. 1994.

175. Maksim Yusin, "Poslednya podlodka otchalit v Tegeran," *Izvestiya*, 30 Sept. 1994.

176. *Izvestiya*, 12 Apr. 1995.

177. Mikhail Karpov, "My evropeitsy," *Nezavisimaya gazeta*, 2 Dec. 1994.

178. Yuri Kovalenko, "Parizh kak i Moskva ne khochet skoropalite'nogo rasshireniya NATO," *Izvestiya*, 15 Dec. 1994.

179. Nezavisimaya gazeta, 14 Mar. 1995.

Chapter 3

Russia and the "Near Abroad": The CIS as a Regional Organization

For Russia the "near abroad" is a critical barometer of foreign policy intentions. Conflict or rivalry with the West will impact on policy toward the "near abroad," increasing the pressure on the Moscow government for a more assertive posture. Since 1992, internal pressure within Russia for a dominant position in this area has grown appreciably, fueled by frustrations with the West, the demand for a great power role, and the security and economic exigencies of the area. Local instability and economic needs may draw Russia into greater involvement in the "near abroad" beyond what the West would tolerate. The inherent instability of the area has the potential to disrupt Russia's relationship with the West and may entice the nationalists and the proponents of empire into assuming a more prominent role in policy formulation.

The Commonwealth of Independent States (CIS) was a temporary and expedient answer to the problem of devising a basis for Russia's relationship with the "near abroad." It was a product of the conditions of late 1991 as the Soviet Union steadily disintegrated and was an unsatisfactory accommodation of two contradictory needs. The first was the demand for sovereignty on the part of the former Soviet republics while the second was the obvious need to maintain coordinated relations in both economic and security fields. Gorbachev grappled with the proposal for a new union treaty with the constituent republics without being able to surrender the idea of a strong central control. Only after Gorbachev's position had been undermined as a consequence of the events that followed the August 1991 attempted coup was Yeltsin able to assert his own proposal for a union treaty, which would, as he put it, liberate Russia from the Soviet Union. Yeltsin's desire to destroy the Soviet Union was based on a belief that Russia was the first victim of Soviet oppression and, moreover, that the Soviet command system was an obstacle to economic reform.

THE FORMATION OF THE CIS

First Deputy Chairman of the Supreme Soviet Sergei Filatov revealed that the formation of the CIS was most unexpected indicating that little had been planned beforehand. Kozyrev wrote that when Yeltsin met with Ukrainian and Belarus leaders in Belovezhsk outside Minsk on 8 December 1991, he was faced with the demand for complete sovereignty. The Russians proposed variants such as a "union of democratic governments" but the Ukrainians were only interested in recognition of their sovereignty.[1] The resultant agreement that was achieved between Yeltsin, the Ukrainian President Leonid Kravchuk and Belarus Supreme Soviet Chairman Stanislav Shushkevich announced the formation of the CIS. Kravchuk expressed the desire of the leaders to preserve a basis for economic integration of which he was a proponent, but without supranational institutions.[2] An accompanying statement issued by government representatives, Gennadii Burbulis, Belarus Premier Vladislav Kebich, and Ukrainian Premier Viktor Fokin emphasized the importance of preserving and developing closer economic ties. In that statement, the heads of government stressed the need to secure a "united economic space" on the basis of the existing monetary unit—the Russian ruble; they called for an interbank agreement to control the money supply and a common system of accounts; coordinated customs policies to facilitate the free transit of goods; and common external economic policies. They also agreed to regulate the accumulated debt of Soviet enterprises and to prepare an inter-republican economic agreement.[3]

From the outset three points could be noted. First, the agreement was reached between the three Slavic states at a time when considerable interest was aroused in Moscow in relation to the formation of a Slavic grouping. Shushkevich when asked whether the intention was to create a purely Slavic grouping referred to the communiqué of the 8 December meeting where it was stated that membership was open to all other governments of the Soviet Union.[4] Yeltsin declared that the future of the Soviet Union could not be decided by three leaders alone and required the participation of all the sovereign states. Yeltsin proclaimed the goal of a "union treaty of sovereign states" toward which the Belovezhsk declaration was a first step.[5] Second, the intention was to dismantle the Soviet political and security superstructure while retaining the integrated economic structures. The hope was that the states concerned could coordinate economic and market reform in a way that would adapt these economic linkages to market conditions. The leaders concerned were fully aware of their interdependent economies and had no intention of forcing the process of sovereignization to the point where these economic ties would be disrupted. Third, security cooperation was only touched on in passing in the Belovezhsk declaration that mentioned the need to establish united control over nuclear weapons and the prevention of nuclear proliferation. Yeltsin expressed the Russian desire for defense and security cooperation but neither Shushkevich nor Kravchuk agreed. Both non-Russian leaders insisted that cooperation in the post-Soviet space would be limited to the economic field, and to joint control of nuclear weapons.

Subsequently, Yeltsin faced strong criticism from the Supreme Soviet where deputies reacted with anger to the termination of the Soviet Union. To this day many former CPSU members cannot, as was expressed to this author, forgive Yeltsin for having presided over the collapse of the Soviet Union without any effort to consult with the nation. Many accept Vladimir Lukin's view that three men had no mandate to dissolve the Soviet Union and that other less drastic alternatives were possible at that stage. Yeltsin, however, in his speech to the Supreme Soviet on 12 December stressed that the collapse of the Soviet Union was triggered by the failure of the August 1991 coup and an irreversible process of sovereignization that followed. According to the president, the Soviet Union had already collapsed by the time of the Belovezhsk declaration and the intention was to prevent further disintegration within Russia that could have resulted in catastrophe. On 12 December 1991, a joint session of both houses of the Supreme Soviet abrogated the decision of the International Congress of Soviets of 30 December 1922, which resulted in the formation of the Soviet Union, and ratified the Belovezhsk declaration.[6]

Despite the attempt to disavow any intention to create a Slavic group the impression was created that Russia had attempted to cast off Central Asia and the Muslim World. Kazakh leader Nursultan Nazarbaev later claimed in an interview that after the Belovezhsk meeting, discussions continued about the creation of a Slavic union with the corresponding specter of a separate Islamic organization. Nazarbaev joined the other Central Asian leaders—Askar Akaev, Islam Karimov, Suparmurad Niyazov, and Rakhmon Nabiev—at the Turkmen capital Ashkhabad on 13 December. Central Asian leaders reacted quickly to their exclusion from the Belovezhsk declaration and declared that the CIS should not be formed along ethnic or religious lines. They proclaimed their readiness to be equal members of the CIS as founding members.[7] Accordingly, a separate meeting was convened in the Kazakh capital Alma Ata on 21 December 1991 that resulted in the formation of an extended CIS including those who did not join the Belovezhsk declaration. Membership was extended from three to eleven including the five Central Asian states, Armenia, Azerbaijan, and Moldova. The Alma Ata agreement made a provision for a CIS council of heads of state and a council of premiers as coordinating institutions.[8] Nazarbaev expressed his desire for a strongly coordinated CIS and declared that he had done everything possible to prevent the formation of separate Slavic and Asiatic blocs.[9]

Significance of the CIS for Russia

What did the CIS mean for Russia? Debate has continued over the significance of the CIS and how relations with the "near abroad" should be approached. Proponents of the pro-Western foreign policy course downgrade the importance of the "near abroad" and see Russia's future in Europe as part of an integrated community. For them the CIS is an instrument of dissociation from the "near abroad" and a means to alleviate the security and economic burdens that the area represents for Russia. In this sense, equality and respect for state sovereignty work to Russia's advantage since by repudiating the imperialist past Russia would share security and economic responsibility for the area with the world community or with international institutions. Proponents of this view have been called economic isolationists and can be found in the newly-created democratic parties or within the academic community.[10] There are deeper historical and political reasons behind the espousal of this view. The democrats among the intelligentsia recognize that Russia's historical expansion into what is now known as the "near abroad" was accompanied by the imposition of an oppressive autocracy that crippled Russia's social and political development. The assumption of a new imperialist role in the "near abroad" would be incompatible with Russian democracy.

At the other extreme are the nationalists and the geopoliticians who insist on a predominant role in the "near abroad." The nationalists may demand great power status for Russia by right while the geopoliticians regard Russia's role in this area in terms of strategic necessity. Their views tend to converge and become fused in relation to the means of policy though the ends may differ somewhat. They argue that Russia's security depends on the stability of the "near abroad" in what is an inescapable geopolitical linkage for Moscow's rulers. Russia, according to this view, cannot isolate itself from the "near abroad" and simply reorientate itself to the West while the area remains unstable and threatens to involve other external powers. Russians often bemoan the fact, as one commentator told the author, that their neighbors are not Switzerland or France, in which case stability along the peripheries could be assured. In the absence of this assured stability the quest for secure borders that motivated Russia's expansionism in the past continues with all the attendant dangers of a reversion to neo-imperialism.

For many Russians, the idea of a Russia without a dominant role in the "near abroad" conflicts with their sense of history and nationalism. Former Vice-President Aleksander Rutskoi has given expression to these views by his consistent emphasis on Russia's great power role. In his campaign for the 1995 parliamentary elections, Rutskoi joined a political grouping appropriately called *derzhava* (power, state) and declared that the aim of the movement would be the restoration of Russia within the borders of the USSR.[11] The chief proponent of Russian hegemony in the "near abroad" has been Andranik Migranyan who argued that Russia should declare to the outside world that the former Soviet Union was a "sphere of its own vital interests."[12] According to Migranyan, Russia's role in this area could not be defined by a relationship with the West but had to be shaped by Russia.

The proponents of a hegemonial role tend to regard the CIS as an error, or an interim measure, that unjustifiably restrains Russia from assuming its rightful role in the "near abroad." According to this group, the idea of sovereign equality does not match the reality of Russia's security and economic predominance. Russia, moreover, should structure relations with the region in a way that reflects that dominance and which would provide a basis for the pacification and stabilization of a troubled area. They see little difference between America's role in Latin America under the Monroe Doctrine and their own desire for a sphere of influence in the "near abroad," which should be recognized by the international community. For them, the CIS should be restructured and its integrative features gradually strengthened to overcome what is seen as the aberrant divisions created in the wake of the disintegration of the Soviet Union. Their dissatisfaction with the CIS impels them to strengthen existing CIS institutions, given their view that the ultimate goal is the revival of the Soviet Union in a new form.

Kozyrev and his democratic supporters would have preferred to avoid the difficult entanglements of the "near abroad" but they were relentlessly attacked by the Supreme Soviet for failing to address Russia's interests. Before the sixth Congress of Peoples's Deputies in April 1992, Kozyrev defended himself and claimed that most of the president's time was devoted to the CIS. Deputies accused Yeltsin of the Belovezhsk conspiracy and of having presided over the collapse of the Soviet Union while Sergei Baburin called for Kozyrev's removal.[13] Both Baburin and Nikolai Pavlov were prominent in demanding recognition for the "near abroad" as Russia's top foreign policy priority and in calling for a revival of the Soviet Union.

There were three specific interests that required attention in the "near abroad" and which, according to critics, were being ill-served by Kozyrev's pro-Western approach. First, the area was identified as a zone of low intensity war by the Council of Foreign and Defense Policy that was alarmed by the outbreak of ethnic and local conflicts along Russia's southern borders. The council feared the consequent Yugoslavization of the "near abroad," in which case the Russian federation with its 21 constituent republics and autonomous regions would go the way of the Soviet Union.[14] Second, Russia has significant economic interests in the "near abroad." The structure of the Soviet economy was such that interdependent industries were located in different republics for security as well as economic reasons. The military industries of East Ukraine and Belarus were linked with those in Russia in a way that was severely disrupted by the Soviet collapse. Moreover, Russia is a natural market for the agricultural products of Ukraine, Moldova, and Central Asia whose traders flood Russian markets. Third, the issue of the ethnic Russians who found themselves in the "near abroad" after the collapse of the Soviet Union emerged as perhaps the most significant factor in Russia's relationship with the "near abroad."

The Russians in the "Near Abroad"

The issue of the Russians in the "near abroad" has had a pernicious effect on Russia's relations with the CIS states. It was unclear at first whether Russia should protect ethnic Russians or Russian language speakers. If the former, ethnicity must be proved in other ways beside language; in the latter case the number of Russian language speakers would swell dramatically. Nazarbaev pointed out that some 99 percent of Kazaks speak Russian and, moreover, almost everyone in Moldova speaks Russian.[15] Moscow's concern, however, has been with the ethnic Russians in the "near abroad" as a product of nationalist accusations that they have been neglected. Russians had become used to a privileged status in these republics during the Soviet period and have found the conditions fostered by the newly-independent states demeaning. Within the new CIS states, governments have introduced policies promoting positive discrimination and have designated indigenous languages for administrative purposes. In the European CIS, the Russian population was generally untroubled but in Kazakhstan and Kyrgyzstan the emigration of Russians has been stimulated by local nationalism. In Tajikistan's case, political instability has been the major factor behind the Russian emigration.

Accurate figures on the number of Russians in the CIS are unavailable. According to the 1989 Soviet census there were 23.33 million Russians in the CIS area and there has been some emigration to Russia since. Russia's Federal Migration Service has conducted periodic registrations of refugees from the former Soviet Union and according to June 1994 figures provided by this service from 1989–1993, 2,309,200 Russians emigrated to Russia from the CIS area, but 1,233,600 Russians emigrated to the CIS area within the same period (see Table 1).[16] Over this period the result was a drop of 1,075,600 in the Russian population of the CIS area, in which case the total figure for 1994 would be 22,254,000. This figure is at variance with the 25 million estimated for the Russian population in the CIS by Valerii Tishkov of the Institute of Ethnology and Anthropology in Moscow, which is higher than the corresponding figure from the 1989 census.[17]

Table 1

Emigration of Russians between Russian Federation and the CIS (in thousands)

	1989	1990	1991	1992	1993
Migration to Russia from CIS area	374.5	464.1	369.4	556.7	544.5
Migration to CIS area from Russia	318.2	278.5	264.7	200.3	171.9
Balance	56.3	185.6	104.7	356.4	372.6

Source: Federal Migration Service of Russia

Moscow has promoted the notion of dual nationality for the Russians in the "near abroad" as a guarantee of their protection. The rationale has been that with this obvious reassurance from Russia, emigration from the CIS would be reduced considerably and those states most concerned about the loss of qualified Russian technical personnel would benefit accordingly. Moscow's demand that a provision for dual nationality be included in separate bilateral treaties with the CIS states has met with various reactions. Most CIS states have regarded the demand as a blatant effort to perpetuate the privileged status of Russians and a threat to their sovereignty. Those that have been more dependent on Russia have been more accommodating.

Moscow signed its first treaty on dual nationality with Turkmenistan on 23 December 1993, and Yeltsin upheld it as a model for relations with other CIS states. Karimov of Uzbekistan rejected the idea outright when Kozyrev pressed him in November 1993, while Nazarbaev of Kazakhstan evaded the issue and refused to meet the Russian foreign minister. The then premier of Kazakhstan, Sergei Terashchenko, criticized the proposal for its obvious inequity and wondered whether the Kazaks in Russia would receive similar treatment.[18] Askar Akaev of Kyrgyzstan, perhaps the most concerned of all Central Asian leaders over Russian emigration, was prevented from acceding to Moscow's demands by internal opposition and cited as a reason the constitution that called for equal treatment of all groups.[19] In negotiations with the Ukraine for a comprehensive treaty, Moscow also pressed for recognition of dual nationality in a way that was considered odious.

Nevertheless, in 1994 Moscow moved to strengthen relations with Russians in the "near abroad" in various ways. The Foreign Ministry proposed that bilateral treaties be negotiated with CIS countries to define the political and economic rights of the Russians on the basis of dual nationality.[20] The Foreign Ministry outlined a special program of assistance for Russians in the CIS including Russian radio and television programs; finance for Russian schools; a mechanism for the evacuation of Russians in time of conflict; conditional credits for CIS countries with the attached demand that 20–30 percent be used to assist Russians; and resort to economic levers against CIS states that violate the human rights of Russians.[21] The Foreign Ministry's proposals were incorporated into a presidential decree dated 11 August 1994. On 10 October 1994, the Duma Committee on CIS Affairs conducted hearings on the issue to recommend further protective measures considering that 80 million Russians have family links in the "near abroad." Moscow simply could not be indifferent to the political significance of these human ties as their votes could become important in Russian elections.[22] An assembly of Russian compatriots was created to provide emergency economic support for Russians in the "near abroad," including preferential credits to allow them to establish their own businesses.[23]

Yeltsin's government has come under increasing pressure from the nationalists to defend the interests of the Russians in the "near abroad." This trend has been noticeable since the December 1993 elections when Zhirinovsky's LDP emerged with increased votes. The problem for Moscow is that political needs are conflicting. The demand for protection of the Russians undermines attempts to promote CIS regionalism. No other factor could provoke hostility toward Moscow and could stiffen resistance to CIS integration more than the demand for privileges for Russians. Moscow may justify the demand for dual nationality in terms of a general move toward "CIS citizenship" which, however, remains a distant goal at this stage. In the meantime, statements such as those issued by Andrei Kozyrev in April 1995 to the effect that Russia may consider all means, including military force, to defend the Russians in the "near abroad" can only damage Russia's relations with the CIS.[24] In this respect, the Russian government can be its own worst enemy in the CIS.

Integrative Trends in the CIS

Moscow was seriously committed to promoting integrative trends within the CIS but faced an acute dilemma. The experience of the Russian bureaucracy dictated a centralized approach toward the CIS that was very much modeled on the Soviet Union. Many within the Russian government involved with the CIS thought that the aim was the re-establishment of the Soviet Union and used the opportunities presented to pursue this goal. The heavy handed top down approach based on the Soviet model was a reflex action for Russian bureaucrats and resulted in proposals and formulations that were plainly incompatible with the sovereignty of the participatory states. This was particularly the case in the military/security field where the military personnel attached to the CIS structure laboriously pressed for a familiar Soviet-style structure. As long as the Moscow government remained entangled in the forms of the past, successful integration within the confines of the CIS could hardly be expected. The Soviet experience was a dead weight around the necks of the proponents of CIS integration and prevented them from utilizing the opportunities presented more resourcefully.

Gennadii Burbulis declared that independence was a necessary phase for the constituent states and that a new period of collaboration would begin after the euphoria of independence disappeared.[25] The Council of Foreign and Defense Policy declared that a post-imperial integrationist course should follow the example of the European Union and should entail reintegration on a new basis. The council advocated the establishment of intergovernmental economic and security organs that would regulate relations within the CIS.[26] Nonetheless, geopoliticians and policy realists pointed out the differences between the European situation and the "near abroad" that made the comparison misleading. First, Russia could not wait for the euphoria of independence to vanish as Burbulis suggested since the problems and conflicts that Russia faced required immediate remedial action. Second, integrative trends within Europe had the benefit of existing stability and secure state structures that provided the foundation for a European economic community. The ethnic and communal conflicts that plagued interstate relations in the CIS were absent within Western Europe. Moreover, European integration was facilitated by a situation of balanced relations among several major integrating actors without the threat of a single hegemon. In the "near abroad" not only was there the problem of unstable state structures but the obvious inequality between Russia and the other states turned it into the dominant partner and natural hegemon, threatening the independence of the newly-independent states.

Military-Security Integration

A major expectation within the military at the time of the formation of the CIS was that the integrated defense and security system that had been imposed during the Soviet era would be maintained. Geopolitically, the defense of Russia was closely tied to the security of the CIS as a whole, and it made sense from Moscow's perspective to retain the security framework that had been developed during the Soviet era. The Soviet military pressed Yeltsin on this point and Soviet Chief of General Staff Vladimir Lobov demanded that the centralization of the armed forces be recognized in the union treaty.[27] How centralization of the armed forces would be compatible with the independence of the republics was unresolved. Yeltsin, recognizing the political aspirations of the republics, limited centralization to strategic and tactical nuclear weapons that would allow each republic to have its own army.[28] Yeltsin's approach was a product of an agreement reached with Ukrainian President Leonid Kravchuk, who accepted the need for a centralized control over strategic nuclear weapons. Kravchuk, however, in 1991 asserted the Ukraine's right to have its own army within three years.[29]

The agreements which brought the CIS into being made no reference to centralized defense functions beyond the control of nuclear weapons. In his speech to the Supreme Soviet on 12 December 1991, Yeltsin declared that the CIS would maintain a united military strategic space but the means to attain this goal were not identified here or in any of the other documents.[30] Members of the CIS at least agreed on maintaining centralized control over nuclear weapons which was included in the Belovezhsk declaration of 8 December 1991. A separate protocol to the Alma Ata agreement confirmed the idea of a general military space under united command as well as united control over nuclear weapons. In an accompanying agreement, the four nuclear-armed states of the CIS—Russia, Kazakhstan, Ukraine, and Belarus—agreed to a common nuclear policy (Article 3); the full liquidation of nuclear weapons from Ukraine and Belarus (Article 4); Ukrainian and Belarus membership of the Nuclear Non-Proliferation Treaty (Article 5); and the removal of tactical nuclear weapons from the Ukraine, Belarus, and Kazakhstan to Russia for destruction by 1 July 1992.[31]

At minimum, the CIS could agree on centralized control of both strategic and tactical nuclear weapons that in practice meant Russian control. Belarus and Kazakhstan were pleased to surrender their nuclear weapons to Russia, and though the Ukraine dithered over strategic weapons it fulfilled the agreement on tactical nuclear weapons. Problems arose, however, when the Russians attempted to give substance to the idea of a common security space by promoting defense integration within the CIS. The Russian demand for closer integration continually clashed with the sovereignty of the republics who utilized their newly established independence to resist Russian blandishments. The CIS never went beyond this conflict in which the Soviet model of integration continued to be promoted against the obvious resistance of the sovereign republics.

It was Yevgennii Shaposhnikov who attempted to realize the goal of a united CIS defense structure. Shaposhnikov was the last Soviet defense minister and was appointed Supreme Commander of United CIS Forces in December 1991. He strove to create a united defense force, which was one of the aims of the Minsk CIS meeting of 14 February 1992. Shaposhnikov's proposal for united command over conventional forces received varied support in a meeting that revealed the depth of the divisions within the CIS. Seven republics agreed to the proposal with the Ukraine, Azerbaijan, Belarus, and Moldova resisting. Based on this agreement, a council of CIS defense ministers was formed between Russia, Armenia, Kazakhstan, Tajikistan, and Uzbekistan that emerged as the core group within the CIS. The Minsk meeting also examined the issue of united command of strategic nuclear forces and attempted to define the distinction between strategic and conventional forces. Russia pressed for a wider definition of strategic forces to include the navy, while the Ukraine insisted that each republic would decide this issue for itself.[32]

Shaposhnikov and his staff clearly understood that their positions depended on Russia's subservience to the CIS defense structure. Once Russia established its own Defense Ministry, however, Shaposhnikov and the united CIS command became irrelevant. On 7 May 1992, Yeltsin decreed the formation of Russia's armed forces while on 17 May 1992 Pavel Grachev was appointed Russian Defense Minister. Tensions immediately resulted from this arrangement that left the relationship between Russia's national command and the CIS defense structure ill-defined. In this situation, Shaposhnikov could only affirm his relevance by pushing for an expansion of CIS defense and security functions. A CIS chiefs-of-staff committee was formed on 6 July 1992 with Viktor Samsonov as chairman, that was to coordinate efforts toward collective security, a common defense policy, and to oversee the restructuring of the armed forces.[33]

There were, however, several significant developments that arose from the effort to promote common security within the CIS. The Tashkent Collective Security Treaty of 15 May 1992 reflected a need within the CIS for integrated security but without the centralized command structure promoted by

Shaposhnikov. Only six states signed the treaty—Russia, Kazakhstan, Armenia, Tajikistan, Turkmenistan, and Uzbekistan. The Ukraine declared its opposition to a united CIS defense structure, or anything that may lead in that direction. Belarus avoided the issue on the grounds that its Supreme Soviet was opposed to membership of military alliances. Georgia was not a member of the CIS at that stage, and Azerbaijan had accused the CIS of supporting Armenia in the conflict over Nagorno-Karabakh and had little interest in joining. The collective security treaty was virtually a Russian-Central Asian arrangement with the inclusion of Armenia, which was dependent on Russian support in any case.[34] Under Article 2 of the treaty, members were only obliged to consult in the event of a threat to the security, territorial integrity, and sovereignty of any one of their number. Under Article 4 an attack on one member would be considered an attack on all and the other members would be obliged to show "necessary assistance, including military support." Under Article 3, a council of collective security was formed that was to include the heads of government and the commander of CIS Armed Forces.[35]

Shaposhnikov claimed that the collective security agreement would form the basis of a single united CIS force in 2–3 years and a future CIS military alliance.[36] Accordingly, he proposed, at the Tashkent CIS defense ministers's meeting of July 1992, that a common military doctrine and policy should be added. The Tashkent Collective Security Treaty survived precisely because it avoided centralization allowing Georgia, Azerbaijan, and Belarus subsequently to join, resulting in a total of nine states by February 1994—the Ukraine, Moldova, and Turkmenistan remained outside the agreement. CIS collective security was basically a misnomer as Russia was the only effective military actor with the other members depending on Russian support in varying degree. Russia attempted to invoke the Tashkent Collective Security Treaty over Tajikistan but discovered that it was shouldering the effort on its own. The Russian military, in any case, placed greater emphasis on bilateral military arrangements with the CIS countries such as the defense agreement reached with Turkmenistan in June 1992 or the military treaty reached with Georgia in January 1994. Resistance against centralization pushed Russia toward belateral relationships in the effort to strengthen a position in the CIS.

The CIS Defense Council continued to meet under Shaposhnikov concerned mainly with strategic nuclear issues. After Yuri Maksimenkov resigned in November 1992, Shaposhnikov himself assumed the position of commander of strategic rocket forces. The Defense Council discussed which forces should be regarded as strategic and which conventional and all CIS states sent representatives to the council while this issue was discussed.[37] Conflict with Grachev's Defense Ministry intensified because a CIS centralized command could not coexist with a Russian national command, and Shaposhnikov was perceived as a threat.[38] In June 1993, CIS defense ministers eventually agreed to dismantle the centralized structure that had proved to be a contentious issue. The CIS Supreme Command was disbanded and

Shaposhnikov was replaced by Victor Samsonov as chairman of a new coordinating committee on CIS military cooperation. The CIS defense ministers's council was retained with Lt.-General Leonid Ivashov installed as secretary beginning in May 1992. Deputy chairman of the new coordinating committee Colonel-General Boris P'yankov, articulated a low profile approach toward security cooperation that avoided the over-centralized Soviet model promoted by Shaposhnikov. P'yankov declared that the political climate was not yet conducive for the goal of united CIS forces and laid the emphasis on coordinating the programs and policies of the CIS national armies, rather than indulging in the futile exercise of compelling their integration.[39]

Throughout 1994, various proposals were raised that would go beyond the existing bilateral military ties that Russia had developed with selected states. Some of those proposals continued to emphasize an unacceptable degree of centralization of the kind previously promoted by Shaposhnikov. Ivashov, for example, proposed the idea of a united command, a common system of strategic planning, and a permanent supporting structure.[40] There was the hope by the Russians that time would make the other CIS members more receptive to the idea of greater integration. The Ukrainian observer at the July 1994 CIS Defense Council meeting, Chief of the General Staff Anatolii Lopata, declared a need for cooperation over military/defense issues in the CIS. Lopata's presence at the meeting and his statement indicated a shift in position by the Ukrainians who began to examine the positive benefits of cooperation within the CIS. Nonetheless, the Ukrainian observer emphasized that his country would not enter any military bloc and proposals for greater integration within the CIS had to take this into account.[41]

Ivashov emphasized the need for a decentralized approach that indicated a change of strategy toward the CIS. This approach called for independent security sub-systems that would be formed in four regions of the CIS: Eastern Europe including Belarus, Russia and Kaliningrad; the Caucasus including South Russia, Azerbaijan, Armenia and Georgia; Central Asia divided into east and west zones; and East Asia including East Kazakhstan and Russia. Each sub-system would have its own defense council and coalition command, and would interact with the other systems within an umbrella collective security system.[42] Major-General Vasilii Volkov from the Council of CIS Defense Ministers similarly argued for regionally-based security structures coordinated by a center in Moscow. Volkov proposed that the separate regions of the CIS organize their own security while the center would be responsible for wider legal and organizational issues.[43] As a somewhat different emphasis, Volkov also proposed a collective security system where countries would participate according to their special interest, which allowed for varying degrees of commitment.[44] The idea of a multilevel approach toward security within the CIS gained wider acceptance within Moscow as a reflection of political realities. At one level, an integrated approach would be pursued involving Russia and its closest allies in the CIS; at another level Russia would be linked with the remaining members in loose arrangements that would take account of specific interests and political conditions.[45] CIS security cooperation could be structured in no other way except on the basis of differentiated membership.

Defense and security cooperation within the CIS, however, remained a bilateral affair and attempts to develop an overarching multilateral system simply strengthened existing fears of Russian hegemony. That military and security effectiveness could be sacrificed for the sake of sovereignty was a new experience for Moscow's defense planners who were conditioned by their background to propose Soviet-style integrative approaches. The CIS was too complicated a place for the imposition of Soviet-style models with no allowance for the sovereignty that the states there had recently obtained. Russia could develop security ties with a core group of allies—Armenia, Georgia, Kazakhstan, Tajikistan, and Uzbekistan—but only bilaterally and according to specific needs. The CIS summit of October 1994 agreed on the idea of united CIS air defenses and a coordinating committee on the subject was created under the Council of CIS Defense Ministers. Russia hoped to involve the Ukraine, Georgia, and Armenia in this venture but Ukrainian participation would only be obtained if a centralized system were avoided.[46] The effectiveness of a decentralized system of air defenses, in which cooperation is negotiated, must remain open to question.

CIS Border Security

There are several functional areas where security cooperation within the CIS may accelerate based on need. Perhaps the most salient is the issue of border protection for which the newly-independent CIS members were ill-prepared. Border protection and control were previously the responsibility of the KGB border troops and the disintegration of the Soviet Union left many of the new states dependent on Russia for this service. Russian border forces, subject to a command structure separate from the army, remained in place along critical CIS external borders patrolling the external borders of Georgia and Armenia under agreements that were concluded during the Soviet era. Similar border agreements were signed with Kyrgyzstan, Tajikistan, and Turkmenistan allowing Russian border forces to patrol the borders with China, Afghanistan, and Iran respectively. Along Azerbaijan's borders with Iran, however, Russian border forces were removed by June 1993 when their presence became a political issue within that country.

General Andrei Nikolaev, Commander of Russian Border Forces, attempted to obtain greater recognition of the need for common border protection from within the CIS. He argued that the protection of Russia's borders went hand in hand with CIS border security—the two were inseparable. In April 1994, Nikolaev convened the first Conference of CIS Border Guards and declared that the aim was to create a CIS command for border forces.[47] Subsequently, Nikolaev proposed the outer borders concept that entailed common defense of external CIS borders on the basis that these borders were easier to control than Russia's borders within the CIS. The idea was that external or outer borders were to be tightly controlled as international frontiers but internal CIS borders would be loosely patrolled. Nikolaev's major concerns were narcotics trafficking, arms smuggling, and organized crime and he proposed integrated border forces under the CIS and a system of mutual security guarantees.[48] One particularly difficult area was Azerbaijan's border with Iran, which Russian border forces had previously vacated. The problem, as Viktor Samsonov lamented, was that Russia's border with Azerbaijan was virtually unpatrolled (as was Azerbaijan's border with Iran) which left a gap in Russia's defenses.[49] Nikolaev met Azerbaijani President Heidar Aliev and called for Azerbaijani cooperation, without which the CIS southern borders in the Caucasus could not be protected.[50] On 15 August, Aliev had already promised Iranian Foreign Minister Ali Akba Velayati that Russian border forces would not return to the area, which in any case was largely controlled by Armenian forces. Nikolaev signed various bilateral agreements with Aliev allowing Russia to provide training and equipment for Azerbaijani border forces but Russian forces would not return.

Peace-keeping in the CIS

Moscow has attempted to organize CIS peace-keeping forces under the terms of the Tashkent Collective Security Treaty to defuse the ethnic conflicts that erupted during and after the collapse of the Soviet Union. At the Tashkent meeting of CIS defense ministers in July 1992 Shaposhnikov called for a CIS peace-keeping force in a proposal that was resisted by the CIS states as another attempt to establish centralized forces under Russian control. The South Ossetian experience in July 1992 was cited as a successful case of CIS peace-keeping when Russian forces collaborated with their Georgian and Ossetian counterparts to defuse an existing conflict. Since then Moscow has begun to campaign for UN and CSCE recognition of CIS peace-keeping under the terms of a mandate that would allow the global community to finance CIS peace-keeping operations. Specific problems have been raised by Moscow's demands, which may promise a means of regulating conflict but also allows Moscow an opportunity to assert its own interests in CIS disputes. In this sense, Moscow may utilize a CIS peace-keeping mandate as a means of affirming its own hegemony.

At the Stockholm CSCE meeting in December 1992, the Russian delegation called for recognition of CIS peace-keeping, arguing that a CSCE mandate would be a guarantee that Russia would not return to imperialist policies. The Russians called for separate zones of responsibilities for NATO, the CSCE, and the CIS claiming that the CSCE was too weak for CIS peace-keeping operations.[51] In his address on 28 February 1993, Yeltsin declared that the UN should award Russia special powers as a guarantor of peace and stability in the CIS. This demand was subsequently justified by Moscow on the basis that no international organization was prepared to assume the responsibility of peace-keeping in the CIS, which was a regional concern in any case. Both the UN and the CSCE resisted Moscow's demand stressing that successful peace-keeping required the involvement of forces from countries that were not parties to the dispute thereby disqualifying Russia.

Kozyrev argued a case for a new form of peace-keeping that went beyond the classic model and would allow Russia to invoke a UN mandate. Kozyrev claimed that Russian peace-keeping efforts in Ossetia and the Transdniester republic did not conflict with the UN Charter and that peace-keeping has to reflect reality. Kozyrev deplored the unwillingness of the UN and CSCE to become involved in CIS peace-keeping, in which case Russia had no choice but to step in itself.[52] Kozyrev subsequently addressed the UN General Assembly on 27 September 1993 calling for UN financial assistance for CIS peace-keeping, the creation of a special fund for this purpose and for a UN War Command to be established under the UN Secretary-General.[53] Later Kozyrev was confronted by what one interviewer called the documented facts of Russia's support for Abkhazian separatists, which in the eyes of the UN/CSCE, disqualified Russia from assuming the role of a peace-keeper. The Russian foreign minister adroitly side-stepped the point and admitted that there were many areas for improvement in CIS peace-keeping.[54]

Kozyrev continued to press the issue, and at the Prague CSCE Conference in June 1994, the organization accepted the idea of Russian peace-keeping subject to two conditions that Moscow rejected. First, that all sides should agree. Second, that peace-keeping forces should be withdrawn after a reasonable period of time.[55] The conflict between Russia and the CSCE over CIS peace-keeping resulted in a stalemate at the Budapest CSCE Conference of December 1994, which approved the dispatch of 3,000 peace-keepers from various European countries to Nagorno-Karabakh. Both the UN Secretary-General Boutros Boutros Ghali and Western representatives insisted that Russian units participate in this force under UN or CSCE command. The Budapest Conference identified the procedures for CIS peace-keeping operations under UN mandate that would require an agreement between the conflicting sides, a UN resolution to approve the introduction of peace-keepers, and UN/CSCE command over the peace-keeping forces.[56]

Russia contested these conditions, pressing for the acceptance of mainly Russian peace-keeping forces under Russian, instead of UN or CSCE command. Fundamentally, Moscow objects to the involvement of international organizations in peace-keeping operations in the CIS, regarding them as instruments of the West. From the Western position the Russian demand for financial support, and a mandate for CIS peace-keeping without accepting external command was a brazen attempt to obtain international endorsement of the CIS as a Russian sphere of influence. While Russian and Western positions over this issue remain deadlocked, no further progress in UN/CSCE sponsored peace-keeping in the CIS can be expected.

Economic Integration within the CIS

Similar efforts have been made to maintain economic unity in the face of the political disintegration of the Soviet Union. Most CIS states continue to be economically dependent on Russia in some way. Mutual economic dependence was reflected in the statistics for inter-republican trade in the Soviet Union, which as a percentage of value national product in 1988 was calculated to be 13 percent for Russia, 27 percent for the Ukraine, 29 percent for Belarus, and between 34–50 percent for the other republics.[57] M. A. Korolev, Chairman of the Statistics Committee of the CIS, claimed that as a consequence of the disintegration of the Soviet Union, the value national product of the CIS countries had been reduced by 30–50 percent, industrial production fell by 10–18 percent, in Turkmenistan, the Ukraine, and Belarus; 24–31 percent in Moldova, Kazakhstan, Azerbaijan, and Russia; and 39–60 percent in Tajikistan, Kyrgyzstan, Armenia, and Georgia.[58] Such statistics were used to justify the Russian view that economic integration within the CIS was a necessity given that many of the states faced catastrophic economic conditions and could not survive independently. Reconciling their obvious interdependence with their sovereignty and political independence was the major task.

Within Russia, various views have developed in relation to economic integration within the CIS. Radical democrats have regarded the CIS an economic burden for Russia demanding energy supplies at less than market prices and other concessions. Russia, in their view, can find alternative markets for its energy products at world market prices that could promote its own economic transformation as well as that of the CIS states in general. At the other extreme are the nationalists and Communists who seek to restore the Soviet Union, and who regard economic cooperation as a means of promoting security integration under Russian aegis. Economic dependence is regarded by them as a lever to re-establish a Russian hegemony that had been impulsively conceded by Yeltsin when he pushed for the formation of the CIS in December 1991. Of interest are the views of Russia's new business class that has developed since 1992, that are as yet inchoate but seem to support the idea of CIS economic integration on a basis similar to that of the EU. Members of the new business class have expressed the view that the CIS is a vast economic hinterland for Russia that would encourage its growth.

The three leaders who signed the Belovezhsk declaration of 8 December 1991 noted in Article 7 the need to collaborate in the development of a "common economic space, a European and Eurasian market and customs union." Article 7 also mentioned cooperation in transport, the environment, migration policy, and against crime. The same formulation in relation to the development of a common economic space was included in the Alma Ata declaration, which shows that the intention was not just to destroy the Soviet Union and to create independent states that had little to do with each other but to maintain existing interdependence. The task then became to negotiate a framework for economic cooperation that would preserve the key features of that interdependence without challenging the sovereignty or independence of the states concerned. The Ukraine opposed the idea of a centralized CIS and consistently sought the path of greater economic integration with Europe, but it participated in the economic deliberations of the CIS and supported those proposals that called for decentralized economic cooperation. In view of the economic deterioration of the Ukraine since it left the Soviet Union, the country had little choice but to move closer to the CIS as its industries were dependent on Russian energy supplies and were tied to Russian markets. According to the Russian Ministry of Economics the Ukraine was the second largest trader within the Soviet Union after Russia. While Russian trade within the Soviet Union up to the 1990s was 38 percent of all inter-Soviet trade, the figure was 21 percent for the Ukraine, considerably higher than the 8.3 percent for Belarus, or the 6 percent for Kazakhstan.[59] The discrepancy between the political aspiration for complete independence from Moscow and the reality of economic dependence was greater in the case of the Ukraine than any other CIS state and pushed its leaders into contradictory positions. Nonetheless, in relation to economic cooperation, the Ukraine maintained a steady course.

At the Minsk meeting of CIS leaders in February 1992, the first attempt was made to give effect to the idea of the common economic space, which was based first and foremost on the use of the Russian ruble. Leonid Kravchuk supported the idea of retaining the ruble as the unit of accounting for the CIS. It was Nazarbaev, however, who emerged as the major proponent of greater economic integration calling for a payments or accounts union that would simplify inter-republican transactions and the lifting of trade barriers. The Russians similarly pressed for a multilateral accounting system and demanded that all CIS states accept the guiding direction of the Russian Central Bank if the ruble zone were to be maintained.[60] At that stage, the IMF pressed for retention of the ruble zone in the expectation that centralized control over the money supply would stabilize inflation. The IMF promoted the idea of the CIS as an economic region linked strongly with Russia; it urged the CIS to adopt a common monetary policy and opposed the introduction of national currencies by individual states. A stable ruble zone was then regarded as an important factor in the successful transition to a market economy, which in the view of the IMF could not be achieved in Russia or in any other republic in isolation.[61] Yeltsin appealed to the CIS to accept a common monetary policy by 1 September 1992 that entailed subordination before the Russian Central Bank. Political developments, however, prevented a return to the monetary centralization of the Soviet era.

The collapse of the ruble zone was a result of the inability to reconcile the demand for monetary centralization with the political independence of the CIS states. As Grigori Yavlinskii pointed out, instead of one central bank controlling monetary policy eleven de facto central banks emerged issuing credits on their own with little central direction. Monetary stabilization could not be achieved in Russia without effective coordination of budget and credit policies within the CIS. According to Finance Minister Boris Fyodorov, about one-third of the rubles in circulation flowed into the CIS as credits issued by the Russian Central Bank for trading transactions or budgetary support.[62] Deputy Head of the Russian Central Bank Vyacheslav Solovev explained that the CIS states could not live up to the demands of sovereignty and that their requests for credits were strengthened by Russia's move toward world prices. In this sense, Russia's internal economic problems spilled over into the CIS and a vicious circle of indebtedness was created.[63] Fyodorov complained of the absence of control over the Russian Central Bank that was subordinate to the Supreme Soviet and claimed that $17 billion in credit (21.4 percent of Russia's GDP) had been given to the CIS states in 1992.[64] The Russian Central Bank continued to operate as though the Soviet Union still existed on the basis of previously determined standard operating procedures. The result was the peculiar situation in which the republics issued their own rubles that traded at different exchange rates, with the Ukrainian ruble valued at 30 percent of the Russian.[65]

Russia began to reduce the credits given to the CIS states as IMF policy changed over the wisdom of maintaining a ruble zone that was plainly unworkable. The IMF's response to the monetary chaos that erupted in the CIS was to press for the introduction of separate national currencies as a means of restoring financial discipline. After negotiations with the IMF in May 1993, Russia began to tighten credit policies toward the CIS. This change was outlined in a Russian government statement of 18 June 1993 in which the introduction of national currencies by the CIS states was regarded as a precondition for economic collaboration and a means of restoring monetary stability within Russia.[66] Moscow demanded the fulfillment of two conditions from those states that wanted to remain in the ruble zone. The first was that they accept subordination before Russia's Central Bank and the second, that they deposit gold or hard currency with Russia as collateral. Most CIS states introduced their own currencies starting with the Ukraine in November 1992, then Kyrgyzstan in May 1993, Georgia in August 1993 and Armenia, Kazakhstan, Moldova, Turkmenistan, and Uzbekistan in November 1993. Azerbaijan followed in January 1994 leaving Tajikistan to rely on old Russian rubles.

Proposals for CIS economic integration were simply stillborn while the debate continued over the value of the ruble zone for Russia and whether it should be retained. Central Bank Director Viktor Gerashchenko pushed for the retention of a ruble zone but advocates of a separate currency for Russia were found in the Economics and Finance Ministries. In 1992, Nazarbaev had already emerged as the major proponent of greater CIS integration as he saw Kazakhstan's future as closely linked with Russia. In September 1992 Russia and Kazakhstan concluded an economic agreement according to which a clearing accounts system was to be established to handle trade between the two countries. Various commercial and state banks would be used for this purpose with one bank designated a clearing bank for strategic products. Nazarbaev declared that Kazakhstan's bilateral relationship with Russia was to be a model for other countries in the ruble zone.[67] Nazarbaev's vision of an integrated CIS was based on a two-tiered structure; the first tier would include the ruble zone states, the second would include the non-ruble zone states that sought to maintain a relationship with the ruble zone. Nazarbaev also proposed that an international bank be created together with a CIS council to coordinate economic policy.[68] The proposals were resisted by other CIS members and the Ukrainians in particular believed that Nazarbaev was promoting a Russian plan. Kravchuk declared that Nazarbaev wanted to restore the old imperial center, a task that Russia could not attempt on its own.[69]

The Bishkek CIS summit of October 1992 considered Nazarbaev's proposals. Two agreements were signed, one that covered the establishment of a united monetary system and the second that concerned the creation of an intergovernmental bank. There was no agreement on the ruble zone though six states agreed to retain united monetary policy—Russia, Belarus, Kazakhstan, Armenia, Uzbekistan, and Kyrgyzstan. There was also no agreement on the idea of a coordinating economic council, though a much less significant working commission was established.[70] Indeed, the agreements signed with such fanfare remained unimplemented as fundamental uncertainty existed over the structure of economic relations that was to be established within the CIS. There was common acceptance of the need for economic cooperation but beyond that little consensus on practical implementation. The Russians were moving away from the idea of a ruble zone as revealed by Aleksander Shokhin, who in December 1992 assumed the position of deputy premier responsible for external economic ties. Shokhin argued a case for Russian policy toward the CIS based on bilateralism that would circumvent the political resistance to economic institution-building depicted above.[71] Nazarbaev, however, argued that an intergovernmental economic coordinating mechanism was required to regulate relations and that the chaos created by the collapse of the Soviet Union could not be overcome by bilateral relations alone. Nazarbaev's contentious idea claimed that the CIS could move toward a market economy through government regulation of the conditions of interaction.[72] The very thought that the pace of Russia's economic reform should be tied to the other CIS states, some of whom were opposed to liberalization, was anathema to the Russian proponents of the free market.

Subsequent meetings and summits confirmed this paralysis, which was barely masked by the political declarations that were produced. Nonetheless, the most significant development was the change of attitude within the Ukraine that was coming under increasing economic strain. President Kravchuk denied publicly that the CIS was a means of ensuring a civilized divorce from Russia, which was the initial Ukrainian view. He now stated that the Ukraine had an interest in an equal economic association and would support economic integration within the CIS. Moreover, the Ukraine's new premier (as of October 1992) was Leonid Kuchma who represented the industrial sector that was deeply in crisis, and who pressed for the re-establishment of economic relations with Russia. The Ukrainian leadership was subject to competing pressures from the nationalists, who were hostile to Russia, and the industrial lobby, which saw its salvation in the CIS. At the Minsk CIS meeting of January 1993, Kravchuk refused to sign the CIS charter but supported the broad declaration without, however, accepting the idea of supranational integration.[73]

Polarization emerged between the Ukraine and Kazakhstan as Nazarbaev pressed for closer integration based on a two-tiered structure including those inside and outside the ruble zone. Kravchuk resisted Nazarbaev at the subsequent CIS meetings in Minsk (April 1993) and Moscow (May 1993) and declared that the documents signed expressed only the intention to form an economic union. Yeltsin retained a balanced position between both leaders.[74] President Niyazov of Turkmenistan, who regularly was absent from such summits, apparently believed that economic unions were unnecessary.

CIS leaders failed to move beyond the level of the impressive rhetoric that their meetings generated. In July 1993, Russia, the Ukraine, and Belarus signed an economic agreement according to which they were to negotiate a free market and various joint projects.[75] This declaration was widely regarded as a move to defuse tension between Russia and the Ukraine over Sevastopol. On 23 September 1993, a CIS economic treaty was signed by nine CIS states without the Ukraine, Turkmenistan, and Georgia. As a move toward economic union, the treaty again expressed intentions without identifying concrete measures. Article 2 of this treaty called for the free movement of goods, capital and labor. Signatories agreed to coordinate credit, budgetary, and taxation policies. Under Article 4 parties agreed to staged coordination of the above, while in Article 6 they agreed to create a general tariff and customs union. In Article 7 they agreed to the formation of an economic regime that would govern their economic integration.[76] At the Ashgabat CIS meeting of 24 December 1993, the parties similarly agreed to collaboration in investment activity, the development of production cooperatives, and the establishment of direct ties between enterprises in the CIS states.

CIS meetings constantly issued statements of intention with the same proposals being recycled while a consensus among the members in regard to their practical implementation was absent. In many respects, the declarations of 1993, including the economic treaty, were intended to offset the divisive impact of the termination of the ruble zone when Russia pushed the CIS states to introduce their own currencies. On 1 July 1993, the Russian Central Bank phased out the old rubles and introduced new bank notes in a traumatic move for those states reliant on the ruble zone, which were then compelled to issue their own currencies. Negotiations over a united ruble zone included the drafting of documents on the harmonization of taxes, customs, and banking legislation and continued even while Russia was preparing to destroy it. The Russian Central Bank granted ruble credits to the CIS assuming that the ruble zone would be maintained in what was a disturbing example of uncoordinated activities between Russian government agencies.[77] Toward the end of 1993, the debate as to whether and to what extent Russia should bind itself to the CIS was revived in view of changing conditions caused by the termination of the ruble zone. Deputy Premier Aleksander Shokhin argued that reform would be made easier if Russia's economy were separated from the CIS but supported, nonetheless, the idea of coordinated policies over a wide range of issues.[78]

The following year witnessed an intensification of the debate about the future of the CIS, its role, and function. In January, a ministry for cooperation with the CIS, headed by Vladimir Mashchits was established. Nazarbaev again proposed the idea of a Eurasian union when he met Moscow Mayor Yuri Luzhkov on 28 March 1994. Initially Nazarbaev did not fully explain the idea, simply saying that the union would be formed on the basis of equality and that every member would have veto power over decision-making.[79] When Nazarbaev visited Tokyo he was asked to explain but his responses were vague, indicating that he had not developed his proposal beyond a few ideas.[80] Nazarbaev declared that the intoxication of sovereignty had passed and that the countries of the CIS could not advance without some institutional framework that demanded supranational organs. He identified the need for a CIS parliament, a council of ministers, and a secretariat, following the model of the EU. In Nazarbaev's view, the new union should be voluntary with a common citizenship for which the language would be Russian.[81]

The proposal aroused such interest within Russia that Nazarbaev was induced to elaborate on the details on 3 June in a document entitled "Project for the Formation of the Eurasian Union." Nazarbaev developed his idea of Eurasian integration based on economic measures such as the coordination of legislation and export policies. Nazarbaev argued that CIS economic development required closer integration, otherwise individual efforts by separate sovereign states would be doomed to fail. According to Nazarbaev, economic integration with the "far abroad" was illusory and the benefits of regionalism could only be obtained within the context of the "near abroad." The union was to be implemented through national referenda or separate acts of parliament resulting in the signature of a treaty on an equal basis.[82] Nazarbaev declared his dissatisfaction with the CIS claiming that over 400 documents that were all largely unimplemented had been signed during various meetings. He confirmed his interest in supranationalism as a principle and stated that he was not afraid of surrendering sovereignty.[83]

Only later did Nazarbaev publicly link his idea of a Eurasian union with the Eurasian movement within Russia though the connection was obvious from the start. In a television interview on 17 September 1994 he called for an "integrated cultural and spiritual space" involving a common market, common borders, common institutions, and a common foreign policy.[84] Director of the Kazakh Institute of Strategic Studies Umerserik Kasenov added that the Eurasian proposal was intended to "overcome the chaos and conflict in the post-Soviet space," a task for which the CIS was unsuited. Kasenov emphasized that the new union would embody the principle of supranationalism while stressing that relations would be based on equality. Realization of the new union would only be possible if Russia avoided the temptation to act as an elder brother and resisted from attempting to restore the Soviet Union. He emphasized that the new union would prevent the disintegration of the former Soviet Union along civilizational lines—Orthodox Slav and Muslim—which had been Nazarbaev's concern since 1991. Moreover, only in the context of the Eurasian union could a Russian military presence in the "near abroad" be regarded as an acceptable means of ensuring security once fears of Russian domination are removed.[85]

The Eurasian union proposal was motivated by a concern on Nazarbaev's side to avoid the fragmentation of the former Soviet Union and to ensure that Russia would remain engaged in Central Asia. Kazakhstan's fortunes were more closely linked with Russia than with any other Central Asian country and the prospect of Russia turning its back on the region to join the Slavic states in a union was a source of apprehension. As a proposal that expressed a Russian aspiration for greater unity within the "near abroad," it was coldly received by Russian leaders. There was no clear response from either Yeltsin or Chernomyrdin as both were reluctant to concede to Kazakhstan a major role in defining policy toward the "near abroad."[86] Nazarbaev's proposal, however, received support from First Deputy Premier Sergei Shakhrai and Chairman of the Federal Assembly's Upper House Vladimir Shumeiko.

Russian proponents of CIS supranationalism understood clearly that Russia was disqualified from pressing the issue and that Nazarbaev at least could prepare the ground for its wider acceptance. Nonetheless, Nazarbaev failed to obtain support within the CIS for various reasons. Uzbekistan's President Islam Karimov opposed the proposal against the background of historical Uzbek-Kazakh rivalry in Central Asia.[87] Moreover, Karimov's special relationship with Moscow, which had been forged over the political instability of Tajikistan, would be threatened by supranational regionalism. Karimov claimed that Nazarbaev had agreed to withdraw the Eurasian proposal from the agenda of CIS heads of state meetings, but this did not prevent the Kazakh president from continuing to campaign on the issue.[88] Nazarbaev traveled to Kiev on 10 August 1994 to explain his proposal to the Ukrainians who had little interest in supranationalism.[89] The Eurasian proposal continued to be discussed within Russian circles but there was little basis for its realization within the CIS.

CIS heads of state meetings continued to deliberate and issue impressive declarations of intention. On 15 April 1994, CIS leaders again decided to establish a permanent body to deal with trade issues. They signed another free trade agreement and yet again discussed the idea of payments union. Nazarbaev did not attend this meeting in protest against Russian indifference toward his Eurasian proposal. Despite the repetitive nature of the discussions the meeting registered an expansion of CIS membership which gave its proponents some cause for optimism. Georgia had joined the CIS in October 1993 as Shevardnadze had declared that he needed Russian support. Moldova officially joined the CIS at this meeting as a result of economic dependence on Russia.[90] Most significant was the treaty that Russia concluded with Belarus on 12 April 1994 that provided for a monetary union between them and which committed the Russian Central Bank to subsidize Belarus's currency. Belarus would also obtain oil and gas from Russia at below world market prices.[91] In return, Russia obtained the free lease of military bases in Belarus, transit for its goods through Belarussian territory to Europe, and the lifting of tariffs and customs duties. The agreement was strongly criticized by Finance Minister Boris Fyodorov as creating another burden for the Russian economy.

Subsequently, the debate over the future of the CIS intensified within Moscow. In view of the continual difficulties in promoting economic cooperation within the CIS, there were those who argued for bilateral arrangements on the lines of the monetary union with Belarus. Proponents of this approach argued for differentiated relationships within the CIS based on the specific needs and desires of the countries concerned. Democrats and economists questioned the value of the CIS for Russia's economy and saw the various members developing in different directions as they established new relationships with Western trading partners. Nonetheless, within government and parliamentary circles the CIS was considered important for Russia and had to be strengthened if Russia's economy was to improve. The weight of orthodox thinking pushed Russia toward a continuation of the previous approach based largely on institutional structures and functional integration imposed from above.

Chairman of the Statistical Committee of the CIS, M. A. Korolev, sent his observations of the CIS on 23 May 1994 to Konstantin Zatulin, Chairman of the Duma's Committee on the CIS. Korolev noted that Russia was losing markets in the CIS, members were becoming increasingly oriented toward the "far abroad." Not only did the CIS countries seek investment from the "far abroad," they also began to import machinery and machine products that were previously supplied to them by Russian industries. For example, in 1993 Kazakhstan and Uzbekistan were compelled to purchase large and small diameter pipes from the "far abroad" for their oil industries because of declining Russian deliveries. Russian exports to the "far abroad" were also increasing but while raw materials (such as energy products) may find ready markets elsewhere, the products of Russian industries were generally uncompetitive outside the CIS. Korolev concluded that "without restoration of economic ties between Russia and the other CIS countries it would be hardly possible to stabilize the (Russian) economy and production as a whole."[92]

Similarly, V. A. Gustov, Chairman of the Committee on the CIS in the Federation Council, claimed that trade and economic relations with the CIS would be an important factor in overcoming the collapse of Russia's economy. Russia's participation in a CIS economic union was an objective need that arose from the mutual dependence of the CIS economies.[93] Deputy Minister for the CIS, V. Pokrovskii claimed that 30 percent of Russia's overall drop in production could be attributed to the rupture of economic relations caused by the collapse of the Soviet Union. Russia had no choice but to turn to the CIS as the expectation of massive Western support was simply unfounded. Pokrovskii argued for the formation of an economic alliance within the CIS since the "normalization of trade and economic ties with the CIS is a necessary condition for the renewal of Russia's economy." Russia, said Pokrovskii, should be the catalyst for CIS integration and should constantly assume a leadership role in the effort to form an economic alliance. Russia, he claimed, needed an effective response to Nazarbaev's Eurasian proposal, which was an indication of Russian officials's concern that the Kazakh president would seize the initiative within the CIS. As for specific measures, the deputy minister identified the need for a customs union, an effective payments or accounts mechanism, and an effort to implement the many agreements already signed.[94]

Minister of External Economic Relations Oleg Davydov similarly advocated stronger measures to realize an economic union within the framework of the CIS. Davydov noted the difficulties of the CIS, including the disagreements over policy, the ineffectiveness in executing CIS agreements, and increasing competition between CIS states in third markets. He claimed, however, that during the Soviet era a foundation for economic and production ties had been established that did not exist to the same degree within the EU. Davydov saw the September 1993 Economic Agreement as a basis for strengthening integration through a free trade association and a customs and currency union. He emphasized the need for voting within CIS economic organs to be based on economic strength, rather than the principle of equality, which would allow Russia to defend its economic interests. Davydov was critical of Nazarbaev's Eurasian proposal claiming it undervalued the significance of economics. According to the external economic minister, Nazarbaev's proposal conflicts with the CIS, takes the emphasis away from economics, and "does not take into account the economic potential of Russia."[95] V. J. Meshcheryakov, Deputy Chairman of the State Customs Committee, called for a system of united external tariffs and the elimination of tariffs between CIS states to form a customs union. Nonetheless, Meshcheryakov lamented that interest in economic working bodies within the CIS was declining. As Russia reduced its tariffs in relation to the external world the CIS states obtained access to Russia's market without allowing Russia a corresponding access to their own.[96] Konstantin Zatulin's Committee for CIS Affairs conducted hearings within the Duma on the issue of the future of the grouping on 5 July 1994. One common view expressed was that the CIS did not meet the need for closer integration but the alternatives discussed, including a Slavic union, the Eurasian union, a Russian-Belarus merger, and repudiation of the 8 December 1991 CIS Agreement, were unrealistic or incomplete.[97]

Within Moscow attempts again were made to move the CIS toward the aims identified above. On 28 July, the Speaker of the Federation Council and Chairman of the CIS Inter-Parliamentary Assembly, Vladimir Shumeiko, called for the transformation of the CIS into a confederation with the expectation that political unity would lead the way to economic integration.[98] Russia's CIS Ministry began to table proposals for supranationalism that included a system of mutual accounts through central and commercial banks to allow transfers of funds between CIS countrie, a payments union that would lead to a currency union eventually, and the elimination of tariffs on internal transport within the CIS as one of the greater barriers to trade.[99] These proposals were discussed at the CIS meeting of prime ministers the following September.

From 7–8 September, the 1994 CIS Coordinating Committee of Deputy Premiers met in Moscow and agreed to consider the formation of an interstate economic committee (IEC), the first supranational body within the CIS. This committee was to be the standing executive body of the CIS economic union and was to preside over the development of its integrative features—the payments and monetary union and the free trade zone.[100] At the CIS prime ministers's meeting of 9 September the proposal to establish the IEC was approved in principle. The committee was to include a permanent executive presidium and an administrative board or collegium, both to be based in Moscow. It was to make decisions binding on all CIS members relevant to transnational economic activities. True to the principle of enshrining economic weight in voting rights, Russia was given 50 percent of the voting rights within this committee, the Ukraine 14 percent, Belarus, Kazakhstan, and Uzbekistan 5 percent each, others were given 3 percent. 80 percent of the votes were required to pass a resolution, which meant that Russia could block any motion, but no motion could be passed without the agreement of major CIS states. The meeting again revealed the deep divisions within the CIS, with Armenia, Belarus, and Georgia being the chief proponents of economic integration. Azerbaijan and Turkmenistan refused to sign the agreement, while Leonid Kuchma declared that the Ukraine would only participate over matters of interest to itself. Moldova agreed to the IEC with the condition that it be granted no supranational powers.[101]

Aleksander Shokhin made the unsupported claim that the IEC would be an equivalent of the European Commission.[102] The specific powers of the IEC were not defined and outside of the few active proponents of economic integration and supranationalism there was little enthusiasm. The CIS summit was held in

Moscow on 21 October 1994 when the IEC was placed top on the agenda, but the meeting, as expected, failed to identify the functions and specific powers of the IEC and some conflict of opinion was stimulated accordingly.[103] Yeltsin subsequently declared that the decision to establish the IEC was one of the few unanimous acts of the CIS. He added that the role of the IEC would be defined later and claimed that the Ukrainian view of economic integration had changed, given that Leonid Kuchma had raised no objections.[104] Yeltsin's adviser Dmitri Ryurikov, however, revealed on 25 October that the CIS summit had only given limited powers to the IEC over the preparation of documents for meetings of CIS officials, though there was the hope that it would acquire executive functions over time.[105] The first meeting of the IEC was held in Moscow on 18 November chaired by Russian Deputy Premier Aleksei Bolshakov who was responsible for CIS affairs. The body moved ahead with the formation of a supporting administrative organ and discussed various economic issues such as a customs union and a common market but otherwise decided little.[106] In effect, the much heralded supranational body became one of the many CIS committees that regularly meet to demonstrate activity in the absence of progress.

CIS INTEGRATION—THE FUTURE

Despite Russian efforts over the past three years, economic integration within the CIS has made little headway. The CIS survived despite initial skepticism and various members, including the Ukraine, strengthened their interest in economic cooperation, though not in the terms proposed by Russian leaders. One of the basic problems was the Russian effort to preserve an integrated system based on command economies that failed to accommodate the sovereignty of the CIS states. The Soviet-style top down approach toward economic integration demonstrated its self-defeating quality by continuing to provoke opposition from among those CIS states that would otherwise participate. Russian representatives argue that economic weight and the security vulnerabilities of the states along their peripheries compel Russia to assume a leading role over subordinate actors. They also claim that Russia is the only effective actor in the area and that the common security and economic interests of all demand that Russia shape and guide the CIS toward greater integration. Supposed security and economic realities result in the continual effort to revive a variant Soviet model for the CIS that has been repeatedly rejected. The Russians, too often, have the expectation that deteriorating conditions will compel a change of view within the CIS, which will become more receptive toward the idea of greater security and economic integration and a dominant role for Russia. Over time, however, a much more complicated picture of Russia's relations with the CIS is likely to emerge that will hardly justify these expectations. Rather than an integrated framework imposed from above, a complex pattern of bilateral relationships on various levels will be the probable result of present trends. Russia's relations with the CIS will be structured around existing political obstacles and will be compelled to accommodate the area's disparate interests. The result is likely to be a multilevel organization with areas of tight integration as well as peripheral membership.

The idea of a multilevel regional structure is not a new one and has been discussed within Moscow circles over the past few years as an accommodation to reality in the CIS. The Council of Foreign and Defense Policy in December 1992 recommended that Russia conduct a differentiated policy toward the CIS, that multileveled groups and associations were required based on different levels of integration.[107] The idea of differentiated membership of the CIS was examined at the Minsk summit meeting of January 1993 and associate member and observer status for various states was proposed.[108] At one level, there would be the overarching regional organization that will include all CIS members in a loosely structured body similar to the Organization of American States (OAS). At another level, there would be the disparate subregional groups that would adopt coordinated policies over various issues whether economics or protection of borders. The CIS, indeed, is moving in this direction.

NOTES

1. Andrei Kozyrev, *Preobrazhenie*, Mezhdunarodnye Otnoshenie, Moscow, 1994, p. 168-170.

2. *Rossiiskaya gazeta*, 10 Dec. 1991.

3. *Rossiiskaya gazeta*, 10 Dec. 1991.

4. *Rossiiskaya gazeta*, 10 Dec. 1991.

5. *Rossiiskaya gazeta*, 10 Dec. 1991.

6. The vote was 161 for, 3 against, 9 abstained, *Verkhovnogo sovieta RSFR Bulletin*, no. 21: joint session of Soviet of the Republic and Soviet of Nationalities, 12 Dec. 1991; also *Rossiiskaya gazeta*, 13 Dec. 1991.

7. *Rossiiskaya gazeta*, 17 Dec. 1991.

8. *Rossiiskaya gazeta*, 24 Dec. 1991.

9. *Reuters Textline*, 19 Feb. 1992.

10. Emil Pain, "Russia and Post-Soviet Space," *Moscow News* (8), 25 Feb./3 Mar. 1994.

11. *Radio Free Europe/Radio Liberty Daily Report* (39), 25 July 1994.

12. *Rossiiskaya gazeta*, 4 Aug. 1992.

13. Vera Kuznetsova, "S'ezd priznal SNG," *Nezavisimaya gazeta*, 21 Apr. 1992.

14. "Strategiya dla Rossiya," *Nezavisimaya gazeta*, 19 Aug. 1992.

15. See Ion Sofronie (Press Secretary, Government of Moldova), "Rossiya ne otkazalas ot imperskikh prityazanii," *Izvestiya*, 29 Apr. 1994.

16. T. M. Regent, *Sovremenie tendentsii v migratsionnom obmene rossii s gosudartsvami blizhnego zarubezh'ya*, Memorandum from Federal Migration Service to Yu. E. Voebode, Deputy Head of Duma Committee on CIS, 4 July 1994.

17. *Nezavisimaya gazeta*, 20 Jan. 1994.

18. Sergei Kozlov, "Nazarbaev ne vstretilsya s Kozyrevym," *Nezavisimaya gazeta*, 18 Nov. 1993.

19. *Nezavisimaya gazeta*, 19 Jan. 1994.

20. Liana Minasyan, "Russkie v SNG—ne inostrantsy," *Nezavisimaya gazeta*, 5 Mar. 1994.

21. Yevgennii Bai, "Moskva razrabotala programmu zashchity 30 millionov russkikh v blizhnem zarubezh'e," *Izvestiya*, 17 Feb. 1994.

22. Aleksander Kodintsev, "Rossyane vne Rossii i natsional'nya bezopastnost' R.F.," *Nezavisimaya gazeta*, 13 Oct. 194.

23. *Radio Free Europe/Radio Liberty Daily Report* (171), 8 Sept. 1994.

24. Konstantin Eggert, Maksim Yusin, "Kozyrev stanovitsya silovym ministrom," *Izvestiya*, 20 Apr. 1995.

25. *Nezavisimaya gazeta*, 29 Jan. 1992.

26. "Strategiya dla Rossiya," *Nezavisimaya gazeta*, 19 Aug. 1992.

27. V. Tkachemko, A. Chernyak, "Armiyu delit ne budem," *Pravda*, 9 Sept. 1991.

28. *Krasnaya zvezda*, 10 Dec. 1991.

29. *Krasnaya zvezda*, 2 Nov. 1991.

30. *Rossiiskaya gazeta*, 13 Dec. 1991.

31. *Rossiiskaya gazeta*, 24 Dec. 1991.

32. Aleksei Luzin, "Sodruzhestvo—eto poka embrional'noe obrazovanie," *Nezavisimaya gazeta*, 15 Feb. 1992.

33. *Itar Tass*, 31 Aug. 1992.

34. "O kollektivnoi bezopasnosti pozabotilis' shest' respublik, otkryty dveri i dla ostal'nykh," *Krasnaya zvezda*, 19 May 1992.

35. For text of the Tashkent Treaty see *Rossiiskaya gazeta*, 23 May 1992.

36. Yevgennii Shaposhnikov, "Natsional'naya i kollektivnaya bezopasnost' v SNG," *Krasnaya zvezda*, 30 Sept. 1992.

37. *Itar Tass*, 4 Nov. 1992; *Nezavisimaya gazeta*, 25 Jan. 1993.

38. Interview of Boris P'yankov, *Nezavisimaya gazeta*, 24 June 1994.

39. *Nezavisimaya gazeta*, 24 June 1994.

40. Leonid Ivashov, "Ot desintegratsii k ob'edineniyu," *Nezavisimaya gazeta*, 6 July 1994.

41. *Nezavisimaya gazeta*, 27 July 1994.

42. Leonid Ivashov, "Vozmozhen li voenno-politicheskii soyuz?" *Nezavisimaya gazeta*, 18 Oct. 1994.

43. Vasilii Volkov, "Kollektivnaya bezopasnost' sodruzhestva," *Nezavisimaya gazeta*, 20 Aug. 1994.

44. *Radio Free Europe/Radio Liberty Daily Report* (159), 23 Aug. 1994.

45. Dmitri Trenin, "Kollektivyaya bezopasnost' i kollektivnaya oborone," *Nezavisimaya gazeta*, 4 Nov. 1994.

46. *Nezavisimaya gazeta*, 21 Feb. 1995.

47. *Nezavisimaya gazeta*, 7 Apr. 1994.

48. *Radio Free Europe/Radio Liberty Daily Report* (217), 15 Nov. 1994.

49. *Pravda*, 17 Feb. 1994.

50. *Nezavisimaya gazeta*, 23 Aug. 1994.

51. Sergei Geivandov, Sergei Samuilov, "SBSE i OON: bor'ba za miro-tvorchestvo," *Rossiiskaya gazeta*, 30 Dec. 1992.

52. Andrei Kozyrev, "Rossiya fakticheski v odinochku," *Nezavisimaya gazeta*, 22 Sept. 1993.

53. *Nezavisimaya gazeta*, 30 Sept. 1993.

54. *Nezavisimaya gazeta*, 24 Nov. 1993.

55. *Radio Free Europe/Radio Liberty Daily Report* (112), 15 June 1994.

56. *Izvestiya*, 9 Dec. 1994; *Nezavisimaya gazeta*, 8 Dec. 1994.

57. P. E. Kandsl, *SNG: dva s polovinoi goda spusta*, Moscow 1994, p. 3.

58. M. A. Korolev, *Rossiya i strany SNG*, Statisticheskii komitet sodruzhestva nezavisimykh gosudarstv (State Statistical Committee for CIS), 23 May 1994.

59. P. E. Kandsl, *SNG: dva s polovinoi goda spusta*, Moscow, 1994, p. 4.

60. *Nezavisimaya gazeta*, 28 Apr. 1992.

61. *Izvestiya*, 27 Apr. 1992, *New York Times*, 20 June 1992.

62. *Izvestiya*, 14 July 1993.

63. *Rossiiskaya gazeta*, 9 Feb. 1993.

64. *Izvestiya*, 14 July 1993.

65. *Economist*, 19 Sept. 1992.

66. *Rossiiskaya gazeta*, 11 Aug. 1993.

67. Ivan Zasurskii, "Nad natsional'nyi rubl' ne nravitsya rossiiskomu ministru," *Nezavisimaya gazeta*, 17 Sept. 1992.

68. *Nezavisimaya gazeta*, 22 Sept. 1992.

69. Vitalii Portnikov, "Kravchuk protiv Nazarbaeva," *Nezavisimaya gazeta*, 22 Sept. 1992; also "Niyazov, Karimov, Akaev, protiv novogo soyuza," *Nezavisimaya gazeta*, 1 Oct. 1992.

70. Vera Kuznetsova, "Itogi vstrecha v Bishkeke," *Nezavisimaya gazeta*, 10 Oct. 1992.

71. Aleksei Shokhin, "My interesovany v inostrannykh investitsiykh no ne na lyubykh usloviyakh," *Nezavisimaya gazeta*, 31 Oct. 1992.

72. "Khaos i anarkhiya k rynku ne vedut," *Rossiiskaya gazeta*, 20 Nov. 1992.

73. Igor' Sinyakevich, Vladimir Skachko, *Nezavisimaya gazeta*, 26 Jan. 1993.

74. Vitalii Portnikov, "Ekonomicheski soyuz mozhet sostoyat'sya," *Nezavisimaya gazeta*, 19 May 1993.

75. *Izvestiya*, 15 July 1993.

76. *Dogovor o sozdanni ekonomicheskogo soyuza*, Moscow, 24 Sept. 1993.

77. Ivan Zhagel', "Obmen deneg sposoben peressorit rossiyu s ee partnerami po SNG," *Izvestiya*, 31 July 1993.

78. Vera Kuznetsova, "SNG stanovitsya ekonomicheskim soyuzom po tipu konfederatsii," *Nezavisimaya gazeta*, 8 Sept. 1993.

79. Vitalii Portnikov, "Evraziiski soyuz po Nazarbaevu," *Nezavisimaya gazeta*, 31 Mar. 1994.

80. Sergei Agafonov, "Kazakhskii debyut v Yaponii," *Izvestiya*, 9 Apr. 1994.

81. "Eiforiya soverinitetov proshla," *Rossiiskaya gazeta*, 31 Mar. 1994.

82. "Ne SSSR, no i ne SNG," *Nezavisimaya gazeta*, 8 June 1994.

83. "Nursultan Nazarbaev: ne nado iskat togo chego net," *Nezavisimaya gazeta*, 11 June 1994.

84. *Radio Free Europe/Radio Liberty Daily Report* (179), 20 Sept. 1994.

85. Umerserik Kasenov, "Razmyshleniya o evraziiskom soyuze," *Nezavisimaya gazeta*, 11 Oct. 1994.

86. Vitalii Portnikov, "Evraziiski soyuz po Nazarbaevu," *Nezavisimaya gazeta*, 31 Mar. 1994.

87. "Ot ekonomicheskogo soyuza k evraziiskomu," *Pravda*, 16 Apr. 1994.

88. *Radio Free Europe/Radio Liberty Daily Report* (96), 20 May 1994.

89. *Radio Free Europe/Radio Liberty Daily Report* (152), 11 Aug. 1994.

90. Vitalii Portnikov, "Dvustoronnya diplomatiya," *Nezavisimaya gazeta*, 16 Apr. 1994; "Lidery SNG sobralis' v Moskve," *Nezavisimaya gazeta*, 15 Apr. 1994.

91. Mikhail Berger, "Belorussiya obmenyala chast' svoego suverniteta na rossiiskie ruble," *Izvestiya*, 14 Apr. 1994; *New York Times*, 13 Apr. 1994.

92. M. A. Korolev, *Rossiya i strany SNG*, Staticheskii komitet sodruzhestva nezavisimykh gosudarstu (State Statistical Committee for CIS), submission to K. F. Zatulin, head of Duma's Committee on CIS and Coethnics, 23 May 1994.

93. V. A. Gustov, *Po itogam parlamenstkikh slushanii; o problemakh formirovaniya ekonomicheskikogo soyuza gosudarstv—uchastnikov SNG*, Komitet po delam sodruzhestva nezavisimykh gosudarstv, soviet federatsii, federal'nogo sobraniya rossiiskoi federatsii (Committee on CIS Soviet of Federation), 3 June 1994.

94. V. Pokrovskii, *Rossiya i ekonomicheskii soyuz gosudarstv sodruzhestva*, memorandum from deputy minister for collaboration with governments of the CIS to head of Duma's Committee on CIS Affairs and Ties with Coethnics (VP-168), 1 July 1994.

95. Memorandum of O. D. Davydov, Minister of External Economic Ties of the Russian Federation to Yu. E. Voevode, Deputy Chairman of the Duma's Committee on CIS Affairs and Ties with Coethnics (no. 10-10/2426), 30 June 1994.

96. Memorandum of V. I. Meshcheryakov, Deputy Chairman of State Customs Committee to K. F. Zatulin, Chairman of the Duma's Committee on CIS Affairs and Ties with Coethnics (01-33A/752-4), 1 July 1994.

97. *Nezavisimaya gazeta*, 13 July 1994.

98. *Radio Free Europe/Radio Liberty Daily Report* (143), 29 July 1994.

99. *Izvestiya*, 25 Aug. 1994.

100. *Radio Free Europe/Radio Liberty Daily Report* (172), 9 Sept. 1994.

101. *Izvestiya*, 9 Sept. 1994; *Radio Free Europe/Radio Liberty Daily Report* (173), 12 Sept. 1994.

102. John Lloyd, "CIS Strengthens Economic Unity," *Financial Times*, 10/11 Sept. 1994.

103. *Radio Free Europe/Radio Liberty Daily Report* (201), 21 Oct. 1994.

104. *Nezavisimaya gazeta*, 22 Oct. 1994; *Financial Times*, 22/23 Oct. 1994.

105. *Radio Free Europe/Radio Liberty Daily Report* (205), 27 Oct. 1994.

106. *Radio Free Europe/Radio Liberty Daily Report* (220), 21 Nov. 1994.

107. Aleksander Salmin, "Dezintegratsiya Rossii?" *Nezavisimaya gazeta*, 10 Dec. 1992.

108. Nezavisimaya gazeta, 20 Jan. 1993.

Chapter 4

Russia and the "Near Abroad": Bilateralism and Subregionalism

The previous chapter examined Moscow's difficulty in promoting integration within the CIS and noted the trend toward differentiated or selective integration on the basis of subregionalism. Within the CIS area there are three main subregions or areas of interaction: the European, Caucasian, and Central Asian. They are distinct geographically and culturally although cross linkages exist between them. As the dominant actor in all these subregions Russia strives to impose an overriding regional framework to turn the CIS into a coherent structure. Nonetheless, the members of the various subregional areas have developed their own economic and security linkages with Russia but otherwise have little in common. The European and Caucasian members of the CIS have minimum interest in the Central Asian members, who have resisted involvement in the other subregions. Russia has developed bilateral relations with these subregions that serve as the basis for policy in the "near abroad." These relationships differ considerably in terms of their significance for Moscow, and their ability to facilitate the development of a CIS regionalism.

EUROPEAN CIS

The European CIS comprises the Ukraine, Belarus, and Moldova—states that differ in their relations with Moscow and their commitment to CIS regionalism. On independence, the Ukraine appeared most likely to break with Moscow over the CIS and to move toward the West. Moldova faced strong pressure for reunification with Romania and its interest in the CIS was dubious. Both, however, developed an interest in the CIS over time with the Ukraine in particular insisting on equality. Belarus, never comfortable with a separate identity, moved toward integration with Russia for ethnic, cultural, and economic reasons.

The Ukraine

There has been no greater challenge for Moscow within the CIS than the Ukraine, which shares history, ethnicity, and religion with Russia. In April 1992, a group of Russian and Ukrainian academics examined what they regarded as positive and negative factors in this complicated relationship. As positive factors they identified: a common Slavic background and Orthodox Christianity; the need to coordinate their economies; common security interests, and overlapping populations. There are some 12 million Russians living in the Ukraine and some 13 million mixed Russian-Ukrainian families, including that of the nationalist Aleksander Rutskoi whose mother was Ukrainian. Among the negative factors they included the Ukrainian concern over the fragility of Russian democracy, the absence of an effective security system in the region and suspicions that Russia intended to dominate the CIS.[1] Political relations between Russia and the Ukraine are paradoxically exacerbated by ethnic and cultural familiarity that strengthens the Russian perception of the Ukraine as an extension of Russia.[2] It was Rutskoi who claimed that Russia and the Ukraine were "two brother nations" and that attempts on the part of the Ukrainian nationalists to remove the Ukraine from "Russian political space" would trigger political conflict. Rutskoi condemned the Ukrainian nationalists who wanted to "destroy the relationship with Russia" to seek entry into Europe.[3]

Ukrainian nationalists accuse Russia of not respecting Ukrainian independence and sovereignty, of attempting to destabilize the country to push it into a dependent relationship with Moscow, and of fomenting political tensions and conflict. Russians have had particular difficulty in accepting an independent Ukraine, but Russian decision-makers would in no way benefit from an unstable Ukraine. With its population of 53 million, the Ukraine is the second largest state in the CIS and holds a critical position for Russia's relationship with Europe. A destabilized Ukraine would invite what Moscow seeks to avoid—NATO involvement—and any attempt by Russia to intervene would simply justify NATO's expansion eastward. Heavy Russian pressure on the Ukraine would strengthen the existing tendency on the part of Ukrainians to look toward Europe and would, moreover, ensure greater receptivity to the Ukraine within Europe. Either the Russians accommodate an independent Ukraine or they will hasten its integration with Europe with consequences that would be self-defeating for Moscow.

Similarly, the Ukraine cannot circumvent Russia's presence and the first few years of independence have witnessed a dangerous polarization between the nationalist West which is oriented toward Europe, and the Russian-speaking and industrial East, which remains strongly linked with Russia. The nationalists and intellectuals demanded the Ukraine's withdrawal from the CIS and were critical of President Leonid Kravchuk whom they regarded as a product of the Communist *nomenklatura* (Communist Party apparatus). Leader of the nationalist movement *Rukh*, Vladislav Chornovil claimed that the Ukraine could not participate in the CIS until it was a state with all the attributes of separate statehood, which Russia should respect.[4] The economic pragmatists and the industrial managers from the East sought to re-establish links with the Russian economy and attempted to negotiate with Russia over critical supplies of energy. For them the CIS was a necessary framework to maintain an economic relationship with Russia and to prevent a dangerous deterioration in relations.[5] The Ukrainian president was buffeted by these conflicting political forces that explains to a considerable extent the Ukraine's ambiguous relationship with the CIS and Russia.

From the outset, Ukrainian representatives held different views of the CIS and a consensus was noticeably absent. The then Chairman of Parliament Ivan Plyushch expressed the view popular with nationalists and intellectuals that the CIS was a means by which the Ukraine could obtain a civilized divorce from Russia. The pro-European nationalists perceived the CIS without purpose and saw the Ukraine's future in Europe.[6] President Leonid Kravchuk, on the other hand, thought that the CIS could play an important role and that it was not the Ukraine's intention to destroy it. Kravchuk believed that the CIS should not be a screen for Russian domination and claimed that U.S.-Canada relations should be a model for Russian-Ukrainian relations.[7] Premier Leonid Kuchma claimed that over the longterm the CIS had no future, but an economic alliance was required without an institutional superstructure. Kuchma was a representative of the industrial lobby group from the East and emphasized the idea of economic cooperation on an equal basis and without supranationalism. Kuchma also chided his nationalist compatriots who thought that Europe was an alternative to the CIS declaring that "no one expects or awaits us."[8]

Three issues bedevilled Russian-Ukrainian relations that were constant reminders of the extent to which these countries were tied together. Despite the nationalist aspiration for a civilized divorce from Russia, economics and politics bound these countries and their separation would be a destructive act. The nationalist Russian insistence on recognition of a predominant Russian role in this relationship would conflict with the reality of the Ukraine's legal and sovereign status, which Russia is bound to uphold if it wishes to preserve the CIS. Any Russian encroachment on the sovereignty of the Ukraine would be contemptuous and would undermine the CIS and poison relations with other states in the "near abroad." The two are locked in a relationship that has provoked much animosity and political friction, and if the Ukraine cannot escape Russia, neither can Russia command the Ukraine to resume its previous subordinate status.

The first issue has been the economic relationship. The Ukraine remains highly dependent on Russian energy supplies, importing some 85 percent of its oil needs, and 52 percent of its gas supplies from Russia. Turkmenistan provides another 25 percent of its gas. Russia has been supplying energy to the Ukraine at less than market prices and, moreover, Ukrainian officials have admitted to siphoning gas from Russia's pipeline to Germany without which the Ukraine's steel and energy industries would collapse.[9] The Ukraine has accumulated huge debts, to both Turkmenistan and Russia that demand rescheduling. By September 1994, the Ukraine had received $3.4 billion in credits from the CIS; $2.7 billion was owed to Russia, $671 million to Turkmenistan; and $28 million to Moldova.[10] Ukrainian nationalists habitually accuse the Russians of manipulating energy supplies to coerce the Ukraine into submission. The Russians retort that a country should pay its bills according to the terms of the commercial transaction and that if the Ukraine is independent it should no longer request special prices from Russia for energy supplies. In answer to the threat to increase energy prices to world market levels the Ukrainians, as First Deputy Premier Igor' Yuzhnovski has pointed out, could move to world prices for their agricultural products.[11] Indeed, Russian markets are filled with Ukrainian traders selling their fruits and vegetables and increases in Russian energy prices may have an impact on their prices in time. In any case, the Ukrainian dependence on Russia for energy is matched by a Russian concern for the stability of the country. Russia could not terminate energy supplies to the Ukraine as though it were a commercial relationship without exacerbating conditions in that country with unpredictable consequences.

The second issue is the Crimea that Khrushchev granted to the Ukraine in February 1954 to commemorate the 300th anniversary of the Ukraine's union with Russia. The Crimea was never part of the Ukraine historically, has a predominantly Russian population (70 percent Russian out of a population of 2.7 million), and is regarded as part of Russian history. Russian forces defended the fortress of Sevastopol for 11 months in 1854–1855 against the British and French during the Crimean War and against the Germans for a month in June–July 1942. Russian nationalists cannot reconcile themselves to the loss of the Crimea and Rutskoi demanded self-determination for the Russian population, which he said cannot be subject to Ukrainianization.[12] The Russian Supreme Soviet voted on 23 January 1992 to re-examine Khrushchev's decision of February 1954 to transfer the Crimea, which was regarded as an inalienable part of Russia, to the Ukraine. On 21 May 1992, the Supreme Soviet actually voted to annul the transfer, as deputies pushed for self-determination for the Crimea, stimulating hostile reactions from the Ukraine.[13] In 1993, the Supreme Soviet formulated its own policy toward the Crimea, which it regarded as an internal issue. Deputy Chairman of the Supreme Soviet Valentin Agafonov sent a letter to his Crimean counterpart advocating membership of the CIS as an independent state.[14] On 9 July 1993, the Supreme Soviet passed a resolution declaring Sevastopol a Russian city, that the transfer of Crimea to the Ukraine was illegal, and that the Black Sea Fleet would remain undivided, contrary to Yeltsin's agreement with Ukrainian President Kravchuk. Both Yeltsin and Kozyrev condemned the action as being in conflict with the Russian government's position on all these issues.[15] Ukrainian Foreign Minister Anatolii Zlenko appealed to the UN Security Council while Russia's representative stressed that the Supreme Soviet resolution did not represent the Russian position, and that Russia had no territorial claims on the Ukraine.[16]

A Crimean independence movement began in August 1991, represented by the Republican Movement of Crimea and headed by Yuri Meshkov. On 29 April 1992, the Ukrainian Supreme Soviet granted autonomy to Crimea while on 5 May 1992 the Crimean Supreme Soviet passed its own act of independence. On 20 January 1994, Yuri Meshkov was elected president of Crimea after campaigning for unification with Russia. However, Meshkov desisted when he realized that Moscow withheld support and began to argue for reconciliation with the Ukraine. This change provoked accusations of betrayal from the nationalist movement *Rossiya*, which he had previously led.[17] Russian leaders, including Yeltsin, have avoided conflict with the Ukrainians over the Crimea, insisting that the issue is an internal matter for the Ukraine.

The third issue is the Black Sea Fleet, which nationalists declare part of Russia's history. The Black Sea Fleet cannot return to Russian command while the Ukraine asserts its claim, neither can it be divided or subject to joint command without destroying its effectiveness. The Black Sea Fleet is a case where overlapping claims have become entangled beyond the point where a clear division would be possible. Various attempts at a resolution have led nowhere. On 3 August 1992, Yeltsin and Kravchuk met at Yalta and agreed to place the fleet under joint Russian-Ukrainian command for three years. Negotiations on the details including logistics, symbols, and flags were to follow.[18] On 17 June 1993, both presidents agreed to divide the fleet on a 50:50 basis that was to include the vessels, facilities, and supporting infrastructure.[19] On 3 September 1993, the presidents agreed that the Ukraine would sell its share of the fleet to Russia in return for a cancellation of debts. Sevastopol would be leased by the Ukraine to the Russian navy. The Ukrainian nationalists opposed this agreement and Kravchuk was compelled to backtrack.[20] A new agreement was reached on 15 April 1994, under which the Ukraine would retain 15–20 percent of the fleet and would sell the remainder of its share to Russia.[21] The Russians accused the Ukrainians of backing away from this agreement as well, and a dispute erupted when the Ukraine allowed Russia the use of Sevastopol as a supporting base while the Russians demanded a series of facilities. The Russian military is strongly against any division of the fleet, and while the dispute continues its operational utility steadily declines and vessels fall into disrepair and are taken out of service. The headquarters of the fleet claimed on 5 June 1995 that of 894 vessels in April 1994 some 840 were accounted for one year later, a decline of 54.[22]

The above three issues illustrate the extent to which Russia and the Ukraine, for better or for worse, are linked and their common problems can only be resolved by close cooperation. The election of Leonid Kuchma as Ukrainian president on 11 July 1994 was widely regarded as an event that would bring the Ukraine closer to Russia within the CIS. Kuchma campaigned on a platform of better relations with Russia and the CIS and his election was indicative of the electorate's concern for the country's economic plight. On 20 June, Yeltsin declared that the Ukrainian elections demonstrated the aspiration of the people to move closer to Russia.[23] Nonetheless, the issue of the Black Sea Fleet remains unresolved and Yeltsin refused to visit Kiev to conclude a formal treaty with the Ukraine pending resolution of this issue. Kuchma may be more receptive to cooperation within the CIS but continues to insist on equality and opposes supranationalism. Among the Russians today there is a greater realization that these problems can be resolved only as part of a wider integrative process that would demand a change of attitude. Nikolai Gonchar, Chairman of the Budget and Finance Committee in Russia's Upper House, identified the Crimea as a possible "kernel of an integrative process" that may embrace the CIS as a whole. Gonchar stated that Russia should act to support the proponents of integration within the Ukraine and quoted Kuchma as saying that the greatest threat to the Ukraine's independence is "economic stupidity."[24] It may take time for Russia and the Ukraine to overcome the past but ultimately there is no alternative for either.

Belarus

Ethnic and cultural proximity, coupled with economic need has bound Belarus closely to Russia. Unlike other Slavic peoples, such as Ukrainians or Poles, the Belarussians have not developed a nationalism directed against Moscow.[25] While Stanislav Shushkevich was Belarussian leader from 1992–July 1994 an effort was made to strengthen Belarus's sovereignty by declaring a policy of neutrality and non-participation in military blocs. On 19 March 1992, Belarus's Supreme Soviet announced that it would withdraw the country from CIS combined forces in pursuit of military neutrality. Nonetheless, pressure for closer cooperation with Moscow came from the industrial lobby, represented by Premier Vyacheslav Kebich that sought access to markets in Russia. In July 1992, Kebich signed an economic cooperation agreement with Russia, which Yegor Gaidar hailed as the first step toward confederation in the CIS and an example for other states.[26]

Premier Kebich was a proponent of closer ties with Moscow and viewed the disintegration of the Soviet Union as a tragedy. In April 1993, he called for an economic union involving Belarus, Russia, and Kazakhstan that would entail a united budget and common financial and customs policies.[27] Subsequently, Belarus joined an economic alliance with Russia in November 1993 when a series of economic agreements was signed. These agreements included a united monetary/credit system and common laws for external trade. Despite opposition from the national front, which regarded the agreements as a betrayal of the national interest, 264 deputies voted in favor in the Supreme Soviet, only 4 were against and 4 abstained.[28] Even the opposition understood how closely Belarus's economy was linked with Russia and economic pragmatism outweighed nationalist sentiment in the voting patterns of the

Supreme Soviet. The 12 April 1994 monetary union with Russia was simply a further stage along a consistent path. Indeed, Premier Kebich commented that "without union with Russia there would be no hope for Belarus" as both Russia and Belarus, he said, form one united economy.[29]

No greater supporter of Russia in the CIS could be found to rival Alyaksandr Lukashenka who campaigned against Shushkevich during Belarus's first presidential elections in July 1994. As presidential candidate, Lukashenka spoke to the Russian Duma and called for the reunification of Russia, Ukraine, and Belarus into a single state, and lambasted the creation of the CIS an error.[30] In the elections of July 1994 Lukashenka emerged with 80.1 percent of the vote—his nearest rival was Kebich with 14.1 percent. Lukashenka's electoral victory was rewarded by a Russian credit of 750–800 billion rubles for energy supplies.[31] His policy of leaning on Moscow was strongly criticized by Moscow's reformers as a substitute for market liberalization and economic reform. Nonetheless, despite the economic burden that Belarus represented, Moscow gained politically through its interest in economic integration that could influence the Ukraine to assume a more positive attitude toward the CIS. Further steps in Belarus's steady integration with Russia followed on 7 October 1994 when both agreed to coordinate border defenses.[32] The most significant step in this direction was taken on 14 May 1995 when Belarussians voted in a referendum in favor of four propositions: economic union with Russia; equal status for Russian as a Belarussian state language; the adoption of Soviet symbols and flag; and presidential power to dissolve Parliament.[33] Russia was to prepare a similar referendum to pave the way for eventual merger of the two countries in a confederation.

Moldova

As a country torn between ethnic affiliation with Romania and economic dependence on Russia, Moldova has reassessed the significance of the CIS. Sixty-five percent of a population of 4.4 million speak a language closely related to Romanian. In 1989, Russians constituted 13 percent and Ukrainians 14 percent of the population. When Moldova declared independence from the Soviet Union on 17 August 1991, the Popular Front for Moldova and the Christian Democratic Party campaigned for reunification with Romania. Romania regarded reunification as the rectification of a historical injustice perpetrated when tsarist Russia first prized Moldova, then called Bessarabia free of the Ottoman empire in 1812. Romania had annexed Bessarabia in 1918 but lost it again to the Soviet Union as a consequence of the 1939 Molotov-Ribbentrop Pact. Romanian leaders, including President Iona Ilescu, regarded reunification as inevitable and saw no basis for a separate Moldova. The reunification movement in Moldova, however, split the country ethnically. The predominantly Russian speaking area of Transdniester proclaimed an autonomous republic (TDR) on 2 September 1990 and threatened to secede entirely. The 150,000 Christian Turks in the South—the Gaugaz—similarly declared autonomy in August 1990.

Moldova was nearly destroyed in the ethnic conflict that followed in 1992 that demonstrated that its independent existence was conditional on its refusal to countenance reunification with Romania. Rutskoi traveled to the TDR capital of Tiraspol in April 1992 and declared his support for the Russian republic, which had threatened to declare independence entirely if Moldova joined Romania.[34] Violence flared in the city of Benderi over 19–23 June 1992 when Moldovan police moved in to restore authority. The TDR militia, with the aid of units from the Russian 14th Army deployed across the Dniester, resisted and counterattacked resulting in a reported 300–400 deaths. Rutskoi accused Moldovan President Mircea Snegur of attempting to impose Moldovan rule on the TDR while Yeltsin declared on 21 June that Russia would defend its own people.[35] Russia's Defense Ministry denied Moldovan accusations that it had ordered the 14th Army into action and claimed that its units had acted independently.[36] The Benderi clash was the occasion for the appointment of Major-General Aleksander Lebed' as commander of the 14th Army in July 1992. He declared the TDR part of Russia and rejected demands for the withdrawal of the 14th Army.[37]

The conflict demonstrated to Moldova the inherent dangers of reunification with Romania and the risk of war with Russian forces. Moldova was compelled to recognize Russia's geopolitical interests as an essential constraint on its own policies and was subsequently required to adjust its foreign policy orientation accordingly. Yeltsin and Snegur negotiated a cease-fire agreement on 21 July that made a provision for a ten kilometer cease-fire zone along the Dniester River and the introduction of peace-keeping forces from Russia, Moldova, and the TDR; the introduction of six battalions of Russian peace-keeping forces, plus three battalions of Moldovan forces and two battalions of TDR forces.[38] On 14 August, negotiations were conducted in Moscow over the future of the 14th Army that Moldova wanted withdrawn as its presence was incompatible with Moldovan sovereignty. The head of the Russian delegation, Deputy Defense Minister Boris Gromov, declared that the withdrawal of the 14th Army depended on general stability in Moldova, though at that stage the Russians agreed to a phased withdrawal over several months.[39] The Russian position hardened in response to the appeals of TDR leader Igor' Smirnov who continued to play the nationalist card. Aleksander Lebed', when promoted to Lt.-General, declared that the 14th Army was a guarantee of stability in Moldova and its withdrawal depended on the negotiation of an acceptable political status for the TDR.[40] It was unclear what that status would entail but the Russians seemed to demand federation while Moldova was reluctant to go beyond local autonomy.

Russia's position over this issue had been defined by local actors because of their ability to manipulate nationalist fears within Moscow to their own advantage. As Lebed' declared with characteristic forcefulness:

> While the status of this territory [TDR] is not defined, while peace will not be guaranteed at the international level we will not leave. So all think and I share these views. Politicians may consider this or not but there is this factor. If the existing problems are not solved there the nation will not permit the army to withdraw.[41]

Chairman of the Moldovan Parliament Alexandru Mosanu pointed to imperialist circles within Moscow as Moldova's real enemy and spoke against Moldova's membership to the CIS, calling for closer cooperation with Romania.[42] Nonetheless, President Snegur opposed reunification with Romania in a speech to Parliament in January 1993. Snegur cited Moldova's ethnic heterogeneity and the geopolitical interests of external powers as essential restrictions and called for the suspension of all talk of reunification.

The Moldovan economy was highly integrated with the Soviet system and was dependent on the CIS for 97 percent of its energy supplies and 90 percent of its raw materials. By 1994, after the country had experienced ethnic conflict and the effects of economic deterioration, Moldova was ready to join the CIS. As a consequence of the parliamentary elections of 27 February 1994, a majority was formed in favor of CIS membership. Proponents of the CIS were the Agrarian Democrats who won 56 of the 104 seats in the new legislature and who regarded Russia as a market for Moldovan agricultural products. In addition, the leftist bloc, the Socialists and the Russian Party *Yedinstvo* (unity), which had also called for stronger ties with Russia, won a total of 28 seats. The Popular Front, which had campaigned for reunification with Romania, faced declining support and won nine seats in Parliament. It boasted around 50 percent of the deputies in the old Supreme Soviet when the last elections were held in 1990.[43] Moldova's entry into the CIS, which was formalized during the April 1994 CIS summit, followed this change of attitude.

Support for reunification with Romania steadily declined within Moldova. A survey undertaken by the Moldovan Academy of Sciences and first published on 7 September 1994, discovered that in 1992 9.4 percent of those interviewed favored reunification, in 1993 the figure was 7.7 percent, while in 1994 it had dropped to 5.6 percent.[44] Many Moldovans apparently saw Romania as plagued by economic difficulties and perceived no economic benefits in reunification. Moldovan-Romanian relations deteriorated after this rejection and Romanian leaders found it difficult to accept Moldovan independence and continued to refer to Moldova as a Romanian state. Relations between Moldova and Romania were deadlocked under the negotiation of a bilateral treaty while Romania insisted on the formula two Romanian states, one nation.[45] Difficulties in the relationship with Romania will be another factor pushing Moldova toward the CIS. If it were possible to reach a solution with Russia over the TDR and the withdrawal of the 14th Army, the friction with Romania would be an assurance of better relations between Moldova and the CIS.

Agreement was reached between Russia and Moldova over the future of the 14th Army during the tenth round of negotiations on 10 August 1994 when its withdrawal was linked to the granting of status to the TDR. Though the details were not made public, Russia and Moldova signed a withdrawal agreement on 21 October 1994. It was unclear what kind of status was being given to the TDR given that the Moldovans had opposed federation of their state.[46] Moscow, it seems, was prepared to allow the situation to stabilize naturally without resolving the intractable problem of the status of the TDR. Moreover, the withdrawal of the 14th Army proved to be a politically difficult operation since it involved the removal of Aleksander Lebed'. This eventually occurred when the general resigned his command in June 1995 and moved into politics.

CAUCASIAN CIS

The Caucasian CIS comprises Armenia, Georgia, and Azerbaijan and is situated in a regional crossroads that has been the scene of past rivalry between Russia and the Islamic World, and between Islamic powers—Turkey and Iran. Armenia and Georgia have been Christian outposts along the frontier with Islam and have turned toward Russia for protection in the past. Armenia has been a staunch ally of Moscow since independence due to its conflict with Azerbaijan. Georgia became an ally once again as a consequence of the experience of ethnic separatism and Russian pressure. Azerbaijan, initially avoiding the CIS, subsequently affirmed its membership in recognition of Moscow's role in the Caucasus.

Armenia

Christian Armenia has regarded itself as a country besieged by Islamic neighbors and has historically turned toward Russia for protection against Turkey. More recently, Armenia's role as an ally of Moscow has arisen from the Nagorno-Karabakh dispute that pits Armenians against Azerbaijanis (whom the Armenians regard as Turks). The Nagorno-Karabakh area is predominantly Armenian but has been ruled by Azerbaijan formally since July 1993. Conflict with Azerbaijan over the issue erupted on 20 February 1988 when the Armenians of Nagorno-Karabakh called for self-determination and merger with Armenia. With the collapse of the Soviet Union, Nagorno-Karabakh declared independence in January 1992 and prompted Armenia into military action in support. For Armenians, the conflict stimulated fears of extinction that cast the issue in terms of cultural and racial survival.[47]

Armenian dependence on Russia was confirmed by the Turkish blockade imposed in 1991, which limited the transit of supplies by railway from Turkey to food supplies only. Armenia was reliant on the Russian gas pipeline that went through Georgia for its energy supplies, though the Georgians availed themselves of Armenian gas.[48] Armenia either seized Soviet military stores or was given military equipment by Soviet commanders sympathetic to the Armenian cause. The Armenian offensive against Azerbaijan of June 1992 was spearheaded by armor and equipment obtained from the former Soviet 15th and 164th motorized divisions. This was sufficient to form three motorized brigades with artillery and anti-air support.[49] Subject to Azerbaijani counterattacks, Armenian President Levon Ter Petrosyan called on the CIS for support and Moscow stepped in as a mediator to negotiate a cease-fire agreement on 3 September 1992, one among many that was subsequently disavowed. Nonetheless, Levon Ter Petrosyan declared that he was pleased with the development of relations with Moscow and that all political forces in Armenia were supportive of relations with Russia.[50] First premier of independent Armenia Vazgen Manukyan declared that Russia was regarded as the ultimate guarantor of Armenia's survival.[51] Russia, at least shared Armenia's concern in regard to Turkish domination of the Caucasus as the basis for a longterm alliance between them.

The impact of the Turkish factor on Russian-Armenian relations was evident in 1992 when the Russians feared Turkish involvement in the Nagorno-Karabakh conflict. On 9 May, Azerbaijani forces seized the town of Shushi that was strategically located on the corridor connecting Nagorno-Karabakh with Armenia. It seemed that Azerbaijan would establish a blockade around Nagorno-Karabakh and isolate it from Armenia. The Armenians counter-attacked at several points and on 20 May the Turkish commander declared a state of alert along the border with Azerbaijan (at the Nakhichevan enclave), which Armenian forces were threatening. Within Turkey there were calls for Turkish involvement in support of Azerbaijan causing the Russians to react with alarm. Yevgennii Shaposhnikov declared that the danger of war would arise if Turkey were involved.[52] Nonetheless, on 26 May, Russia and Turkey issued a joint statement appealing for an end to the use of force and the seizure of territory, and called for a resolution of the conflict by political means.

On the one hand, traditional rivalry with Turkey over the Caucasian region compelled Russia to maintain a position in the area and to cultivate Armenia as an ally. On the other hand, Russia had interests that went beyond Armenia and that limited its support for Armenian objectives in the Nagorno-Karabakh war. Russia also wanted to involve Azerbaijan in the CIS, and indeed, unmitigated Russian support for Armenia would strengthen the Azerbaijan-Turkish connection thereby impairing Russia's position in the Caucasus. Moscow's interests demanded a balanced position between Armenia and Azerbaijan with the longterm objective of bringing both under Russian influence within the CIS. For this reason, Russia's Foreign Ministry criticized Armenian seizure of territory in May 1992 as annexationist.[53] Russia moved to mediate between the warring sides, beginning with the abortive cease-fire of September 1992. Defense Minister Pavel Grachev negotiated the Sochi cease-fire agreement of 9 April 1993 with Armenian and Azerbaijani defense ministers, and similar agreements were negotiated in February 1994 and on 16 May 1994.

Despite Russian efforts, however, no resolution of the issue seemed possible while Armenia insisted on recognition of Nagorno-Karabakh as a partner in the negotiations. Azerbaijan refused to acknowledge Nagorno-Karabakh as anything other than a part of its own territory and demanded a withdrawal of Armenian forces from all occupied Azerbaijani territory. Negotiations continued with the Russians calling for the introduction of CIS peace-keeping forces, which would be one-third Russian. The Azerbaijanis requested that Turkish peace-keepers be involved, while President Ter Petrosyan declared that only Russian peace-keepers could ensure the stability of the area. Armenia with Russia's endorsement rejected any Turkish involvement in peace-keeping operations.[54]

Russia accordingly presses for a negotiated solution over the Nagorno-Karabakh dispute while maintaining Armenia as an ally. The two may be incompatible. Russian support for Armenia makes compromise less likely in the dispute with Azerbaijan and ensures that the Armenians will continue to pursue a military solution. That may be the longterm result of the Russian efforts to strengthen the alliance with Armenia in 1994. Pavel Grachev visited Yerevan from 8–10 June 1994 and came to an agreement with President Ter Petrosyan for the establishment of Russian bases in Armenia in Yerevan and Gyumri. Russia was to pay no rent for 25 years and reports claim that Armenia wanted a greater Russian military presence as a means of breaking the Turkish blockade. Grachev's intention was to locate rapid reaction forces in Armenian bases as part of an expanded Caucasian military defense system. Armenia also accepted a role in the CIS Air Defense System that the Russian side had been promoting.[55] Grachev declared that Russia and Armenia shared the same strategic space and announced that a total of five bases would be established as Russia's defense line in the Caucasus—the two bases in Armenia would be supplemented by an additional three in Georgia.[56] Vladimir Shumeiko, Speaker of the Federal Assembly's Upper House, declared that Russia's relationship with Armenia was closer than with any other former Soviet state. He claimed it was too early to propose a Russian-Armenian confederation, though the idea had been suggested by the Russians.[57]

Georgia

Georgia has emerged as another Caucasian ally of Russia after a troubled start to its independence when it came close to disintegration. Historically, Russia has acted as a guarantor of Georgian territorial integrity against Islamic power in the Caucasus. Georgia's Erekle II negotiated an agreement with Catherine the Great in July 1783 according to which Georgia became a Russian vassal state in return for Russian protection against encroaching Iran. At that time, Russia failed to act against the Iranian ruler Agha Mohammed Khan Qatar but later, by engaging in military campaigns against Iran and Turkey, Russia ensured Georgia's survival. The price, however, was incorporation into the Russian empire and subjection to Russification and forced assimilation under Tsar Aleksander III (1881–1894).

Georgia collapsed as a state after independence was attained in 1992. Zviad Gamsakhurdia came to power in May 1991 on the crest of a populist reaction against Soviet intervention into Tbilisi in April 1989 to suppress a local revolt. An admirer of Stalin, Gamsakhurdia attempted to impose a centralized state and Georgian control on the many minorities of Georgia. The result was the eruption of three conflicts—with the Ossetians, the Mingrelians, and the Abkhazians—and the consequent collapse of state authority internally. In this situation Georgia had no interest in the CIS, while nationalist opinion blamed Moscow for the interventions of 1989. Gamsakhurdia, in any case, was overthrown on 6 January 1992 by leaders of the National Guard, Tengiz Kitovani, and Dzhaba Ioseliani, and escaped with his followers, eventually to commit suicide.

Russia became deeply involved in Georgian affairs as the Russian military supported local separatists against a Tbilisi regime that was hostile toward Moscow. Georgia's recognition of its status as ally of Moscow was a product of the experience of separatism manipulated and encouraged by the Russian military. In Tbilisi it was understood that Georgia survived on the basis of Moscow's sufferance. Russia emerged as the champion of minority rights to control Georgia and to ensure a role for itself in the central and western Caucasus as an arbitrator of events. Georgia's status as a Russian ally was a product of manipulation and coercion. It was understood within Tbilisi that there were few options.

Russia supported South Ossetia against the Georgian National Guard when its Supreme Soviet accused Georgia of genocide and called on Moscow for protection. A referendum was conducted in South Ossetia on 19 January 1992 with the majority calling for autonomy within Russia and union with North Ossetia, which was part of the Russian federation.[58] The conflict that had been provoked while Gamsakhurdia was in power was conducted between the Georgian National Guard and Ossetian units. Speaker of the South Ossetian Supreme Soviet Torez Kolembekov appealed to Russia to dispatch a contingent of forces as protection. On 24 June, Yeltsin and new Georgian leader Eduard Shevardnadze agreed to a cease-fire in South Ossetia, an agreement that included representatives of both North and South Ossetia. Some 300 Russian peace-keeping forces entered South Ossetia on 14 July as part of a combined force which included a company from North Ossetia and a battalion from Georgia. The Russian forces, under the command of Col.-General Valerii Patrikeyev, remained until 20 August.[59] Russia defused the conflict in South Ossetia and thereby established its necessity for Georgian stability in a way that clearly demonstrated the fragility of Georgian statehood.

The extent to which Georgia became dependent on Russia was illustrated by the case of Abkhazia in Western Georgia. Conflict erupted when Defense Minister Tengiz Kitovani despatched troops to Abkhazia to enforce Georgian rule on 14 August 1992. The Abkhazi Supreme Soviet turned toward Russia to support its claim for independence and a crisis in Russian-Georgian relations followed. Premier Tengiz Sigua accused Russia of instigating conflict by arming the Abkhazi, and Shevardnadze claimed that the Russian Supreme Soviet goaded the Abkhazi into conflict with Tbilisi.[60] Russia had been conducting negotiations with Georgia over a treaty under which Russian forces would be deployed in Georgia as part of the Caucasian military district.[61] As a consequence of Russian intervention into Abkhazia, Georgia's Parliament reacted against Moscow and declared that negotiations on the treaty would continue only after Georgian demands concerning Abkhazia had been met.[62] As a reaction to the above the Abkhazi Supreme Soviet declared a willingness to sign a status of forces agreement with Russia and declared that Georgian insistence on the removal of Russian forces was interference into the affairs of a sovereign republic.[63]

The Russian role in the Abkhazi revolt against Georgia is still somewhat obscure. Russian forces were introduced into Abkhazia in September 1992 and comprised two assault units under the direct command of the Defense Ministry in Moscow, not the Caucasian military district. Emboldened by the Russians, Abkhazia demanded the complete withdrawal of Georgian forces while the Georgians refused to withdraw from what it regarded as its own territory. The Abkhazi attack on Sukhumi on 17–18 March 1993 convinced the Georgians that the Russians were directly involved in the conflict. The Georgians claimed that the SU-25 aircraft that had been shot down after attacking their positions was Russian. On 19 March, the Georgian Parliament issued an appeal to the UN and the world accusing Russia of conducting an aggressive policy toward Georgia.[64] Similarly, in April and over 1–2 July, when Abkhazi attacks on Sukhumi were renewed, the Georgians claimed that MI-24 helicopters, SU-25s and some 500 Russian advisors were involved on the Abkhazi side. Several Russian captives were shown to Western military attachés and CSCE representatives.[65] Abkhazia had received heavy equipment from the Russian military but it was unclear whether this was part of Russia's strategy or whether local commanders were simply selling weapons. The Abkhazi admitted that Russian volunteers fought on their side alongside others from the north Caucasus and Turks from the U.S. and Germany.[66]

Russia pursued various interests in supporting the Abkhazi revolt against Georgia. On 23 February 1993, Pavel Grachev expressed the Russian military's interest in the Black Sea coastline that would be ensured if Russia were to maintain influence over Abkhazia.[67] Deputy Premier Sergei Shakhrai declared that Russia acted as a guarantor of stability in the region by ensuring Abkhazian autonomy and simultaneously protecting Georgian territorial integrity. Shakhrai pointed to a Russian interest in manipulating conflicts to ensure a position of influence.[68] Russia, accordingly, utilized the conflict to push Georgia into a renewal of the negotiations over the military relationship. In November 1992, a Russian delegation arrived in Tbilisi with the intention of concluding various agreements: a treaty of friendship and collaboration; a treaty on the status of Russian forces in Georgia that comprised 12 motorized divisions; a similar treaty governing the presence of Russian border forces; and an agreement over rail transport.[69]

Negotiations continued through 1993 on the treaty governing the status of Russian forces. Georgia insisted on a timetable for their withdrawal with the deadline set at 31 December 1995 while the Russians hoped to obtain an agreement that would ensure their retention for a longer period. Details under negotiation included the use of camps, air fields, Russian military assistance, and the training of officers as well as legal jurisdiction over Russian forces.[70] Shevardnadze, who had been elected chairman of Parliament and head of state in October 1992, declared that Georgia could not protect its own frontier with Turkey and was agreeable to a continuation of the current situation in which Russian border forces would patrol the area.[71] Throughout 1993 Shevardnadze continued to balance between the radical nationalists, who wanted a Russian withdrawal of forces from Georgia, and the Social Democrats who were more receptive to a Russian presence. Opinion within Georgia's Parliament eventually backed Russia, and on 22 October 1993 Shevardnadze accepted Georgia's membership to the CIS. By then, the security situation in Georgia had deteriorated further and an alliance with Russia was seen as a matter of survival.[72]

Subsequently, on 3 February 1994, Russia and Georgia concluded a treaty intended to govern their security relationship over the next ten years. Russia declared its interest in the territorial integrity of Georgia but Yeltsin called for a special status for both Abkhazia and South Ossetia in a new Georgian constitution. Russia was to assist with the training and development of the Georgian armed forces and had obtained the right to use three new military bases on Georgian soil—at Batumi, Akhalkalaki, and Vaziani.[73] Shevardnadze explained that Georgia had no alternative but to seek Russian support and protection. Georgia, he declared, had a ruined economy and the Tbilisi government was hardly in control of the country. He stated that with the assistance of Russia he hoped to restore control over Georgia and when criticized for assisting the rebirth of the Russian empire retorted that he was attempting to prevent it.[74]

The Georgian leader had attempted to avoid this dependence on Russia by involving the UN in peace-keeping and peace-enforcing activity but admitted his disappointment. Shevardnadze came to the unpalatable conclusion for Georgia's nationalists that without Moscow's help Georgia would not be able to overcome new outbreaks of conflict.[75] Georgia had ceased to exist as a functioning state as a result of five years of internal strife. Mingrelia and West Georgia were under opposition control, the southern Armenian regions had their own armies, and the Azerbaijani areas were virtually independent. Population centers had their own militias as defense against marauding bandits and the political parties had similarly created security forces for their own protection.[76] It was the chairman of the Russian Duma's CIS Committee, Konstantin Zatulin, who claimed that Russia had confirmed Georgia's territorial integrity at a time when it had collapsed. In Zatulin's view, Russia had saved Georgia.[77]

Azerbaijan

President Ayaz Mutalibov signed the Alma Ata Agreement of 21 December 1991, bringing Azerbaijan into the CIS. Without the endorsement of the Milli Mejlis or parliament while it was dominated by the Nationalist People's Front. Turkic speaking and Islamic Azerbaijan attempted to shrug off any association with the CIS, and its leaders at first sought to develop alternative relations, above all with Turkey. The attempted reorientation of Azerbaijan away from Russia, and the north toward Turkey and the Islamic south, however, was fraught with difficulties. Russia was particularly concerned about the development of Azerbaijani-Turkish relations, fearing that its position in the Caucasus would be undermined. While Azerbaijan was heavily engaged in a war with Armenia over Nagorno-Karabakh Russia could exert pressure on its in the effort to induce a readjustment of attitude. A new leadership under Heider Aliev realized that Azerbaijan could not afford to alienate Russia and ratified the Alma Ata Agreement as a result. Nonetheless, Azerbaijan's relationship with Russia could never be close and the CIS was simply a means of defusing potential conflict, and not necessarily a path toward integration with Russia[78]

Azerbaijani-Turkish relations became a critical factor in Azerbaijani-Russian relations in a linkage that Azerbaijani leaders could not avoid. As a major oil producer, Azerbaijan has not been as dependent on Russian energy supplies as the Ukraine and Moldova, but over 50 percent of its gas supplies were imported from Russia and Turkmenistan. Azerbaijan previously was the Soviet Union's center for oil equipment manufacturing but has attempted to diversify outlets for its products by developing business ties with Turkey. Reduced economic dependency on Moscow and expectations of alternative markets gave the Azerbaijani leadership the confidence to implement the desired reorientation of policy that was, with hindsight, somewhat misplaced. Mutalibov soured his relationship with Yeltsin by supporting the August 1991 Moscow coup and continued to irritate the Russians by developing relations with Turkey. He visited Ankara in January 1992 and declared that Turkey may have a mediatory role in the Nagorno-Karabakh dispute agreeing to send cadets to Turkish military academies for training.[79] Mutalibov was later forced out of office as a consequence of various events, including losses in the Nagorno-Karabakh conflict. Far more critical for relations with Moscow was the election of popular front leader Abulfaz Elchibei as president in June 1992.

Described as an uncomplicated and open person, Elchibei genuinely believed that he could link Azerbaijan more closely with Turkey. He claimed that the renaissance of Azerbaijan was a matter of returning to its Turkic roots and that it was only natural that Turkey would be an important factor in Azerbaijan's foreign policy. Elchibei also announced his opposition to Azerbaijan's membership in the CIS[80] and demanded the withdrawal of the remaining Russian forces, the 366th Motorized Regiment, which remained in Azerbaijan after independence. Mutalibov clashed with Yevgennii Shaposhnikov over the presence of these forces in Azerbaijan during the Minsk CIS meeting in February 1992 in what was described as a heated discussion.[81] Under Elchibei, an agreement was reached in October 1992 for their removal by 31 August 1993.[82]

Elchibei's policies exacerbated relations with Iran as well, demonstrating that the Islamic World was divided and that popular Russian and Western notions about Islamic unity were fallacious. Elchibei accused Iran of abusing the rights of the Azerbaijani population of northern Iran that numbered around 20 million, more than double the 7.5 million population of Azerbaijan. Despite the fact that Azerbaijanis shared a common Shiite Islamic heritage with Iran, the ethnic factor as exacerbated by Elchibei proved to be more significant than religious affinity for relations with that country. Elchibei's pro-Turkish orientation was an additional factor causing strain in relations with Iran that prompted the development of Iranian relations with Armenia. Armenia sought deliveries of Iranian natural gas to break the blockade imposed by Azerbaijan and Turkey.[83] Protracted negotiations came to fruition when Armenian Prime Minister Hrant Bagratyan visited Teheran in May 1995. Bagratyan signed an agreement under which Iran was to supply Armenia with electricity and natural gas over a 20-year period through a pipeline that was yet to be constructed.[84]

Elchibei's policy of building bridges with Turkey resulted in tensions with both Russia and Iran. Without compensatory support from Turkey, Azerbaijan came under increasing pressure from Russia over the Nagorno-Karabakh dispute. Turkey could not come to Azerbaijan's assistance over this dispute without aggravating relations with Moscow. Turkey's President Suleiman Demirel was a supporter of closer relations with Moscow in view of the Kurdish card, which both Russia and Armenia could play. Turkish leaders remained concerned over Armenia's harboring of separatist Kurdish elements and the ties that developed between the Armenian Nagorno-Karabakh leadership and the Kurdish Workers Party.[85] Various Kurdish movements have appeared in Moscow with official sanction, including the National Liberation Front of Kurdistan formed early in 1994, and the Confederation of Kurds of the CIS formed on 1 November 1994 with the support of Russia's Foreign Ministry.[86]

In early 1993, Azerbaijan faced greater Russian pressure through the Nagorno-Karabakh conflict. Azerbaijan's Foreign Ministry claimed that Armenian offensives were being assisted by Russian servicemen from the 7th Army in Armenia. In the Milli Mejlis, Elchibei declared that the Russian military gave Azerbaijan an ultimatum to accept the continued presence of

Russian forces. Azerbaijani rejection, said Elchibei, resulted in the participation of 7th Army units in the Armenian attacks in northern Karabakh.[87] In September 1992, six Russian servicemen were captured by Azerbaijanis and tried as mercenaries in April 1993. They were *spetznatz* members assigned to the 7th Army in Armenia and may have been given specific missions against Azerbaijani forces.[88] Grachev, however, at a press conference on 17 May claimed that they were deserters.[89] The issue of Russian involvement in these Armenian offensives was not satisfactorily resolved, though suspicions remain strong. In any case, Elchibei admitted that Armenian forces had occupied more Azerbaijani territory and that the loss of Kel'badzhar was a great defeat for Azerbaijan. Elchibei blamed the defeat on the passivity of other countries—the U.S., Britain, and Russia.[90]

Elchibei could not survive the defeats and was toppled in a coup on 17 June 1993, and formally removed from power by referendum on 28 August. His rival and successor Heidar Aliev was once First Secretary of the Azerbaijani Communist Party, then Soviet First Deputy Premier, and later a member of the Soviet politburo from November 1982. Aliev returned to Azerbaijan and immediately after the August 1991 attempted coup in Moscow was elected chairman of the Mejlis of the Nakhichevan enclave that shares a 137 kilometer border with Iran. Aliev found himself in conflict with the National Front based in Baku that he claimed attempted to destabilize him.[91] He neither shared the National Front's hostility toward Russia nor Elchibei's indifference toward Iran in recognition that both countries were significant for Azerbaijan's position. As Aliev maneuvred Elchibei out of power, he rectified one key omission by having Azerbaijan's membership to the CIS ratified on 20 September 1993 despite being strongly criticized domestically for taking Azerbaijan back into the Russian orbit.[92]

Despite the domestic criticisms that he was conducting a pro-Russian policy, Aliev was simply removing the sources of needless conflict with powers that Azerbaijan could not afford to offend. Aliev moved to develop balanced relations with both Russia and Iran in recognition of their historical role as arbiters of the Caucasus. Azerbaijan had little alternative but to acknowledge Russia's role in the Caucasus in terms of an ability to influence the outcome of the Nagorno-Karabakh conflict. Rather than dismissing Moscow as Elchibei had attempted to do, it made better strategic sense to engage Russia and convince Moscow's rulers that Azerbaijan offered greater benefits than Armenia. Azerbaijani Vice Premier Abbas Abbasov thought that Russia could consider Azerbaijan a bridge to Turkey and Iran, or Russia's window into the Islamic World.[93] Aliev avoided giving Turkey a special position in his statements on foreign policy and stressed the idea of harmonious relationships with all neighbors. Iranian President Rafsanjani visited Baku in October 1993 and reactivated a relationship that had deteriorated under Elchibei.[94] Aliev returned the visit in July 1994 hoping to prevent further collaboration between Iran and Armenia.[95]

Tension remained in Russian-Azerbaijani relations that were inherent in Aliev's attempts to retain a balance. Moscow wanted to integrate Azerbaijan more closely into the CIS security and defense system, which Azerbaijan resisted. On 8 October 1993, Aliev rejected the Russian proposal for the deployment of Russian border forces along the Azerbaijani-Iranian frontier in view of Iranian objections.[96] In August 1994, Commander of Russian Border Forces General Andrei Nikolaev pressed Aliev to cooperate with the CIS over this issue, but the Azerbaijani leader had previously promised Iranian Foreign Minister Ali Akba Velayati that Russian forces would not return to the Iranian frontier.[97] While Azerbaijan resisted Moscow over this issue it could never be assured of Russian support over the Nagorno-Karabakh conflict that continued without resolution.

Azerbaijan obtained no appreciable benefits from membership to the CIS in relation to the Nagorno-Karabakh dispute. Russian Defense Minister Pavel Grachev attempted to negotiate a cease-fire with his Armenian and Azerbaijani counterparts on 10 February 1994 and later in May. Russia's Vladimir Shumeiko insisted on 28 April that the Karabakh side be involved in the negotiations as a third party, which demonstrated that Russia had not moderated its support for Armenia.[98] Armenia established control over much of the frontier with Iran and attacks continued in 1994. Azerbaijani units withdrew into Iran and there were reports in November 1993 of Armenian artillery fire on Iranian villages.[99] Because of an unfavorable military position, Azerbaijan reduced its previous demands and from 4–5 May 1994 agreed to accept Nagorno-Karabakh as a party in negotiations only for the purpose of the peace plan. This concession was subsequently attacked as an act of betrayal by the opposition within the Milli Mejlis.[100] At the CIS summit of 15 April 1994, Aliev found the Russians promoting a peace plan for Nagorno-Karabakh that entailed the introduction of Russian peace-keeping forces, which he opposed.[101] Aliev appealed for external support over this conflict from the CSCE and the UN in the realization that Russia was no more willing to push Armenia into a resolution of the dispute than previously. He called on the CSCE Minsk group to provide peace-keeping forces, with no single state providing more than 30 percent of the total contingent.[102] In an address to the UN General Assembly on 29 September 1994, Aliev called on the world body to compel the withdrawal of Armenian forces from Azerbaijani territory.[103]

There was, however, another dispute between Russia and Azerbaijan that was linked with the Nagorno-Karabakh conflict. On 20 September 1994, Azerbaijan signed an agreement with a Western consortium of companies to develop three oil fields on the Caspian Sea shelf. The agreement involved an $8 billion investment over 30 years in the development of these fields and included the Russian oil company, Lukoil, which was awarded a 10 percent stake.[104] In his address to the UN nine days later, Aliev revealed his motives other than economic in concluding the deal. He declared that the oil contract could only be realized if the world community would take a more active role in restoring peace in the area.[105] Whether or not world community support could be mobilized for a resolution of the Nagorno-Karabakh conflict was an open question. Nonetheless, the declaration indicated the extent to which Aliev had become disillusioned with the Russians.

The oil deal promised new clashes with Moscow as the Russian Foreign Ministry declared its opposition to the deal because the Caspian Sea is a lake and not a sea. Its resources were, accordingly, the common property of the five littoral states: Russia, Azerbaijan, Kazakhstan, Turkmenistan, and Iran.[106] The Foreign Ministry argued that the oil deal contravened two treaties concluded with Iran on 26 February 1921 and 25 March 1940. The first treaty, however, related to Iran's right to maintain naval vessels on the Caspian Sea while the latter governed the issue of sea passage. Neither could be construed as regulating Caspian Sea resources. Russian Premier Viktor Chernomyrdin had no objections to the deal and conveyed his support to Aliev during the CIS summit of 21 October 1994. Yeltsin, however, supported his Foreign Ministry and had previously circulated a memorandum dated 21 July that included the possibility of sanctions against Azerbaijan.[107]

Azerbaijan's role in the CIS integrative process is somewhat minimal. Having little interest in closer economic ties with Russia, Azerbaijan regards the CIS in terms of conflict prevention and management strategy to reduce the risk of alienating Russia. Azerbaijan's formal membership to the CIS has not altered Russia's role over the Nagorno-Karabakh dispute and relations with Moscow generally remain strained. Moscow attempts to integrate Azerbaijan into its Caucasian security system; this would entail a reorientation toward Russia that would be domestically unacceptable. Russia may utilize further pressure over the Nagorno-Karabakh conflict to induce Azerbaijan to accept Moscow's demands for a security relationship of the kind concluded with Armenia and Georgia. However, Moscow cannot go to excessive lengths in pressing Azerbaijan over this issue without destabilizing the area and drawing in Turkey or Iran, the very powers it seeks to exclude.

CENTRAL ASIAN CIS

Over the past three years, Central Asia has stimulated much debate within Moscow between the proponents of involvement and the advocates of disengagement. Moscow's radical democrats have called for a withdrawal from the region on the basis that a Russian position there is the legacy of the colonial past that is incompatible with Russia as a democracy. The radical democrats regard the colonial expansionism of the tsarist period as having contributed to autocracy within Russia and see a similar parallel today. Moscow supports authoritarian regimes in Central Asia in the name of stability which, according to the democrats, have an impact on Russian attitudes toward democracy within Russia. Until Moscow successfully completes the process of decolonization, which was initiated with the collapse of the Soviet Union, the development of democracy within Russia will be hindered and perhaps obstructed. Nonetheless, Moscow's democrats and others who profess indifference toward Central Asia are outweighed by those who argue for continued involvement for geopolitical reasons.

Vladimir Lukin claimed that Russia can assume a critical stabilizing role in Central Asia and saw no basis for Russia other than forward engagement. In Lukin's view the strategic task for Russia was to prevent the struggle for influence in the area on the part of Turkey, Iran, Afghanistan, Pakistan, and China, and to avoid destabilizing consequences.[108] The Council of Foreign and Defense Policy identified Central Asia as a zone of instability into which Islamic fundamentalism may spread.[109] The proponent of Russian activism Andranik Migranyan, claimed that there was the danger of Turkish influence in Central Asia and that Russia needed to maintain the balance of power against Turkey by supporting Iran and Armenia.[110] Giving a military view Colonel S. Pechorov identified Russia's interests in Central Asia in terms of countering fundamentalist Islam and preventing ballistic missile proliferation among Islamic states that could be hostile to Russia.[111] Colonel Mustafin claimed that there was the danger of the emergence of an arc of conflict in the Islamic World from former Yugoslavia, the Caucasus, and along the belly band of the CIS or Central Asia.[112]

The idea of the threat from the Islamic south tended to dominate discussions about Central Asia that was designated the "near Islamic abroad" (blizhn'ee islamskie zarubezh'e).[113] A widespread view was that the major trend of the 1990s would be the rise of Islamic fundamentalism in Central Asia. This justified the articulation of a Russian version of the domino theory—if Tajikistan was overthrown the rest of Central Asia would follow.[114] The domino theory was endorsed by Deputy Foreign Minister Georgi Kunadze who, though trained as a Japan expert, had assumed responsibility for the Central Asian region after the Foreign Ministry's Japan fiasco. Kunadze declared that it was in Russia's interest to maintain stability in Central Asia, to prevent Islamic extremist penetration of the region, and to protect the Russian language speakers there.[115] There were, however, alternative views of Central Asia and Russia's role within it that avoided the idea of conflict or confrontation inherent in the identification of Islam as a source of threat.

Director of the Institute of Africa Aleksei Vasil'ev argued that Russia is inside the Islamic World and cannot turn against its own Islamic roots. Vasil'ev claimed that Islamic fundamentalism was no real danger for Russia and that the threats arise from ethnic, social, or economic instability. Vasil'ev added that Russia's role in the new world order depended on its relations with the Islamic World, which in his view should be seen as an ally.[116] These views were echoed by Aleksei Malashenko from the Institute of Oriental Studies who claimed that part of the Islamic World is in Russia, itself the home of 15 million Muslims. Malashenko feared that Russians were fated to become second class Europeans and argued a case for greater attention to be given to the Islamic World.[117] Former Justice Minister Nikolai Fyodorov asserted that Islam is not foreign to Russia but an important element of Russian cultural life. Russia, he claimed, could not confront Islam without going against part of its own history. Fyodorov argued against the tendency to equate Islam with fundamentalism, stating that true Islam was opposed to fundamentalism.[118] For this reason, the Russian Foreign Ministry, according to Malashenko, used the term extremism rather than fundamentalism.[119]

Three essential views struggled for a hearing within the prolonged and often confusing debate about Central Asia. First, those that called for engagement were concerned about the danger of instability stimulated by ethnic differences, socio-economic discrepancies, and Islamic fundamentalism. The military and members of Russia's security establishment have viewed Central Asia in these terms. The second view was disengagement whose proponents were a minority not represented in government, though the author has come across this view within the Federal Assembly. Third, there are those who counsel prudence and appeal for an understanding of the potential for collaboration with the Islamic World. The scholars and specialists who argue this way point to the very real danger of demonizing Islam if the essential distinctions between Islam and fundamentalism, ethnicity and religion are confused.

Moscow's approach toward Central Asia has been based on the idea of engagement with the attendant assumption that fundamentalist Islam represents a potential threat. This assumption results in an effort to mobilize the CIS behind the existing secular leaders of Central Asia, who for the most part are products of the Communist *nomenklatura*. Russia involves the CIS in supporting existing political structures with their social and economic inequalities, which has the effect of stimulating ethnic-based or religious-inspired opposition. The dangers of supporting the political status quo are well understood by those familiar with the region who argue that Russia's efforts should also embrace a longer-term process of social and economic change. In this sense, Russia and the CIS should not be limited to supporting existing political structures but should devise policies that accommodate ethnic or Islamic opposition groups as well. Those that argue this way have apparently little influence on policy. Moscow has acted to buttress the existing leadership through bilateral military and economic agreements under the CIS umbrella, which critics claim has contributed to the political polarization between government and Islamic opposition.

Central Asia represents Russia's salient security concern that is not necessarily shared by the rest of the CIS. The European and Caucasian CIS member have little interest in Central Asia and regard the area as a Russian problem. The other members of the CIS resent Russian efforts to involve the CIS as a group in Central Asian security and confront Russia with a dilemma. Russia cannot extend CIS security collaboration to Central Asia in any meaningful way without exacerbating this resentment and provoking further opposition against centralization. Moscow could avoid the problem by managing Central Asia outside the CIS framework but that would be an open admission of the irrelevance of CIS security cooperation for its greatest challenge. While Moscow holds fast to the vision of the CIS as the multilateral security vehicle for the "near abroad" it will continue with its efforts to involve it in the security of Central Asia. In reality, however, Moscow will act on a bilateral basis utilizing the CIS as ex post facto justification.

Kazakhstan

Nursultan Nazarbaev of Kazakhstan is Russia's most reliable ally in Central Asia and an advocate of greater unity within the CIS. The factors bearing on Nazarbaev's loyalty to Moscow are both demographic and geopolitical, which point to the fragility of Kazakhstan and its dependence on Russian goodwill. Kazakhstan shares an extensive border with Russia and has a sizeable Russian minority that, according to the 1989 Soviet census, constituted 6.2 million of a population of 16.5 million, or 38 percent; Kazakhs themselves were 40 percent of the population with Germans 5.8 percent, Ukrainians 5.4 percent and Uzbeks 2.0 percent. From 1989–1993, however, growing Kazakh nationalism has stimulated Russian emigration though figures reported vary considerably—from a high of 1.4 million to a net total of 350,000. The Russian minority as a percentage of total population may have dropped to 33 percent–36 percent by 1994. The Russians are located in the urban areas as well as in the northern regions where the Russian secessionist movement called LAD has its base.[120]

Russian resentments have been fueled by Nazarbaev's policy of promoting Kazakhs in government as part of a process of reverse discrimination. The Kazakh language has been made the language of administration, and Russians are under-represented in the national Parliament. Russian nationalists have called for the inclusion of the Russian-speaking areas of Kazakhstan into Russia and have described the present border as artificial. Before his return to Russia in July 1994, Aleksander Solzhenitsyn expressed the view that Russia's borders with Kazakhstan should be redrawn to include the predominantly Russian-speaking areas, which precipitated a nationalist outburst within Kazakhstan.[121] Nazarbaev has had to balance delicately between his Kazakh constituency and the Russian minority, and in many respects his pro-Moscow policies can be regarded as a necessary corollary of the Kazakhization of government. By declaring loyalty to Moscow, he may disarm the Russian nationalists and allow himself greater freedom to promote pro-Kazakh policies than he would otherwise. Nazarbaev's position has been made more difficult by the absence of unity within his own Kazakh constituency. Tribalism and clan politics are the realities of Central Asia in which nationalism has played a subordinate role. The Kazakhs are divided in three *orda* or tribal groupings that made it easier for the Russians to conquer them in the nineteenth century. The process of tribalization was accelerated by Kazakhstan's independence and the divisions between the west, the central/north east and the south *ordas* were entrenched. The south, in particular, is more strongly Islamised and includes an Uzbek minority, from which was drawn the *nomenklatura* of the Soviet years including Nazarbaev. Nazarbaev is also compelled to maintain equilibrium between the *orda* and cannot risk conflict with the Russian minority while the Kazakhs are divided.[122]

For Russia, Kazakhstan is seen as a buffer against southern Islamic influence that would otherwise reach Russia's borders and infiltrate its Muslim population. The debates in Moscow, in relation to Central Asia, assess Kazakhstan's strategic value for Russia in terms of a shield against fundamentalism in the south. Russia can not afford to destabilize Kazakhstan over issues that are properly regarded as domestic, such as the treatment of the Russian minority or the promotion of Kazakh nationalism. Nazarbaev, as one *Nezavisimaya gazeta* commentary put it, is a political gift for Russia.[123] Those who argue for a Russian withdrawal from Tajikistan still emphasize the importance of maintaining a position in Kazakhstan and converting its border with the rest of Central Asia into Russia's border with the Islamic World.[124] Aleksander Solzhenitsyn modified his ethnically-defined view of Russia's role in the CIS when he declared that Russia and Kazakhstan should jointly protect the border with the rest of the Islamic World.[125]

Nazarbaev has feared the emergence of nationalism or Slavic chauvinism in Russia that would result in the division of the CIS along cultural or civilizational lines. He orchestrated the negative Central Asian reaction to the Belovezhsk declaration of December 1991 when it seemed that Islamic Central Asia was to be excluded from an essentially Slavic post-Soviet grouping. Nazarbaev reminds Russia that it cannot define itself as a Slavic power and cannot define its relationships on the basis of a Slavic identity without undermining its position in Central Asia. A post-Soviet world divided according to racial or cultural groups would entail the disintegration of Kazakhstan and possible intercommunal conflict. Moreover, without a stable Kazakhstan, Moscow's southern borders with the Islamic World would be jeopardized and its security threatened.

To Western observers it may seem that Nazarbaev demeans himself by accepting the position of a vassal to Moscow. Yeltsin has unfortunately treated Nazarbaev as a competitor or a hindrance and has frequently angered his ally. Throughout 1992–1993 Russia and Kazakhstan declared their intention of preserving a common economic space including the use of the Russian ruble, and Nazarbaev emerged as the leading proponent of coordinated economic policies in the CIS. In September 1992, Russia and Kazakhstan concluded a bilateral economic agreement that included a provision for a clearing accounts system. Nazarbaev began to promote the idea of a coalition of ruble zone states in the CIS with supporting economic institutions.[126] Subsequently, however, Russia took resolute measures to terminate the ruble zone, compelling

Kazakhstan to issue its own currency (*tenge*) in November 1993. Nazarbaev was angered by this action and his relationship with Yeltsin was affected accordingly. Yeltsin's dismissal of his Eurasian union proposal was yet another disappointment, which was the reason why Nazarbaev did not attend the April 1994 CIS summit.

Nazarbaev's behaviour toward Russia is understood within Moscow as a Central Asian characteristic in which smaller powers are able to influence the actions of larger powers. Russians regard this behaviour as Asian in which the larger power is manipulated by professions of loyalty or vassal status. By declaring himself Moscow's loyal ally, Nazarbaev obtains freedom of action for himself not only domestically but in terms of foreign policy as well. Nazarbaev has accordingly claimed the freedom to promote the idea of Central Asian regionalism that was discussed by the five regional leaders when they met in Tashkent in January 1993. Moscow has been wary of Central Asian regionalism fearing that it may result in Russia's exclusion. At the Tashkent meeting various proposals were raised for economic cooperation and for an inter-republican coordinating council.[127] In July 1994, Central Asian leaders met again in the Kazakh capital of Alma Ata where a Central Asian economic union was proposed involving a regional bank to be located in Alma Ata.[128] Nazarbaev cleverly announced that the idea of a Central Asian economic union was part of the Eurasian union. Moreover, Nazarbaev was able to promote relations with Turkey without provoking Russian alarm about Turkish penetration of Central Asia. Nazarbaev attended the second Summit of Turkic Speaking Peoples that was held in Istanbul in October 1994. The meeting brought together four Central Asian leaders with the Azerbaijani President Aliev and Turkish President Suleiman Demirel. The conference proposed a great oil pipeline from Central Asia to Europe via Turkey following the old silk road. Nazarbaev responded to Russian concerns by claiming that cooperation among Turkic-speaking states would not conflict with the Eurasian union proposal.[129]

Perhaps there was no better example of Nazarbaev's skillful effort to expand ties with the outside world without provoking a Russian reaction, than in the case of the Chevron oil deal under negotiation since 1991. Chevron had developed an interest in Kazakhstan's Tengiz oil fields, and on 6 April 1993 signed an agreement with Nazarbaev that allowed it a 20 percent stake over a 40-year period. As oil production in the Tengiz fields is due to increase, new and more convenient pipeline outlets will have to be constructed. During his second visit to Washington in February 1994, Nazarbaev emerged as a critic of Russia and declared that he wanted a more reliable outlet than the present Russian pipeline that connects Kazakhstan's oil fields to Novorossyisk on the Black Sea. He said that he preferred a pipeline through the Persian Gulf or the Mediterranean, which would in effect exclude Russia.[130] To defend himself against Russian protests, Nazarbaev subsequently confirmed that Russia would be one of the parties in this project and that considering the volume of oil involved there may have to be several outlets. Nazarbaev affirmed that despite what the press says, Russia remains Kazakhstan's main partner, even while he was openly seeking alternatives.[131]

Tajikistan

Tajikistan has been in the throes of an agonizing and destructive civil war since 1991 when ethnic and clan conflicts, which were suppressed during the Soviet era, erupted. The conflict was essentially clan-based in that the northern Leninabad or Khojand group, in alliance with the southern Kulyab group, had maintained a hold on power and refused to share that power with other regional clans. The Leninabad region was the most developed area of Tajikistan drawing most of the investment and attention under the Soviet Union. It was, moreover, heavily populated with Uzbeks that added the danger of secessionism to the conflict. Tajikistan's president after the 27 November 1991 elections, Rakhmon Nabiev, was drawn from the north (as were all his predecessors). Under Russian pressure, a coalition government was established in May 1992 that included the opposition (the Democratic Party, the Islamic Renaissance Party, and Rastokhez). The northern group was unreconciled to the coalition government that provoked the outbreak of civil war. Conflict broke out between clan supporters of the government and opposition in the Kurgan and the Kulyarb regions, which was aggravated by the collapse of the Najibulah regime in Afghanistan in April 1992. Complicated linkages were established with Afghanistan as the Tajik opposition received much support from Gulbidden Hekmatyar's Mujahidin. Nabiev was forced out of office on 7 September 1992 and was replaced by Imamali Rakhmonov on 16 November as chairman of Parliament. Rakhmonov was formerly chairman of the Kulyab Oblast Executive Committee; his appointment signified the cementing of the Leninabad-Kulyab alliance and the consequent destructive escalation of civil war.[132]

Traditional tribal and clan conflicts were exacerbated by the Islamic-democrat opposition against the Communist *nomenklatura* in the north. The situation has been characterized in terms of a conflict between the old Communist forces, which were supported by Brezhnev's Soviet Union, and the new political wave that was a product of Gorbachev's *perestroika*.[133] The Democratic Party represents urban non-Communist intelligentsia, the Rastokhez movement appeals to Tajik nationalism and stands for a Persian Tajik identify while the Islamic Renaissance Party drew support from the southern Kurgan region which was more disposed toward fundamentalism. The picture was one of a complicated inter-clan conflict overlaid by broader political and religious movements that had emerged in this collapsed state. Nonetheless Nabiev, who represented a leadership that had been traditionally supported by Moscow, portrayed the conflict in terms of a struggle against fundamentalism in an attempt to ensure Moscow's continuing involvement.[134] Nabiev attempted to involve Russia's 201st motorized division, which had been deployed in Tajikistan since the Soviet era, in the civil war that his group had largely provoked.[135]

Russia's position in Tajikistan was based on a strategy of forward deployment that was intended to shield Tajikistan from the destabilizing influences of Afghanistan. On 21 July 1992, Russia concluded a border agreement with the Tajik government based in Dushanbe according to which Russian border forces would be deployed along the Tajik-Afghan and Tajik-Chinese borders.[136] Russian border guards were immediately involved in the attempt to interdict crossborder traffic, and over the period of 7 May to 10 September 1992 it was reported that seven border guards were killed.[137] On 6 November 1992, a second agreement with the Dushanbe government was concluded outlining the rules of engagement of the 201st motorized division. At the request of the Dushanbe government, the 201st division could support curfew measures, protect special buildings and installations, secure road transport, prevent the illegal transfer of weapons, and disarm terrorist and criminal groups. Russian forces were not to be involved directly in the civil war and were only to assist the Dushanbe government in extraordinary situations.[138] In practice, however, the distinction between the above contingencies and the civil war was nonexistent and Russian forces moved to support the Dushanbe government as a consequence of the overthrow of Nabiev in September. The poorly paid conscripts of the 201st division became part of the problem as reports circulated of Russian soldiers selling weapons and contraband from Afghanistan.[139]

Moscow became involved in the Tajik civil war as a consequence of its perceived need to maintain a forward position in Central Asia. The logic of the domino theory and a receptivity to the idea of Islamic fundamentalist penetration of the region led to the conviction that Russia's security was to be defended along the Tajik-Afghan border. Kozyrev declared that Russia could not withdraw from Tajikistan without creating a threat to Russian territory and its neighbors, and that the security of Russia's borders demanded political stability in Central Asia.[140] Nonetheless, significant differences emerged in the implementation of Russian policy with Kozyrev's Foreign Ministry calling for the creation of a state council (gos soviet) in Tajikistan as a temporary organ of power. This state council would include representatives of all regions in Tajikistan, the opposition as well as the Dushanbe government, and was in essence a proposal to revive the coalition government of May 1992.[141] The coalition collapsed because of the hostility of the Leninabad group and their Kulyab allies who opposed the idea of the state council. While the Foreign Ministry's concern with national reconciliation was blocked, Russia drifted toward closer military support of the Dushanbe government in a way promoted by the local Russian commanders, the military and, it seems, Yeltsin himself. Russia's security establishment was swayed by notions of fundamentalism that were disseminated by the Dushanbe government and the emphasis was placed on military support for the incumbent regime. On 25 May 1993, Russia concluded a military cooperation agreement with the Dushanbe government that strengthened Moscow's commitment to the regime. Rakhmonov declared that without Russian assistance Tajikistan would not exist and Yeltsin announced his intention to dispatch additional forces there, a move opposed by the Supreme Soviet.[142]

On 13 July 1992, some 20 to 25 Russian border guards were killed as an armed group of 200 men crossed the Pyandzh River that separates Afghanistan from Tajikistan. The incident itself signified no new escalation of conflict but provided Yeltsin with the justification to overcome Supreme Soviet resistance against an increase of forces in Tajikistan, and allowed his government to solicit CIS support for the Dushanbe government. At this point Deputy Foreign Minister Georgi Kunadze made public the idea of the domino theory. Declaring that Russia's borders should be protected as far from the north as possible, Kunadze outlined the strategic argument that it was easier to defend the 1,400 kilometer Tajik-Afghan border than the 6,000 kilometer Russian-Kazakh border. He claimed that there was no basis for a border between Kazakhstan and Kyrgystan or Uzbekistan in any case. Kunadze, however, identified the Foreign Ministry's reluctance to accept an open-ended commitment to the Dushanbe government, declaring that Russia's involvement would be dependent on its willingness to promote national reconciliation with the opposition. According to Kunadze, if the Dushanbe government refused to widen its social basis by involving the opposition clans Russia would withdraw.[143]

The idea of the domino theory, however, was not compatible with the willingness to withdraw since Kunadze had already declared that there was no other position to which Russia could withdraw. Andrei Kozyrev identified Russia's interests in Tajikistan as: protection of Russian language speakers—around 200,000, the maintenance of a shield against extremism and prevention of its spread to the north, and prevention of ballistic missile proliferation. Kozyrev emphasized that Russia was not just supporting the Communist regime in Dushanbe but was pushing for national reconciliation and dialogue between the various clan and ethnic groups. Russia, declared Kozyrev, would not compensate for the absence of political will in Tajikistan and would not fight Dushanbe's war. Soviet involvement in Afghanistan in the 1980s would not be a precedent for Russia's role in Tajikistan in the 1990s.[144]

The dilemma that Moscow faced was one well understood by the U.S. in earlier decades in Vietnam. A government of a country declared as strategically vital lost all incentive to promote political reforms and increasingly relied on its great power ally for a military solution to communal war. Strategic necessity would drive the great power into supporting that government, thereby creating a vicious cycle of dependency and further involvement. The Foreign Ministry expected that the Dushanbe government would pursue national reconciliation and yet the only pressure it could apply was the threat of withdrawal, which was an unrealistic one. For Moscow's security establishment there was no alternative to the maintenance of a forward position in Tajikistan and the situation called for a strengthened commitment. Defense Minister Grachev declared after the July 1993 border clashes that Russian border forces required heavy equipment, tanks, artillery and aircraft, to enable them to do their job effectively. Grachev revealed that the Defense Ministry had proposed to the Supreme Soviet that an appeal be directed to all CIS parliaments to dispatch peace-keeping forces to Tajikistan.[145]

Yeltsin convened a meeting with the Central Asian leaders on Tajikistan in Moscow on 7 August 1993 in an attempt to involve them in the Tajik imbroglio in the name of the CIS. The Moscow meeting declared that "the Tajik-Afghan border is to be considered a CIS border and is to be defended collectively," a statement included in the two documents signed at the meeting. Yeltsin invoked the Tashkent Collective Security Treaty of May 1992 and pressed the Central Asian governments to make contributions to peace-keeping in Tajikistan and again called on the Dushanbe government to engage in dialogue with the opposition.[146] The meeting decided that Tajikistan was to be given additional military and humanitarian aid as well as support for the creation of national armed forces. In practice that support was to be almost entirely Russian. Moreover, it was also decided that the present Russian force in Tajikistan would be strengthened with units from Kazakhstan, Kyrgyzstan, and Uzbekistan.[147]

The Moscow meeting marked a new stage in Moscow's commitment to Tajikistan and revealed familiar conflicts of purpose. First Deputy Foreign Minister Anatolii Adamshin claimed that one important intention behind the meeting was to induce external actors—Afghanistan, Pakistan, Iran, and Turkey—to assist in the political resolution of the dispute.[148] The reaffirmation of Tajikistan's strategic value for Moscow, however, gave the Dushanbe government no reason to accept a political resolution. Second, Moscow's attempt to involve the Central Asian governments engendered a similar dilemma in that there was little incentive for those governments to assume commitments in Tajikistan in view of Moscow's deepening involvement.

Subsequently, Moscow promoted the idea that Tajikistan was to be the responsibility of a CIS collective security system based on the Tashkent Collective Security Treaty. In October 1993, forces deployed in Tajikistan were designated as CIS collective peace-keeping forces as Russia sought a UN mandate for peace-keeping in Tajikistan. Nonetheless, the term collective was a misnomer and barely concealed the extent to which the commitment was largely a Russian effort. Commander of Russian forces in Tajikistan Colonel-General Boris P'yankov claimed that he had to travel to the Central Asian capitals to request the respective governments to fulfill the commitments they had accepted at the Moscow meeting.[149] Russia requested a commitment of forces from Kazakhstan in the previous year and in December 1992 Nazarbaev announced an intention to dispatch forces but the plan was opposed by Parliament. In April 1993, a battalion of Kazakh internal security forces was designated for Tajikistan but had not arrived by the end of 1993.[150] Kyrgyzstan despatched a reduced battalion that served in the Pamirs in Badakhshan.

Russia established a special relationship with President Islam Karimov of Uzbekistan on the basis of a common concern for the security of Tajikistan. Karimov has consistently described Moscow as the guarantor of peace and stability along the external borders of Central Asia.[151] Karimov told the Russians that conflict in Tajikistan threatens the peace in Central Asia and in September 1992 (over Russian television) accused Moscow of not fulfilling its duties in defending the southern frontiers of the CIS. The Uzbek president understood the debates that were being conducted in Moscow when he declared that if Russia did not identify its strategic interests in Central Asia its southern borders would move toward the Islamic World.[152] Karimov also called Tajikistan a time bomb and claimed that power in that country had been captured by the fundamentalists.[153]

Karimov's militancy over Tajikistan and the obvious effort to involve Moscow were products of particular Uzbek concerns. Conflict between Tajiks and Uzbeks had been exacerbated by the Soviet demarcation of Central Asian frontiers in 1924 that divided Tajik and Uzbek populations and included centers of Tajik culture—Bukhara and Samarkhand—in Uzbekistan. According to the 1989 Soviet census, 4.7 percent of Uzbekistan's 23 million population was Tajik, while 23.5 percent of Tajikistan's 5 million was Uzbek, mainly in the north. Some Russian observers have claimed that the Tajik-Uzbek ethnic conflict could tear apart Central Asia.[154] Karimov has strongly supported the Uzbek-populated north against the south and reports claim that Uzbeks have assisted the Dushanbe government in the training of special security units. Dushanbe government units can use safe havens in Uzbekistan and Uzbek forces have been involved in operations on the government side.[155] Moreover, Karimov was also a supporter of the Uzbek commander in northern Afghanistan, Abdul Rashid Dostum. That part of the Tajik-Afghan border controlled by Dostum, who was based in Mazar Sharif, was considered safe. Dostum apparently met regularly with Uzbek intelligence and has had good relations with Moscow as an ally against fundamentalism.[156]

For Moscow, Karimov was indeed a stabilizer in the region and an indispensable ally. Nonetheless, Moscow could not rely on Karimov without exacerbating the Uzbek-Tajik ethnic conflict and so undermining the goal of national reconciliation. Among the Tajik intelligentsia, Uzbekistan was regarded as the main enemy of the Indo-European Tajiks who saw themselves as an island surrounded by Turkic nations. In this context, Tajikistan was regarded as the victim of Uzbek chauvinism and Russia was criticized for its support for Karimov.[157] Karimov initially resisted the idea of national reconciliation but under Russian pressure gave his endorsement. Karimov, like the Russian military, has had little faith in diplomacy and continues to pursue a military solution. Whether Moscow can obtain the benefits of Karimov's role as a stabilizer while promoting a diplomatic solution to the conflict is seriously open to question. The danger is that by relying on Karimov, Russia increasingly becomes a captive of Uzbek-Tajik conflict.

Aside from Uzbekistan only Kyrgyzstan answered the Russian call to dispatch forces to Tajikistan as part of a CIS contingent. President Askar Akaev joined Yeltsin and Nazarbaev in September 1992 in signing a declaration on Tajikistan that affirmed the inviolability of the southern borders of the CIS. It stressed that the three presidents would strengthen support for the brotherly Tajik nation.[158] Akaev declared that without Russian's support it would be impossible to establish security in Central Asia and claimed that he fully supported Russian efforts.[159] President Niyazov of Turkmenistan, however, deflected all Russian pressure for involvement in Tajikistan. When Kozyrev met Niyazov in September 1992, the Turkmen president declared his neutrality in relation to the conflict. Indeed, the Turkmen Foreign Minister Kuliyev Avdy described the conflict as an internal affair and in this context emphasized the role of UN and international organization.[160]

Russia was unable to coordinate Central Asian, let alone CIS responses to the problem of Tajikistan. Russia requested both Georgia and Belarus to contribute units to Tajikistan and the Belarussians responded by claiming that the dispatch of forces abroad contravened their Constitution. Russia was left to assume the major military burden in Tajikistan that did not prevent the designation CIS peace-keeping forces from being applied to the mainly Russian forces there. The CIS Council of Defense Ministers, however, used the term collective defense forces operating on the basis of the Tashkent Collective Security Treaty. As Boris P'yankov explained, the purpose of those forces could not properly be described as peace-keeping while no ccase-fire had been achieved.[161] Nonetheless, for CIS political leaders the term peace-keeping was applied to allow Russia to claim a UN mandate for its military role in the CIS.

Russian policy toward Tajikistan could not overcome an essential conflict of intentions. The Foreign Ministry continued to emphasize the importance of national reconciliation and when Kozyrev visited Dushanbe again in November 1993 he explained that Russia would not "endlessly fight for it."[162] The message was repeated the following month when Kozyrev visited Dushanbe with First Deputy Defense Minister Boris Gromov who, as the last Soviet commander in Afghanistan, had grave misgivings about Russia's involvement in Tajikistan.[163] Kozyrev pushed the Dushanbe government to negotiate with the opposition over the holding of new elections involving the participation of all regions. Throughout 1994, three rounds of negotiations between the Dushanbe government and the opposition were held: the first round was in Moscow in April, the second in Teheran in June; and the third in Islamabad in October. The opposition demanded a cease-fire, a general amnesty for political prisoners, the return of the 80,000 Tajik refugees who had fled to Afghanistan and a power-sharing arrangement. All these demands were consistently rejected by the Dushanbe government, convinced as it was of the support of Moscow and Karimov.

Russia's military saw little purpose in negotiations with an opposition that was regarded as dominated by fundamentalists anyway. The difficulty of harmonizing the Foreign Ministry and Defense Ministry positions may have been a reason for the delay in the first round of Tajik negotiations, which were initially scheduled for 16 March but that began on 5 April 1994. Russia's commander in Tajikistan Boris P'yankov publicly doubted if Tajik negotiations could succeed and claimed they were simply a political gesture.[164] The Russian military in Tajikistan consistently supported Dushanbe government operations. For example, when Dushanbe sent food convoys to Badakhshan to relieve the effects of the opposition's blockade, units from the 201st motorized division provided protection. Rakhmonov visited Badakhshan with an armed escort of Russian soldiers.[165] Nonetheless, Russian operations in Tajikistan were less than effective in many ways. Relations between Russian forces and the local population have been reportedly bad and as a result the Russian military has suffered from poor intelligence and difficulty in coping with local formations, which have more effective intelligence networks. Moreover, the 201st division was badly equipped, its officers were on rotation from other areas and often lacked incentive. The division cannot properly support the border forces that are under different command and lack air support and bases.[166]

The idea of the political gesture tended to characterize the Dushanbe government's view of national reconciliation as it continued to receive Moscow's support. Moscow supported 70 percent of the Tajik budget allowing credits to Tajikistan that were denied to other CIS states.[167] Bowing to external Russian and UN pressure the Dushanbe Parliament passed a resolution on 20 July 1994 calling for presidential elections and for a referendum for a new constitution. Rakhmonov visited Moscow on 16 August to solicit Russian political support and to seek additional credits from Chernomyrdin; the credits were refused as Moscow attempted to push Dushanbe into serious political dialogue.[168] The Tajik presidential elections were held on 8 November under conditions that prompted an opposition boycott. Neither the UN nor the CSCE sent observers because it was understood that the Dushanbe government had planned Communist-style elections to confirm the power of the incumbents. Rakhmonov was proclaimed president and declared that he would develop even closer ties with Russia and the CIS.[169]

Russia had bound itself to the defense of an unrepresentative regime in Tajikistan because of assumptions of threat from the Islamic south, and its own version of the domino theory. The commitment to Tajikistan distorted Russia's involvement in Central Asia and elevated a specific security issue into a major criterion for Russian relations there. Russian critics of Moscow's commitment were concerned about the danger of being drawn into a second Afghanistan as Russian intervention exacerbates the existing civil war and prevents the Dushanbe government from compromising with the opposition. Moreover, Russian democrats perceive the political dangers of a situation in which Moscow supports the Communist *nomenklatura* in Central Asia against its democratic and Islamic opposition. In 1992, Moscow was willing to provide asylum for Central Asian dissidents but subsequently began to side with the regimes against their democratic critics. Moscow's support for the local regimes pushes the Central Asian opposition toward extremist measures to seek external support in what could be a self-fulfilling prophecy as far as fundamentalism is concerned.

Kyrgyzstan and Turkmenistan

Both Kyrgyzstan and Turkmenistan have attempted to develop bilateral relations with Moscow apart from the Tajikistan issue. Neither has been particularly involved in the CIS (of which they are members) and Turkmenistan in particular has maintained a consistent indifference toward the CIS. Kyrgyz President Akaev has been concerned about the steady emigration of ethnic Russians which he declared a catastrophe for both Kyrgyzstan and Russia. Russian emigration had been stimulated by declining living standards, the designation of Kyrgyz as the official language, and preferential treatment for Kyrgyz in government appointments. Russians constituted 21.2 percent of the population in 1990, a percentage which dropped to 17 percent in 1994 according to Akaev.[170] The emigration of Russian technical personnel was affecting Kyrgyzstan's local defense-related industries to the extent that Akaev was considering the granting of dual nationality to Russians. The Kyrgyz president allowed the formation of a Slavic university in October 1992 that was to meet Russian concerns for the higher education of their children.[171] Russian-Kyrgyz military agreements were concluded on 21 July 1994 that allowed Russia to train and equip the Kyrgyz army and Russian officers to serve in the Kyrgyz military.[172]

Turkmenistan's views of the CIS were expressed in First Deputy Foreign Minister Boris Shikhmoradov's statement on foreign policy in October 1992. Turkmenistan was to emphasize positive neutrality as a temporary measure until the country could move to absolute autonomy. As the third largest producer of natural gas in the world Turkmenistan, unlike any other CIS state, had a unique opportunity for independent development. Turkmenistan opposed the idea of a centralized CIS, which would include a collective security organization and coordinating councils, but agreed to tolerate multilateral structures temporarily.[173] Turkmenistan attempted to devise alternative transport outlets to the south to avoid Russia and a railway was proposed from Ashkhabad to Teheran and similar routes were under negotiation with Pakistan.[174] Despite the declaration of intention, however, President Suparmurad Niyazov steadily drew more closely to Moscow to strengthen his unreformed authoritarian regime. Niyazov miscalculated when he supported the August 1991 coup attempt in Moscow and later adapted to change in Moscow when he renamed his Communist Party the Democratic Party without any essential changes. Niyazov hosted a CIS summit in Ashkhabad in December

1993 and on 21 December concluded a defense agreement with Yeltsin that allowed for joint Russian-Turkmen defense of the border with Iran and Afghanistan.[175] In January 1994, Turkmenistan joined the CIS Economic Union under Russian pressure as Russia moved to integrate Central Asia within the CIS framework. Turkmenistan's bilateral relationship with Moscow was cemented when Niyazov visited Moscow in May 1995 and declared Russia to be Turkmenistan's ally and partner. Niyazov was most concerned about the decline of trade with Russia, which fell from 60 percent of Turkmenistan's trade in the Soviet era to 8 percent by 1995. Various economic agreements were signed at this meeting as well as an agreement that protected the Russian minority in Turkmenistan, the first of its kind for the CIS.[176]

Central Asian Regionalism

The consolidation of Russia's position in Central Asia has been driven by several motives. Aside from the specific security concern that Tajikistan represents, Moscow attempts to prevent the states's involvement in regional organizations sponsored by Islamic powers—Turkey, Iran, or Pakistan. Moscow also strives to forestall the formation of indigenous regional organizations which would reduce Russia's influence over the area, or which may promise to draw in external Islamic powers. Central Asian states had an incentive to join external associations or to create their own form of regionalism that would increase their options and provide balance against Moscow. Despite such intentions, Moscow's presence in Central Asia has been overwhelming and the alternatives explored have so far been disappointing and ineffectual.

Immediately after the collapse of the Soviet Union several arrangements were proposed that would link Central Asia more closely with the Islamic World. The Organization for Economic Development, founded in 1965, held a summit in Teheran in February 1992 and included Azerbaijan, Uzbekistan, Tajikistan, and Turkmenistan. Iran also proposed a Caspian Sea grouping involving Russia, and a cultural organization involving Persian-speaking peoples in Afghanistan and Tajikistan.[177] Turkey competed with Iran for influence in Central Asia and while Turgut Özal was president sought to promote relations with the area on the basis of pan-Turkic sentiment. His successor Suleiman Demirel when interviewed by the Russian press declared that Turkey had a moral duty to develop relations with Central Asia and to strengthen the independence of the countries there.[178] Turgut Özal sponsored the first summit of Turkish-speaking peoples which was held in Ankara in October 1992, and included the four Turkish-speaking Central Asian states as well as Azerbaijan. In October 1994, Suleiman Demirel organized a second meeting in Istanbul that called for closer political, cultural, and economic cooperation, and offered support for Demirel's proposal for an oil/gas pipeline connecting Central Asia with Europe via Turkey. Russia's Foreign Ministry regarded the meeting as evidence of growing Turkish influence in Central Asia and rising pan-Turkism.[179] Alarmist reports appeared in the Russian press about Turkish influence in Central Asia and notions of a greater Turkestan which include the Muslim parts of Russia. In reality, however, the vision of pan-Turkism was unfulfilled and Turkey's role in Central Asia remained constrained by its own economic problems.

Attempts at indigenous regionalism among the Central Asian states were intended to provide an assurance of an alternative should the CIS fail. In April 1992, a Bishkek summit of Central Asian leaders was held that declared that Central Asia was one economic and political space. The summit confirmed the territorial integrity of the regional states and the sanctity of existing borders and agreed to strengthen the CIS as well as to develop relations among themselves.[180] In January 1993, Central Asian leaders met at Tashkent when a series of proposals was agreed to including a comprehensive defense and economic union. The Central Asian leaders in their proposals replicated the CIS and included the idea of a Central Asian bank as well. It was Karimov who revealed the purpose of the meeting when he deplored the failure of the CIS to fulfill any of the agreements signed. This made it clear that CIS ineffectiveness stimulated Central Asian regionalism as an alternative.[181] This was an incentive for Russia to promote the CIS and to ensure the region's integration in CIS economic structures to forestall the emergence of an independent Turkestan. Central Asian leaders continued to launch various regional initiatives and Karimov, Akaev, and Nazarbaev met in Alma Ata in April 1994 to propose, yet again, an economic alliance.[182] These initiatives had the particular diplomatic purposes of pushing the CIS into greater effectiveness and repairing the strained relationship between Karimov and Nazarbaev.

CIS: The Future

No doubt trends from 1992–1994 appear encouraging to Moscow's rulers as virtually all states have strengthened their commitment to the CIS for various reasons. The Ukraine, under President Kuchma, has adopted a more positive view of the CIS while Moldova, Georgia, and Azerbaijan either joined or confirmed their membership. Even Turkmenistan, which under President Niyazov initially attempted to follow an autonomous path, eventually gravitated back to Moscow. Nonetheless, these trends confirmed not so much the value of regional integration as the importance of bilateral relations with Moscow for diverse purposes. Such purposes included security against external attack or instability (Armenia, Uzbekistan), against disintegration, or internal revolt (Georgia, Tajikistan, Turkmenistan, Kazakhstan), for diplomatic balance (Azerbaijan) or for economic benefit (Belarus, Ukraine, Kazakhstan, Turkmenistan). Moscow has attempted to direct what has been a need for bilateral Russian security or economic support into an endorsement of CIS regionalism. For most CIS states this endorsement has been a necessary diplomatic gesture to ensure the desired benefits of the relationship with Moscow. What passes as CIS regionalism is actually a series of bilateral relations that Moscow has strengthened with the CIS states in their respective subregions.

Moscow's ability to shape the direction of CIS regionalism has been constrained by the nature of the relationships it has developed, both bilaterally and at a subregional level. Moscow's involvement in Central Asia and the Caucasus causes apprehension within the members of the European CIS and removes any desire on their part to endorse security multilateralism. Moscow cannot involve the CIS as an organization more deeply in the affairs of Central Asia or the Caucasus without intensifying existing strains. The tension between Moscow's immediate needs, which are served by separate bilateral relationships, and Moscow's vision of CIS regionalism will spur the development of a CIS subregionalism that will become increasingly evident.

NOTES

1. Yuri Leonov, "Russiya i Ukraina posle gibeli SNG," *Nezavisimaya gazeta*, 18 Apr. 1992.

2. On the historical background see Zenon E. Kohut, "History As a Background: Russian-Ukrainian Relations and Historical Consciousness in Contemporary Ukraine" in S. Frederick Starr (ed.), *The Legacy of History and the New States of Eurasia: The International Politics of Eurasia*, vol. 1, M. E. Sharpe, Armonk, New York, 1994. For the historical basis of Ukrainian nationalism see Ronald Grigor Suny, *The Revenge of the Past: Nationalism, Revolution and the Collapse of the Soviet Union*, Stanford, 1993, pp. 43–51.

3. "Oslepenie," *Rossiiskaya gazeta*, 20 May 1992.

4. *Rossiiskaya gazeta*, 31 Oct. 1992.

5. Vladimir Skachko, "Ot Kravchuka potrebuyet plana konkretnykh deistvii po otnosheniyu k SNG," *Nezavisimaya gazeta*, 21 Oct. 1992.

6. *Nezavisimaya gazeta*, 12 Feb. 1992.

7. *Izvestiya*, 18 June 1992.

8. "Rossii i Ukraine neobkhodim ekonomicheskii soyuz," *Rossiiskaya gazeta*, 13 Jan. 1993.

9. *Radio Free Europe/Radio Liberty Daily Report* (276), 1 Dec. 1994.

10. *Radio Free Europe/Radio Liberty Daily Report* (172), 9 Sept. 1994. Over 1992-July 1994 Russia provided the Ukraine with $5 billion to finance imports of energy, *Financial Times*, 5 Dec. 1994.

11. *Nezavisimaya gazeta*, 20 Jan. 1993.

12. "Oslepenie," *Nezavismaya gazeta*, 20 May 1992.

13. *Nezavisimaya gazeta*, 22 May 1992.

14. *Nezavisimaya gazeta*, 14 Apr. 1993.

15. "Oborona sevastopolya," *Nezavisimaya gazeta*, 13 July 1993.

16. *Izvestiya*, 13 July 1993.

17. *Nezavisimaya gazeta*, 4, 6 Oct. 1994.

18. *Itar Tass*, 9 Sept. 1993.

19. *Itar Tass*, 17 June 1993.

20. *Itar Tass*, 4 Sept. 1993.

21. *Nezavisimaya gazeta*, 22 Apr. 1994.

22. *Open Media Research Institute Daily Digest*, 6 June 1994.

23. *Izvestiya*, 31 July 1994.

24. *Nezavisimaya gazeta*, 16 Aug. 1994.

25. See Ronald Grigor Suny, *The Revenge of the Past: Nationalism, Revolution, and the Collapse of the Soviet Union*, Stanford, 1993, pp. 30–35.

26. Vitalii Portnikov, "Rossiya i Belarus' sozdaet novyi soyuz," *Nezavisimaya gazeta*, 22 July 1992.

27. *Nezavisimaya gazeta*, 2 Apr. 1993.

28. Vitalii Tsyganov, "Rossiya i Belarus' ob'edinyayut deneszhyesistemy," *Nezavisimaya gazeta*, 20 Nov. 1993.

29. *Pravda*, 29 Apr. 1994.

30. *Radio Free Europe/Radio Liberty Daily Report* (94), 18 May 1994.

31. *Nezavisimaya gazeta*, 9 Aug. 1994.

32. *Radio Free Europe/Radio Liberty Daily Report* (193), 11 Oct. 1994.

33. *Open Media Research Institute, Daily digest*, 16 May 1994.

34. *Nezavisimaya gazeta*, 8 Apr. 1992.

35. *Nezavisimaya gazeta*, 23 June 1992.

36. *Rossiiskaya gazeta*, 24 June 1992.

37. *Moscow News* (24), 5-12 July 1992.

38. Vera Kuznetsova, "Uregulirovanie v pridnestrov'c," *Nezavisimaya gazeta*, 23 July 1992.

39. *Nezavisimaya gazeta*, 15 Aug. 1992.

40. A. Lebed', "V den' kogda mirotvorcheskie sily uidut iz pridnestrov'ya . . .," *Izvestiya*, 26 Feb. 1993.

41. A. Lebed', "V den' kogda mirotvorcheskie sily uidut iz pridnestrov'ya . . .," *Izvestiya*, 26 Feb. 1993.

42. *Nezavisimaya gazeta*, 21 Jan. 1993, *Rossiiskaya gazeta*, 22 May 1993.

43. *Izvestiya*, 2, 10 Mar. 1994.

44. *Radio Free Europe/Radio Liberty Daily Report* (172), 9 Sept. 1994.

45. *Radio Free Europe/Radio Liberty Daily Report* (202), 24 Oct. 1994.

46. Nikolai Plotnikov, "Rossiya i Moldova dogovorilis," *Nezavisimaya gazeta*, 13 Aug. 1994; *Pravda*, 21 Oct. 1994.

47. For the background to the Nagorno-Karabakh conflict and for Armenian views see Richard G. Hovannisian, "Historical Memory and Foreign Relations: The Armenian Perspective," in S. Frederick Starr (ed.), *The Legacy of History in Russia and the New States of Eurasia: the International Politics of Eurasia*, vol. 1, M. E. Sharpe, Armonk, New York, 1994.

48. Liana Linasyan, "Armenia pered ugrozoi katastrofy," *Nezavisimaya gazeta*, 11 Dec. 1992.

49. Pavel Fel'gengauer, "Rossiiskie mirotvortsy v zapadne," *Nezavisimaya gazeta*, 11 Aug. 1992.

50. *Nezavisimaya gazeta*, 13 Nov. 1992.

51. *Nezavisimaya gazeta*, 8 Apr. 1994.

52. *Nezavisimaya gazeta*, 28 May 1992.

53. *Nezavisimaya gazeta*, 28 May 1992.

54. *Radio Free Europe/Radio Liberty Daily Report* (129), 11 June 1994.

55. Armen Khanbabyan, "Pavel Grachev dovolen vizitami u Yerevan i Tbilisi," *Nezavisimaya gazeta*, 11 June 1994. *Radio Free Europe/Radio Liberty Daily Report* (108), 9 June 1994.

56. *Radio Free Europe/Radio Liberty Daily Report* (200), 20 Oct. 1994.

57. *Radio Free Europe/Radio Liberty Daily Report* (194), 12 Oct. 1994.

58. *Nezavisimaya gazeta*, 25 Mar. 1992.

59. *Nezavisimaya gazeta*, 14 July, 4 Sept. 1992.

60. *Nezavisimaya gazeta*, 6 Oct. 1992.

61. Guga Lolishvili, "Voennoe prisutsvie Rossii v Zakavkaz'e," *Nezavisimaya gazeta*, 11 Dec. 1992.

62. *Nezavisimaya gazeta*, 19 Dec. 1992.

63. *Nezavisimaya gazeta*, 22 Dec. 1992.

64. *Nezavisimaya gazeta*, 20 Mar. 1993.

65. *Izvestiya*, 7 July 1993.

66. *Izvestiya*, 28 July 1993; *Nezavisimaya gazeta*, 1 Oct. 1993.

67. *Nezavisimaya gazeta*, 25 Feb. 1993.

68. *Izvestiya*, 15 July 1993.

69. Guga Lolishvili, "Rossiisko-gruzinskii dogovor o druzhbe skoro budet podpisan," *Nezavisimaya gazeta*, 18 Nov. 1992.

70. *Nezavisimaya gazeta*, 13 Feb., 19 Mar. 1993.

71. *Nezavisimaya gazeta*, 19 Feb. 1993.

72. *Nezavisimaya gazeta*, 22 Sept. 1993.

73. *Nezavisimaya gazeta*, 4 Feb. 1994.

74. *Izvestiya*, 2 Feb. 1994, 17 Feb. 1994.

75. Mikhail Dolidze, "Tbilisi nadeetsya na pomosh' NATO," *Rossiiskaya gazeta*, 29 Mar. 1994.

76. Aleksander Iskandaryan, "Shevardnadze nadeetsya, chto dogovor s rossei pomozhet emu . . .," *Izvestiya*, 17 Feb. 1994.

77. *Nezavisimaya gazeta*, 5 May 1995.

78. On the background to Azerbaijani-Russian relations see Tadeusz Swieto-chowski, "Azerbaijan's Relationship: The Land Between Russia, Turkey and Iran" in Ali Banuazizi and Myron Weiner (eds.), *The New Geopolitics of Central Asia and Its Borderlands*, I. B. Tauris, London, 1994.

79. *Nezavisimaya gazeta*, 29 Jan. 1992.

80. *Moscow News* (24), 14/21 June 1992.

81. *Nezavisimaya gazeta*, 15 Feb. 1992.

82. *Nezavisimaya gazeta*, 13 Oct. 1992.

83. Aidyn Mekhtiev, "Azerbaizhano-Iranskii dogovor ne za gorami," *Nezavisimaya gazeta*, 28 Oct. 1993. Mamed Safarli, "Tegeran-Baku: protivorechiya na fone dobrososedestva," *Nezavisimaya gazeta*, 5 July 1994.

84. *Open Media Research Institute, Daily digest* (90), 10 May 1995.

85. Osman Iyldyrym, "Ankara ozabochena aktivizatsiei kurdskogo soprotivleniya," *Nezavisimaya gazeta*, 5 Nov. 1993.

86. *Radio Free Europe/Radio Liberty Daily Report* (210), 4 Nov. 1994.

87. Aidyn Mekhtiev, "Baku obvinyaet rossiiskikh desantnikov," *Nezavisimaya gazeta*, 26 Feb. 1993.

88. Thomas Golts, "Letter from Eurasia: The Hidden Russian Hand," *Foreign Policy*, no/. 92, fall 1993.

89. *Krasnaya zvezda*, 18 May 1993.

90. *Nezavisimaya gazeta*, 5 May 1993.

91. *Rossiiskaya gazeta*, 29 Oct. 1992.

92. *Nezavisimaya gazeta*, 16 Sept. 1993.

93. Abbas Abbasov, "Azerbaidzan mezhdu Rossiei Turtsiei," *Nezavisimaya gazeta*, 16 Sept. 1994.

94. Aidyn Mekhtiev, "Azerbaidzano-Iranskii dogovor ne za gorami," *Nezavisimaya gazeta*, 28 Oct. 1993.

95. *Nezavisimaya gazeta*, 5 July 1994.

96. *Nezavisimaya gazeta*, 28 Oct. 1993.

97. *Nezavisimaya gazeta*, 23 Aug. 1994.

98. *Nezavisimaya gazeta*, 30 Apr. 1994.

99. *Nezavisimaya gazeta*, 27 Nov. 1993.

100. *Nezavisimaya gazeta*, 19 May 1994.

101. *Nezavisimaya gazeta*, 16 Apr. 1994.

102. *Radio Free Europe/Radio Liberty Daily Report* (139), 25 July 1994.

103. *Nezavisimaya gazeta*, 5 Oct. 1994.

104. *Radio Free Europe/Radio Liberty Daily Report* (180), 21 Sept. 1994.

105. *Nezavisimaya gazeta*, 5 Oct. 1994.

106. Aidyn Mekhtiev, "Rossiyu ne ustraivaet nyneshnii status kaspiya," *Nezavisimaya gazeta*, 15 June 1994.

107. Aidyn Mekhtiev, "U Chernomyrdina pretenzii k kontraktu veka net," *Nezavisimaya gazeta*, 15 Oct. 1994.

108. "Rossiya i ee interesy," *Nezavisimaya gazeta*, 20 Oct. 1992.

109. "Strategiya dla Rossiya," *Nezavisimaya gazeta*, 19 Aug. 1992.

110. *Rossiiskaya gazeta*, 4 Aug. 1992.

111. Colonel S. Pechorov, "Geostrategicheskie ugrozy Rossii, oni realny ili mnimy?" *Krasnaya zvezda*, 20 Mar. 1992.

112. Lt.-Colonel R. Mustafin, "Islamskii faktor: on bespokoit mnogikh," *Krasnaya zvezda*, 9 Apr. 1992.

113. *Rossiiskaya gazeta*, 6 May 1992.

114. V. Yefimov, "Islamskii fundamentalizm, ugroza dla Rossii?" *Svobodnaya mysl'* (16), 1993.

115. *Nezavisimaya gazeta*, 29 July 1993.

116. Aleksei Vasil'ev, "Trudnosti preodolimy," *Nezavisimaya gazeta*, 11 Mar. 1994.

117. Aleksei Malashenko, "Rossiya i Islam," *Nezavisimaya gazeta*, 22 Feb. 1992.

118. Nikolai Fyodorov, "Islam ne navyazan Rossii izvne," *Rossiiskaya gazeta*, 14 May 1993.

119. Aleksei Malashenko, "Islam kak faktor vosstanovleniya SSSR," *Nezavisimaya gazeta*, 18 Aug. 1993.

120. Ahmed Rashid, *The Resurgence of Central Asia, Islam or Nationalism*, 2nd ed., Oxford/Zed, London, 1994, chapter 5. Ahmed Rashid, "Renewed Hegemony," *Far Eastern Economic Review*, 24 Feb. 1994.

121. *Radio Free Europe/Radio Liberty Daily Report* (103), 1 June 1994.

122. Sergei Kurginyan, "Soderzhanie novogo integratsionizma," *Nezavisimaya gazeta*, 7 July 1994.

123. Vitalii Portnikov, "Rossiisko-Turkestanskii soyuz," *Nezavisimaya gazeta*, 6 Aug. 1993.

124. Dmitri Trenin, "Kollektivnaya bezopasnost' i kollektivnaya oborona," *Nezavisimaya gazeta*, 4 Nov. 1994.

125. Radzad Safarov, "Reformator Solzhenitsyn i musul'manskii vopros," *Nezavisimaya gazeta*, 25 Aug. 1994.

126. *Nezavisimaya gazeta*, 22 Sept. 1992.

127. *Itar Tass*, 4 Jan. 1993.

128. Yevgennii Denisenko, "Soyuz trekh ozhidaniya i realnost'," *Nezavisimaya gazeta*, 8 July 1994.

129. Aidyn Mekhtiev, "Tzentral'no-Aziatsko sodruzhestvo mozhet stat' al'ternativoi SNG," *Nezavisimaya gazeta*, 21 Oct. 1994.

130. *Izvestiya*, 18 Feb. 1994.

131. Vladimir Ardaev, "V odinochku tango ne tanstuyut," *Izvestiya*, 25 Feb. 1994.

132. On Tajikistan see Barnett R. Rubin, "The Fragmentation of Tajikistan," *Survival*, winter, 1993/94, vol. 35, no. 4; Aziz Niyazi, "Tajikistan" in Mohiaddin Mesbahi (ed.), *Central Asia and the Caucasus after the Soviet Union: Domestic and International Dynamics*, University Press of Florida, Gainesville, Florida, 1994. Russian sources include Aleksei Malashenko, Aziz Niyazi, "O Tadzikistane bez pristrastiya," *Nezavisimaya gazeta*, 3 Mar. 1993; Cheslav Putovski, "Chto takoe narodnyi front Tadzhikistana?" *Nezavisimaya gazeta*, 16 Dec. 1992.

133. Malashenko, Aziz Niyazi, "O Tadzhikistane bez pristrastiya," *Nezavisimaya gazeta*, 3 Mar. 1993.

134. Oleg Panfilov, "Nabiev idyot v nastuplenie," *Nezavisimaya gazeta*, 6 Aug. 1992.

135. *Nezavisimaya gazeta*, 22 Aug. 1992.

136. *Nezavisimaya gazeta*, 15 Aug. 1992.

137. *Nezavisimaya gazeta*, 16 Sept. 1992.

138. Igor' Rotar', "Dva za Andreya Kozyreva," *Nezavisimaya gazeta*, 7 Nov. 1992.

139. Igor' Rotar', "Voina bez pobeditelei," *Izvestiya*, 30 Sept. 1993.

140. Igor' Rotar', "Moskva pytaetsya pogasit' tadzhiksuyu mezhdousobitsu," *Nezavisimaya gazeta*, 11, Nov. 1992.

141. Igor' Rotar', "Moskva pytaetsya pogasit' tadzhiksuyu mezhdousobitsu," *Nezavisimaya gazeta*, 11, Nov. 1992.

142. Igor' Rotar', "Rossiya vtyagivaetsya v novyu nenuzhnyu voinu?" *Nezavisimaya gazeta*, 27 May 1993.

143. *Nezavisimaya gazeta*, 29 July 1993.

144. Andrei Kozyrev, "Chego khochet Rossiya v Tadzhikistane," *Izvestiya*, 4 Aug. 1993.

145. *Nezavisimaya gazeta*, 16 July 1993.

146. Vera Kuznetsova, "Itogi obsuzhdeniya v Moskve tadzhikskoi problemy neodnoznachny," *Nezavisimaya gazeta*, 10 Aug; 1993.

147. "Ofitsial'noe soobshchenie," *Rossiiskaya gazeta*, 10 Aug. 1993.

148. "Ofitsial'noe soobshchenie," *Rossiiskaya gazeta*, 10 Aug. 1993.

149. "My obyazany utverdit' mir v Tadzhikistane," *Krasnaya zvezda*, 9 Nov. 1993.

150. Boris Vinogradov, "Prizrak vtorogo afghana," *Izvestiya*, 3 Mar. 1994.

151. *Nezavisimaya gazeta*, 2 June 1992.

152. Semen Novoprudskii, "Islam Karimov preduprczhdaet," *Nezavisimaya gazeta*, 4 Sept. 1992.

153. *Itar Tass*, 8 Aug. 1992; *Far Eastern Economic Review*, 15 Oct. 1992.

154. Igor' Rotar', "Voina bez pobeditelei," *Izvestiya*, 30 Sept. 1992.

155. Igor' Rotar',"Tashkent pomogaet anti islamistam," *Nezavisimaya gazeta*, 11 Dec. 1992.

156. Oleg Panfilov, "Novye trevogi rossiskikh diplomatov," *Nezavisimaya gazeta*, 16 Nov. 1993.

157. Khabib Nazrulsoev, "Strasti po tadzhikistanu," *Nezavisimaya gazeta*, 10 Apr 1993.

158. *Nezavisimaya gazeta*, 5 Sept. 1992.

159. *Izvestiya*, 3 Aug. 1993.

160. *Nezavisimaya gazeta*, 6 Nov. 1992.

161. "My ne khotim pugat' mir," *Nezavisimaya gazeta*, 24 June 1994.

162. Igor' Rotar', "Andrei Kozyrev vernulsya iz Dushanbe v Moskvu," *Nezavisimaya gazeta*, 19 Nov. 1993.

163. *Nezavisimaya gazeta*, 16 Mar. 1994.

164. Gul'nara Khasanova, "General P'yankov ne verit . . .," *Izvestiya*, 12 Mar. 1994.

165. *Nezavisimaya gazeta*, 5 July 1994.

166. Sergei Grigor'ev, "Rossiskaya armiya v tadzikskoi voine," *Nezavisimaya gazeta*, 16 Sept. 1993.

167. *Izvestiya*, 30 Nov. 1993.

168. *Nezavisimaya gazeta*, 17 Aug. 1994.

169. *Radio Free Europe/Radio Liberty Daily Report* (213), 9 Nov. 1994.

170. *Radio Free Europe/Radio Liberty Daily Report* (111), 14 June 1994.

171. *Nezavisimaya gazeta*, 13 Oct. 1992.

172. *Radio Free Europe/Radio Liberty Daily Report* (138), 22 July 1994.

173. Igor' Zhukov, "Ramki sodruzhestva tesny dla Turkmenii . . .," *Nezavisimaya gazeta*, 7 Oct. 1992.

174. *Izvestiya*, 14 July 1993.

175. *Izvestiya*, 24 Dec. 1993.

176. *Rossiiskaya gazeta*, 18, 19 May 1995.

177. *Middle East economic digest*, 28 Feb. 1992.

178. *Izvestiya*, 6 July 1994.

179. Aidyn Mekhtiev, "Tsentralnoaziatsko sodruzhestvo mozhet stat' al'ternativoi SNG," *Nezavisimaya gazeta*, 21 Oct. 1994.

180. Igor' Rotar', "Bishkekskie dogovoronnosti ne protivorechat printsipam SNG," *Nezavisimaya gazeta*, 25 Apr. 1992.

181. *Nezavisimaya gazeta*, 6 Jan. 1993.

182. *Nezavisimaya gazeta*, 8 July 1994.

Chapter 5

Russia and the Asia-Pacific Region

Initially, the Asia-Pacific was a subordinate priority for Russia and policy toward it was largely an extension of policy toward the West. When Kozyrev outlined the principles of Russia's foreign policy in March 1992 the emphasis was placed on the West and the Asia-Pacific region was treated in passing.[1] Subsequently, Moscow's interest in the region was elevated by the need to resolve the territorial dispute with Japan, and by a recognition of the importance of China and the Korean Peninsula. At one level of policy, the idea of the balance of power dominates Russian attitudes toward the region as the traditional approach toward foreign policy. Vladimir Lukin identified Russia's policy toward the Asia-Pacific in terms of the maintenance of a balance of power between the major actors, Japan and China in particular.[2] Beyond this most basic level of policy Moscow is strongly guided by Gorbachevian multilateralism, the contents of which were spelled out in the Vladivostok speech of July 1986. Gorbachevian multilateralism is seen as a means of integrating Russia into the Asia-Pacific and minimizing the negative effects of an unregulated balance-of-power system, which include protracted tensions and possible conflicts.

The tension between the balance of power approach and Gorbachevian multilateralism is one that has shaped both the aims and the conduct of Russian diplomacy toward the region. The Asia-Pacific region has witnessed the impact of domestic political forces on Russian foreign policy that have undermined Moscow's ability to chart a consistent course. Domestic political influences in the form of a revived nationalism have been stimulated by the territorial dispute with Japan and have altered the direction of Moscow's policy toward that country. Moreover, local Far Eastern interests have claimed a role in policy toward the Asia-Pacific in view of Moscow's distance from the area and its overriding concern with Europe and the West. Conflict between federal and local authorities has influenced Russian behavior toward Japan and China. Policy toward the Asia-Pacific cannot be conducted by Moscow alone in this situation. Moscow has attempted to formulate a coherent policy toward the Asia-Pacific but has found itself responding to contradictory internal and external pressures.

MOSCOW'S MULTILATERALISM

In the Vladivostok speech, Gorbachev emphasized the need to normalize relations with China, which was achieved in May 1989, and stressed the importance of an overriding multilateral security framework for conflict prevention and regulation. The idea of security multilateralism in its various forms continued to be expressed by Gorbachev in subsequent speeches and became orthodoxy for the Soviet Foreign Ministry. The Gorbachevian legacy retains a similar position for the Russian Foreign Ministry whose representatives have continued to emphasize the importance of security multilateralism, and have made specific proposals to give it effect. Moscow has obtained an opportunity to articulate its views on this issue through the annual Association of South East Asian Nations (ASEAN) Foreign Ministers meetings that have included Russia as a special guest since 1992. Russia has pressed ASEAN to grant it the status of a dialogue partner, of which there are seven—the U.S., Japan, the EU, Australia, New Zealand, Canada, and South Korea. From the ASEAN perspective, however, dialogue partner status is awarded to states or regional groupings with extensive economic ties with the ASEAN region, a criterion which excludes Russia. In any case, Kozyrev spoke at the 25th ASEAN Foreign Ministers's meeting in Manila in July 1992 as a special guest and declared that Russia intended to be constructively engaged in the Asia-Pacific region. He proposed a series of confidence building measures (CBMs) and measures to limit naval exercises within designated "zones of peace" and suggested security cooperation with the ASEAN states.[3]

ASEAN countries had invited both Russian and Chinese foreign ministers as special guests at their 1992 Foreign Ministers's meeting to prepare for a post-Cold War regional order in which both China and Russia would assume a role. Among the ASEAN countries, the widespread expectation was that Russia would serve to support regional equilibrium in a balance-of-power system that would prevent the emergence of a hegemon. The Russian naval facility at Cam Ranh Bay in Vietnam, which had been regarded as a threat by Thailand, Singapore and the West during the Cold War years, came to be viewed differently. As regional concerns switched to China, a Russian presence at Cam Ranh Bay was seen as useful insurance by those ASEAN countries who are concerned about the South China Sea emerging as an area of possible conflict. The Russian presence at Cam Ranh Bay has been reduced significantly, however; the last major surface vessel, a destroyer, was withdrawn in December 1991 and all military advisers were removed in May 1992. U.S. Undersecretary of Defense for Policy Paul Wolfowitz declared in August 1992 that in practical military terms there was no longer a Russian presence at Cam Ranh Bay.[4] Nonetheless, Russian Naval Chief Felix Gromov stated that Cam Ranh Bay would remain a resupply and repair stop for Pacific Fleet vessels provided that Moscow could reach a satisfactory agreement with Vietnam over rent and its future use.[5]

ASEAN countries sought Moscow's affirmation of the post-Cold War regional equilibrium and so allowed Russia access to Asia-Pacific security fora and related bodies. Russia, however, was in no position to act as a major support for regional order that would entail balancing China, while its leaders placed so much importance on maintaining a relationship with Beijing. Moreover, Russia's ability to contribute to regional security had declined dramatically since the end of the Cold War and made it dependent on a regional order underpinned by other external powers—the United States in particular. The inherent contradictions in Russia's approach to the region gave added impetus to the search for an Asia-Pacific security multilateralism. Moscow wanted to avoid a dependence on the United States in managing tensions on the Korean Peninsula or in counterbalancing China. As a result, Russian representatives became fervent proponents of Asia-Pacific security multilateralism as an alternative.

Yeltsin, during his address to South Korea's Parliament on 14 November 1992, stressed that Russia geopolitically was part of the Asia-Pacific region and that its national interests dictated that it become a full partner of the region.[6] He called for a mechanism for multilateral negotiations in the Asia-Pacific region as well as its subregions. He also proposed a system of conflict regulation and regular discussions between regional security experts as a conflict prevention measure.[7] At the 26th ASEAN Foreign Ministers's meeting, which was held in Singapore in July 1993, Kozyrev proposed that Russia assume the role of a guarantor of an Asia-Pacific security system that would be developed over time. He declared that his aim at the 26th Foreign Ministers's meeting was to affirm Russia's role in the region in terms of maintaining a political stronghold for comprehensive Russian involvement in regional affairs.[8] Kozyrev also suggested that a Russia-ASEAN committee be established, but this and other proposals were ignored. ASEAN showed little interest in a body or committee to conduct relations with Russia similar to the ASEAN-China Senior Officials Committee. Nonetheless, Russia was included as a member of the ASEAN Regional Forum (ARF) that met in July 1994; this security body now includes 19 members—Russia, the six ASEAN countries and their seven dialogue partners, China, Vietnam, Cambodia, Laos, and Papua New Guinea. At the meeting, Kozyrev proposed that a center for the study of conflict be established and called for greater transparency in arms sales and military doctrines. The ARF was regarded by the Clinton administration as the security equivalent of Asia-Pacific Economic Cooperation (APEC), as a means to engage China in dialogue and to promote specific security-related measures. Russia's inclusion in this body was an achievement but one that masked the extent to which its participation was regarded as a matter of diplomatic courtesy.

Indeed, Russia's Foreign Ministry was concerned that the debates within the Asia-Pacific region were being conducted without Russia.[9] Russia had been included in ARF in the expectation that it may have a stabilizing role in the region but it had been excluded from the APEC process, despite its eagerness to join. Russia's proposals in the Asia-Pacific region had fallen on deaf ears because, as *Izvestiya* correspondent Sergei Agafonov put it, Russia suffered from an outsider syndrome whereas in Europe it has been an accepted actor.[10] Kozyrev complained that reactions to his proposals at ARF were restrained if not sour, as though they were intended for propaganda purposes.[11] Geographic propinquity has been an inadequate basis to claim a right of involvement in the Asia-Pacific region in the face of Moscow's European orientation. Cultural differences and administrative and economic chaos have made Russia one of the least attractive potential partners for the region. Eurasianists and others may assert Russia's Asian identity and may proclaim Asia to be as important for Russia as the West. For the Asia-Pacific region at large Russia is not part of of Asia or at least lies within another part of Asia and is somewhat alien to the Sino-Confucian cultures along the peripheries of its Far Eastern borders. The outsider syndrome alone would not be sufficient to bar Russia's entry into the Asia-Pacific region; when allied with economic disorder and the absence of economic links with the major economies there this factor becomes a justification.

Part of the problem has been that Russian representatives act according to a policy framework and continue to table proposals as though Russia were still a superpower. This status previously allowed Moscow the prerogative of assuming participatory rights in the Asia-Pacific region, particularly over security issues, but the demand is unjustifiable today. Some of the proposals raised by Russian representatives relate to an era of superpower naval rivalry that has since passed, others are simply impractical or repetitive. The expectation that the region would treat Russia's proposals seriously is a legacy of the Gorbachev period when every new Soviet initiative was applauded. The realization of irrelevance that has since dogged Moscow's efforts in the Asia-Pacific region has been a bitter experience for a people who once claimed equality with the United States.

Russia has related to the region in terms of bilateral relationships that have not been harmonized with the multilateralism espoused. Moscow's relationship with Japan has been hostage to the territorial dispute allowing Japan to exercise silent veto power over Russia's entry into APEC, or its membership of other regional fora. China is a geopolitical and economic priority for Russia and stable relations with Beijing are necessary for Russia's security. Nonetheless, closer Russian relations with China, either through expanded arms sales or from perceived geopolitical necessity, may become an Asia-Pacific concern, and would reduce Russia's ability to assume the role of a regional guarantor. In relation to both Japan and China, bilateral relationships have undermined Moscow's ability to pursue multilateralism. In relation to the Korean Peninsula, however, bilateral relationships have suffered as a consequence of Moscow's emphasis on multilateralism, the results of which have fallen short of expectations. This confusion has prevented Moscow from devising a coherent Asia-Pacific policy that would reconcile bilateral relationships with the multilateralism espoused.

IMPASSE WITH JAPAN

Moscow's democrats moved to resolve the territorial dispute with Japan; this was to be their first significant foreign policy act after the Soviet collapse. The salient motive behind this intention was related to the nature of the post-Soviet domestic order that they wanted to establish in Russia, which required an act of repudiation of the Stalinist past. In their eyes, the four island groups in question, which the Russians call the South Kuriles and the Japanese the hoppô ryôdo, were obtained illegally in September 1945 when they were occupied by Soviet forces. The process of expurgating Russia of its Stalinist past demanded the establishment of a legal order and a corresponding foreign policy based on legality. Russia, claimed the pro-Western democrats, had to ensure that its border would have the sanction of international law and thus foreign policy would be realigned with new domestic priorities. Russia's border with Japan, as Foreign Ministry Director Solov'ev declared, required the foundation of international legality.[12] Behind this view was the democrats's concern to establish an enduring legal basis for Russia's border security as a reorientation away from the excessive reliance on power during the Soviet era.

The expectation of economic benefit constituted an additional reason that was highlighted when Gorbachev visited Tokyo in April 1991. The economic factor has had contradictory significance for the Russians. There were some who argued that economics would compel Japan to meet Moscow's terms because of a need for Russia's resources. This theory of limitless resources as an attraction for Japan was debunked by those with an understanding of Japan's trade relations with alternative suppliers of those raw materials, but it still retained a following.[13] Gorbachev, however, went to Tokyo expecting Japanese economic support for Soviet perestroika on the basis that economic relations could be separated from the territorial issue.[14] The economic factor was also salient in Ruslan Khasbulatov's visit to Tokyo in September 1991 when he talked in terms of a staged resolution of the dispute. Khasbulatov claimed that Moscow required $8–15 billion from Japan in economic support.[15] The most Japan was willing to offer was a $2.5 billion assistance package that was announced on 8 October immediately after Khasbulatov's visit. This decision followed the EEC's granting of $1.5 billion to the Soviet Union and was viewed as a necessary measure to promote stability after the attempted coup of August 1991.

The views of the political figures who were subsequently to become leaders of independent Russia were shaped in 1990–1991 during a period of conflict and interaction with Soviet authorities. Yeltsin's position was characteristically ambiguous and impulsive, and depended on his political audience. During his visit to Tokyo in January 1990 he proposed a five-stage resolution of the issue which comprised: official recognition of the territorial problem; a peace treaty without the precondition of a settlement of the territorial dispute; the formation of a free enterprise zone around the islands; demilitarization of the area; and a final solution to be left to future generations.[16] This was the first occasion that a Russian official had recognized the existence of the problem and gave the Japanese some hope. Nonetheless, Yeltsin soon afterward visited the islands and declared to the Russian settlers there that they were on Russian territory and that he had no intention of handing them over to Japan.[17] It was Yeltsin in his capacity as Chairman of Russia's Supreme Soviet who bound Gorbachev's hands with a declaration of Russian sovereignty on 12 June 1990. Point 8 of this declaration stated that Russian territory could not be altered without the will of the people as expressed through a referendum. As a representative of the Soviet Union, Gorbachev was deprived of legal authority over Russia and consequently lost the authority to negotiate the issue with the Japanese during his April 1991 visit to Tokyo.

Andrei Kozyrev, as Russia's Foreign Minister was invited by Soviet Foreign Minister Aleksander Bessmertnykh to join Gorbachev's delegation in Japan. Kozyrev stressed the importance of recognizing the existence of the territorial problem and establishing an acceptable post-war border with Japan. He emphasized that there could be no sale of Russian territory. The intention of a sale had been attributed to Gorbachev by commentators and by the notorious parliamentary deputy Artyem Tarasov.[18] Kozyrev's position subsequently became clearer as he identified the Soviet-Japanese Agreement of 19 October 1956 as the basis for the regulation of the issue; two islands, Shikotan and Habomais, would be returned to Japan.[19] Georgi Kunadze, Kozyrev's deputy who had previously specialized on Japan at the Institute of Oriental Studies in Moscow, emphasized the need to resolve the issue on the basis of legality.[20] Kozyrev was strongly criticized by Soviet Foreign Ministry representatives for undermining the Soviet position during this short period in 1991 when Russian and Soviet Foreign Ministries competed. The Soviet position rested on the 1945 Yalta Agreements that allowed Soviet forces to occupy the islands and Article 2(e) of the 1951 San Francisco Treaty that deprived Japan of sovereignty over the Kurile Islands. The Soviet Foreign Ministry insisted that the disputed islands were part of the Kurile Islands and that the 1956 agreement had lost its validity after Japan signed the Mutual Defense Treaty with the U.S. on 19 January 1960.

Russia's democrats moved to prepare the public for negotiations over the issue with Japan. Russia's renowned Japan specialist, Konstantin Sarkisov of the Institute of Oriental Studies, claimed that a resolution of the issue required changes in the thinking of the Russian people who had been programed by the Soviet Union to regard the territory in dispute as unquestionably Russian. Sarkisov and Cherevko cited material obtained from the archives of the Soviet Foreign Ministry to demonstrate that the islands had never been Russian territory before 1945. According to this material, Foreign Minister General Putyatin received instructions from Tsar Nicholas I dated 24 February 1853 to negotiate a border between Russia and Japan. The island of Urup was designated the last point of Russian territory, reflected in the 1855 Treaty of Shimoda. This treaty established the border where Russian and Japanese patterns of settlement met in the late eighteenth century. Russian settlers had followed the Kurile Islands from the Kamchatka Peninsula as far as Urup, which they occupied until they were forced out by the Japanese in 1807. The Japanese reached Etorofu in 1798 and were motivated by a desire to establish a barrier against further Russian movement south. The islands in questions were never settled or claimed by the Russians until Soviet forces expelled the 17,000 Japanese residents in 1945.[21] The issue was discussed at an emergency session of the Russian Supreme Soviet on 23 October 1991 when Sergei Baburin and Nikolai Pavlov declared their nationalist credentials by opposing either complete or partial transfer of the islands to Japan. Both Baburin and Pavlov had support within the Supreme Soviet when they called for an annulment of the 1956 agreement while Kozyrev was sarcastically asked what price Russia would sell the islands to Japan.[22]

This issue, more than any other, aroused public opinion within Russia to become an important factor in foreign policy. Russia's democrats attempted to prepare the public for a resolution of the dispute that to nationalist circles appeared as a capitulation before Japan. Those pro Western democrats who based their arguments on legality could find little support from a Russian public that had minimal experience or understanding of this idea. The attempt to demonstrate that the islands in question were never Russian before 1945 simply bred distrust and suspicion among a public inured to the manipulative campaigns of their leaders. Russian democrats drew back from confrontation with the nationalists and moved to resolve the issue over the heads of the public in Soviet fashion. Paradoxically, the democrats acted undemocratically with the conviction that the public had been deeply socialized by the Soviet system and would not understand the significance of the issues involved. As the democrats resorted to secrecy in preparation of a resolution of the issue, a broad opposition coalition was formed, particularly in the Supreme Soviet. The consequence was that nationalist public opinion emerged as a barrier that prevented any movement over the dispute, thereby confirming the impasse in Russian relations with Japan.

This issue demonstrated the extent to which local administrative figures could emerge with significant influence on Asia-Pacific policy. In this case, Valentin Fyodorov, as representative of Sakhalin *Oblast,* assumed the role of guardian of the interests of the Russian settlers of the disputed islands and subsequently emerged as a champion of Russia's national interests. Fyodorov was pro rector at the Moscow-based Plekhanov Institute of National Economy from 1985 to April 1991 when he was elected as chairman of the executive committee of Sakhalin *Oblast* administration. His intention in moving to the Far East was to introduce a free market experiment in the area and to test economic theory. Fyodorov was thrown into public prominence when, before and during Gorbachev's visit to Japan, he campaigned against a return of the islands to Japan. He then threatened to establish a political party to oppose the transfer of the islands in return for economic aid.[23] It was Fyodorov who declared that "to sell ancient Russian land is a crime" and who demonstrated a deeper intuitive understanding of the symbols and slogans that motivate Russians than the democrats. The term ancient Russian land (*iskonnoe russkoe zemlya*) captured the public's imagination despite the fact that the territory in question had never been under Russian occupation until recently.[24]

Fyodorov's role was surprisingly ambiguous and he never was the national patriot his sloganeering made him appear to be. He used nationalist slogans to prevent a resolution of the territorial issue by Moscow alone but his intention was to preserve the necessary freedom to conduct his economic experiment. He declared that the territorial issue could be resolved if borders were eliminated in an economic union that embraced Sakhalin and Hokkaidô.[25] On 27 May 1991, Russia's Supreme Soviet conferred the status of a free enterprise zone on the Sakhalin region but the experiment was again threatened toward the end of the year when it seemed that preparations for a resolution of the issue were being reviewed. Fyodorov was the first among Far Eastern governors to support Yeltsin during the August 1991 coup attempt and was rewarded accordingly. On 12 October 1991, Fyodorov was promoted by Yeltsin to head of *oblast* (Russian territorial sub-division) administration and on 23 December the title of governor was conferred on him by *oblast* deputies. His campaigns against the democrats over the territorial issue developed in stridency and confrontative style in a way that provided a precedent for Russia's national patriots. Though not a national patriot himself Fyodorov invoked the symbols of Russian nationalism that aroused the involvement of nationalist groups. Their hard line and rancorous views of the territorial dispute would make Fyodorov's economic experiment impossible because it demanded Japanese participation. Fyodorov ironically undermined his own intentions.

Fyodorov called for public protests against Khasbulatov's visit to Japan when it seemed that a deal was being arranged and insisted that any resolution of the issue required the participation of Sakhalin *Oblast*.[26] When Kunadze declared that he would be guided by the 1956 agreement, Fyodorov alluded to the deputy foreign minister's Georgian ethnicity announcing that he did not have the moral right to manage the issue of ancient Russian land.[27] In a speech in Kunashiri, Fyodorov declared that if the Soviet Union attempted to return the islands to Japan he would consider campaigning for full independence for the Russian Far East.[28] Indeed, during the Supreme Soviet hearings on the issue on 23 October, Fyodorov repeated the warning that the problem could lead to the establishment of a Far Eastern republic.[29] Fyodorov also popularized the notion that the islands constituted an important economic asset for Russia in terms of its fishing resources.[30]

When the Soviet Union collapsed, the pro-Western democrats saw this issue as an opportunity to make a declaration of future behavior on the basis of legality and accepted international norms. When Soviet Foreign Minister Boris Pankin hosted his Japanese counterpart Tarô Nakayama in October 1991 a Soviet-Japanese working group was established to develop bilateral relations.[31] This body first met as a Russian-Japanese committee at deputy foreign minister level in February 1992 during which discussions focused on the territorial issue. Russia's chief delegate, Georgi Kunadze, claimed that Russia would scrap the Andrei Gromyko declaration of 29 January 1960, which repudiated the October 1956 Soviet-Japanese joint statement. This declaration followed the signature of the Japan-U.S. Mutual Defense Treaty on 19 January.[32] In February 1992 Yeltsin's visit to Japan was fixed for September and a special commission headed by Gennadii Burbulis was established, which called for a solution based on the 1956 joint statement.

The Japanese perceived an opportunity for a resolution of an issue that had been left hanging since the war. The *hoppô ryôdo* issue did not touch on public opinion in Japan and if not for the lobbying activities of the Northern Islands Association many Japanese would have been unaware of a problem that was so remote from their lives. The issue was a matter of state interest for Japan's official representatives for whom the distinction between non-Japanese territory, which had to be surrendered after World War II as imperial conquest, and homeland territory, which would always be Japanese, was a real one. The Japanese Foreign Ministry or *Gaimushô* as the custodian of Japan's state interests, has been concerned that homeland territory should not be confused with imperial conquests. Moreover, the territorial issue was the touchstone of relations with Moscow, which could not develop effectively unless Russia disavowed the consequences of what the Japanese regarded as the illegal occupation of their territory. The then Japanese Foreign Minister, Michio Watanabe, told Russian audiences that the real issue was trust, without which there could be no effective and sound relationship with Moscow. Watanabe revealed what most concerned the older Japanese generation about Russia when he pointed to Soviet treatment of Japanese POWs after the war and the violation of the April 1941 Neutrality Pact when the Soviet Union joined the war against Japan. Watanabe declared that Japanese business would not be interested in Russia without the restoration of trust in the relationship, which required a satisfactory resolution of the territorial issue.[33]

Among the Japanese there were significant differences of views between the *Gaimushô* and the then ruling Liberal Democratic Party. LDP Secretary-General Ichirô Ozawa visited Moscow in March 1991 and declared that the LDP would drop the demand for an immediate return of all four islands and spoke in favor of their phased return according to the 1956 declaration. Without referring to Ozawa by name Kozyrev wrote that before Gorbachev's trip to Tokyo one of the LDP leaders proposed a $28 billion deal in return for the islands.[34] On his return to Tokyo, however, Ozawa met Prime Minister Kaifū and on 23 March issued a statement that Japan demanded the return of all four islands together and that the 1956 agreement was insufficient as a basis for the resolution of the issue.[35] Similar differences could be noted over whether Japan should offer limited economic assistance to Russia irrespective of the territorial dispute. The *Gaimushô* tended to resist this move while the LDP Special Committee on Foreign Economic Aid stressed the importance of contributing to political stability in Russia.[36] By early 1992 the *Gaimushô* had endorsed the idea of a phased return of the islands, and in February 1992 Watanabe declared that Japan could accept the return of two islands under the 1956 agreement, provided Russia accept Japanese sovereignty over all the islands.[37]

The Japanese accepted the need to assist the Russian settlers of the islands in order to remove a Russian complaint that could hinder negotiations over the issue. The then Prime Minister, Kiichi Miyazawa, declared that Japan may consider granting permanent residency to Russian residents who wanted to stay and housing assistance for those who wanted to leave the islands rather than live under Japanese rule.[38] Nonetheless, the property rights of the Japanese settlers who were forcibly evicted in 1945 would be restored if Japan obtained the islands, and the position of the remaining Russians would be dubious. According to a Soviet census, there were 24,600 Russian settlers on the islands as of 1 January 1991—11,000 on Etorofu and 13,600 in Kunashiri and Shikotan;[39] in addition there were some 7,000 armed forces personnel. Since 1991, emigration from the islands to the mainland has accelerated and by 1994 there were 14,000 residents and services personnel.[40] Not surprisingly, some of the Russian settlers were actually in favor of returning the islands to Japan to benefit from better living conditions. A poll was conducted among the residents that showed that 6 percent of 3,000 people when asked agreed to live under Japanese jurisdiction in 1989 while in 1991 when 11,704 people were asked the figure rose to 22 percent.[41]

The stage was set for a gross misunderstanding between Russia and Japan over this dispute. The Moscow pro-Western group prepared for a resolution of the issue behind the scenes in order to avoid a nationalist backlash. Supreme Soviet Deputy Aleksei Surkov claimed that the Committee of International Relations held hearings on the issue at the beginning of the year and concluded that the territory had been illegally included in the Soviet Union and should be returned to Japan. Surkov declared that foreign policy could no longer be based on amorality and had to be firmly grounded in law, and opined that a majority of Supreme Soviet deputies would support this position.[42] Supreme Soviet deputy Vladimir Ispravnikov headed a parliamentary delegation that visited Tokyo in May 1992 and declared that the territorial problem would be resolved when Yeltsin visited Tokyo. At the Munich G-7 meeting in July 1992, Yeltsin talked freely about the possibility of concluding a peace treaty with Japan in exchange for substantial economic assistance.[43]

Japanese expectations were stimulated by such public pronouncements which made it seem that all would hang on Yeltsin's visit. Miyazawa had declared on 3 February that the issue would be settled when Yeltsin visited Japan.[44] In separate interviews with Vitalii Tret'yakov, main editor of *Nezavisimaya gazeta*, the various Japanese leaders outlined their heightened expectations. Watanabe said that Yeltsin intended to sign a peace treaty with Japan during his visit and reiterated a willingness to be flexible over the terms and conditions of the return of the islands. Miyazawa seemed less certain than before that the problem would be finally disposed of during Yeltsin's visit but expressed hope that negotiations would result in the resolution of the controversy. He declared that when the issue is settled large-scale financial assistance for Russia would be possible.[45] Japanese statements linking financial assistance to a final resolution of the problem aggravated existing divisions among the Russians. Those around Yeltsin who prepared for his visit to Japan had additional incentives to work for a resolution of the issue. Those who were fundamentally opposed to a compromise over the islands had additional reasons to strengthen their opposition and to suspect that a betrayal of Russia's interests was indeed being planned. The consequence was a polarization of views and the formation of a broad opposition group directed not only against the idea of compromise over this specific dispute, but against Kozyrev's foreign policy in general.

A key event in the formation of this opposition coalition was the holding of the Supreme Soviet hearings during the visit on 28 July 1992. The hearings were organized by Oleg Rumyantsev who was head of the Constitutional Commission and whose ambitions pushed him into the sphere of foreign policy. Rumyantsev's foray into foreign policy was a result of the ill-defined relationship that existed between executive and legislature and of an attempt to strengthen the legislature's role. In an interview in May 1992, Rumyantsev outlined his approach that contained three key points. First, he insisted that there was to be no forced resolution of the issue and no revision of the results of World War II. If Russia's borders were revised in the East said Rumyantsev they could be revised in the West, where other countries had claims on Russian territory. In the case of a territorial revision ultra-nationalist forces in Russia would be strengthened, which would add to existing political instability. Second, the 1956 agreement must be presented to the Supreme Soviet for endorsement in which case the support of the conservatives may be negotiated. Third, any decision to transfer all or part of the islands, according to Rumyantsev, may require a referendum.

The situation was very unclear at that stage but it was known that efforts to formulate a new constitution, which were being orchestrated by Rumyantsev himself, could be strongly affected by moves to surrender territory as part of a deal with Japan. Various proposals were tabled within the Constitutional Commission to prevent territorial changes without specific approval either of the Supreme Soviet or by the people through a referendum. According to Article 75 of the draft constitution, which had been approved by the Sixth Congress of Peoples's Deputies, a proposed territorial change required the approval of the republic, *krai* (Russian territorial sub-division, similar to *oblast* but including a small minority) or *oblast* in question, and a referendum within the Russian Federation. Moreover, the Constitutional Commission contemplated strengthening the Supreme Soviet's power's over foreign policy by allowing it to ratify and denounce international treaties (Article 80) and the authority to conduct national referenda (Article 85).[46] While the Supreme Soviet claimed these powers, as well as the authority to define the basic direction of foreign policy (Article 85/B) its involvement in events relating to the territorial dispute with Japan was assured.

On the eve of the hearings Kunadze declared that a peace treaty with Japan had been prepared, and that the issue should not be subject to internal political conflict.[47] The Foreign Ministry and its supporters on this issue adopted the view that the territory in question was not Russian territory anyway and had been illegally acquired by Soviet occupation, therefore draft constitutional provisions had no bearing on the issue. On this basis the executive could act alone according to the dictates of international law. The attitudes associated with this view were regarded as contemptuous by Supreme Soviet representatives. Deputy Head of the Committee on International Relations Ion Andronov declared that a conspiracy had been hatched to return the islands to Japan within three stages, for which he blamed Kozyrev and Lukin.[48] The head of the committee, Ambartsumov, stated publicly that there was too much pressure from Japan and the utility of Yeltsin's visit to Japan was in question.[49]

The hearings, subsequently published in *Rossiiskaya gazeta,* were notable for the range of views expressed. They provide insight into foreign policy attitudes in general as well as a specific record of mounting opposition over this issue. Twenty-nine deputies (out of 52 invited) gave their views in closed door hearings. Sergei Filatov, who opened the hearings, supported the Foreign Ministry's position to the effect that affirmation of the 1956 agreement would provide a legal basis for Russia's relationship with Japan. This position was supported by Ambartsumov, Japan specialist Konstantin Sarkisov, and Director of the Institute of International Economics and International Relations (IMEMO) V. A. Martynov. Contrary views were expressed by Ambartsumov's deputy Andronov who pointed to the effect that return of the islands would have on Chinese or Finnish territorial claims on Russia. R. V. Petrov of the Far Eastern Institute claimed that the issue had become an internal political issue and that any political figure who transferred the islands to Japan would sign his own death warrant. The nationalist Nikolai Pavlov proposed that the Foreign Ministry be investigated for its willingness to cede territory to Japan and demanded that not even a meter be given away. N. N. Vorontsov from the

Kurile Islands reminded the deputies of the fishing resources of the islands and proposed a Japanese Russian condominium.

Most interesting from the perspective of general foreign policy was the reaction to the presentation of the military's view. The Russian military similarly expressed different views of the issue that reflected the condition of society at large. Major-General Georgii Mekhov argued that the islands in question were necessary for the security of Russia's Far East, detailing the following reasons: the islands covered access to the Sea of Okhotsk; the unfrozen sea straits of the southern Kuriles were most suitable for all-year-round deployment of naval vessels; the islands were important for the air defense of the Far East; and return of the islands would allow Japan to transform them into a military forepost against Russia. Mekhov, however, concluded that a compromise based on a return to Japan of some of the islands was possible.[50] A document was circulated during the hearings under the name of Chief of General Staff Col.-General Viktor Dubynin that included the above strategic observations and added a number of political arguments. Return of the islands created the danger of a chain reaction of territorial demands on Russia and would weaken Russia in relation to China. Moreover, within Russia anti-government protests and rebellions would result if the islands were returned, which would strengthen separatism.[51] The military was also represented at the hearings by V. P. Zaloman from the General Staff and Rear Admiral Yuri Kaisin who argued that even a return of some of the islands was out of the question in view of the danger that Japan and the U.S. posed for Russia in the Far East.[52] In Soviet times, the views of the military would have had unquestioned authority but times had changed and deputies reacted negatively to Kaisin's views in particular. Ambartsumov declared his rejection of the military's argument that the islands were necessary for future war while S. F. Zasukhin retorted "Comrade Admiral, there is no need to frighten us."[53] Military considerations were very much subordinated to political priorities during these hearings, which demonstrated the extent to which Russia differed from the Soviet Union.

The demand that the president postpone Poltoranin's trip to Japan was raised during these hearings. Feelings were exacerbated by Kunadze's declaration that the president's official position over this issue would be declared only during the visit. This may have reflected Yeltsin's vacillations but otherwise strengthened the suspicion that a conspiracy had been organized. Kunadze added that it was not the Supreme Soviet's role to become involved in the actual negotiations, which simply added fuel to the fire.[54] Rumyantsev had organized the hearings in order to ascertain the president's position before he went to Japan, and to ensure that the Supreme Soviet would retain a role in formulating foreign policy over issues such as proposed territorial adjustments. Rumyantsev's own views were reflected in a pamphlet published by the Constitutional Commission entitled "Russian-Japan Relations and the Problem of the Territorial Integrity of the Russian Federation." Rumyantsev argued that the president should not visit Japan without a defined position over the issue formulated in collaboration with the Supreme Soviet and the Congress of Peoples's Deputies. He rejected the Foreign Ministry's argument that Russia's Constitution did not apply to the islands since they were not considered Russian territory and insisted that a referendum would be required to change their status. He claimed that Russia has imperfect title to the islands but Japan has no title at all, except for Habomais for unexplained reasons. The 1956 agreement which was regarded as the basis of a solution by the Foreign Ministry was, according to Rumyantsev, conditional in that it was to be activated on the fulfillment by Japan of certain conditions, which included the signing of a peace treaty. Japan, he argued, never fulfilled this condition and therefore, the 1956 declaration cannot be accepted as a one-sided obligation for Russia, irrespective of the conditions initially attached. Rumyantsev came to the conclusion that the most rational solution for the dispute would be the retention of Kunashiri and Etorofu under Russian jurisdiction and the establishment of joint Russian-Japanese sovereignty over Shikotan and Habomais in a condominium.[55]

The hearings revealed that public opinion, which the president could not ignore, had emerged as a key factor in Russian foreign policy. The president himself said little about the issue but it was Sarkisov's view that by August he had decided that the time was not propitious for a visit to Japan. Yeltsin had understood the mood and how isolated the Foreign Ministry and its supporters had become over this matter. On 8 August, Deputy Prime Minister and Information Minister Mikhail Poltoranin were sent to Japan to prepare for the president's visit. Speculation was stimulated by the selection of Poltoranin for this task rather than the foreign minister and it was thought that Kozyrev's resignation was imminent.[56] Kozyrev wrote that Poltoranin's trip to Japan was sheer slapstick as he knew little about foreign policy and did great damage to the Foreign Ministry and to Russian diplomacy.[57] Poltoranin rather innocently declared that the president would propose a two-stage solution to the dispute and was the first high-ranking minister who revealed his view. In Japan he emphasized that the 1956 agreement would be the basis of Russia's position and that the Okinawa model would apply to the remaining islands, Kunashiri and Etorofu. They would remain under Russian rule for 15–20 years before they would be transferred to Japan. All property and financial problems arising were to be resolved during this period. Moreover, Poltoranin stressed while in Japan that no referendum would be required over the transfer since the islands were not Russian territory.[58]

Poltoranin represented no one but himself over the issue and went further than the Foreign Ministry and the Burbulis commission, which based their positions only on the 1956 agreement. He naively played into the hands of the opponents of the president's visit who could claim that a sellout had indeed been planned. Viktor Sheinis, a Supreme Soviet deputy and member of Ambartsumov's Committee on International Relations, had opposed the visit during the hearings. He claimed that after Poltoranin's visit 52 deputies wrote to the president calling for a return to Soviet policies over the issue and declared that it should be left for future generations to resolve.[59] Stanislav Kondrashov of *Izvestiya* wrote that Parliament was the guardian of Russia's national interest and stressed that the matter must be resolved democratically with Parliament's full involvement. Kondrashov claimed that in the current mood even the radical democrats would not press for the return of the islands to Japan out of concern for their reputations.[60]

If the president was still wavering, his meeting with Watanabe in Moscow on 2 September removed all doubt that the visit should be postponed. The meeting lasted 35 minutes, and when Yeltsin was asked what his position was he replied that he would declare it in Tokyo, and insisted that the issue could not be resolved under pressure.[61] The president subsequently told reporters that the political timing was not right for a settlement of the dispute. When Watanabe returned to Tokyo he declared that Yeltsin required more time and had proposed the demilitarization of North East Asia. The issue of sovereignty over the islands according to Yeltsin's view was to be left to future generations, a proposal which the Japanese rejected outright.[62]

First Deputy Head of the president's Security Service Boris Patnikov complained that the president's security could not be guaranteed because the service was not allowed to take weapons to Japan. He claimed that he was alarmed by the situation in Japan and the danger posed to the president by nationalist extremists in that country. On 3 September he sent a fax to the president recommending postponement of the trip for security reasons.[63] This was an unprecedented statement and it was not the business of the president's Security Service to join public debates. The suspicion remains that the public was being prepared for the postponement of the visit.

Yeltsin announced his decision not to visit Tokyo during the Security Council meeting of 9 September. He telephoned Roh Tae Woo in Seoul first, then called Miyazawa to announce postponement of the trip.[64] For the Japanese, the decision was sudden and characteristic of Yeltsin's erratic behavior. The head of the president's administration, Yuri Petrov, had traveled to Japan in mid-August and was convinced that the visit should be postponed in view of Japanese insistence on an immediate resolution of the issue. When interviewed, Petrov said he could not explain the Security Council decision since he was not a member. It is certain, however, that Petrov lobbied behind the scenes against the visit and may have been responsible for the Security Service's unusual public statement.[65] Kozyrev claimed that during the Security Council meeting Rutskoi, Skokov, and Security Minister Barannikov launched an attack on the visit and demanded its postponement, which was accepted without voting.[66] Kunadze said that the decision was made by Yeltsin himself but it was unlikely to be opposed, least of all by the Foreign Ministry.[67]

In terms of Russia's relationship with Japan, the cancellation demonstrated clearly the impact of Russian domestic political forces that eliminated all prospect of a resolution of the territorial issue in the foreseeable future. Policy toward Japan was made a hostage to domestic politics and relations with that country slid into an impasse from which they have not been extricated. Yeltsin assumed a populist pose indicating the extent to which his attitude to the dispute had been influenced by domestic politics. The president was preparing to face another round of conflict with the 7th Congress of Peoples's Deputies, to be convened in December 1992. He had no intention of provoking further opposition among the many conservatives and nationalists within the congress by pushing an unpopular resolution of the territorial dispute with Japan. *Izvestiya* correspondent, Konstantin Eggert argued that Yeltsin sacrificed foreign policy to preserve his own domestic policy and protect it from attack. Concessions to Japan over the territorial dispute would have given ammunition to the opponents of domestic economic reform who had taken up the struggle against Yeltsin's government within the Congress of Peoples's Deputies.[68]

Maksim Yusin of *Izvestiya* wrote that the decision tilted the equilibrium of forces within the Russian government against Kozyrev and the Foreign Ministry that had been tainted by the suspicion of wanting to capitulate before Japan.[69] Certainly the ability of the Foreign Ministry to assume the role of an active formulator of foreign policy had been much undermined by this decision. The possibility of further foreign policy innovations to bring Russia into line with the West over other outstanding issues had been blocked by this decision. All talk of a solution to the territorial dispute with Japan was dropped as the innovative period in Russia's relationship with Japan had passed. Both sides had attached so much importance to the territorial dispute that they found it difficult to move to a normal functioning relationship apart from it. The failure to resolve the dispute cast its shadow over the relationship and ensured that mutual suspicions and muted hostility would set the tone for the future. The Russian leadership was prompted to look beyond Japan in the Asia-Pacific and attempted to develop compensatory relationships with South Korea and China. The deadlock that was reached in the relationship with Japan at least compelled Russia to face the wider Asia-Pacific region if only to minimize the repercussions of failure.

The cancellation of the visit had a marked effect on Japanese perceptions of Russia and of Yeltsin in particular. In a country where diplomatic form and ceremony are deeply ingrained, the cancellation was seen as primitive behavior and provided further evidence of the unreliability and unpredictability of Russians. Japan lost diplomatic ground, however, as the Western world applied pressure on the country not to insist on an urgent resolution of the territorial dispute. U.S. Undersecretary of State Frank Wisner called on Japan to appreciate Yeltsin's political predicament, embroiled as he then was in conflict with his conservative opponents in the Supreme Soviet and the Congress of Peoples's Deputies.[70] Lady Margaret Thatcher visited Tokyo later in September 1992 and urged Japan to be flexible, while U.S. Senate Armed Forces Committee Chairman Sam Nunn reminded the Japanese that the disputed islands would never be returned if Yeltsin were replaced by a hard line ruler.[71] Helmut Kohl visited Tokyo in March 1993 and pressed the Japanese to coordinate efforts to ensure stability in the former Soviet Union.[72] Yeltsin, indeed, reaped diplomatic benefits from the cancellation of the visit while he could portray himself as the embattled champion of democracy and free-market reform in Russia. The Japanese were placed on the defensive over the issue and beat a tactical retreat.

The hapless Watanabe, who was accused of rigidity over the issue by his own colleagues in the LDP, was replaced as foreign minister by Kabun Mutô in April 1993. Those groups within the ruling LDP, represented by economic policy-maker Hiroshi Mitsuzuka and critical of the hard line position pushed by Watanabe, had the opportunity to press for a more balanced approach toward Russia. After meeting with Kozyrev on 13 April Kabun Mutô declared that Japan had removed the link between a resolution of the territorial issue and economic aid.[73] Japan had come under sustained pressure from its G-7 partners to contribute to Russia's economic stabilization and the tactical adjustment was a means to ward off further pressure. Within the LDP there was little interest in economic assistance for Russia as Japan's business community was attracted by the opportunities in China and Indochina. Japan's commercial interest turned toward Central Asia rather than Russia and trade delegations were sent to all Central Asian republics except Tajikistan. Central Asian leaders visited Tokyo with the hope of attracting investment; Japan hosted Askar Akaev in April 1993, Nazarbaev in April 1994, and Islam Karimov in May 1994.

Conflict within the Russian government continued in relation to Japan in the wake of the cancellation of the visit. Yeltsin, strongly supported by the Foreign Ministry and his circle of advisers, was still eager to visit Japan to reduce the negative consequences of the cancellation of the 1992 trip. Nonetheless, others were concerned that Yeltsin would make idiosyncratic and impulsive concessions to the Japanese that would complicate policy. Governor Fyodorov who had stimulated Russian nationalism over the territorial dispute, retired from Russian politics on 2 April 1993. He returned to Moscow at his own request, tired by the effort to establish a free-market zone in Sakhalin and rejected by his own deputies.[74] His replacement, Yevgennii Krasnoyarev, similarly expressed opposition to any territorial deal with Japan but in this case local views had high level support. Chernomyrdin himself assumed the mantle of guardian of Russia's interests as if to commit the Russian government to a clear position well before Yeltsin visited Japan. On 18 August, Chernomyrdin visited Yuzhno-Sakhalinski (Sakhalin) and declared to local residents "this problem for us does not exist, we will not discuss it and we don't intend to return them [the islands]." On 19 August, Yeltsin responded by stating that Chernomyrdin had simply pointed to one of the various solutions being discussed. On 20 August, Chernomyrdin traveled to Khabarovsk where he reiterated his position.[75] He subsequently explained that "Russia had no intention of giving the Kurile islands to anyone. We don't need anyone else's

[land] but we will keep our own." The Russian premier sought to establish a consensus over the issue within the council of ministers and to develop relations with all countries in the Asia-Pacific region as a way of balancing Japan.[76]

Gennadii Burbulis continued to express his view of the territorial problem as senior adviser to Yeltsin. On 31 August, he claimed that Chernomyrdin's remarks did not reflect the views of the president's office, thus illustrating again the divisions between the administrative structures represented by Yeltsin and Chernomyrdin.[77] During his own visit to Tokyo in early September, Burbulis remarked that the islands would be returned to Japan sooner or later and that the development of broad and active cooperation between Russia and Japan would lead to a speedier resolution of the dispute.[78] The presidential office and its supporters had been encouraged by the end of the LDP rule in Japan in August 1993 and the emergence of the Hosokawa coalition which seemed more receptive to Russian needs. Hosokawa had emphasized that Japan would strive for full normalization of relations with Russia. His Foreign Minister Tsutomu Hata had stressed the need to support Moscow's democratic and economic reforms.[79] *Izvestiya* correspondent Sergei Agafonov, nonetheless, criticized what he called naive hopes among the Russians that a new Japanese government would result in a change of Japanese attitudes toward the territorial problem.[80]

Yeltsin finally visited Japan in October 1993 after being assured that impossible demands would not be raised by the Japanese. His visit took place from 11–13 October, only a week after he had ordered his army to fire at the Supreme Soviet building. This action undermined his authority in the eyes of the Japanese. It was unclear whether he was the champion of political reform in the way he had presented himself or whether indeed his position as president was secure. Sergei Agafonov found the Japanese pessimistic about the future of Russian-Japanese relations and the political future of Yeltsin himself.[81] In Tokyo, Yeltsin declared that a new psychological climate had developed in relations with Japan, which was hardly the case as the old climate still prevailed.[82] He met Emperor Akihito and in a gesture that did not fail to impress his hosts apologized for Soviet treatment of Japanese POWs during and after World War II.[83] He told Hosokawa that Russia was the heir of the Soviet Union and would observe all treaties and obligations from the Soviet era. When asked whether the 1956 agreement was included, Yeltsin replied, "naturally, I have in mind this agreement."[84] In a joint press conference with Hosokawa, Yeltsin claimed that a territorial demarcation between the two countries would follow the five-phase plan he had earlier proposed, and that Moscow officially accepted and recognized the existence of the territorial problem.[85]

Yeltsin's visit was an attempt to make amends for the cancellation of his earlier trip and not a move to unravel the territorial problem. Soon afterward, Zhirinovsky emerged triumphant at the parliamentary elections of December 1993 thereby dampening any emerging enthusiasm in Japan about relations with Russia. On 13 December, on German radio Zhirinovsky denied that there was any territorial dispute with Japan and claimed that "we will create new Hiroshimas and Nagasakis" and that "I won't hesitate to deploy atomic weapons."[86] Zhirinovsky confirmed the Japanese perception of Russia as capricious, unpredictable, and potentially dangerous. Other factors in this perception included the difficulty in determining who was responsible for policy in Moscow in relation to the territorial dispute and the demilitarization of the islands. Force reductions began in 1992 and the 40 MIG-23s that were deployed in Etorofu in 1983 had been reduced to 10 by May 1993.[87] The Japanese pressed for the complete demilitarization of the islands and the removal of the 7,000 soldiers and border guards.

In May 1992 when Yeltsin met Watanabe he promised that forces stationed there would be withdrawn, while Grachev as the new Russian Defense Minister told an audience of army officers that those forces would remain. The Foreign Ministry explained that Yeltsin was referring to the longterm while Grachev pointed to the immediate future. At this point, Sergei Agafonov lamented the absence of an official position in Russia's young democracy.[88] When Yeltsin met Hosokawa in October 1993 he told the Japanese prime minister that 50 percent of the forces there had been withdrawn, with the rest to follow soon so the islands would be fully demilitarized. One year later in October 1994 Grachev declared that there was no intention to remove the forces deployed there and emphasized the importance of the Far Eastern Military District for Russian security.[89] Who indeed was to decide this issue? It seems that Yeltsin was characteristically indulging in diplomatic courtesies and that Grachev expressed a position that the president would not repudiate in view of his need for the army's support.

Sergei Agafonov wrote from Tokyo that Japan had lost interest in Russia and saw little need to assist Russia economically. According to the Japanese, the momentum given to the attempt to resolve the territorial dispute by both Gorbachev and Yeltsin had been exhausted and the Russian leadership was incapable of further moves, constrained as it was by domestic politics.[90] Tsutomu Hata visited Moscow in March 1994 and stated that the territorial problem should not be a barrier to the development of dialogue between Russia and Japan and that a peace treaty should be signed as quickly as possible.[91] Hata had intended to maintain a channel of communication between Russia and Japan and both sides agreed to exchange visits at foreign minister level at least twice a year.

Various levels of cooperation were developed between the countries but in a relatively low-key manner. Japanese companies Mitsubishi and Mitsui joined a Western consortium to negotiate agreements for the exploration of oil along the Sakhalin shelf. The first agreement was signed in June 1993; a second followed in June 1994 but such ventures were placed in jeopardy by the absence of legislation in Russia that would clarify property rights and taxation obligations. Various assistance projects were unveiled when Russian Deputy

Premier Oleg Soskovets visited Tokyo in November 1994. Japan's Ministry of International Trade and Industry (MITI) announced a program to assist small and medium businesses in Russia and to train Russian executives in Japan, with the intention of strengthening Russia's industrial and export potential. Japan's Export-Import Bank also proposed a $400 million loan for various industrial projects and a $500 million loan for humanitarian assistance. The Russian demand for Japanese participation in a free-trade zone including the disputed territory was ignored by the Japanese.[92] Low-level security dialogue was also developed during the regularly held meetings of Russian and Japanese senior officials. Russian Foreign Ministry and defense officials have also been involved in the North East Asian cooperation dialogue that was initiated in October 1993, and the trilateral forum on North Pacific security problems launched in early 1994.[93]

Relations have been troubled by the problem of Japanese fishing in disputed waters—regarded as poaching by the Russians. The Russian ability to police these waters was severely reduced during the last days of the Soviet Union because of a lack of fuel. During the 1980s, four patrols a day were maintained around the islands, reduced to one a day by October 1991, then becoming irregular.[94] The Sea of Okhotsk became open to Taiwanese, South Korean and Polish fishing, which the Russians could not prevent. The Foreign Ministry complained of Japanese poaching around the disputed islands, a charge which the Japanese rejected on the basis that the fishing was conducted in Japanese waters. Foreign Ministry figures for Japanese poaching were 7,555 cases in 1991, 7,932 in 1992, and 7,690 in 1993.[95] On 14 August 1994, when Russian patrol boats fired on Japanese fishing vessels, several casualties resulted and in another incident on 4 October a Japanese fishing vessel was sunk. Commander of Pacific Ocean Border District Lt.-General Vitalii Sepykh complained that Japanese vessels were impudently intruding into Russian waters and declared that he would defend Russia's exclusive economic zone (EEZ) and would open fire on delinquent vessels.[96] Deputy Foreign Minister Aleksander Panov similarly condemned illegal Japanese fishing in the area and supported the border forces, declaring that they were operating according to law.[97] The Russian Foreign Ministry called for joint patrols with the Japanese around the islands while Oleg Soskovets proposed that the Japanese pay a fishing fee for the right to fish in the area.[98] Sakhalin Governor Yevgennii Krasnoyarov proposed that Japan pay $10 million annually in fishing rights—to be paid directly to the Sakhalin *Oblast.*[99] The Japanese rejected any proposal that implied recognition of Russian sovereignty over the islands and were left with the unpleasant impression that the incidents reflected an attempt to extract yet more money.

Both sides would like to move beyond the territorial problem to improve relations, hoping that widening cooperation would work to their advantage. The Russians expect the dispute to be either circumvented or made more capable of resolution in a different context should relations improve. The

Japanese hope that a more stable Russia would be better able to resolve the issue without forgetting the matter entirely. An improvement of the relationship in certain limited areas is possible without a solution to the dispute, but ultimately both sides are strongly influenced by the past, which casts a heavy weight on any effort at reconciliation.

From the perspective of foreign policy in general, the territorial dispute was the occasion for the assertion of a role for public opinion in foreign policy. In Russia, public opinion expressed itself through the Supreme Soviet and through political and administrative figures who influence the nation. The democrats around Yeltsin (who pressed for a quick resolution of the issue) found themselves, paradoxically, accused of using Soviet methods that conflicted with the values they claimed to represent. The secrecy with which the Russian government conducted its deliberations over the problem was seen as conspiratorial behavior by its opponents in the Supreme Soviet. The effort to side step public opinion was a product of the understanding that the Russian public was not ready for such concessions and that it had been socialized during the Soviet period to view the territory in question as indisputably Russian. Nonetheless, after the collapse of the Soviet Union, Russia declared itself a democracy and the involvement of public opinion could not be avoided. Russia was in a weakened position in 1992 when it was threatened by disintegrative trends, and Russian public opinion reacted in alarm to the idea of concessions to Japan. Only when Russia has overcome these disintegrative trends and becomes more stable would a solution to the territorial dispute based on the 1956 agreement be possible.

RUSSIA–CHINA

China is of inestimable significance for Russia's security in a way belied by the attention given to the West. Russia fears a reassertion of Chinese claims to the Russian Far East that were raised publicly in 1963 when Sino-Soviet polemics were intensified. Added to that is the fear of a renewal of border clashes of the kind that occurred on the Ussuri River in March 1969, which could have a destabilizing impact on the security of Russia's Far East. Russia has a concern for the political stability of China as it undergoes its own economic transformation. As the forces released by this transformative process clash with the political order in China, a dangerous factionalism may result leading to a deteriorating security situation along the border. Moreover, China is seen as a major economic partner for Russia. Trade with China has been an important factor in the economy of Russia's Far East, a means through which food and consumer goods could be obtained. China has been regarded as a customer for Russia's arms industries that have suffered badly since state procurement dropped dramatically in 1992. Russia's state industries have attempted to revive relationships with their Chinese counterparts, which were first established during the Soviet era. Some in Russia, such as Arkadii Vol'skii of the Union of Industrialists, have regarded China as a model for Russia in which economic change would be pursued in advance of political reform. This view, however, is not widespread among Russians.

China has also been a controversial subject for the various opinion groups that have attempted to shape Russian foreign policy. Russia's pro-Western democrats tend to minimize the significance of China, whose Communist system reminds them of their own Soviet past. For these democrats, China belongs to another world separated by political and ideological values and by a disrespect for human rights that they find repugnant. The geostrategists and geopoliticians among the Russians regard China as a country essential for Russian security and one that cannot be alienated without detrimental consequences for Russia. From their perspective China is a major priority for Russia and this should be reflected in foreign policy statements in a way that demonstrate Russia's interests clearly. They point to the absurdity of having difficult relations with China and Japan simultaneously, which would be the case if Russian policy toward Beijing simply followed the West. From the perspective of the practitioners of the balance of power, China is a means to balance Japan and to pressure the Japanese leadership to improve relations with Russia. For Russia's nationalists and Communists the picture becomes blurred. The author encountered hostility toward China among Zhirinovsky's supporters, but most other nationalist groups reserved their hostility for the West.

Political and ideological differences damaged relations between Russia and China as Russia's democrats reacted with abhorrence to the Tiananmen Square events of June 1989. Yeltsin publicly criticized the Chinese leadership for the suppression of the student demonstrations and President and Party Chairman Jiang Zemin avoided him when he visited Moscow in May 1991. Russians suspect that the leaders of the August 1991 coup informed the Chinese of their plans in advance seeking them as an ally against Gorbachev. When Russia emerged from the ruins of the Soviet Union its pro-Western leaders brought with them the negative perceptions of China that had been forged the previous few years and during the Maoist years of the Cultural Revolution. Nonetheless, the pro-Western leadership had to accommodate the strategic reality of China and its significance for Russia's security, which resulted in an agonizing conflict of priorities. When the advocate of pro-Westernism, Kozyrev, visited Beijing in March 1992 he stayed only 30 hours in a visit marked by acute political differences. Kozyrev declared that human rights constituted an integral part of Russian foreign policy toward China and that Russia was in no hurry to conclude agreements with China. He admitted that Asian civilization places society above the individual but claimed he disagreed with the Chinese over human rights. Nonetheless, according to Kozyrev, Russia and China should cooperate to ensure mutual security.[100] *Izvestiya* correspondent Maksim Yusin wrote that Russia's relationship with China would remain tense and that those who crushed the students's revolt cannot expect the sympathy of Russian leaders.[101] This was an assessment, however, that was not shared by Russian society at large.

Beyond the pro-Western group, views of China varied from that of a necessary geopolitical partner to a potential ally. Vladimir Lukin in his assessment of China claimed that Russia's relationship with that country should be as important as its relationships with Europe or Japan as a way of maintaining a balance in foreign policy.[102] This view of China's role for Russia was included in the Foreign Policy and Defense Council's report according to which China should be a priority comparable to Europe and the U.S.[103] Sergei Goncharov argued that Russia's proximity to the West or the U.S. may create tensions along the border with China and that the relationship with China should be independent of the West. Accordingly, human rights or minority rights should not be emphasized in the relationship with China.[104] A definite China lobby exists in Russia that has continually pressed for closer relations with Beijing on the basis of geopolitical or economic need. Some have regarded China as Russia's main foreign policy partner given that both are multiethnic countries with a shared interest in maintaining each other's territorial integrity.[105] Vice Premier Aleksander Shokhin represented interests within the Russian government eager to develop economic ties with China. According to Shokhin, Russia had better reasons for trading with China than with the West, which was essentially a closed market for Russian products.[106]

Security overrode other considerations when both Russia and China ratified the border treaty that had been concluded with the Soviet Union on 15 May 1991. Negotiations for this treaty began in 1987 under Gorbachev and were spurred by a Russian desire to prevent the re-emergence of border tensions over disputed areas. Gorbachev accepted the Thalweg principle according to which the main channel along the Amur/Ussuri Rivers would decide the ownership of the many islands there. The treaty covered the Russian-Chinese border from North Korea to Mongolia (4,300 kilometers); negotiations were to continue on a treaty for China's border with Central Asia. The treaty was ratified by Russia's Supreme Soviet on 10 February 1992 with 174 votes for, 2 against, and 24 abstentions. Kozyrev explained to the Supreme Soviet that for the first time the entire border had been defined by treaty. Russia, he said, would have "about half" of 1,845 islands. The treaty, however, left undetermined the status of several islands near Khabarovsk—Bol'shoi Ussursiiski, Tarabarov, and Bol'shoi island on the River Argun. Lukin told the Supreme Soviet that the treaty was exceptionally beneficial for Russia as it gave the border the sanctity of international law and avoided an alteration of state borders.[107] On 26 February, China's National Peoples's Congress ratified the treaty and Kozyrev arrived in Beijing on 18 March to exchange the instruments of ratification. Demarcation of the border began in the spring of 1993 and was to continue for 3–4 years.

An agreement covering a 55 kilometers stretch where Russia shares a border with China between Mongolia and Kazakhstan was signed when

China's Head of State Jiang Zemin visited Moscow in September 1994. Negotiations on China's border with Central Asia, Kazakhstan, Kyrgyzstan, and Tajikistan (which included Russia as a partner) began in 1990. In dispute was the border along the Pamir Mountains with Tajikistan for which few documents existed. While civil war raged in Tajikistan, China was in no hurry to conclude a border agreement for this section. A separate border accord with Kazakhstan was signed when Chinese Premier Li Peng visited Alma Ata in April 1994. Negotiations similarly continued on force reductions along the Russian-Chinese border and 15 rounds of talks were held by May 1995 without success. Russian troop levels dropped from 400,000 to 200,000 in 1992 but further reductions were complicated by a disagreement over the width of the demilitarized zone. Russian troops were deployed within 100 kilometers of the border because of geography, infrastructure and transport connections while Chinese troops were deployed further back, some 300–400 kilometers from the border.

China proposed a 100-kilometer demilitarized zone which would keep its own forces intact while requiring the withdrawal of Russian troops. Deputy Russian Foreign Minister Aleksander Panov explained that a withdrawal of Russian forces was opposed by the military as new barracks and infrastructure would have to be constructed for which funds were absent.[108] Nonetheless, other measures were proposed to ensure stability along the border when Russia's Chief of Border Forces Col.-General Andrei Nikolaev visited China in November 1993. He came to an agreement with his Chinese counterparts over multilevel collaboration between both border forces, commanders of armies, and military districts.[109] Grachev accompanied Nikolaev and concluded a five-year agreement with the Chinese on measures to enhance confidence and security. Both countries were to notify each other prior to the holding of mass military exercises along the border and agreed to an exchange of visits by senior officers.[110]

Yeltsin attempted to make amends for his earlier hostility to the Chinese Communist leadership. As his foreign policy had provoked the ire of the Supreme Soviet he moved to defuse domestic hostility by promoting a more balanced foreign policy. His trip to Beijing in December 1992 was largely a product of domestic politics as his pro-Western course in foreign policy came under increasing criticism from the Supreme Soviet and the Congress of Peoples's Deputies. In Beijing, Yeltsin declared that his government was accused of Americanization and that he came to seek a balance in foreign policy. According to him there was to be no military alliance or bloc, only "mutually advantageous good neighborly relations" with China.[111] Kunadze examined the specific interests behind this visit, emphasizing that a territorially stable China was vital for Russia, and that China's interest was similarly in a strong Russia. China would be a market for Russia's defense industries without, as Kunadze stressed, disturbing the balance in the Asia-Pacific region. In relation to human rights, the Russian deputy minister struck an ambiguous note that reflected the dilemma faced. Kunadze declared that Russia could not resort to double standards by condoning human rights abuses in China but China's Confucian tradition placed the collective above the individual. In this context he claimed that ultima could not be used to promote human rights.[112]

During the Beijing visit, Yeltsin signed a joint declaration on the fundamentals of relations with the Chinese leadership that stated both countries regarded each other as friendly states. They pledged not to join military alliances directed against each other and not to conclude treaties detrimental to the security of the other side.[113] This declaration was cited by the Russian opponents of NATO's Partnership for Peace Program to demonstrate that any links that Russia may forge with NATO would clash with its relations with China. Yeltsin achieved his immediate objective of restoring relations with the Chinese leadership (which he had vilified) but he failed to interest them in a non-aggression pact. Other proposals included an agreement to prevent incidents along the border and a plan to create a zone of stability around the border to a distance of 200 kilometers.[114] Yeltsin, however, failed to meet Deng Xiaoping and shortened his visit by a day citing trouble with the 7th Congress of Peoples's Deputies as his reason to return to Moscow on 19 December.

For a while it seemed that Taiwan would emerge as a problem in Russia's relationship with China since Moscow had developed closer relations with Taipei in the last days of the Soviet Union. Taiwan's Foreign Minister John Chang visited Moscow in January 1990 and the following March Taiwan lifted restrictions on direct trade with the Soviet Union. In June 1991 Taiwan declared a willingness to offer the Soviet Union direct financial assistance.[115] After the dissolution of the Soviet Union and Moscow turned toward the West, interest in Beijing temporarily waned. Russia's defense industries began to make soundings of Taiwan as a possible client for Russian weapons. In March 1992, First Deputy Minister for Foreign Economic Relations, Sergei Glaziev revealed that Taiwan had already approached Moscow about purchasing of weapons. Glaziev claimed that weapons sales to Taiwan could exceed transfers to China by billions.[116] Several high-ranking Russian naval officers visited Taiwan in July 1992, including former Commander of the Pacific Fleet Admiral Vladimir Sidorov and Rear-Admiral (reserves) Anatolii Shtyrov. The purpose of the visit was not clearly explained but Sidorov did not exclude the possibility of arms sales to Taiwan.[117]

Arms interests were poised to dictate policy toward Taiwan but Russia's commitment to Beijing was too significant to be challenged by the defense lobby. The Foreign Ministry protested vigorously against this intrusion into foreign policy and Beijing was confirmed as a major priority. In view of Russia's relationship with China, the idea of arms sales to Taiwan was absurd and the idea was dropped. Nonetheless, Moscow wanted to preserve a relationship with Taiwan for trade purposes in a way that would be acceptable to Beijing. On 24 June 1992, it was revealed that Moscow and Taipei would establish coordinating commissions to manage their relationship. Yeltsin's decree of 15 September on relations between the Russian Federation and Taiwan formalized the position of Moscow's supposed non-governmental body which would conduct relations with Taiwan. Oleg Lobov, who became head of the Security Council, was made its director.[118] Stanislav Kondrashov of *Izvestiya* complained about the privatization of diplomacy in relation to Taiwan against the protestations of the Foreign Ministry. Lobov, after all, had de facto official status and visited Taiwan with government representatives.[119] Kondrashov referred to the rules of the game according to which Russia could maintain a lowlevel relationship with Taiwan without offending Beijing. As Kunadze explained Russia sought the kind of relationship that Western countries themselves had established with Taiwan.[120] Yeltsin's need to visit China in December 1992 sealed the fate of Russia's Taiwan lobby and the issue was not raised again.

Moscow had hoped that trade with China would arrest the decline of Russia's economy and prove to be the salvation of the defense industries in particular. Chinese state enterprises retained relationships with their former Soviet equivalents and required new machinery and spare parts for factories constructed during the 1950s according to Soviet designs and specifications. During 1992–1993 China was Russia's second trading partner (after Germany) while in 1993 Russia was only the seventh for China. Russia had a $2 billion surplus in 1993 and 40 percent of this trade comprised Russian industrial goods, machinery, and industrial equipment destined for Chinese state enterprises. Some 63 percent of the trade in 1993 was crossborder business between the Russian Far East and the Chinese province of Heilongjiang. Border trade allowed Chinese consumer goods, food supplies, and fruits and vegetables, which were otherwise in short supply throughout Russia, to flow into the Russian Far East. It would be no exaggeration to say that during the difficult years, 1991–1993, trade with China sustained the Russian Far East. In European Russia, however, Chinese goods had to compete with imports from Europe that inundated Russian markets.

Russian hopes for an expanding arms market in China have been only partially fulfilled. China concluded a deal with the Soviet Union in April 1991 for the purchase of 26 Sukhoi 27s, which were delivered in stages from 1991–1993. Yegor Gaidar declared that arms sales to China would keep Russia's stagnating defense industries afloat and announced that China was one of Russia's top priorities in foreign policy.[121] At the 7th Congress of Peoples's Deputies in December 1992, Gaidar revealed that $1 billion in weapons had been sold to China but he did not mention the period involved.[122] China expressed interest in Russian assistance to upgrade its air defenses including ground-based radar and ground-to-air missiles and the SA-10 Grumble, the Russian equivalent of the U.S. Patriot.[123] The U.S. Defense Intelligence Agency reported that China purchased some 100–150 SA-10 launchers at a cost of $1.5 billion under a contract signed in 1992.[124] China reportedly also purchased 400 T-72 tanks in early 1992 and in the following year deliveries of 50 T-80 tanks were noted at a reported cost of $125 million; China intended to purchase another 200 T-80s according to Russian reports.[125] In addition, Russian defense scientists worked in China on contract; the figure has varied from about 200 in early 1992 to 300–400 in 1993.[126]

Russia was also assisting China in developing an engine for the new Super 7 fighter that originally was to benefit from U.S. technology but fell victim to bans on strategic exports to China.[127] When Vice Admiral Zhang Lianzhong, Commander of the Navy, visited Moscow in April 1993 a Russian role in the development of the Chinese Navy, including the purchase of Russian vessels, was on the agenda.[128] Vice Chairman of the Central Military Commission Liu Huaqing visited Moscow in June 1993 and negotiations commenced on the purchase of Russian kilo-class submarines, air defense systems, and additional SU-27s.[129] An agreement to sell four kilo class submarines was concluded in November 1994 at a total cost of around $1 billion.[130] China agreed to buy an additional six kilo-class submarines over the next five years to strengthen its conventional naval capability.[131] China has displayed an interest in purchasing a Russian aircraft carrier, and in 1992 negotiations were conducted over the Varyag which was being completed in the Ukraine. In November 1994, Russian Naval Commander Felix Gromov revealed that the two sides could not agree on a price.[132] Gromov, however, came to an agreement with the Chinese on technological assistance and training, under which Chinese naval crews would be trained in Russia.[133] Should China decide to construct its own aircraft carrier, Russia would have a major role under these agreements in providing technology and training.

Despite the expansion of defense cooperation between Russia and China it has fallen short of Russian expectations. Indeed, on the basis of objective indicators (such as the size of the Chinese market and the scale of Russia's defense industries) more would have been expected than has been recorded to date. China has faced an American ban on weapons and arms sales since the Tiananmen Square events and the deteriorating political relationship between the United States and China should have redounded to the benefit of Russian defense industries. Despite these circumstances several factors have acted to constrain the development of this defense relationship. The Chinese have been less interested in purchasing equipment than in manufacturing under licence. When Grachev visited Beijing in May 1995, China again expressed interest in the SU-27, of which the Russians hoped to sell an additional 100–150. The Chinese, however, pressed for technology transfers and the right to manufacture the SU-27 under licence.[134] Certain essential purchases of Russian equipment will be made to fill immediate needs but over the longterm the Chinese intent is to manufacture and eventually design their own. Moreover, in cases where purchases are negotiated, China has insisted on payment either wholly or partially in bartered goods. The Chinese understand Russia's eagerness to sell and have undertaken negotiations to extract maximum benefits from Russia's weakness. Ultimately, the Russians have few other markets and

China can turn elsewhere for its purchases, though at much higher cost. For these reasons, the anticipated revival of Russian defense industries based on Chinese orders can not be expected.

There have been other problems in the Russia-China relationship that have dampened the enthusiasm expressed by Russia's pro-China lobby. The border treaty that was to be the basis of stability in this relationship has been subjected to heavy criticism from local authorities in Russia's Far East who regard it as detrimental to their own interests. In the context of a strained relationship between Russia and the Far East, and whose authorities have complained bitterly of Moscow's control, this problem has taken on the dimension of a struggle over foreign policy. Toward the end of 1993, the conflict between center and periphery became obvious when local Far Eastern authorities lodged protests with the Russian National Boundary Demarcation Committee, when it became clear that some river islands would be handed to China. This committee included representatives from Far Eastern administrations at regional *krai* and *oblast* levels and some, reportedly, refused to participate in a visit to China.[135] Representatives of Russia's border forces defended the treaty and described as irresponsible the criticism that it resulted in significant concessions to China.[136]

Local Far Eastern authorities complained that the border treaty was negotiated in secret and that there was little opportunity for them to express their views. The return of Damansky/Chen Pao Island to the Chinese was especially galling for local residents. The island had been the site of the March 1969 border clashes between the Soviet Union and China and had, in these residents's eyes, been somehow sanctified by the loss of Russian blood. The Foreign Ministry attempted to explain to local residents that as a consequence of the Zhou Enlai-Kosygin Agreement of September 1969 Moscow had relinquished the island to Chinese control.[137] Another problem was the river islands near Khabarovsk, Tarabarov, and Bol'shoi Ussuriiskii whose transfer to China was strongly opposed by Viktor Ishaev, the governor of Khabarovsk *Krai*. In a letter to Premier Chernomyrdin dated 15 September 1993, which was circulated in subsequent Duma hearings on China, Ishaev explained his objections. The status of these islands, he explained, was fixed by the Treaty of Peking of 16 July 1861, which determined the border between Russia and China in this area. Ishaev pointed to Article 8 of the 1991 border treaty according to which Chinese vessels were allowed to follow the main channel of both the Amur and Ussuri rivers. Russia had accepted that the main channel represented the border under Article 5 of this treaty. Ishaev complained that since the autumn of 1992 Chinese naval vessels had been taking the liberty of navigating along the main channel of these rivers that brought them past Khabarovsk city itself, intruding into Russia's internal waters. He added that the treaty allows an uncontrolled flow of Chinese into Khabarovsk and chastized Moscow for coming to an agreement with China without consulting local authorities. He called on Chernomyrdin to prevent the Foreign Ministry from resolving the issue without local participation. Above all, wrote Ishaev, the islands cannot be the subject of negotiations that infringe on the rights of citizens living in Khabarovsk and the Far East.[138]

Primorski Governor Yevgennii Nazdratenko also expressed his opposition to the border treaty, claiming that it results in the loss of three important areas. He threatened to lobby against the treaty in Federal Parliament where he had support from the Deputy Speaker of the Soviet of Federation, Anatolii Dolgolaptev, who referred to the injustice of the border treaty.[139] Kozyrev was compelled to visit Beijing and to reassure his Chinese hosts that Russia would fulfill its obligations under this treaty and that federal authorities in Moscow decided this issue.[140] Nonetheless, because of the opposition of Far Eastern authorities the work of the border committee in demarcating the border in the Primorsk region was blocked. The border agreement will not be implemented until Moscow re-establishes control over its Far Eastern peripheries.

In addition, border trade with China has come under increasing criticism within Russia in a way that, again, pitted federal against local authorities. Chinese traders had visa-free access to the Far East from 1992–1993 but on 29 January 1994 the Moscow side reintroduced the visa requirement. Moscow also imposed higher import duties on trade with China to control the import of Chinese products. The concern was that border trade conducted by Chinese *Chelnoki* or shuttletraders was to Russia's disadvantage. Russia's economists argued that barter trade with China resulted in the outflow of Russian resources in exchange for Chinese manufactured goods for which there was no other market. The price of Chinese consumer goods was governed by artificial shortages in the Far East, which meant that Russian resources were being traded at less than their value in other markets. The much vaunted joint Russian-Chinese venture was seen as a means to channel Russian resources to China at these prices. In addition, Russia's exports of machinery to China were actually declining for a variety of reasons including production difficulties in Russia and the existence of alternative sources of machinery for China.[141] As a consequence of the new requirements pushed by Moscow a 40 percent drop in Russian-Chinese trade was recorded in the first quarter of 1994. Chernomyrdin visited Beijing in May 1994 when the new measures became the subject of discussions with the Chinese.[142]

Conflict between Moscow and Far Eastern business interests that profited from trade with China followed the introduction of these measures. S. I. Lopatin, head of external economic relations of Khabarovsk *Krai,* outlined his concern in a memorandum to federal authorities prepared for parliamentary hearings on China in April 1994. China, he said, played a leading role in the Khabarovsk economy and accounted for 45 percent of its trade in 1993. He emphasized that the Khabarovsk economy was increasingly orientated away from Russia and the CIS toward the external market and China. According to Lopatin, trade with China was a way of getting out of the present crisis situation as the Khabarovsk region imports a significant part of its grain, sugar, meat products, fresh fruits and vegetables, clothes, and textile materials from China. He stressed that in view of the region's dependence on China the impact of higher duties would be an increase in prices of essential commodities for the people of the region.[143]

Deputy head of the Amur administration's Department for Foreign Relations A. A. Kuleshev similarly lodged a protest with federal authorities in relation to the new visa regime. Kuleshev admitted that problems had arisen in relation to the "intense development of economic relations with the states of the Asia-Pacific region" because of the free entry of the citizens of these countries into the *oblast*. He stated, however, that Amur *Oblast* had lobbied Moscow throughout 1993 not to introduce a visa regime and when such a regime was introduced in 1994, to return to the previous visa-free system. He declared that the task of federal authorities was to create favorable conditions for Amur *Oblast's* collaboration with China.[144] A memorandum prepared by Amur *Oblast* noted that trade with China was not just a matter of satisfying food needs, but a livelihood for those engaged in the re-exports of Chinese goods. The measures introduced by federal authorities had deprived the region of Chinese workers and had significantly reduced business profits that would affect the taxes paid to city and *oblast* budgets. The financial losses for the first quarter of 1994 were calculated as 5 billion rubles for the firms involved and some 2 billion rubles in customs duties for the federal budget.[145] A letter from various company directors from Blagoveshchensk in Amur *Oblast* similarly registered protests against the administrative measures imposed by Moscow on the Far East. The company directors claimed that for the first time in the history of the Far East products from Hong Kong, Singapore, and Korea were available in local markets because of trade with China. They argued that the measures hinder the development of projects in which they had invested with their Chinese counterparts and called specifically for reduced import tariffs, the termination of the visa regime, legal guarantees of investment, and an assurance that 50 percent of the customs duties collected would remain in the region.[146] In contrast, local security organs were in favor of the strict visa regime that showed that views varied not only according to region but also according to occupation. Major-General V. A. Balanev of the Khabarovsk administration militia expressed his support for the visa regime and proposed a series of other measures to ensure control over foreigners.[147]

Vice Premier Oleg Soskovets voiced his concern about the economic disintegration of Russia and the problems associated with a Far Eastern enclave that looks toward China and the Asia-Pacific region.[148] Moscow's inability to satisfy the Far East's economic needs spurs the local development of economic links with China and complicates the process of regulating relations with that country by centralized means. The Far Eastern region feels constrained and victimized by Moscow complaining that its interests are being ignored by central authorities. Moscow, however, has to respond to a wider constituency than just the Far East over an issue that has escalated to become a national concern. During the parliamentary hearings on China, Deputy Foreign Minister Aleksander Panov explained that the remaining regions welcomed a stricter visa regime with China for reasons related to the influx of Chinese, which in some circles in Russia has caused alarm.[149]

There are no reliable figures on the number of illegal Chinese settlers in Russia and the issue has been obfuscated by this absence of data. Settlers cannot be distinguished from temporary residents (such as traders) given that border controls have not been effectively enforced. Figures for the illegal Chinese population of Russia vary from 150,000 to 2 million and in the chaotic administrative system in Russia the notion of an illegal entrant may be quite arbitrary. Chinese traders have settled in Moscow where they have purchased apartments and have been a noticeable presence in many local markets. Among nationalist circles there is fear that China's population will spill over into the sparsely settled Russian Far East with its population of 9 million. Even when this figure is added to the population of Siberia, the total is only 32 million, from the Urals to the Sea of Okhotsk. Concern has been voiced that in certain border regions there are twice as many Chinese as Russians. In the border Primorsk regions the ratio is reportedly 1:1.[150]

The issue of the Chinese presence in Russia is linked with a fear of China within nationalist circles which could continue to affect relations with Beijing if left uncontrolled. There is the apprehension that China harbors territorial designs on Russia's Far East that could provide *lebensraum* (living space) for China's surplus population. Some have even speculated that the influx of Chinese is part of a grand design on the part of Beijing to establish control over the Far East. Zhirinovky's LDP has frequently raised the issue, stressing that if the influx continues a referendum would be called in the Far East and the region would be lost to Russia. When Zhirinovsky visited Vladivostok in July 1994 he declared that it was China's intention to colonize the Far East and he warned the residents of the region to learn Chinese.[151] Indeed, in an interview with the LDP's foreign policy expert and deputy head of the Duma's Committee on International Affairs Aleksei Mitrofanov the author was told that the illegal Chinese in Russia should be forcibly removed. Mitrofanov told the author that the idea of a Chinatown in every Russian city was intolerable, as China was an expansionist power and a potential enemy for the LDP. On 25 April 1994, joint hearings on China were conducted by the Committees of International Relations of both the Duma and the Soviet of Federation. The hearings were not published but they were intended to investigate the allegation, promoted by the Security Services within Moscow, that illegal Chinese emigration was part of a grand design on the part of Beijing. The hearings concluded that there was no evidence to support the allegation and it would be surprising if any could be uncovered.[152] Nonetheless, they revealed the difference in views that existed over this issue with central authorities expressing concern over the influx and local business interests seeing it as a necessity.

Beyond the central security organs and the LDP different assessments were made of the same situation. Russian liberals told the author that they would welcome a Chinatown in every Russian city because this would improve the economy and make Chinese cuisine readily available. Governor of the Amur region V. Polevanov stressed that there was in fact no law or authority that could forcibly remove the Chinese.[153] Aleksei Voskresenskii, a commentator on China, wrote that the Chinese have become a Russian national minority and cannot be ejected. Russia, he argued, must involve the Chinese in the economic life of the country and attract investment from the Asia-Pacific region.[154]

However, most troubling for Russians was the idea of a Chinese superpower that they may have to confront in the next century. Optimistic Western predictions about the growth of the Chinese economy have served to feed an anxiety in Russia that cannot be assuaged by the usual diplomatic platitudes. The Far East, some observers note, feels particularly abandoned by Moscow and is haunted by the specter of Chinese expansionism.[155] This specter, however, did not prevent Far Eastern representatives from developing closer economic relations with China or from opposing the strict visa regime imposed by Moscow. Voskresenskii expressed the fear of the emergence of a greater China on Russia's borders, which may resolve its demographic problem by military means.[156] Such anxieties are widespread among the Russians and lead to different conclusions. Nationalist groupings, such as the LDP, see in China an external threat to rouse the nation and to give it a sense of direction. Pro-Western groups and geopoliticians recognize the inherent dangers of provoking an anti-China nationalism and conclude that Russia can only manage the situation by developing a special relationship with China. Only by negotiating the key issues with the Chinese leadership will conflict be avoided and racial scares minimized.

Deputy Premier Sergei Shakhrai's views on China were instructive in this respect. Shakhrai noted that for the first time in 400 years China has overtaken Russia in development, which demands a significant adjustment of Russian views. He bewailed the absence of a coherent view of China within Russia and complained that local authorities see China from their own local perspective, not from the perspective of state interests that unfortunately had not been formulated. Shakhrai stated that the formation of Chinatowns in the Far East should be avoided because it would cause friction between the Chinese and the local population. He concluded that relations with China were too important to be allowed to drift and that a special mechanism was required for cooperation with China.[157] Deputy Minister of External Economic Relations M. E. Fradkov expressed concern about the growing transparency of the Russian-Chinese border and noted the Chinese interest in purchasing property and land in the Far East. He recommended, however, that Russia reach agreement with China in relation to the Chinese influx into the Far East and called for a legal regime to govern the presence of Chinese settlers or citizens in Russia.[158]

China has become of critical importance for Russia in a way that will influence foreign policy orientation. Not only is there the issue of border security, a common concern for the security of Central Asia, but there are trade and economic reasons that necessitate a constructive relationship with China. Moreover, the presence of Chinese traders/settlers may emerge as a domestic political issue that could stimulate nationalist hostility. Those in government well understand that the LDP's position over this issue is dangerous and could provoke conflict with a potential superpower on Russia's borders while Russia itself is in a weakened state. The fear of being pushed into a situation of prolonged hostility with China by nationalist forces compels Russian government representatives to affirm the need for collaborative relations with Beijing. Russians noted the opinions expressed by Chinese Head of State and Party Chairman Jiang Zemin before his trip to Moscow in September 1994. When questioned about the impact of Chinese illegal entrants on the relationship with Russia he stressed that this would not create tension "if relations between Russia and China are sincere, friendly, this will not be a factor of tension. The issue will be gradually regulated."[159] Russia, indeed, has no choice but to strengthen relations with Beijing otherwise the consequences would be obvious.

The need for close relations with the Beijing leadership is a strategic and political imperative for Russia that cannot afford to side with the West in any conflict with China. From Moscow's current perspective, the West's struggle with China over human rights cannot be a Russian concern. China represents a permanent constraint on Russia's relationship with the West that the pro-Western group around the president cannot escape. In the Asia-Pacific region, Russia's inability to assume the role of a balancing factor against China will become more apparent should tensions emerge over Taiwan or the South China Sea. Asia-Pacific security multilateralism has the purpose of preventing tensions from escalating into open conflict, and should China emerge as a security issue for the region Russia will not be able to contribute effectively. Russia, indeed, would be paralyzed. Russia's role in regional security multilateralism will be influenced by China for better or for worse.

RUSSIA AND THE KOREAN PENINSULA

Traditionalism and integrationism as alternative foreign policy approaches have clashed over the Korean Peninsula as well. Historically for Russia, the Korean Peninsula represented an area of rivalry with Japan. Russian penetration of the peninsula was one of the factors that triggered war with Japan in 1904–1905. Consciousness of rivalry with Japan still influences Russian attitudes toward the Korean Peninsula. One way or another Russia's geostrategists and geopoliticians regard both North and South Korea as counterbalances against Japan and as a means of extending influence into the Asia-Pacific region. From their perspective, the Pyongyang regime may be loathsome but it may serve a useful purpose in a balance-of-power strategy that may protect Russia against a resurgent Japan. Russia's main task is to develop relations with both North and South Korea in order to be in a position to benefit strategically from their eventual reunification. A reunified Korea would be a significant actor in a North East Asian balance of power and if Russia were able to forge a relationship with this state its position in relation to Japan would be strengthened considerably. Further pressure could be brought to bear on Japan to downplay the territorial issue and to collaborate with Russia economically.

The pro-Western democrats in Russia view the northern regime as the last vestige of Stalinism while the South represents economic opportunity. Pro-Western groups in the Foreign Ministry and elsewhere reject the balance-of-power approach as one that would involve Russia in conflicts on the Korean Peninsula or with Japan. They support North East Asian integrationism as a component of wider Asia-Pacific integrationism within which the particular security problems identified by the geostrategists and geopoliticians may be managed. For the Foreign Ministry, the denuclearization of the Korean Peninsula is Russia's key interest and demands close collaboration with the West. Rather than involving North or South Korea in a balance-of-power game, which could justify and stimulate the nuclearization of the peninsula, the emphasis should be on removing all basis for its continuation.

Debate has occurred about the purported success and the attendant costs of Yeltsin's particular policy toward the Korean Peninsula. Yeltsin has acted on the assumptions of pro-Westernism in relation to the Korean Peninsula cooperating with the West more than his own Foreign Ministry would have preferred. His critics have argued that he has curried favor with the West at the expense of Russia's interests in the peninsula that demand that it maintain balanced relations between North and South. As a consequence, critics claim, Russia has been dealt out of the game over an area considered important for its security and in which it has a historical interest. Critics argue that Yeltsin's approach over this issue has involved impulsive action and flawed judgment which has given the initiative to the United States and China and has relegated Russia to the sidelines. Defenders of the president's actions argue that Russian options were limited from the begining and that cooperation with the West was the only way toward ensuring the denuclearization of the peninsula.

Russia's geostrategists and geopoliticians claim that loss of influence over the Korean Peninsula was the result of Yeltsin's departure from the aim of balanced relations between North and South. Yeltsin continued with the Gorbachev policy of favoring the South over the North, which arose from the establishment of diplomatic relations between the Soviet Union and Seoul from 30 September 1990. Gorbachev expected to attract South Korean investment into the Soviet Far East in a way that would place pressure on Japanese business to follow. Gorbachev responded to Roh Tae Woo's nordpolitik, a strategy unveiled by South Korea with the staging of the Seoul Olympics in

1988. Seoul had intended to obtain leverage over Pyongyang through this strategy and to prepare for eventual reunification by utilizing the influence of the Soviet Union and other socialist states. The assumption behind Seoul's nordpolitik was that the road to reunification went through Moscow which was an incentive to consider a package loan for the Soviet Union of $3 billion. This loan was announced on 22 January 1991 as consideration for Gorbachev's decision in establishing diplomatic relations with Seoul. Russia's relations with Pyongyang deteriorated accordingly.[160]

With the liberation of Russia from the shackles of the Soviet Union a confusion in policy over Korea became evident as conflicting goals were identified. Kozyrev placed the emphasis on the need to restrain the North's nuclear program and to obtain Pyongyang's agreement to international inspection. Russia agreed to support Seoul publicly over the North's nuclear program, which was an advance on what the Soviet Union was willing to do. When Kozyrev visited Seoul in March 1992 he declared that Russia would do its utmost to press Pyongyang over the nuclear issue, hence stimulating South Korean expectations of Moscow. During this visit, Kozyrev proposed that Seoul sign a treaty of friendship with Moscow to cement their relationship.[161] Indeed, Yeltsin's special envoy Igor' Rogochov visited Pyongyang in January 1992 and on the 29th of that month the northern regime signed the Nuclear Safeguard Agreement with the IAEA. Russia was only one of the factors bearing on Pyongyang over the nuclear issue, but certainly in Seoul's assessment, its role was significant. South Korean Ambassador in Moscow Khong Sun Eng expressed the hope that Russia could disuade the North from producing nuclear weapons, thereby creating peace on the peninsula.[162]

Denuclearization of the peninsula, however, conflicted with the aim of maintaining balanced relations with both North and South. The strategy of balanced relations was promoted by the Korean specialists in the Foreign Ministry who, unlike Kozyrev, perceived a need to maintain relations with the North. Geopolitical and geostrategic logic dictated that Russia take advantage of its unique position, as the only country with diplomatic relations with both Pyongyang and Seoul, to strengthen its position on the peninsula. Kunadze explained in an interview in August 1992 that Russia had no intention of breaking with North Korea but wanted to preserve and strengthen good relations with Pyongyang. Moreover, Kunadze added that a treaty would be signed with Seoul when Yeltsin visits South Korea toward the end of the year. Russia would then have treaty relations with both Seoul and Pyongyang. Russia, claimed Kunadze, could then play an important role on the peninsula.[163] Head of the Korean Section of the Foreign Ministry Georgi Toloraya claimed that Korea was Russia's natural partner and that Russia's interests required a peacefully united Korea. He emphasized that there was no alternative but to maintain the relationship with Pyongyang and that ideology should not hinder the development of neighborly relations with the North.[164]

Geopolitical and geostrategic logic pushed Russia toward the position outlined by Kunadze, hoping that a relationship be maintained with Pyongyang. Integrationist logic, ideology, and economics drew Russia's leadership toward South Korea and undermined the notion of balanced relations on the peninsula. Russia's pro-Western leadership maintained an abhorrence of Pyongyang that conflicted with the diplomatic pragmatism required to ensure the success of the aims Kunadze identified. Deputy Premier Mikhail Poltoranin expressed this abhorrence of Kim Il Sung's regime when he announced his expectation that it would soon collapse. He urged the Japanese not to pay compensation for the suffering inflicted on the Korean people by Japanese colonialism, as demanded by Pyongyang, as this would ensure its survival.[165] The emphasis placed on the denuclearization of the peninsula turned Russia into a partner of the West over this issue. Russia lost whatever influence it may have had with Pyongyang as a result.

As Russia moved into a closer relationship with Seoul, the South raised its own demands that entailed the elimination of Russia's remaining links with the North. The South was to exact a price for this relationship—Russia's sacrifice of the 1961 treaty of friendship with the North. As Russia prepared for Yeltsin's trip to Seoul, southern pressure on Moscow became manifest. In July 1992, the Defense Minister Lee Jong Ku called on Moscow to terminate the 1961 treaty. Yeltsin told South Korean Foreign Minister Lee Sang Ok that the treaty had lost its effectiveness and retained its name only.[166] The Russian president seemed to exhibit little interest in the treaty and was willing to accommodate Seoul's demands. The Foreign Ministry, on the other hand, resisted this pressure and refused to make a decision solely in favor of Seoul that would have completely destroyed the strategy it was promoting. Kunadze protested that Russia cannot accept pressure from the South in relation to "our obligations to a third party." Kunadze added that any attempt to review Russia's commitments to North Korea "can lead to confusion" and could remove the legal basis of Russia's policy toward the peninsula.[167]

Considerable confusion has surrounded the status of this treaty that was automatically extended for five years in 1991. The South Korean press, for obvious reasons, has persistently claimed that Russia would terminate or revise the treaty. The controversy focused on Article 1 of the treaty which states that in the event of an attack on one party the other would quickly offer support. The Foreign Ministry wanted to maintain a relationship with Pyongyang while avoiding the prospect of being drawn into a conflict on the Korean Peninsula. Kunadze declared that Article 1 of the treaty still applied in the event of unprovoked aggression against the North.[168] The Foreign Ministry, however, declared that Russia would be relieved of any legal obligation to support the North against the consequences of its own provocative actions. Foreign Ministry sources told the author that Pyongyang was advised of this reinterpretation of commitment before Yeltsin visited Seoul in November 1992.

The basis of the geopolitical strategy promoted by the Foreign Ministry was undermined when China established diplomatic relations with Seoul on 24 August 1992. There were no evident ideological controversies in Beijing in relation to Pyongyang and China emerged as the North's only effective ally, providing it with necessary oil and grain shipments. In 1993, China supplied North Korea with a reported 72 percent of its food imports and 75 percent of its oil imports.[169] China, accordingly, assumed the unique position to which Russia had aspired of having relations with both North and South. It became clear to Seoul that the road to Pyongyang now went through Beijing and that China's support was more important than Russia's to push the North to accept international inspection of its nuclear program. Russia maintained a minimal relationship with the North, supplying it with 25,000 tons of crude oil in 1992 for which Pyongyang sent 20,000 laborers to Siberia.[170] Russia continued to deliver spare parts to North Korea for military equipment previously purchased. When Kunadze visited Pyongyang in January 1993 it was obvious, however, that Russian relations with the North had reached a nadir. Kunadze pressed for the International Atomic Energy Agency (IAEA) to inspect the North's nuclear facilities and was bluntly told by his counterpart, Kang Sok Ju, that it was not Russia's concern. Kunadze complained of the North's tough attitude that made it difficult to reach agreement over anything including the North's debt to Russia which was estimated at $3.3 billion.[171]

Yeltsin and Kozyrev had pursued the aim of promoting relations with Seoul while allowing the relationship with the North to deteriorate. The Foreign Ministry's Korean specialists believed, however, that without an effective relationship with the North, relations with Seoul would suffer accordingly. Yeltsin and his entourage dismissed this geopolitical logic claiming, as did Kozyrev, that a relationship with an ideological ally of the Soviet Union such as Pyongyang would be a hindrance to relations with the South.[172] Moreover, as a member of a global coalition against nuclear proliferation, Russia would carry more weight on the peninsula. The affirmation of the principle of nuclear non-proliferation and international inspection of nuclear facilities would serve Russia's interests more than would the maintenance of a decrepit treaty with Pyongyang. Those within the Foreign Ministry and president's administration who supported this position had their eyes on Russia's Islamic neighbors who may be tempted to follow North Korea's example by embarking on the nuclear path. Russia had to side with the West to confirm the principle of nuclear non-proliferation as a higher security interest which went beyond Russia's specific interests in the Korean Peninsula. For those immersed in the geopolitical logic of foreign policy, however, Yeltsin's one-sided choice for Seoul was inexcusable.

An attempt was made by Moscow in 1992 to use Seoul against Tokyo in the hope that the Japanese would be less strident over the territorial issue. Its failure demonstrated a flaw in the geopolitical strategy of using South Korea as counterbalance to Japan. In January 1992, Moscow negotiated a fishing agreement with Seoul that set quotas for fish caught in each other's fishing zone. South Koreans were allowed to catch 30,000 tons from Russian waters, which included the islands claimed by Japan.[173] The Japanese Foreign Ministry protested and brought pressure to bear on Seoul. Trilateral negotiations over the issue were later conducted including Japan, and Seoul called for the fishing zone to be transferred elsewhere.[174] Subsequently Watanabe met with Lee San Ok in Kyoto and told his South Korean counterpart that Japanese relations with Seoul would be undermined if either made a hasty move toward Russia. Watanabe criticized the fishing agreement and warned that it could affect Japan's stance on the North's nuclear program.[175] The fishing agreement was shelved as Japan had assumed greater significance for Seoul than Russia.

Expectations of South Korean economic support were similarly shown to be exaggerated. First, South Korea's $3 billion loan had been frozen by Russia's failure to repay interest. The first tranche of $1.473 billion ($1 billion in cash loans, $473 million for the export of consumer goods to Russia) had been disbursed to the Soviet Union. The second tranche, however, had been suspended pending clarification of Russia's obligations for what had been a loan to the Soviet Union. During his visit to Seoul in March 1992 Kozyrev attempted to persuade the South Koreans to disburse the second tranche. In May 1992, Russia declared that it could not pay $32.5 million interest on the first tranche and wanted to negotiate a new repayment schedule.[176] South Korea borrowed from the international money markets to extend these credits to Russia while it was facing its own current account deficit. The loans were strongly criticized by South Korea's opposition and no further credits could be expected.

Second, though South Korean investment in Russia showed a slight increase in early 1992, China subsequently emerged as the preferred destination. South Korean reports revealed that $3.66 million had been invested in the Soviet Union in 1991 and $7.02 million in Russia from January–June 1992 showing that Russia had an auspicious start. Goldstar Communications invested $1.5 million in a switchboard factory, Dongwon Industries invested $1.24 million in a fisheries project, and Halla Heavy Industries invested $1.91 million in a gas turbine factory in St. Petersburg; Samsung invested $710,000 in a Nakhodka fisheries project; and Pusan Shipbuilding invested $800,000 in a project in Sakhalin.[177] These projects were relatively insignificant and the Russians began to complain that South Korea was losing interest in Russia as the Chinese market opened up. South Korean business was drawn by the potential of China and 55.8 percent of Seoul's direct investment in 1992 went to that country, 15.4 percent to Vietnam and 10.8 percent to ASEAN.[178] Investment in Russia (around 5 percent) was minor.

Even before Yeltsin's visit to Seoul in November 1992 the rather modest results of Russia's Korean policy, when measured against earlier expectations, became clear.[179] Despite Yeltsin's and Kozyrev's intentions, Russia's relationship with Seoul remained weak and the anticipated economic benefits were not forthcoming. Ironically, China had displaced Russia as the key actor on the peninsula by appropriating the strategy advocated by Russia's Foreign Ministry Korean experts. Yeltsin's trip to Seoul was in this context a diplomatic show that failed to achieve the expected results. The visit took place after the cancellation of Yeltsin's visit to Tokyo and was intended to remind the Japanese that Russia had alternative relationships in the Asia-Pacific region. Similar pressures arose from Russia's domestic politics which pushed the president to demonstrate an Asian orientation to Russia's foreign policy to balance the Western. This pressure will explain Yeltsin's enthusiasm to ensure the success of the diplomatic show, even to the point where additional confusion was created in policy toward Korea.

In his address to the South Korean Parliament, Yeltsin declared that "today our foreign policy is shifting from the U.S. and Western Europe to Asia and the Pacific. I think this visit is the beginning of this process." He told his South Korean hosts that Russia and Korea had never been enemies and that South Korea had become one of Russia's major trading partners in the Asia-Pacific region.[180] Yeltsin used the opportunity to demonstrate Russia's interest in the region, which showed a desire for a political platform there—whether it was to be Seoul or Tokyo did not really matter. The grand statements were not justified by the minor gains achieved during the visit and, though Yeltsin called for full-scale economic collaboration with the South and the creation of joint enterprises, no new investments or credits were obtained. The Russians proposed the construction of a pipeline to convey natural gas from Yakutsk to South Korea via North Korea, over 5,000 kilometers; the estimated cost was to be $15–20 billion and it was to be a 50:50 joint venture.[181] The proposal attracted interest but major issues had to be settled before it could be seriously negotiated, issues such as finance and North Korea's participation.

Foreign Ministry official Georgi Toloraya explained that the visit was to be the occasion for the signing of a treaty of friendship with South Korea, with specific provisions that would exclude its use against any third party.[182] No such treaty resulted as Seoul resisted the proposal while Yeltsin was unwilling publicly to pronounce the 1961 treaty with the North inoperative. Yeltsin declared that the relationship with the South would not be detrimental to Russia's relations with the North, which showed that the president refused the South's demand for Russia to break with the North.[183] He said that the 1961 treaty should be terminated or drastically revised, claiming that Russia had no intention of providing the North with assistance in the event of conflict under Article 1.[184] This Article, said Yeltsin, would be removed, a statement that went beyond what his Foreign Ministry had intended. What emerged from the visit was an agreement on the principles of bilateral relations that the Russians called a treaty. In addition, on 20 November, a memorandum on defense collaboration was also signed, under which the two sides could exchange visits at defense minister and chief of general staff level.[185] Yeltsin also declared that Russia was ready to supply military equipment to Seoul and offered the MIG-29 and naval vessels. South Korean president Roh Tae Woo raised the issue of arms deliveries to the North and Yeltsin responded that military assistance to Pyongyang had been suspended.

Russia failed to obtain the desired treaty in order to demonstrate the success of its diplomacy toward South Korea. Neither was there any progress in terms of the stated economic objectives of the visit. From the Yeltsin-Kozyrev perspective the visit failed its major aim of strengthening relations with the South in the terms desired. Yeltsin's public statements and desire to please the South reflected on the relationship with the North and put another nail in the coffin of the geopolitical strategy that the Foreign Ministry attempted to promote. The one major benefit for Moscow was in highlighting Russia's interest in the Asia-Pacific region after the cancellation of the president's visit to Japan. For this the South Korean National Assembly where Yeltsin delivered his address acted as a sounding board.

As the North Korean regime used its nuclear program in an attempt to establish a relationship with the United States, Russia struggled for a role. In March 1993, Pyongyang declared that it would withdraw from the Nuclear Non-proliferation Treaty, and in June 1993 it announced that it had suspended its withdrawal. Kim Il Sung's New Year address delivered on 1 January 1994 called for a joint statement with the U.S. to facilitate a settlement of the nuclear dispute.[186] In the same month, Pyongyang agreed to submit seven nuclear facilities to IAEA inspection that took place in March 1994. IAEA inspectors were not permitted access to two nuclear dumps which could have provided information on Pyongyang's nuclear program. The United States again raised the issue of UN sanctions against the North. Momentarily at least, Moscow's fortunes in the peninsula were revived as a member of the UN Security Council. Policy toward the peninsula came under prolonged debate in Moscow. Kunadze, on 17 December 1993, had expressed his opposition toward sanctions as dangerous and capable of triggering war on the peninsula.[187] Kunadze, however, was appointed ambassador to South Korea in January 1994 and was moved out of Moscow. Deputy Foreign Minister Aleksander Panov became responsible for Asia-Pacific affairs and voiced his support for sanctions, declaring that Russia did not want to appear close to an odious Communist regime.[188]

Support for sanctions was a logical continuation of the Yeltsin-Kozyrev line of identifying with the West. The removal of Kunadze from Moscow meant that the major advocate of the geopolitical strategy, which could not accommodate the idea of sanctions, had been effectively neutralized. Nonetheless, by agreeing to UN sanctions Russia would deprive itself of a role in the peninsula and the key arbitrators of Korea's destiny would be the United States and China, both of which had greater influence with Pyongyang. On 24 March 1994, aiming to re-establish a role for Russia, the Foreign Ministry proposed an international conference on the Korean Peninsula that would bring together both Koreas, Russia, the U.S., China and Japan as well as the UN and the IAEA. Moscow's proposal, however, was ignored by the major actors as China called for negotiations between North and South Korea, the U.S. and China involving the IAEA as well.[189] South Korean president Kim Yong Sam similarly called for negotiations involving the U.S., Japan, Korea and China; Russia was not considered.[190]

In the public debate that continued in Moscow Kozyrev declared that a North Korea "lobby" existed in the Duma, some members of which reportedly favored secret negotiations with Kim Il Sung to restore Russia's relationship with the North.[191] Kim Il Sung's death on 7 July 1994 confronted the Russians with an uncertain situation. One supporter of North Korea was Korean specialist Yuri Banin of the Institute of Oriental Studies in Moscow. Banin complained that the democrats were indifferent to Russia's interests on the peninsula and that a close relationship should be maintained with Russia's "closest neighbor in the Asia-Pacific region." Banin argued that the nuclear crisis had been artificially stimulated by the United States, which wanted the destruction of the "last remaining Communist state" in the region. Some representatives of Russian external intelligence dismissed the claim that North Korea was even close to developing nuclear weapons and were more skeptical about Pyongyang's potential in this area than were their American counterparts.[192] Banin was hostile toward the idea of sanctions against "our old ally" and opposed the idea of an international conference that could end up as a tribunal directed against the North. Banin, in an endorsement of the geopolitical strategy that apparently had no high-level advocates, claimed that hostile or unfriendly actions against the North do not promote Russia's authority with South Korea.[193] A similar view was propounded by Yevgennii Aleksandrov who declared that no other example could be found in the history of international relations of the Foreign Ministry's "trashing of an ally." He claimed that deteriorating relations with Pyongyang will not bring stability to the peninsula and will retard its reunification.[194]

A second critical approach was developed by Vladimir Lukin who argued that influence over Pyongyang was required in order to resolve the issue of the North's nuclear program. For this reason he criticized Russian policy for failing to maintain a relationship with the North. Lukin claimed that the Korean crisis was more important to Russia than was Yugoslavian conflict because of the danger of chain reaction nuclear proliferation. He emphasized that there should be no nuclear arms race near Russia's borders, a position that brought him close to the Foreign Ministry he had often criticized. He also stressed that it was time to renew Russia's dialogue with Pyongyang at the deputy foreign minister level, which had been suspended when Moscow established diplomatic relations with Seoul in September 1990. He declared that the freezing of Article 1 of the 1961 treaty was an error and he was opposed to the United States's use of heavy pressure against the North.[195]

Moscow was flattered that all was not lost when Kim Young Sam arrived in June 1994 to ascertain Russian views on the possible imposition of sanctions on the North. The South Korean president had already visited China in March 1994 to consult with Beijing over sanctions (which revealed his priorities). South Koreans understood the significance of the debate over Korean policy in Moscow and wanted to prevent a possible reorientation of policy toward Pyongyang as a backlash against Russia's marginalization over the issue. In Moscow on 2 June 1994, the South Korean president addressed the Council of Federation, or Parliament's Upper House, and later called for Russia's support for sanctions. Kozyrev said this support would be forthcoming if the idea of the international conference fails. Yeltsin indicated his agreement to the application of sanctions and the South Koreans apathetically endorsed international conference proposal. The issue of Russia's delivery of spare parts to the Northern regime's military was raised but Moscow used this to place pressure on Seoul to consider purchases of Russian weapons. The Russians said they were unwilling to lose a market for their weapons in the North without corresponding compensation from Seoul. A Russian-South Korean working group was formed to examine arms purchases by Seoul.[196]

The South Koreans questioned the Russians about their commitment to the North under the 1961 treaty and whether or not Russia would be involved should war break out. Aleksander Panov stated in March 1994 that Article 1 was still in force and that the Russian leadership would exercise its own judgment as to whether to react in time of conflict. Panov claimed that in 1996 a new treaty will be negotiated with Pyongyang, or the old treaty will be extended automatically.[197] Yeltsin, however, told the South Korean president that Article 1 of the treaty had been corrected and that the treaty would not be reviewed when it expires in 1996. Foreign Ministry officials subsequently supported Panov's statements to the author, who emphasized the need to maintain the treaty, but in modified form. Throughout 1994, debate continued over the significance of the treaty between those around the president, who wanted to discard it, and those in the Foreign Ministry, who saw a need to retain it.

Kozyrev met Warren Christopher in Istanbul on 11–12 June and agreed that an international conference would be supplementary to the issue of sanctions. On 16 June, Kozyrev wavered, claiming that since Russia had not been consulted he opposed the idea of applying sanctions. In a speech to the Duma on 17 June, he referred to the danger of a nuclear belt emerging along Russia's southern borders by the end of the millennium and declared his support for sanctions. He told the deputies that sanctions should be applied in stages and only if it could be proved that North Korea had succeeded in developing nuclear weapons.[198] Russian relations with North Korea deteriorated when Russian counter-intelligence revealed on 15 June that five North Korean diplomats had been expelled from Moscow for attempting to obtain nuclear material. Head of the Duma's Committee on Defense, Sergei Yushenkov criticized Pyongyang for conducting "outrageous nuclear blackmail."[199]

North Korea succeeded in establishing a relationship with the United States when an agreement covering the nuclear program was reached in Geneva on 21 October. The basis of the agreement was that the international community would pay Pyongyang to freeze its nuclear program, which critics described as a reward for blackmail. Under the agreement, an international consortium including Japan and South Korea would build two light water reactors (at a cost of $4 billion) for Pyongyang if it closed its graphite reactors, capable of producing weapons grade plutonium. The U.S. agreed to supply crude oil to Pyongyang to compensate for energy losses and the North agreed to allow the IAEA full access to all nuclear facilities when the first of the light water reactors has been constructed.[200] The Clinton administration argued that the agreement averted a dangerous crisis and would ensure that North Korea would be free of nuclear weapons. To achieve this agreement, the Clinton administration not only resorted to financial rewards but also agreed to move toward "full normalization of political and economic relations" with the North. Provisions were made in this agreement for a reduction of trade and investment barriers, the opening of liaison offices in both capitals (Pyongyang and Washington) and, eventually, the upgrading of bilateral relations to ambassadorial level.[201]

Russia had been entirely excluded from this agreement. The United States had been confirmed as the major external actor on the Korean Peninsula leaving Moscow to lament the consequences. Russia had not been involved in the international consortium to provide Pyongyang with lightwater reactors though the North insisted on Russia's participation. Within Moscow the reaction to the agreement was one of acute chagrin that Russia, which had followed the United States and the international community and had sacrificed its own relationship with the North, had been pushed out.[202] Kunadze revealed that in 1993 Moscow had cancelled the delivery of three nuclear plants to Pyongyang (estimated at $4 billion) under a 1991 agreement because of concern over North Korea's nuclear program.[203] The effect was to remove any remaining basis for the promotion of the geopolitical strategy since it was obvious that Russia was irrelevant to the North. The Yeltsin-Kozyrev approach of emphasizing the South over the North was accordingly justified.

Tensions emerged between the United States and South Korea as the U.S. moved closer to the North, the stimulation of which may have been one of the aims of Pyongyang's strategy. This development provided Seoul with an incentive to improve relations with Moscow after the signing of the nuclear agreement in October 1994. The debt issue was finally resolved in December 1994 after Moscow offered to repay interest in aluminium ingots and weapons. Russia's accumulated debt to South Korea (interest plus principal) was calculated at $375 million, which was to be repaid in the form of T-80 tanks, armored personnel carriers, semimanufactured goods, aluminium, and steel.[204] On 10 July 1995, Deputy Premier Oleg Davydov concluded a debt rescheduling agreement with South Korea allowing Moscow to repay its debt in this way.[205]

Moreover, in November 1994 it was announced that the first group of South Korean military officers would be sent to Russia for training under the defense cooperation agreement of November 1992. Eight officers were to be placed in a Russian military academy for a year, which the Russians hope would lead to expanded relations between the militaries of the two countries.[206]

How can Russian policy toward the Korean Peninsula be assessed? According to the criterion of the geopolitical strategy, Russia's policy was an abject and humiliating failure because it failed to prevent the U.S. from emerging as the main actor. Russia squandered its relationship with the North, missed the opportunity of establishing a compensatory position in the South, and was relegated to the sidelines. According to the criterion adopted by the proponents of the Yeltsin-Kozyrev pro-Seoul approach, the nuclear danger has receded and Russia's security has benefited as the peninsula has been made safer through U.S. involvement. Russia's security is ensured, not through unworkable balance-of-power strategies, but through security multilateralism that includes the U.S. Russia was incapable of implementing the geopolitical strategy, which was a chimera from the Soviet past. Russia may have downgraded the relationship with the North but it is still too early to assess the benefits of the relationship with Seoul negatively. Defense relations are developing, bilateral trade is increasing ($860 million in 1992, $1.6 billion in 1993, $2.2 billion in 1994)[207] and South Korean interest in investing in the Russian Far East has been reactivated.

RUSSIA AND THE ASIA-PACIFIC REGION: AN ASSESSMENT

Russia's interest has focused on North East Asia, which constitutes the area of direct contact with the Asia-Pacific region. However, outside of North East Asia, Russia has not established enduring basis for bilateral relationships of the kind that would support its Asia-Pacific ambitions. Russia's relationship with Vietnam (once a staunch ally) has declined considerably since the Soviet era as relations with China have been strengthened. A renewal of the 1978 Soviet-Vietnamese treaty was negotiated when Premier Vo Van Kiet visited Moscow in June 1994. Yeltsin revealed his opinion of Vietnam when he refused to meet his Vietnamese guest.[208] The ASEAN countries have represented an arms market for Russia whose potential was demonstrated when in June 1993 Malaysia announced the purchase of 18 MIG-29s; the price was $550 million with a provision for 25 percent part payment in palm oil. However, Russia has offered MI-7-17 helicopters to Thailand to offset a debt of around $70 million, missile patrol boats to the Philippines, and the MIG-29 to Indonesia without success.

Moscow wants to be assured of a role in the Asia-Pacific multilateralism that has been unfolding. The problem with Moscow's approach toward the region in general is that bilateral relationships in North East Asia have served to undermine Russia's credibility as a regional actor. The impasse in the relationship with Japan has deprived Russia of Japanese, and perhaps wider regional support, for its desire to join APEC. In economic terms Russia is no worse than the Latin American members of APEC, Mexico, and Chile, and has a stronger case for membership on geographic grounds. The dispute with Japan has contributed to Russia's marginalization and has strengthened the outsider syndrome that the region associates with Moscow. Russia's deepening relationship with China prevents it from contributing effectively to a regional security order, which may entail a counterbalance against China. Russia, rightly or wrongly, has lost its previous position of influence on the Korean Peninsula, which brings into question its involvement in negotiations affecting its future. The Gorbachevian policy of engaging the Asia-Pacific region continues to be affirmed without a substantial basis for Russia's involvement as an external actor. Ambitions far outweigh potential when it comes to the Asia-Pacific region.

Part of the problem is that Russian leaders are still influenced by the superpower paradigm on which Gorbachevian grand designs were based. There is the noticeable expectation of a rightful role in the region that has stimulated unrealistic ambitions. The other part of the problem has been the impact of domestic politics on foreign policy and the conflict that has been evident between central and local authorities, particularly in relation to the territorial issue with Japan and to Chinese settlers in Russia's Far East. Domestic political forces have influenced foreign policy in the Asia-Pacific and have rendered ambitious plans for the engagement of the region unachievable. Until Russia develops a satisfactory relationship with Japan, or reduces the domestic conflict over foreign policy it will continue to be characterized in the region as a country of unfulfilled aspirations.

NOTES

1. Andrei Kozyrev, "Vyzov preobrazheniya," *Izvestiya*, 31 Mar. 1992.

2. Vladimir Lukin, "Rossiya i ee interesy," *Nezavisimaya gazeta*, 20 Oct. 1992.

3. Address by A. V. Kozyrev, Ministry of Foreign Affairs at the Consultative Meeting with the ASEAN Ministers of Foreign Affairs, 21 July 1992, Manila.

4. *USIS*, 3 Aug. 1992.

5. *Itar Tass*, 2 Apr. 1993.

6. *Rossiiskaya gazeta*, 20 Nov. 1992.

7. *Itar Tass*, 19 Nov. 1992.

8. *Itar Tass*, 24, 26 July 1993.

9. *Izvestiya*, 9 Nov. 1994.

10. Sergei Agafonov, "Na aziatski politicheskie igry Andreya Kozyreva ne priglashayut," *Izvestiya*, 26 Mar. 1994.

11. Andrei Kozyrev, *Preobrazhenie*, Mezhdunarodnoe Otnoshenie, Moscow, 1994, p. 245.

12. *Krasnaya zvezda*, 9 July 1992.

13. See Sergei Agafonov's attacks on this theory, *Izvestiya*, 1, 4 Apr. 1991.

14. *Izvestiya*, 20 Apr. 1991. On Gorbachev's visit to Japan see Tsuyoshi Hasegawa, "The Gorbachev-Kaifu Summit: Domestic and Foreign Policy Linkages," and Igor' Tyshetskii, "The Gorbachev-Kaifu summit: The View from Moscow" in Tsuyoshi Hasegawa, Jonathan Haslam, Andrew Kuchins (eds.) *Russia and Japan: An Unresolved Dilemma Between Distant Neighbors*, University of California at Berkeley, 1993.

15. *Rossiiskaya gazeta*, 18 Sept. 1991.

16. *Kyodo*, 18 Apr. 1991; *Summary of World Broadcasts* (FE/1050/I), 19 Apr. 1991.

17. A. V. Zagorskii, "Rossiisko-yaponskie otnosheniya: B. N. Yeltsin pered dramaticheskim vyborom," *Znakom'tes' Yaponiya: k vizitu B. N. Yeltsina*, Nauka, Moscow, 1992, p. 20.

18. Elizabeta Leont'eva, "Ostrova kak simbol edinstva," *Rossiiskaya gazeta*, 10 Apr. 1991.

19. *Jiji Press*, 1 Oct. 1991, *Reuters Textline*, 31 Dec. 1991.

20. *Jiji Press*, 21 Oct. 1991, *Reuters Textline*.

21. K. Sarkisov, K. Cherevko, "Putyanu bylo legche," *Izvestiya*, 4 Oct. 1991. See also John J. Stephan, *The Kurile Islands: Russo-Japanese Frontier in the Pacific*, Clarendon, Oxford, 1974.

22. I. Yelistratov, "Otdavat' li yaponstam ostrova?" *Izvestiya*, 24 Oct. 1991.

23. *Izvestiya*, 28 Mar. 1991.

24. *Moskovskie novosti* (15), 8–14 Apr. 1991.

25. *Jiji Press*, 15 Apr. 1991, *Reuters Textline*.

26. "Za kuril'skie ostrova," *Sovietskaya Rossiya*, 3 Oct. 1991.

27. *Komsomolskaya pravda*, 2 Oct. 1991.

28. *Reuters Textline*, 11 Oct. 1991.

29. *Jiji Press*, 24 Oct. 1991, *Reuters Textline*.

30. *Reuters Textline*, 7 Oct. 1991.

31. *Krasnaya zvezda*, 15 Oct. 1991.

32. *Jiji Press*, 12 Feb. 1992, *Reuters Textline*.

33. Aleksander Anichkin, "Vosstanovit' doverie mezhdu rossiei i yaponiei," *Izvestiya*, 7 Sept. 1992.

34. Andrei Kozyrev, *Preobrazhenie*, Mezhdunarodnoe Otnoshenie, Moscow, 1994, p. 295.

35. *Kyodo*, 23 Mar. 1991, *Summary of World Broadcasts* (FE/1030/A2/191), 26 Mar. 1991.

36. *Nikkei Weekly*, 15 Mar. 1992, *Reuters Textline*.

37. *Jiji Press*, 18 Feb. 1992, *Reuters Textline*.

38. *Nihon keizai shinbun*, 10 Feb. 1992, *Reuters Textline*.

39. *Kyodo*, 9 May 1991, *Summary of World Broadcasts* (FE/1062/AR/2), 3 May 1991.

40. *Komsomolskaya pravda*, 26 May 1994.

41. *Moskovskie novosti* (15), 8–14 Apr. 1991.

42. Aleksei Surkov, "Mirnykh dogovor dolzheh byt' zaklyuchen," *Nezavisimaya gazeta*, 16 May 1992.

43. *Nezavisimaya gazeta*, 10 July 1992.

44. *Izvestiya*, 4 Feb. 1992.

45. Vitalii Tret'yakov, "Peredacha ostrovov ne dolzhna byt' nemedlennoi," *Nezavisimaya gazeta*, 14 Mar. 1992.

46. *Proekt konstitutsii rossiiskoi federatsii (sbornik materialov)*, Verkhovnyi soviet rossiiskoi federatsii, Moscow, 1992.

47. *Rossiiskaya gazeta*, 24 July 1992.

48. *Nezavisimaya gazeta*, 17 July 1992.

49. *Nezavisimaya gazeta*, 14, July 1992.

50. Georgii Mekhov, "Voenni aspekt territorial'noi problemy," *Krasnaya zvezda*, 22 July 1992.

51. See document entitled "Zaklyuchenie general'nogo shtaba vooruzhennykh sil rossiiskoi federatsii po probleme territorial'nogo razmezhevaniya mezhdu Rossiei i Yaponiei" (Conclusions of general staff of armed forces of Russian Federation on problem of territorial demarcation between Russia and Japan), *Nezavisimaya gazeta*, 30 July 1992.

52. *Nezavisimaya gazeta*, 30 July 1992.

53. *Rossiiskaya gazeta*, 14 Aug. 1992.

54. *Rossiiskaya gazeta*, 29 July 1992.

55. Oleg Rumyantsev, *Rossiisko-yaponskie otnosheniya i problema territorial'noi tselostnosti rossiiskoi federatsii; devyat' aspektov*, Konstitutsionnaya Komissiya rossiiskoi federatsii, Moscow, July 1992.

56. Vitalii Tretyakov, "Ostavka Andreya Kozyreva"" *Nezavisimaya gazeta*, 31 July 1992.

57. Andrei Kozyrev, *Preobrazhenie*, Mezhdunarodnoe Otnoshenie, Moscow, 1994, pp. 298–299.

58. Vasilii Golovin, "Mikhail Poltoranin otvergaet," *Nezavisimaya gazeta*, 8 Aug. 1992.

59. Viktor Sheinis, "Ispytanie kurilami," *Izvestiya*, 6 Aug. 1992.

60. Stanislav Kondrashov, "Muki zamireniya s Yaponiei," *Izvestiya*, 14 Aug. 1992.

61. *Nezavisimaya gazeta*, 3 Sept. 1991.

62. *Nikkei*, 7 Sept. 1992, *Reuters Textline*.

63. *Rossiiskaya gazeta*, 8 Sept. 1992.

64. Vera Kuznetsova "Yaponskie strasti prodolzhayut sotryasat' Rossiyu," *Nezavisimaya gazeta*, 11 Sept. 1992.

65. Sergei Agafonov, "Vizit otlozhen i Tokio v shoke," *Izvestiya*, 10 Sept. 1992.

66. Aleksei Pushkov, "Uroki otmennogo vizita," *Moskovskie novosti* (38), 20/27 Sept. 1992. Andrei Kozyrev, *Preobrazhenie*, Mezhdunarodnoe Otnoshenie, Moscow, 1994, p. 299.

67. *Nezavisimaya gazeta*, 7 Oct. 1992.

68. Konstantin Eggert, "Moskva delaet stavku na sblizhenie s Seulom i Pekinom," *Izvestiya*, 15 Sept. 1992.

69. Maksim Yusin, "Otmena vizita . . .," *Izvestiya*, 11 Sept. 1992.

70. *Jiji Press*, 29 Sept. 1992, *Reuters Textline*.

71. *Jiji Press*, 16 Nov. 1992, *Reuters Textline*.

72. Sergei Agafonov, "Germano-yaponskii dialog po russkim voprosam," *Izvestiya*, 2 Mar. 1993.

73. *Far Eastern Economic Review*, 20 May 1993.

74. *Itar Tass*, 2 Apr. 1993.

75. Sergei Ponomarev, "Chuzhoi zemli nam ne nado," *Rossiiskaya gazeta*, 24 Aug. 1993.

76. Yuli Lebedev, "Pravitel'stvo RF yedinoe vo mnenii po kuril'skoi probleme," *Nezavisimaya gazeta*, 3 Sept. 1993.

77. *NHK TV*, 31 Aug. 1993, *Reuters Textline*.

78. *Jiji Press*, 9 Sept. 1993, *Reuters Textline*.

79. *Jiji Press*, 23, 27 Aug. 1993, *Reuters Textline*.

80. *Izvestiya*, 21 Sept. 1993.

81. *Izvestiya*, 7 Oct. 1993.

82. *Izvestiya*, 14 Oct. 1993.

83. *Rossiiskaya gazeta*, 13 Oct. 1993.

84. *Nezavisimaya gazeta* 13, 14 Oct. 1993; Charles Smith, "The Bear Hug," *Far Eastern Economic Review*, 21 Oct. 1993.

85. *Rossiiskaya gazeta*, 14 Oct. 1994.

86. *Reuters Textline*, 15 Dec. 1993; *Nikkei*, 20 Dec. 1993.

87. *Jiji Press*, 21 July 1993, *Reuters Textline*.

88. *Rossiiskaya gazeta*, 23 May 1992; *Izvestiya*, 21 May 1992; *Reuters Textline*, 20 May 1992.

89. Sergei Agafanov, "Spor Grachev i El'tsina iz-za yuzhnykh kuril," *Izvestiya*, 26 Oct. 1994.

90. *Izvestiya*, 13, 26 Jan. 1994, 22 Feb. 1994.

91. Dmitrii Gornostaev, "Tokio nastaivaet na skoreishchem zaklyuchenii mirnogo dogovora . . .," *Nezavisimaya gazeta*, 22 Mar. 1994.

92. *Japan Times*, 28, 29 Nov. 1994.

93. *Japan Times*, 23 Dec. 1994.

94. *Itar Tass*, 10 Feb. 1992.

95. *Izvestiya*, 17 Aug. 1994.

96. *Izvestiya*, 17 Aug. 199e.

97. *Izvestiya*, 18 Aug. 1994.

98. *Japan Times*, 26 Nov. 1994.

99. *Izvestiya*, 22 Nov. 1994.

100. Yurii Savenkov, "Tridtsat' pekinskikh chasov A. Kozyreva," *Izvestiya*, 18 Mar. 1992, *Reuters Textline*, 17 Mar. 1992. Kozyrev subsequently wrote that human rights were universal and that no particular national differences would be used to justify

a failure to adhere to them; Andrei Kozyrev, *Preobrazhenie*, Mezhdunarodnoe Otnoshenie, Moscow, 1994, p. 95.

101. Maksim Yusin, "Moskva-Pekin: polosa ispytani," *Izvestiya*, 24 Mar. 1992.

102. Vladimir Lukin, "Rossiya i ee interesy," *Nezavisimaya gazeta*, 20 Oct. 1992.

103. "Strategiya dla Rossiya," *Nezavisimaya gazeta*, 19 Aug. 1992.

104. Sergei Goncharov, "Osobye interesy rossii," *Izvestiya*, 25 Feb. 1992.

105. Vladimir Myasnikov, "Vostochnyi vector dla strany," *Krasnaya zvezda*, 23 Dec. 1993.

106. *Izvestiya*, 8 May 1992.

107. *Moscow Radio, BBC*, 13, 15 Feb. 1992, *Reuters Textline*.

108. Alexander Panov, "Moscow and Beijing Have Agreed on Almost All Points," *Moscow News* (5), 4/10 Feb. 1994. See also Vladimir Skosyrev, "Rossii pridetsya otvesti voiska ot granitsy s kitaem," *Izvestiya*, 2 Dec. 1992, also *Open Media Research Institute Daily Digest* (95), 17 May 1995.

109. *Krasnaya zvezda*, 17 Nov. 1993.

110. *Itar Tass*, 7 Dec. 1993.

111. *Nezavisimaya gazeta*, 18 Dec. 1992; *Itar Tass*, 18 Dec. 1992. Yeltsin said that the visit to Beijing "gives a natural balance to our foreign policy" and that "we are always accused of looking too much to the West," *Reuters Textline*, 17 Dec. 1992.

112. *Nezavisimaya gazeta*, 10 Dec. 1992.

113. *Itar Tass*, 18 Dec. 1992.

114. *Izvestiya*, 17 Dec. 1992.

115. *Izvestiya*, 26 Oct. 1991.

116. *Itar Tass*, 3, 4 Mar. 1992.

117. *Reuters Textline*, 23 June 1992, *Far Eastern Economic Review*, 9 July 1992, *Izvestiya*, 10 July 1992.

118. *Izvestiya*, 10 Sept. 1992.

119. Stanislav Kondrashov, "Chastnaya diplomatiya vokrug Taivanya," *Izvestiya*, 17 Sept. 1992.

120. *Nezavisimaya gazeta*, 10 Dec. 1992.

121. *Itar Tass*, 31 Aug. 1992, *Reuters Textline*, 31 Aug. 1992.

122. *AFP*, 3 Dec. 1992, *Reuters Textline*.

123. *Far Eastern Economic Review*, 26 Mar. 1992.

124. *Far Eastern Economic Review*, 8 July 1993, *Reuters Textline*, 11 June 1993.

125. *Izvestiya*, 30 Mar. 1993.

126. *Far Eastern Economic Review*, 8 July 1993.

127. *Itar Tass*, 10 Nov. 1993.

128. *Itar Tass*, 6 Apr. 1993.

129. *South China Morning Post*, 25 June 1993.

130. *Open Media Research Institute Daily Digest* (11), 13 Feb. 1995, *Japan Times*, 11 Feb. 1995.

131. *South China Morning Post*, 4 Mar. 1995.

132. *Nezavisimaya gazeta*, 2 Nov. 1994.

133. *Radio Free Europe/Radio Liberty Daily Report* (213), 9 Nov. 1994.

134. *South China Morning Post*, 15 May 1995.

135. *Wen wi po* (Hong Kong), 27 Aug. 1993; *BBC*, 3 Sept. 1993, *Reuters Textline*.

136. See Lt.-General Yuri Neshumov, Lt.-Colonel Nikolai Golub, "Govorit ob ottorzhenii rossiiskikh zemel' net osnovanii," *Nezavisimaya gazeta*, 29 Sept. 1993.

137. Boris Gorbachev, "Nasmert bilis' za damanskii," *Nezavisimaya gazeta*, 15 Mar. 1994.

138. V. I. Ishaev (head of administration, Khabarovsk *Krai*), letter to V. Chernomyrdin dated 15 Sept. 1993.

139. *Izvestiya*, 10 Feb. 1995.

140. *Izvestiya*, 3 Mar. 1995.

141. *Pravda*, 11 Jan. 1994.

142. *Izvestiya*, 26 May 1994.

143. S. I. Lopatin (head of Dept. of External Economic Ties, Khabarovsk *Krai*), *Vneshne ekonomicheskie svyazi Khabarovsk kraya i KNR* (undated) (prepared for Duma, Soviet of Federation hearings on China, 25 Apr. 1994)

144. A. A. Kuleshov (Deputy head of Amur *Oblast* Administration for Foreign Relations), *Problemy v reshenii kotorykh neobkhodima pomosh' federal'nykh organov.* (undated) (as above).

145. *Informatsiya ob ekonomicheskom, nauchno-tekhnicheskom i kul'turnom sotrudnichestve amurskoi oblasti s KNR* (undated) (prepared by Amur *Oblast* Administration, as above).

146. *Obrashchanie; predstavitelei delovykh krugov s Blagoveshchenska k deputatam federal'nogo sobraniya i Gosudarstvennoi Dumy v svyazi s parliamentskimi slushaniyami po problemam rossiisko-kitaiskikh otnoshenii*, A. V. Surat, L. A. Khalfin, B. L. Anikin V. I. Gladilov and others. (undated) (as above).

147. V. A. Balanev, Head, Department of Internal Affairs, Khabarovsk *Krai*. *Upravleniya vnutrennikh del khabarovskogo kraya po yporyadocheniyu rezhima prebivaniya inostrannykh grazhdan na territorii rossii* (19/297), 20 Apr. 1994 (as above).

148. *Kommersant*, 26 May 1994.

149. *Izvestiya*, 27 Apr. 1994.

150. *Pravda*, 11 Jan. 1994, *Izvestiya*, 27 Apr. 1994.

151. *Moscow Tribune*, 28 July 1994.

152. *Izvestiya*, 27 Apr. 1994.

153. *Nezavisimaya gazeta*, 1 Feb. 1994.

154. Aleksei Voskresenskii, "Zona sotrudnichestva ili potentsial'nogo konflikta," *Nezavisimaya gazeta*, 3 June 1994.

155. Aleksander Platkovskii, "Kitaiskaya golovolomka," *Moskovskie novosti* (21), 22/29 May 1994.

156. Aleksei Voskresenskii, "Vyzov KNR i rossiiskie interesy," *Nezavisimaya gazeta*, 16 Sept. 1994.

157. Sergei Shakhrai, "Neobkhodima strategiya otnoshenii s kitaem," *Izvestiya*, 30 May 1994.

158. M. G. Fradkov, Deputy Minister of External Economic Relations, *Memo to A. P. Manannikov, Deputy Chairman, Committee on International Affairs, Soviet of Federation*, 22 Apr. 1994.

159. *Izvestiya*, 31 Aug. 1994.

160. On Gorbachev-South Korean relations see Peggy Falkenheim Meyer, "Gorbachev and Post Gorbachev Policy Towards the Korean Peninsula: The Impact of Changing Russian Perceptions," *Asian Survey*, vol. 32, no. 8, Aug. 1992.

161. Maksim Yusin, "Moskva obeshchaet podderzhat' Seul v yadernom spore s pkhen'yanom," *Izvestiya*, 20 Mar. 1992, *Reuters Textline*, 19 Mar 1993.

162. "My partnery v politike i ekonomike," *Rossiiskaya gazeta*, 23 May 1992.

163. Gennadi Charodeev, "Rossiya gotovitsya k podpisaniyu dogovora s yuzhnoi koreei," *Izvestiya*, 13 Aug. 1992.

164. "Nuzhno li Rossii vybirat' iz dvykh korei odnu?" *Rossiiskaya gazeta*, 28 Aug. 1992.

165. *Reuters Textline*, 6 Aug. 1992.

166. Georgi Stepanov, "Rossiya ne khochet delat' odnostoronyii vybor v pol'zy Seula," *Izvestiya*, 31 July 1992.

167. *Izvestiya*, 13 Aug. 1992.

168. *Izvestiya*, 13 Aug. 1992.

169. *Far Eastern Economic Review*, 10 Feb. 1994.

170. *Far Eastern Economic Review*, 3 Dec. 1992.

171. *Itar Tass*, 6 Feb. 1993; Aleksander Zhebin, Vadim Tkachenko, "Kunadze letel v Pkhen'yan cherez Pekin," *Nezavisimaya gazeta*, 17 Feb. 1993.

172. Andrei Kozyrev, "Vyzov preobrazheniya," *Izvestiya*, 31 Mar. 1992.

173. *Itar Tass*, 25 Feb. 1992.

174. Sergei Kukhar', "Igra v poddavki s yaponiei," *Rossiiskaya gazeta*, 10 June 1992.

175. *Jiji Press*, 9 Nov. 1992, *Reuters Textline*.

176. *Reuters Textline*, 22 May 1993.

177. *Yonhap*, 16 Sept. 1992, *BBC*, 2 Oct. 1992, *Reuters Textline*.

178. *Far Eastern Economic Review*, 3 Mar. 1994.

179. Sergei Agafonov, Igor' Golemviovskii, "Bez illyuzii, no s perspektivoi stroyat otnosheniya Moskva i Seul," *Izvestiya*, 12 Nov. 1992.

180. "Vystuplenie B. Yeltsina v national'nom sobranii respubliki Koreya," *Rossiiskaya gazeta*, 20 Nov. 1992. Vera Kuznetsova, "Nachalo aktivnoi politiki rossii na tikhom okeane," *Nezavisimaya gazeta*, 20 Nov. 1992.

181. *Reuters Textline*, 20 Nov. 1992.

182. *Itar Tass*, 13 Nov. 1992.

183. Vladimir Kuzar', "Seul-Moskva: epokha partnerstva," *Krasnaya zvezda*, 20 Nov. 1992.

184. *Itar Tass*, 20 Nov. 1992.

185. Vladimir Kuzar', "Vizit v respubliku Koreya udalsya," *Krasnaya zvezda*, 21 Nov. 1992; also "Novyi start vostochnoi diplomatii rossii," *Krasnaya zvezda*, 19 Nov. 1992.

186. *International Herald Tribune*, 3 Jan. 1994.

187. *Yonhap, BBC*, 18 Dec. 1993, *Reuters Textline*.

188. *Izvestiya*, 1 Apr. 1994.

189. Vladimir Skosyrev, "Pekin i Seul ignoriruyut initsiativu Kozyreva," *Izvestiya*, 30 Mar. 1994.

190. *Izvestiya*, 26 Mar. 1994.

191. *Izvestiya*, 24 Mar. 1994.

192. See Gennadii Yevstafvev's statement, *Moscow News* (2), 17 Jan. 1994.

193. Yuri Banin, "Nakazanie KNDR avtoriteta nam ne dobavit," *Pravda*, 16 June 1994; "Lobbistov ishchut ne tam gde nado," *Pravda*, 29 June 1994.

194. Yevgenni Aleksandrov, "Ne dal'novidnaya politika," *Pravda*, 1 July 1993.

195. Vladimir Mikheev, "Vladimir Lukin predlagaet svoyu ocherednost' shagov v podhode k pkhen'yanu," *Izvestiya*, 11 June 1994.

196. For Kim Young Sam's address see *Soviet federatsii, federalnogo sobraniya: sixth session*, 2 June 1994, Bulletin no. 3 (5). Dmitrii Gornostaev, "Kreml' gotov podderzhat' sanktsii protiv KNDR," *Nezavisimaya gazeta*, 3 June 1994.

197. *Izvestiya*, 31 Mar. 1994.

198. *Radio Free Europe/Radio Liberty Daily Report* (114), 17 June 1994, *Radio Free Europe/Radio Liberty Daily Report* (115), 20 June 1994.

199. *Radio Free Europe/Radio Liberty Daily Report* (113), 16 June 1994.

200. *Far Eastern Economic Review*, 27 Oct. 1994.

201. *USIS*, 24 Oct. 1994.

202. *Izvestiya*, 29 Oct. 1994.

203. *Far Eastern Economic Review*, 29 Dec. 1994/5 Jan. 1995.

204. Sergei Agafonov, "Koreiskie tainy rossiiskoi diplomatii," *Izvestiya*, 23 Dec. 1994.

205. *Japan Times*, 12 July 1995.

206. *Izvestiya*, 10 Nov. 1994.

207. *Far Eastern Economic Review*, 16 June 1994, *Japan Times*, 12 July 1995.

208. *Moscow News*, no. 24, 17/23 June 1994.

Chapter 6

The Future

This study has examined Russia's foreign policy in three areas of immediate security interest—Europe and the West, the CIS, and the Asia-Pacific region. As part of the process of adjusting foreign policy priorities Moscow has conducted a retreat from the globalism of the Soviet era and a reorientation toward contiguous areas. The repudiation of the globalist perspectives of the Soviet Union has provoked anguished criticism from their advocates, those who had given their careers to their definition and formulation. Globalism has grown deep roots in Moscow and the readjustment of Russia's role from a superpower to a regional power has not been without pain. Once an important category for Moscow's leaders and academics, the Third World means very little to Russia today. In any case, the notion of the Third World is a misnomer, a product of the simplistic Procrustean categorization of Soviet times. The lapse of interest in this area has caused few difficulties but there are two regions that have become controversial. Neither lies within the zone of immediate security interest but both have their advocates who have decried what they regard as official indifference toward these areas, namely the Middle East and South Asia. Their advocates insist that linkages enhance the value of both regions for Russia, that they are related to Russia's immediate interests, and that Moscow policy makers neglect these connections to their own detriment.

In relation to the Middle East, Moscow's specialists claim that Russia needs to cultivate relations with the wider Islamic World to be assured of its own security. Russia has veered too close to the West in a way that could negatively impact on relations with the Islamic World.[1] Karen Brutents wrote of the "professional arrogance" of the *zapadniki* (Westerners) who ignore the Arab World and who fail to see the opportunity for Russia to act as a balancing factor. Russia, he argued, can play a major role in overcoming the Arab-Israeli problem.[2] Nonetheless, Moscow's pro-Western leaders have seen no purpose in a Soviet-style balancing strategy that previously involved the Soviet Union in several Middle East wars. Moscow's democrats have no interest in a struggle for influence in the Arab World (which would entail conflict with the U.S.) when their own sympathies are with democratic Israel. Alignment with the Arab World has been replaced by a different approach, evident since the Soviet Union restored diplomatic relations with Israel on 18 October 1991. If Moscow has competed with the United States it has not been through military support of the Arabs against Israel, but in sponsoring a comprehensive resolution of the Arab-Israeli problem. As cosponsor of the Madrid Conference, the Russian Foreign Ministry arranged a Moscow Conference in January 1992 that brought together Israel and ten Arab states. Moscow subsequently promoted the comprehensive approach, but a similar initiative for a new Middle East conference in March 1994 was rejected by the U.S. By then, the U.S. had excluded Russia from the peace process by adopting the bilateral approach in reconciling Israel with the Arabs. The two key agreements between Israel and the PLO (on 13 September 1993 and 4 May 1994) were reached without Moscow's involvement. PLO leader Yasser Arafat attempted to involve Moscow in the process and traveled there in April 1994 to appeal to Russia's leaders. However, if peace returns to the Middle East, it will be without Russia's assistance.

Russia has pursued particular interests in relations with the Arab states, as many were longterm purchasers of Russian weapons. A low-key relationship with Syria has been maintained and Russia concluded a military agreement with that country on 27 April 1994 for the sale of defensive weapons and spare parts.[3] Kuwait has emerged as a purchaser of Russian weapons, probably to prevent Moscow from tilting toward Iraq and by way of a reward for receiving Moscow's support during the 1991 Gulf War. A defense cooperation agreement with Kuwait was signed in November 1993 allowing the sheikhdom to diversify weapons supplies.[4] Moscow acted as an intermediary in the North-South Yemen conflict of early 1994 and negotiated a cease-fire on 30 June 1994.[5] Moscow also pushed for the removal of the UN economic sanctions imposed on Iraq after the Iraqi invasion of Kuwait in August 1990. After Iraqi Premier Tarik Aziz visited Moscow in July 1994, the Russian Foreign Ministry began to press for the lifting of sanctions on the basis that Iraq was ready to recognize Kuwaiti sovereignty. Moscow was guided by several interests including the desire to negotiate the repayment of the $7 billion Iraqi debt as well as the hope that Russian companies would be invited to complete industrial and oil projects commenced before the Gulf War.[6] Lobbyists for the lifting of sanctions include the Russian oil company Lukoil (which hopes to gain access to Iraqi oil fields) and the arms trading company Rosvooruzhenie. A pro-Iraq lobby has formed in Moscow which includes Foreign Ministry officials, Deputy Premier Oleg Soskovets, the Ministry of Foreign Trade, and some military representatives.[7] The West, however, will not consider lifting sanctions unless, in addition to the recognition of Kuwaiti sovereignty, Iraq compensates Kuwait for the devastating occupation during the Gulf War, returns valued objects taken from Kuwait's museums, and accounts for over 1,000 missing Kuwaitis.[8]

A similar process of withdrawal has been noted in the case of South Asia where India was once a major Soviet ally. The alliance was forged in August 1971 when Indira Gandhi reacted against U.S. support for Pakistan during the war of Bangladesh's liberation. The Soviet-Indian alliance had a particular significance when both sides regarded China as a threat and when India viewed the American naval presence in the Indian Ocean in hostile terms. The basic assumptions of this relationship were challenged during the Gorbachev era when Moscow normalized relations with Beijing and repudiated the idea of a continued rivalry with the United States. Russia's pro-Western position and the importance that Moscow attaches to stable relations with Beijing have resulted in a downgrading of India's significance for Russia. India has continued to regard China as an emerging threat in view of its naval modernization and penetration of Burma. This provides Moscow with even less incentive to renew the relationship. Russia and India have drifted far apart.

Within the Russian Foreign Ministry a debate has developed over India's significance for Russia. The view that Russia should maintain a special relationship with India was advocated by the Foreign Ministry's Asian Department. The opposing position was expressed by Kunadze during the Supreme Soviet hearings on foreign policy in January 1993. The deputy foreign minister argued for a balanced position in which the significance of Pakistan should be raised to the same level as India's in Russian foreign policy.[9] Behind Kunadze's position was not only an understanding of China's value for Russia but the recognition that Pakistan may assume an important role in Central Asian security. Moreover, since November 1991 Moscow has supported Pakistan over the proposal for a South Asian nuclear free zone (which India has consistently rejected) and has pushed India to sign the Nuclear Non-Proliferation Treaty. The priority that Moscow now attaches to nuclear non-proliferation has introduced additional stresses in the relationship with India.

Moscow leaders who continued to emphasize India as a priority for Russia included Ruslan Khasbulatov who, during his visit to New Delhi in August 1992, stressed Moscow's traditional friendship with India. Khasbulatov declared that all constitutional means will be adopted to ensure that Russian-Indian relations do not continue to decline.[10] The Supreme Soviet speaker took issue with Moscow's pro-Western leaders over their priorities in foreign policy and was attempting to change their views. Yeltsin himself came down on the side of the pro-India lobby in January 1993 during his visit to New Delhi. Nonetheless, Yeltsin's visit to India was yet another example of diplomatic theater with few longterm results. Yeltsin was prompted to arrest the decline in the relationship for reasons related to economics as well as to domestic politics. After visiting Seoul and Beijing, a trip to India was yet another opportunity to declare Moscow's Asia orientation in foreign policy as part of the struggle with the Supreme Soviet. In India, Yeltsin signed a new treaty of friendship to replace the 20-year 1971 treaty, agreed to resume the delivery of spare parts to India's military (which had been disrupted) and came to an agreement over India's debt to Russia. Yeltsin declared that "now our policy is equally balanced toward both the West and the East."[11]

Once Yeltsin made his declaration and returned to Moscow, policy toward India continued to drift. India's interest in maintaining a relationship with Russia centered around the need to purchase spare parts for the mainly Soviet-supplied Indian military. India was interested also in purchasing new equipment (MIG-29s) and in entering proposed joint ventures with Russia to manufacture MIG-21s, -23s and -27s as well as T-72 tanks under license. Indian Prime Minister Narashimha Rao visited Moscow in June 1994 and discussed the purchase of 36 MIG-29s. Chernomyrdin in turn visited New Delhi in December 1994. On both occasions Indian concerns were stimulated by reports that Russia was considering arms sales to Pakistan—Yeltsin and Chernomyrdin denied this.[12] Russian arms manufacturers together with their supporters in government have in fact been lobbying Moscow to sell MIG-29s and other weapons to Pakistan.

There is more sentiment than reality behind Russia's relationship with India. The pro-Indian lobby group continues to stress the need to maintain a special relationship with New Delhi to ensure Russia's role as a bridge between East and West.[13] Nonetheless, without the geopolitical basis that previously characterized the relationship it has steadily atrophied in a way barely masked by official pronouncements. In future years, leaderships will emerge in both Moscow and New Delhi that will not recall the events of the 1970s and will not be guided by the past or by illusory hopes for the future. Russia's interests in Central Asia will pull it toward a more balanced relationship with South Asia, which will include an upgraded role for Pakistan.

It is unlikely that the Middle East or India will ever be restored as high priorities in Russian foreign policy—that could only occur on the basis of a return to globalism. The revelations of the *perestroika* years have exposed the costs of globalism to the Russian people in terms of a massive diversion of resources to unproductive areas. Russia today suffers the consequences of this. Moreover, the interventionary globalist phase of Moscow's interaction with the outside world was sustained by an ossified ideology and a particular despotic structure of power that has since been repudiated and dismantled. Within the context of this globalist ideology the Middle East, India, and the Third World may have had a role in terms of rivalry with the West. The renunciation of interventionary globalism, however, also entailed the abnegation of a role in these outer areas.

Russia has become a battleground of values that reflects a struggle between past and future, collectivism and individualism, order and disorder. Foreign policy has been part of that battle and has become inseparable from domestic politics. It made sense in the Soviet era to examine foreign policy as the disembodied formulations of a small elite but this is certainly not so today.

Nonetheless, the tradition persists in the West to divorce foreign policy from domestic politics, to expect consistency and logical coherence in foreign policy statements and pronouncements when they may be absent. Foreign policy can be an instrument in domestic political conflict and government statements may represent stages in the evolution of particular domestic positions, not necessarily related to the external environment. In this way Yeltsin's sometimes confusing statements and the contradictions that have emerged with his own ministers can be understood. To expect clarity and coherence at a time of anguish and readjustment would be most unrealistic.

The conflict between past and future runs through this book as a main theme to which other issues may be subsumed. The past represents collectivism, the suppression of alternative views, the imposition of orthodoxy, and in terms of foreign policy the defense of state interests by traditional methods—the use of military force, the quest for power, and the resort to balance-of-power strategies. Traditionalism represents a hostile external environment that has to be subdued by the manipulation of power or by conquest. The future represents pluralism, democracy, and individual responsibility and in foreign policy it entails the pursuit of economic and political integrationist strategies. Integrationism represents a benign external environment that has been made hostile by Russia's past behavior. Whether Russia is unique, in which case the external environment is a hostile one, or an evolving part of an integrated world, is an old conflict that has been revived in a new guise. Behind integrationism stand Russia's pro-Western democrats who see Russia's so-called uniqueness as the characteristics of isolationism and retarded development. Russia's nationalists, Communists, and Eurasianists perceive integrationism as a threat because it will demand the sacrifice of all, which in their minds made Russia unique.

For Russia, the relationship with the West can be regarded as crucial in determining the general direction of foreign policy. The West represents the integrated world that could absorb and reform Russia or rob it of its uniqueness. Joining an integrated world has become an economic and security necessity, yet the process demands adjustments that are seen as humiliating concessions by those who represent the past in Russia. Eventually NATO will expand in Europe and will embrace the Central and East European states in a process that has its origins in a justified fear of Russia's behavior. Russia's nationalists can oppose this process and may lead the country once more into self-destructive isolation. They may search for geopolitical advantages against the West by developing closer relations with China or Islamic states such as Iran. They may also refuse to ratify the START-2 Treaty to maintain Russia's nuclear arsenal as a symbol of great power status and a means of inculcating respectful attitudes toward Russia from the West. Russia, however, is in no position to sustain rivalry with the West for very long though bouts of conflict will no doubt arise.

Eventually, however, Russia will be compelled to return to integrationist policies as the need to modernize and learn from the West is too great to be suppressed. Only then will it be understood that Russia can change Europe's attitude toward it by changing its own behavior, by avoiding traditional methods of conducting power politics, and by eschewing the use of force as a reflex action to cope with complicated issues—such as Chechnya's status in the Russian Federation. Under these conditions NATO may disappear and be replaced by a wider Eurasian security structure of the kind demanded by Russia's present rulers. Then the civilizational divisions that have been regarded as baselines for future conflicts will become blurred, and in their place will arise regional differences that will be testimony to cultural diversity and a source of stimulation and interest.

The relationship with the West touches on Russia's identity and the stresses and difficulties associated with it will not vanish immediately. Those in the West who expected Russia to emerge from the Soviet shipwreck as a ready-made Western country with a functioning free market and democracy were simply naive. Those in Russia who imagine that it represents another civilization or world that is separate from the West are blind. In response to the pressures emanating from the West that demand adjustment to an integrated world one can expect the oscillation effect. Torn between clashing influences and values Russia's behavior will oscillate between cooperation and conflict, the assumption of a power complex and the conduct of the diplomacy of reconciliation. Erratic and unpredictable behavior will continue to characterize Russian foreign policy depending on the influence of particular lobby groups and interests, the impact of the Federal Assembly, as well as political parties and movements. Not until a stable domestic political order has been established will the confusion be reduced and the oscillatory effect eliminated.

The Chechnya conflict was instructive in this sense as it revealed the contradictory impulses within Russian government. The traditional response to the Chechen desire for independence from Russia was to dispatch troops and to intimidate the Chechens by an awesome display of military power. Yeltsin and his Security Council gave way to traditional methods when the troops were ordered into Chechnya on 11 December 1994. Premier Chernomyrdin reverted to negotiations after the Budennovsk hostage-taking incident of June 1995 in a reaction against these traditional methods which had been so destructive. On 30 July 1995, Russia signed a military disengagement agreement with the Chechen leadership and Chernomyrdin declared the war ended. Why throw the troops into Chechnya in the first place if the results of the negotiations could have been obtained earlier in 1994? The political status of Chechnya was as ambiguous then as it is today and the military excursion resolved little. Chechnya was illustrative of a deep conflict of values within Russian government and society at large and the extent to which the past can be a guide to future behavior. As noted above similar oscillations can be expected in foreign policy.

Russian attitudes toward the former Soviet Union are closely linked to this conflict of values surrounding the relationship with the West. Nationalists, Communists, and Eurasianists may seek a revival of the Soviet Union or coercive integration following the Soviet Union as model, but their ability to have their way depends on the success or failure of the relationship with the West. A failed relationship, one that pushes Russia's leadership toward confrontative postures, will enhance the pressure to seek compensatory satisfaction within the former Soviet Union for frustrated great power. Russia may then seek to define itself within the former Soviet Union and may attempt to convert the CIS into an integrated structure based on coercion. Such attempts would accelerate the process of differentiation within the CIS as allies of Moscow will join with Russia but those that fear Moscow will resist its pressure. Russia may gain Armenia, Belarus and the Central Asian states as allies but tensions will be created with the Ukraine that would push Kiev toward the West. Conflicts may be stimulated in the Caucasian and southern Central Asian regions by Moscow's military interference and desire for greater control over outlying regions. The results of an imperial recidivism would be self-defeating for Russia and would include the destruction of the CIS and the rapid expansion of NATO, both of which Russia has attempted to avoid.

The demonstrated success of integrationism in relation to the West would influence attitudes within Moscow and positively impact on Russia's relationship with the CIS. Russian integrationists have often argued that even without any coercion the CIS states would seek a voluntary economic and security association with Moscow. Some CIS states cannot survive economically, others require Moscow's security support, and all realize the benefits of economic integration with larger markets that is the trend of the times, in Europe as well as the Asia-Pacific region. If Russia could curb its imperialist instincts it could go a long way to preparing the basis of a voluntary association that would answer common needs in the CIS, as perceived by states as diverse as the Ukraine and Turkmenistan. Imperialist instincts are deep within the leadership in Moscow and have accumulated over centuries within a people whose collective memory of the outside world has been of danger. The overcoming and sublimation of these instincts will require, amongst other things, a successful relationship with the West to allow integrationist logic to prevail over imperialist tendencies.

In turn, how Russia relates to the former Soviet Union or the "near abroad" can influence relations with the West. Russia acts according to the security imperative in both the Caucasus and in Central Asia—particularly in relation to Tajikistan. Russia's rivalry with Islamic influences along the southern borders of the CIS will continue to motivate the search for reliable allies, for bases and deployment points for military forces and air defenses. Should the situation along the southern borders deteriorate, either because of the collapse of state structures or communal conflict stimulated by external penetration, Russia would be tempted to resort to military power on a greater scale than was the case with Chechnya. A Russia embroiled in a series of local wars along its peripheries would be vulnerable to accusations of human rights abuses and of excessive reliance on force thereby creating significant political tensions with the West. As long as Russia confronts the danger of instability along its borders it may be tempted to resort to military power, which has been a constant feature of its history, complicating relations with European neighbors and justifying the expansion of NATO. For these reasons, assert the traditionalists, Russia cannot disarm and will continue to rely on the exercise of power that will hinder the development of closer relations with the West.

Integrationism also clashes with traditionalism in the Asia-Pacific region. The region is an area where Moscow has promoted an integrationist multilateralism in both economic and security spheres that is the legacy of Gorbachevian new thinking. Nonetheless, the region has witnessed some of the bitterest battles over foreign policy where multilateralist assumptions have been directly confronted by domestic nationalism. Integrationism demanded a resolution of the territorial dispute with Japan to confirm Moscow's adherence to international law and to pave the way for closer economic ties with Japan and economic integration with the Asia-Pacific region. The attempt to resolve this issue in 1992 directly provoked the involvement of domestic political forces that emerged as a constraint on foreign policy. Public opinion was revealed as a powerful weapon in diverting the course of foreign policy, one which policy makers were compelled to accommodate. Russia has particular difficulty in affirming its commitment to multilateralism while China assumes such an important position for security. Integrationism and traditional geopolitical logic have clashed over the Korean Peninsula where, according to the proponents of traditional balance of power policy, Russia has lost. Integrationists, however, see success not in strengthening influence over other states but in overcoming the danger of nuclear proliferation on the peninsula by means of a coalition strategy linking Russia and the West.

The West has an opportunity to shape or influence the future in Russia in view of the significance it has for that country. The West can encourage more open policies toward Russia to strengthen the hands of the democrats and the integrationists against the benighted forces of nationalist isolation. Closer economic relations with the European Community, for example, would demonstrate the benefits of integrationist policies and promote the kind of domestic changes in Russia that over time would contribute to economic stabilization. The West should avoid punitive strategies based on geopolitical pressure or on the balance of power which, for example, would set the Ukraine against Moscow. This behavior would confirm the worst suspicions of the nationalists and traditionalists and would give them cause to rally. The West's emphasis should be on incentives for cooperation and their withholding if need be until Moscow is prepared to respond. In the context of a developing relationship with the West, Moscow would be unlikely to turn to imperialist policies in the CIS, or to actively ally with regimes hostile to the West. Such behavior could be provoked if the relationship with the West deteriorates, if Western leaders lose patience with the pace of change and resort to punitive measures, or if the West simply closes its doors to Russia on the basis of supposedly irreconcilable civilizational differences.

The clash of values and the struggle between integrationism and traditionalism in foreign policy will be strongly influenced by two factors that in many respects interact with each other. Much depends on the success of economic reform and whether or not economic change demonstrates its value to the Russian people before an electoral backlash sweeps aside the democrats and sponsors of market reform. Negative electoral reactions to economic reform could throw Russia into a crisis and may entail the end of democracy as the government would be tempted to declare a state of emergency rather than allow its current policies to be reversed. The benefits of economic change have percolated to small groups in the major cities and the polarization of society between rich and poor has proceeded relentlessly. Some Russian members of Parliament told the author of their concern about a Communist reaction to economic reform in the next and subsequent elections. Certainly, as in Britain and the U.S. in the nineteenth century, economic change in Russia has resulted in great injustices in a loosely regulated system that has been described as wild west capitalism. Should the Moscow government learn from history and introduce regulatory measures to reduce the social polarization, an electoral backlash could be avoided. Required measures would include a reduction of crime, a just and sensible tax regime that would provide a decent living for those on fixed salaries, and the introduction of order and legality into the present chaotic bureaucratic structure.

Russia's geopolitical position will continue to impact on foreign policy in a way that will emphasize the need for Russia to reconcile the West and Asia. Geopolitical position has prompted the formulation of Eurasianism as an ideology of interaction and integration between the cultures that historically have made Russia a crossroads between Europe and Asia, whether Christian Orthodox, Turkic Muslim,, or Mongolian Buddhist. Eurasianism has been influential in Russia either in terms of language or conviction and offers an explanation as to why Russia has not been and may not become a part of the West. Even Nikolai Berdyaev, no supporter of Eurasianist ideology, noted that Russia should recognize itself as East as well as West, should unite itself within two worlds without dividing.[14] Eurasian ideas may gain in popularity and may serve as an ideological basis for future foreign policy. Russia's geopolitical position compels its leaders to be as responsive to the Islamic and Chinese worlds as to the West. In any conflict between the West and Islam, or the West and China over human rights, democracy and fundamental values Russia cannot afford to side wholly with the West. Neither can it join a Western coalition directed against China or its major Islamic neighbors. This is a major constraint on Moscow's foreign policy.

Russia would be faced with a major dilemma in the event of conflict between the West and China or the Islamic World. The West's relationship with China or with Islam may be an important factor bearing on Russian foreign policy attitudes in future years. Pressures emanating from such conflict would exacerbate existing divisions in Russia between pro-Western democrats, nationalists, and others and between European and Far Eastern Russia. At one stage between 1992–1993, there was the fear that Russia would disintegrate under the pressure of its geopolitical position, that Moscow would look to Europe, and that the Far East would join the Asia-Pacific region as a participant in the economic integrative processes being encouraged there. Nonetheless, despite the evident tensions between Moscow and the Far East, Russia will not follow the Soviet Union, neither will the Far East separate from Moscow. Ethnicity and culture remain powerful binding elements between European and Far Eastern Russia which have been strengthened by proximity and contact with neighboring China.

Ultimately, this study of foreign policy reflects a deeper and more complex process of adjustment to modernity and to the integrated world that is being formed with startling rapidity today. Russia is not the only country that has embarked on this troubling path, not the only country that has spawned a tradition of uniqueness for which war and conflict have been invoked. Germany and Japan proclaimed their unique national identities before war and devastation compelled a painful transformation and readjustment. For Russia, the instrument of this corrective process may be the humiliation of the past few years that hopefully will expunge the exaggerated pretensions to greatness and the Messianic nationalism that prevailed under conditions of isolation. Russia, in Arnold Toynbee's terms, is facing the major challenge of its history as "the stimulus of blows."[15] Russia's response to that challenge will shape the next century.

NOTES

1. See Sergei Goncharov, "Osobyenteresy rossii," *Izvestiya*, 25 Feb. 1992, Aleksei Vasil'ev, "Rossiya i musul'manskii mir–partnery ili protivniki," *Izvestiya*, 10 Mar. 1992.

2. Karen Brutents, "Pora vozurashchatsya," *Nezavisimaya gazeta*, 5, 7 Oct. 1994.

3. *New York Times*, 29 Apr. 1994.

4. *Pravda*, 23 Dec. 1993.

5. *Nezavisimaya gazeta*, 1 July 1994.

6. El'mar Guseinov, "Irak nadeetsya podkupit Moskvu," *Izvestiya*, 13 July 1994.

7. *Izvestiya*, 15 Sept. 1994.

8. *Izvestiya*, 15 Sept., 8 Dec. 1994.

9. *Itar Tass*, 25 Jan. 1993.

10. *Rossiiskaya gazeta*, 13 Aug. 1992.

11. *Reuters Textline*, 29 Jan. 1993, Stanislav Kondrashov, "Indiiskie zadachi Borisa Yeltsina," *Izvestiya*, 27 Jan. 1993.

12. Hamish McDonald, "Getting Down to Business," *Far Eastern Economic Review*, 14 July 1994, *Nezavisimaya gazeta*, 21 Dec. 1994.

13. Oleg Malyarov, "Indiiskie zaboty rossiiskogo prem'era," *Nezavisimaya gazeta*, 21 Dec. 1994.

14. Nikolai Berdyaev, *Sud'ba rossii* (reprint of 1918 ed.), MGU, Moscow, 1990.

15. Arnold J. Toynbee, *A Study of History* (abridged ed.), vol. 1, Oxford University Press, London, 1946, pp. 108–111.

Selected Bibliography

RUSSIAN SOURCES

Newspapers

Izvestiya
Krasnaya zvezda
Moskovskie novosti
Nezavisimaya gazeta
Pravda
Rossiiskaya gazeta
Sovietskaya Rossiya

Monographs

Gumilev, L. N. *Ot rysi k rossii*, Progress-Pangeya, Moscow, 1994.

Gumilev, L. N. *Ritmy evrazi: epokh i tsivilizatsii*, Progress-Pangeya, Moscow.

Kozyrev, Andrei. *Preobrazhenie*, Mezhdunarodnye Otnoshenie, Moscow, 1994.

Novikova, L. I.; and Sizemskaya, I. N. (eds.) *Rossiya mezhdu evropoi i aziei; evraziiskii soblazn*, Nauka, Moscow, 1993.

Programma: kommunisticheskoi partii rossiiskoi federatsii (3rd Congress, 22 Jan. 1995), Moscow, 1995.

Rumyantsev, Oleg. *Rossiisko-yaponskie otnosheniya i problema territorial'noi tselostnosti rossiiskoi federatsii; devyat' aspektov*, Konstitutsionnaya Komissiya rossiiskoi federatsii, Moscow, 1992.

Topornina, B. N.; Batukina, Yu. M.; and Orekhova, R. G. *Konstitutsiya rossiiskoi federatsii; kommentari*, Yuridicheskaya literature, Moscow, 1994.

III s'ezd kommunisticheskoi partii rossiskoi federatsii (materialy i documenty), Informpechat', Moscow, 1995.

Zhirinovsky, Vladimir. *Poslednii brosok na yug* , Rait, Moscow, 1994.
Zhirinovsky, Vladimir. *Poslednii vagon na sever*, [s.n.], Moscow, 1995.
Zyuganov, Gennadii. *Derzhava*, Informpechat', Moscow, 1994.

Journals and Articles

Vedomosti; federal'nogo sobraniya rossiiskoi federatsii, no. 1, Jan. 1994.
Yevzerov, Robert. "Evraziiskaya ideya v nezavisimykh gosudarstvakh," S*vobodnaya mysl'*, no. 14, 1993.
Zagorskii, A. V. "Rossiisko-yaponskie otnosheniya: B. N. Yeltsin pered dramaticheskim vyborom," in *Znakom'tes' Yaponiya: k vizitu B. N. Yeltsina*, Nauka, Moscow, 1992.

ENGLISH SOURCES

Itar-Tass (after January 1992)
Moscow News
Open Media Research Institute Daily Digest
Radio Free Europe/Radio Liberty Daily Reports
Radio Free Europe/Radio Liberty Research Reports
Reuters Textline Data Service
Tass (before January 1992)

Newspapers and Weekly Journals

Economist
Far Eastern Economic Review
Financial Times
Guardian
Independent
International Herald Tribune
Japan Times
New York Times
Straits Times
Washington Post

Monographs

Declaration of the Heads of State and Government Participating in the Meeting of the North Atlantic Council Held at NATO Headquarters, Brussels on 10-11 January 1994, NATO International Secretariat, Brussels, 1994.
Gelman, Harry. *Russo-Japanese Relations and the Future of the U.S.-Japanese Alliance*. Rand Corporation, Santa Monica, California, 1993.

George, Bruce. *After the NATO Summit: Draft General Report*, North Atlantic Treaty Organization, Public Data Service, Brussels, 1994.

Impact of IMF/World Bank Policies toward Russia and the Russian Economy, Hearings before the Committee on Banking, Housing and Urban Affairs, U.S. Senate, Washington DC., 1994.

Nimmo, William F. *Japan and Russia: A Reevaluation in the Post-Soviet Era*, Westport, Greenwood Press, 1994.

Nixon, Richard. *Seize the Moment: America's Challenge in a One Superpower World*, Simon and Schuster, New York, 1992.

Niyazi, Aziz. "Tajikistan" in Mohiaddin Mesbahi (ed.), *Central Asia and the Caucasus after the Soviet Union: Domestic and International Dynamics*, University Press of Florida, Gainesville, Florida, 1994.

Rashid, Ahmed. *The Resurgence of Central Asia, Islam or Nationalism*, 2nd ed., Oxford/Zed, London, 1994.

Stephan, John J. *The Kurile Islands: Russo-Japanese Frontier in the Pacific*, Clarendon, Oxford, 1974.

Wachsler, Tamas. *NATO and NAA, Enlargement: Draft Special Report*, NATO International Secretariat, Brussels, 1994.

Articles

Abduvakhitov, Abdujabar. "Islamic Revivalism in Uzbekistan" in Dale F. Eickelman (ed.), *Russia's Muslim Frontiers*, Indiana University Press, 1993.

Adomeit, Hannes. "Russia As a 'Great Power' in World Affairs: Images and Reality," *International Affairs* (UK), 71, 1 (1995).

Afanasyev, Yuri N. "Seems Like Old Times? Russia's Place in the World," *Current History*, Oct. 1994.

Akaha, Tsuneo and Murakami, Takashi. "Soviet-Japanese Economic Relations" in Hasegawa Tsuyoshi *et al.* (eds.), *Russia and Japan*, University of California, 1993.

Akiner, Shirin. "Whither Central Asia?" in Rosemary Hollis (ed.), *The Soviets, Their Successors and the Middle East*, St. Martins, London, 1993.

Aleksei Arbatov, "START II, Red Ink, and Boris Yeltsin", *Bulletin of the Atomic Scientists*, Apr. 1993.

Arbatov, Alexei. G. "Russia's Foreign Policy Alternatives," *International Security*, fall 1993.

Arbatov, Georgi. "Eurasia Letter: The New Cold War," *Foreign Policy* (95), summer 1994.

Belokrenitsky, Vyacheslav Ya. "Russia and Greater Central Asia," *Asian Survey*, Dec. 1994.

Blank, Stephen. "We Can Live Without You: Rivalry and Dialogue in Russo-Japanese Relations," *Comparative Strategy*, Apr./June 1993.

Bluth, Christoph. "American-Russian Strategic Relations: From Confrontation to Cooperation," *World Today*, Mar. 1993.

Bluth, Christoph. "Russia and European Stability," *World Today*, Apr. 1994.

Brusstar, James H. "Russian Vital Interests and Western Security," *Orbis*, fall 1994.

Brzezinski, Zbigniew. "The Premature Partnership," *Foreign Affairs*, Mar./Apr. 1994.

Brzezinski, Zbigniew. "A Plan for Europe," *Foreign Affairs*, Jan./Feb. 1995.

Buszynski, Leszek. "Russia and Japan: The Unmaking of a Territorial Settlement," *World Today*, Mar. 1993.

Buszynski, Leszek. "Russia and the Asia-Pacific Region," *Pacific Affairs*, May 1992.

Chung, Eunsook. "Russia in a Changing International Environment" in Chung Il Yung, Chung Eunsook (eds.), *Russia in the Far East and Pacific Region*, Sejong Institute, Seoul, Korea, 1994.

Cox, Michael. "The Necessary Partnership? The Clinton Presidency and Post Soviet Russia," *International Affairs* (UK), 70, 4 (1994).

Dannreuther, Roland. "Russia, Central Asia and the Persian Gulf," *Survival*, vol. 34, no. 4, winter 1993/94.

Davidov, Oleg V. "Russia's Position towards the North Korea's Development As a Nuclear Power" in Chung Il Yung, Chung Eunsook (eds.), *Russia in the Far East and Pacific Region*, Sejong Institute, Seoul, Korea, 1994.

Falkenheim, Peggy. "Moscow's Relations with Tokyo: Domestic Obstacles to a Territorial Agreement," *Asian Aurvey*, Oct. 1993.

Freedman, Robert O. "Moscow and the Iraqi Invasion of Kuwait" in Robert O. Freedman (ed.), *The Middle East After Iraq's Invasion of Kuwait*, University of Florida Press, 1993.

Fuller, Graham. "Turkey and Russia" in Graham E. Fuller and Ian O. Lessier (eds.), *Turkey's New Geopolitics*, Rand Corporation, Santa Monica, 1993.

Goble, Paul A. "Russia and Its Neighbours," *Foreign Policy*, spring (90), 1993.

Goble, Paul A. "Ten Issues in Search of a Policy: America's Failed Approach to the Post-Soviet States," *Current History*, Oct. 1993.

Goble, Paul A. "Russia as a Eurasian Power: Moscow and the Post-Soviet Successor States" in Stephen Sestanovich (ed.), *Rethinking Russia's National Interests*, CSIS, Washington, DC, 1994.

Goldman, Amy Ravenhorts. "The Dynamics of New Asia: The Politics of Russian-Korean Relations" in Hasegawa Tsuyoshi *et al.* (eds.), *Russia and Japan: An Unresolved Dilemma Between Distant Neighbors*, University of California, 1993.

Goltz, Thomas. "Letter from Eurasia: The Hidden Russian Hand," *Foreign Policy* (92) fall 1993.

Haghayeghi, Mehrdad. "Islam and Democratic Politics in Central Asia," *World Affairs*, spring 1994.

Hasegawa, Tsuyoshi. "The Gorbachev-Kaifu Summit: Domestic and Foreign Policy Linkages" in Tsuyoshi Hasegawa et al. (eds.), *Russia and Japan: An Unresolved Dilemma Between Distant Neighbors*, University of California, 1993.

Haslam, Jonathan. "The Pattern of Soviet-Japanese Relations Since World War II" in Hasegawa Tsuyoshi et al. (eds.), *Russia and Japan: An Unresolved Dilemma Between Distant Neighbors*, University of California, 1993.

Hough, Jerry F. "America's Russian Policy: The Triumph of Neglect," *Current History*, Oct. 1994.

Hovannisian, Richard G. "Historical Memory and Foreign Relations: The Armenian Perspective" in S. Frederick Starr (ed.), *The Legacy of History in Russia and the New States of Eurasia: The International Politics of Eurasia,* M. E. Sharpe, Armonk, New York, 1994.

Ivanov, Vladimir I. "Russia in the Pacific: Prospects for Partnership with China" in Chung Il Yung, Chung Eunsook (eds.), *Russia in the Far East and Pacific Region,* Sejong Institute, Seoul, Korea, 1994.

Jackson, William. "Russia After the Crisis: Imperial Temptations: Ethnics Abroad," *Orbis,* winter 1994.

Katz, Mark N. "Nationalism and the Legacy of Empire," *Current History,* Oct. 1994.

Kim, Won Bae. "Sino-Russian Relations and Chinese Workers in the Russian Far East," *Asian Survey,* Dec. 1994.

Kimura, Hiroshi. "A Positive Sum Solution to the Territorial Dispute," *Japan Echo,* winter 1992.

King, Charles. "Eurasia Letter: Moldova with a Russian Face," *Foreign Policy* (97), winter 1994/95.

Kissinger, Henry. "Russian and American Interests After the Cold War" in Stephen Sestanovich (ed.), *Rethinking Russia's National Interests,* CSIS, Washington DC, 1994.

Kozyrev, Andrei. "Russia: A Chance for Survival," *Foreign Affairs,* spring 1992.

Kozyrev, Andrei. "The Lagging Partnership," *Foreign Affairs,* May/June 1994.

Lukin, Vladimir P. "Russia and Its Interests" in Stephen Sestanovich (ed.), *Rethinking Russia's National Interests,* CSIS, Washington DC, 1994.

MacFarlane, S. Neil. "Russia, the West and European Security," *Survival,* autumn 1993.

Malcolm, Neil "A New Russian Foreign Policy," *World Today,* Feb. 1994.

Meyer, Peggy Falkenheim. "Gorbachev and Post-Gorbachev Policy towards the Korean Peninsula," *Asian Survey,* Aug. 1992.

Mochizuki, Mike M. "The Soviet/Russian Factor in Japanese Security" in Hasegawa Tsuyoshi et al. (eds.), *Russia and Japan: An Unresolved Dilemma Between Distant Neighbors,* University of California, 1993.

Morrison, John. "Pereslav and After: The Russian Ukrainian Relationship," *International Affairs* (London), 1993, no. 4.

Olcott, Martha Brill. "Central Asia's Political Crisis" in Dale F. Eickelman (ed.), *Russia's Muslim Frontiers,* Indiana University Press, 1993.

Olcott, Martha Brill. "Central Asia's Post Empire Politics," *Orbis,* spring 1993.

Olcott, Martha Brill. "The Myth of Tsentral'naia Aziia," *Orbis,* fall 1994.

Panov, Alexander. "The Problem of Regional Stability and Security in the Asia-Pacific Region" in Chung Il Yung, Chung Eunsook (eds.), *Russia in the Far East and Pacific Region,* Sejong Institute, Seoul, Korea, 1994.

Pushkov, Alexei K. "Letter from Eurasia: Russia and America: The Honeymoon's Over," *Foreign Policy,* winter 1993/94.

Rogov, Sergei. "Military Interests and the Interests of the Military" in Stephen Sestanovich (ed.), *Rethinking Russia's National Interests*, CSIS, Washington DC, 1994.

Rozman, Gilbert. "Japanese Images of the Soviet and Russian Role in the Asia-Pacific Region," in Hasegawa Tsuyoshi et al. (eds.), *Russia and Japan: An Unresolved Dilemma Between Distant Neighbors*, University of California, 1993.

Rubbin, Barnett R. "The Fragmentation of Tajikistan," *Survival*, vol. 34, no. 4, winter 1993/94.

Rubinstein, Alvin Z. "The Geopolitical Pull on Russia," *Orbis*, fall 1994.

Rumer, Eugene B. "Eurasia Letter: Will the Ukraine Return to Russia?" *Foreign Policy* (96), fall 1994.

Rybakov, O. "Prospects for the Development of Russia's Economic Relations with States of the Commonwealth," *Problems of Economic Transition*, Jan. 1995.

Sarkisov, Konstantin O. "Russia and Japan: The Territorial Dispute" in Chung Il Yung, Chung Eunsook (eds.), *Russia in the Far East and Pacific Region*, Sejong Institute, Seoul, Korea, 1994.

Sase, Masamori, and Sawa, Hidetake. "Does Yeltsin Deserve Our Support?" *Japan Echo*, autumn 1993.

Segal, Gerald. "China and the Disintegration of the Soviet Union," *Asian Survey*, Sept. 1992.

Smith, Mark. "Russia's New Priorities in the Middle East" in Rosemary Hollis (ed.), *The Soviets, Their Successors and the Middle East*, St. Martins, London, 1993.

Snyder, Jack. "Nationalism and the Crisis of the Post-Soviet State," *Survival*, spring 1993.

Stankevich, Sergei B. "Russia in Search of Itself," *National Interest*, summer 1992.

Stankevich, Sergei B. "Toward a New National Idea" in Stephen Sestanovich (ed.), *Rethinking Russia's National Interests*, CSIS, Washington DC, 1994.

Swietochowski, Tadeusz. "Azerbaijan's Relationship: The Land Between Russia, Turkey and Iran" in Ali Banuaziziand and Myron Weiner (eds.), *The New Geopolitics of Central Asia and Its Borderlands*, I. B. Tauris, London, 1994.

Travkin, Nikolai. "Russia, Ukraine and Eastern Europe" in Stephen Sestanovich (ed.), *Rethinking Russia's National Interests*, CSIS, Washington DC, 1994.

Tyshetskii, Igor'. "The Gorbachev-Kaifu summit: The View from Moscow" in Tsuyoshi Hasegawa et al. (eds.), *Russia and Japan: An Unresolved Dilemma Between Distant Neighbors*, University of California, 1993.

Wolfowitz, Paul. "The US-Russian Strategic Partnership" in Stephen Sestanovich (ed.), *Rethinking Russia's National Interests*, CSIS, Washington DC, 1994.

Yu, Bin. "Sino-Russian Military Relations: Implications for Asian-Pacific Security," *Asian Survey*, Mar. 1993.

Index

About the Author

LESZEK BUSZYNSKI is Associate Professor at the International University of Japan. A specialist on Russian foreign policy, he has authored several books, including *Soviet Foreign Policy and Southeast Asia* (1986) and *Gorbachev and Southeast Asia* (1992).

ISBN 0-275-95585-0

9 780275 955854

HARDCOVER BAR CODE